A LITERARY HISTORY OF *Kentucky*

WILLIAM S. WARD

A LITERARY HISTORY OF *Kentucky*

With a Foreword
by Thomas D. Clark

THE UNIVERSITY OF TENNESSEE PRESS / KNOXVILLE

The paper in this book meets the minimum requirements of the American National Standard for Permanence of Paper for Printed Library Materials. ♾ The binding materials have been chosen for strength and durability.

Library of Congress Cataloging in Publication Data
Ward, William Smith, 1907–
A literary history of Kentucky.
Bibliography: p.
Includes index.
1. American literature—Kentucky—History and criticism. 2. Kentucky in literature. 3. Kentucky—Intellectual life. 4. Authors, American—Kentucky—Biography. 5. Kentucky—Biography. I. Title.
PS266.K4W37 1988 810'.9'9769 88-1277
ISBN 0-87049-577-1 (cloth : alk. paper)
ISBN 0-87049-578-X (pbk. : alk. paper)
ISBN 0-87049-579-8 (deluxe : alk. paper)

Contents

PART THREE *Maturity*

1930–1980

Illustrations

Foreword

Pitching headlong into the ebb tide of two centuries of history, Kentuckians are taking stock of the past. And none of their past accomplishments has sounder validity or merits more study than the collective offerings of their creative writers.

Almost unanimously Kentucky's authors have in some way fallen under the spell of the land and its penetrating environmental influence in molding personality and setting the course of the state's history. If there is such a thing as a composite Kentucky personality, spirit, or sentimentality, it is firmly fixed in the deeply grooved agrarian-rural traditions which have rigidly bonded people in their responses to the subtleties and recurrences of place and land. For both creative writers and historians, however, the land of Kentucky has in willful ways held its mysteries.

Legislators oblivious to the impact of geography in early years looped a set of boundaries around incongruous physical areas and gave them a common political label. Subsequently, writers, historians, newspaper publishers, and politicians have striven to reconcile Kentucky's myriad internal divergencies. From earliest Euro-American penetration of the great western littoral inside Cumberland Gap, Kentucky has survived as a land of distinct parts. It has never evidenced a truly defined way of life, folkways, or social attitudes. While Kentuckians have tolerated common political identification, they have never in a single historical moment truly shared common experiences or responded in kind to common heritages of their land. In no documentation is this fact more vividly revealed than in the books, essays, and poems of their creative writers.

There are not any obvious interlacing threads or themes coursing through Kentucky literature which bind the Commonwealth into a whole. No fictional character has yet personified a core Kentucky. James Lane Allen and John Fox, Jr., the state's first truly representative novelists, did not portray central themes of the entire land, but rather the essentially divisive forces which bore so oppressively upon the destinies of their characters. They were aware of the dissimilar geography, resources, and environments which formed the granitic and divisive social and cultural barriers existing in Kentucky. Repeatedly, those writers who trod in the footsteps of Allen and Fox have validated their forebears' portrayal. Essentially, James Still, Jesse Stuart, Harriette Arnow, Harry Caudill, and others have updated the traditional themes of social and cultural division. Elizabeth Madox Roberts, Elizabeth Chevalier, Wendell Berry, and other agrarians have dredged the abiding themes of man and land.

Strangely, Kentucky writers have ignored the gaping holes which appear in their collective offerings. No novelist has yet probed the depth or breadth of Kentucky's most persistent theme, politics and politicians. True, almost wraith-like, politicians weave in and out of some of the novels, but none is firmly or fully depicted. William Gilmore Simms glorified the Sharpe-Beauchamp Tragedy, and Robert Penn Warren cast it anew in a modern fictional mold. No author, however, has made a Shelby, Clay, Crittenden, Breckinridge, Buckner, or Barkley a focal character or politics a central theme. Miraculously, no Kentucky novelist has exploited the gothic-like Goebel Tragedy with all of its violent implications.

On another theme, the invasion of Kentucky by cash-laden corporations gobbling up rich resources of timber, coal, oil, and gas reshaped social mores and recast the human scene. Although John Fox, Jr., sensed the coming changes, and Harlan Hatcher, Harriette Simpson Arnow, and James Still have delved into the resulting crises of human identity, full literary exploration of the centrality of this aspect of Kentucky life is still to come.

Nevertheless, when the fruits of Kentucky authors' labors are assessed in a history such as Professor William Smith Ward's volume, their contributions become most impressive. With an incisiveness not exhibited in past inventories of Kentucky writers, Professor Ward has applied a modern critical assessment of the subject. Almost as a matter of course, he has brought into focus Kentucky writers' concepts of the lives of divergent people who have often been oblivious to the existence of each other. Professor Ward's history eloquently documents the enduring emotional and divisive forces which have so deeply colored Kentucky's past. This fresh appraisal of Kentucky's creative writers all but closes the books on a past era and points a bold course for new authors who seek to delineate Kentucky life in an age of onrushing and often confusing changes. Professor Ward's history sets a clear backsighting from which to proceed on a certain literary course into Kentucky's future, whatever its fortunes may be.

THOMAS D. CLARK

Preface

General Works on Kentucky Literature

For three quarters of a century Kentuckians have been fortunate in having John Wilson Townsend's *Kentucky in American Letters, 1784–1912* (1913), as a trustworthy source of information about early writers of the Commonwealth. These two volumes, which include discussions of journalists, historians, scientists, and other notable Kentuckians, as well as writers of belles-lettres, are arranged chronologically by author. Each entry is a brief biographical sketch incorporating, in narrative form, a record of the author's works and appending selections from them. In 1974 Dorothy Edwards Townsend, Townsend's widow, reissued these volumes, then out of print; and in 1976, with the assistance of Thelma Scott Kiser, published volume 3 of *Kentucky in American Letters, 1913–1975*, making available (though with a few important omissions) a uniform series dealing with Kentucky authors from 1784 through 1975. These volumes have constituted the most complete account of Kentucky authors in print.

Between the publication dates of volumes 1–2 and 3 of the Townsend series, the original two volumes grew increasingly out of date. In 1963 Ish Richey, with Townsend's permission, published *Kentucky Literature, 1784–1963*, in order to bring Townsend up to date. This he did by copying and updating the Townsend entries, but omitting the selections from the writings and adding new entries on authors who had come on the scene between 1913 and 1963. Richey enhanced his volume by copying entries from *The Kentucky Novel*, published in 1953 by Lawrence and Algernon Thompson. A third general work on Kentucky literature was *Kentucky Authors*, published in 1968 by Sister Mary Carmel Browning, O.S.U., who with her students at

Brescia College assembled the materials for the volume. The work is divided into chapters roughly corresponding to genres, with authors arranged chronologically. There is some inconsistency in the methodology, and the reader may be puzzled by certain imbalances, such as the fact that Archbishop John Lancaster Spalding fills seven pages and Norman C. Cooper, a colleague at Brescia College, fifteen; while James Still is given barely more than two, Harriette Arnow three, and Robert Penn Warren four. The volume can occasionally be used to supplement Townsend and Richey. To be noted also is *Biographical and Critical Materials Pertaining to Kentucky Authors* (1941), edited and supervised by Bess A. Ray, as a part of the Kentucky Work Projects Administration Library Project. Arranged alphabetically by author, the volume contains biographical information not found elsewhere about Kentucky writers. There are brief excerpts from reviews of their works.

Scope and Arrangement of the Present Volume

The present volume is constructed along entirely different lines from these volumes and is something less and something more than any one of them or all of them collectively. It is distinctive in two ways. One is that it is, first, a literary history rather than a set of biblio-biographical author-essays arranged chronologically or alphabetically. Secondly, for major authors in particular, it aims to give insight into authors' works, examine the stages of their development, provide an overall understanding of them as literary figures, and reveal their relationship to their times. Works such as the three Townsend volumes and those of Richey and Browning will therefore still have their usefulness, for they not only include authors who do not appear here but also contain in some cases more extensive biographical information and a more complete list of works.

Attention is also given to social and cultural matters in order to set authors and their works in a context that will enhance the reader's understanding. The account moves forward chronologically, but it is spatial also in order to provide context and depth. This method may be likened to that of weaving: it deals with the warp and the woof of the fabric of Kentucky writing. The warp is linear time, made up of events as they occur in chronological order. The woof, each shuttle containing its own thread, is as diverse as the knowledge of the literary historian permits: weaving in literary genres, social and cultural conditions, the taste and temper of the time, events in the life of the writer and his or her background—anything, in fact, that may have gone into or shaped the literary work. Ideally, the parts should be coordinated as they feed into the loom and should emerge as a work of art. Overcomplexity leading to tedium, however, is a constant risk, so my purpose is to bare the essential threads and let the imagination of the reader do the rest.

In trying to accomplish this I have divided the volume into three parts in chronological order and then divided each part into chapters that group like kinds of authors and works together. For example, genre headings in each of the three parts relate themselves crosswise to other chapter headings in the same part, and at the same time each genre relates itself lengthwise, along the time dimension, to its own kind in successive parts. The same arrangement works with other headings, such as "The Genteel Tradition," "The Agrarians," "The Literature of Protest," "Literary Criticism," "Writers of Eastern Kentucky," and so on. Each heading (or chapter) has its own introduction that provides a background for the section and, as appropriate, relates itself crosswise to other sections. Normally there is one main entry for a major author, but on occasion it is necessary for the reader to turn to a topical, genre, or other chapter that serves more than one author. One can, for example, follow the development of Allen Tate as a literary critic by reading the main entry on Tate, but larger than Tate is the fact that three Kentuckians—Tate, Robert Penn Warren, and Cleanth Brooks—were central figures in the development of what was perhaps the most important critical movement during the first three quarters of the century—the New Criticism. Hence a chapter on literary criticism. Such overlapping necessarily takes place, but there is no duplication; and cross-references and the general index make it easy for the readers to supplement and reinforce their knowledge.

Problems, Procedures, and Definitions

Problems related to the organization of materials are not the only ones that a literary historian confronts. Even the choice of the material is troublesome. It is easy to say that literary merit should be the only criterion, but relativism soon rears its ugly head. For example, should the same standards of excellence be required of an author who wrote during the days of the first settlers as of one who writes in the middle of the twentieth century? Fortunately the only authors who qualify as "first settlers"—Thomas Johnson, Jr., and Gilbert Imlay—were not without talent, but with the turn into the next century post-frontier writers began to write retrospectively, some of them with less talent than that of their two frontier predecessors. The obverse side of the problem, of course, is whether we would include them if they were writing today instead of a century and a half ago.

Another problem is determining which writings of merit to include. Some who have written about Kentucky authors have virtually limited their attention to writings that deal with the Commonwealth. Doubtless a case can be made for such a limitation, but I have steadfastly declined to be so limited. I may have written in more detail about works and authors that focus on Kentucky, but I have declined to reduce any work of merit to a mere mention just because of its subject matter. In the first place, such a study would betray a provincialism that I choose to avoid. In the second place, a reader would be cheated by being exposed to such a narrow representation of many authors' works, and those authors would be done an injustice if the reader perceived them as writers of such narrow range.

Finally, there is the problem of knowing how to appraise an author whose works are judged to merit inclusion. Should, for example, Mary Jane Holmes's *Tempest and Sunshine*, Jane Holt Giles's *The Enduring Hills*, and Harriette Arnow's *The Dollmaker*—for purposes of commentary—be judged by precisely the same standards? The answer, I think, is that they should not. Reviewers and critics are constantly troubled about what to say about one book that sets modest goals for itself and achieves them well and about another book that strives for greatness but doesn't quite attain it. Some kind of injustice has been done if the first one comes off as a success and the other as a failure. But injustice has been done also if the novel with modest goals is judged only by the extent to which it failed to be a *War and Peace*. The reader probably infers from the tone of these comments and my specific evaluations that different standards of judgment are being employed for different kinds of works.

Definitions and ground rules are useful not only in providing the reader with a set of expectations but in helping the historian to keep within bounds. Most important is the definition of what constitutes a "Kentucky writer." Since this is a history of belles-lettres by Kentuckians, it needs to be stated that for our purposes a Kentuckian is a person who was born in the state or was a legal resident of it at some time. Such a definition generally works well enough, but sometimes it is all but a travesty on what constitutes a Kentucky writer. Thus, according to this rule, we should examine the works of an author born in Kentucky but who early moved away and wrote about matters entirely unconcerned with things Kentuckian. By the same definition, authors would be eliminated who were born just across the state line but wrote about Kentucky all their lives. One must indeed have guidelines, but occasional exceptions must be made and attention called to them.

Even establishing a terminal date for this survey was not simple. When the study was begun in the early 1980s, the year 1980—a neat half-century later than the date many literary historians pick as the beginning of the modern era—seemed just right. Now it has become increasingly unsatisfactory, for not only have authors who had written before that date continued to write, but more importantly new and promising authors have come on the scene. The result has been an occasional compromise. I have continued to consider 1980 as the cut-off date for established authors when a publication after 1980 signaled no notable change in direction and appeared not to be a major work. On the other hand, if a promising author began a publishing career after 1980, I have stretched the terminal date to 1985 on the grounds that it is more important to do justice to an author and this record than to be mindlessly intimidated by a date.

Acknowledgments

This volume was written in retirement after a teaching career spent in a field unrelated to Kentucky literature. Thus, most of what I know on the subject has been newly come by, and the secondary sources to which I am indebted are to be measured by the hundreds. Many of these sources have been helpful and are appended in a bibliography of books and articles, even though they were never actually quoted from or alluded to. Whenever I have quoted from a secondary source or used an idea that bears the trademark of a particular scholar or critic, I have tried without fail to acknowledge my indebtedness in the text.

I am also indebted to others who have never written about Kentucky literature and have no particular knowledge of it. These include colleagues who have for some special reason read segments of the manuscript early in its preparation. In particular I must mention John L. Cutler, who has read the manuscript in its entirety and with a suggestion here and a recommendation there improved the flow of the thought and added grace to a phrase or a sentence that otherwise would have just limped along. Wade Hall, of Bellarmine College, has been a source of information on many matters, but most of all I am indebted to him for our conversations about the organization of some unwieldy materials and for criticism that was always forthright, to the point, and helpful. David Burg has also been helpful in a variety of ways, but most importantly he has helped me reduce verbiage and accomplish the purpose Charles Lamb had in mind when he declared in a letter to a friend that "If I had had more time I would have written you a shorter letter." I owe my special thanks to my daughter, Catherine Ward Bishir, who has read every word I have written and with characteristic forthrightness and enthusiasm has helped and encouraged me with comments ranging from "Wordy!" to "Wonderful!" and with page-long suggestions for me to consider. And finally, to my wife, Margaret Byrn Ward, I owe my thanks for suggestions made as she read my manuscript, piece by piece, discussed problems pertaining to it, lent encouragement at all times, and tolerated without complaint the silence of not only the days but of the long evenings that the fun I was having imposed upon her.

W.S.W.

PART ONE

The Early Years

BEFORE 1860

CHAPTER 1

The Beginning

This Other Eden

The literary history of Kentucky began in the Bluegrass region, for it was there the pioneers first settled. It was not that an abundant literature sprang into existence with the arrival of the first settlers, but rather that the land itself and the quest for it were the stuff out of which literature was to grow. Even before June 7, 1769, when Daniel Boone and John Findley first looked westward from the promontory of Pilot Knob toward what today we call the Inner Bluegrass, the region was known as a very special place. Though it had no precisely fixed boundaries, it was labeled "Kentucke" and had shape and form enough to have been set aside by the Indians as a neutral-territory hunting ground where the tribes were free to hunt its abundant game but where no one was allowed to become a permanent resident.

This land into which were to flow almost a quarter of a million settlers by the end of the century was uncommonly fertile, a rich, dark, loamy soil often five feet deep and containing limestone and phosphorus along with abundant organic matter. Unlike the mountainous wilderness through which Boone and Findley had struggled from the East, forests were surprisingly open, with giant trees wide apart and uncluttered with undergrowth. The ground was covered by grasses and clovers of many kinds, including a grass which at pollen time gave off a bluish hue. Everywhere there was an incredible amount of wild game, and the streams teemed with fish.

Matching the munificence of this land was the drama that guided those settlers who followed Boone and Findley through Cumberland Gap, and very shortly thereafter those who came down the Ohio

River from Pittsburgh, landing at Limestone (Maysville) and proceeding southward along a wagon trail. Even as Boone and Findley gazed westward from Pilot Knob, the scene was not only charged with high drama but was interpenetrated with myth. These two men—and Boone in particular—symbolized a people flushed with a new vision breaking through a mountain wilderness into a fertile and beautiful land where they might hope to make their fortune, a people on the threshold of a new life where they could be free and fulfill their destiny. It was indeed the Great Meadow, but it was also "this other Eden" that John of Gaunt describes in *Richard II*, a new land where a new Adam and Eve might have a second chance.

The Settlers Arrive

Over the years, word of this land made its way across the mountains to the colonies through reports of traders, hunters, and explorers who made forays into the new land and of land companies which sent surveyors into the uncharted wilderness. What these forerunners had to say—plus John Findley's earlier experiences as a trader among the Indians—led Boone and Findley to find their way through Cumberland Gap and up the ancient Warrior's Path to Pilot Knob in 1769 and to become the first white men to penetrate so deep into the Bluegrass region, and then led Boone, posing as a hunter, to spend two years studying the topography of the Bluegrass and the general terrain southward toward Cumberland Gap. In April 1775 Boone led Richard Henderson and his Transylvania Land Company up Boone's Trace (later Wilderness Road) to establish Boonesborough just weeks after James Harrod had led another band of settlers down the Ohio River to the mouth of the Kentucky River and thence up the river to found the first permanent settlement at Harrodsburg.

At the very moment that Boone, Harrod, and their followers were building their forts, not without trouble from the Indians, many miles away an event occurred that complicated their problems greatly—the firing of the first shot in the American War of Independence at Lexington, Massachusetts. No British force was ever dispatched to Kentucky to fight a contingent of the Colonial army, but with Kentucky lying just south of the Old British Northwest Territory (Ohio, Indiana, Illinois, Wisconsin, Michigan), Britain foresaw a long-range threat to the territory and proceeded to make alliances with a number of Indian tribes, particularly in Ohio. By the spring of 1777 there were British/Indian attacks on Fort Boonesborough, Fort Harrod, Logan's Station, and elsewhere among the settlements that had been established during the past two years.

As long as the white settlers had shown no signs of becoming residents in the Indians' hunting ground, they were allowed to come and go as much as they liked; but as soon as settlers began pouring across the mountains and down the Ohio River, the Shawnees began to fight desperately to retain their preserve. Thus for the Indians and settlers alike the Happy Hunting Ground became the Dark and Bloody Ground. Despite warfare, however, and despite hardship and privation, discouragements, sickness, and death, the settlers continued to arrive in ever-increasing numbers. Where there had been zero white population in early 1775, there were several hundred in 1780, 74,000 by the time of the first census in 1790, and 220,000 by 1800. On another level of measurement the small area of land in Clark County where Boone, Findley, and their companions had encamped in 1769 would expand vastly; by December 1776 it would become Kentucky County of Virginia; by 1782 the last battle would be fought at Blue Licks and soon a peace treaty would declare that the western boundary of Kentucky—and of the republic—was to be the Mississippi River; by 1792 Kentucky would be admitted as the fifteenth state in the Union; and by 1795 the Shawnees would relinquish all claim to the land. For the Shawnee nation, Kentucky had been a very special place; for the white settlers it was also very special, and numbers and strength were on their side. In winning their objectives and facing the struggles and hardships that constantly tested them, the settlers often saw their hopes dashed and their idealism sorely tried and even tarnished. Still, at the end there was triumph of heroic proportions. The ingredients for literature were there, but in the main the writing of that literature would have to wait for a coloring of imagination to be cast over the whole stirring sequence of events and for time to provide a perspective from which meaning as well as details could be perceived.

Literary Beginnings

It would not be wholly inaccurate to say that Kentucky's literary history began at Pilot Knob with Boone's statement that "from the top of an eminence we saw with pleasure the beautiful level of Kentucke." Almost from that moment onward a sense of beauty, a sense of destiny and of bright hope for a better world played upon the imagination and spread by word of mouth as explorers came and went and settlers returned to their former homes to guide still more settlers across the mountains or down the Ohio. It spread as families wrote letters back to their friends and kinsmen, as travelers wrote books about their experiences, or as notices and accounts appeared as information and news. Some of these settlers were no doubt dull to what they saw, and most were not gifted with language. What they wrote in books, diaries, and letters was not literature in the belletristic sense; but the language was often effective and the content heightened by the metaphor of the Garden Myth, with Boone a new Adam and the land a second paradise.

Literature of the frontier can be said to be of two kinds: that written during the period of the frontier itself and that which included the frontier but was written retrospectively by later authors. Despite the inconvenience to literary historians, however, historical periods and movements are not given to beginning and ending officially by the clock or the calendar. One could pick as the end of the Kentucky frontier period the date 1792, the year Kentucky became a state; or 1795, since in that year the Shawnees relinquished all claims to the land; or even 1800, since it is close by and is a round number. In any event, Kentucky had two frontier authors who fit comfortably within any of these dates, and retrospective writers did not appear till well after 1800.

Thomas Johnson, Jr.

Thomas Johnson, Jr. (ca. 1760–1820) may be said to be something of an exception to a postulate of literary history that, no matter how momentous the events or how deep the stirrings of the spirit on the opening of a new frontier, the demands of daily survival preclude attention to the literary arts. In like manner, Johnson seems to be an exception to the truism of literary studies that satire is produced by a mature, stable, comfortable society inasmuch as the aim of satire is to provoke laughter at the expense of the complacencies and foibles of humankind and its institutions. Too, satire has characteristically flourished in strongly intellectual eras and among societies sufficiently self-confident to be amused at satiric views of themselves. How, then, does one account for the fact that the first belletristic volume published on the Kentucky frontier was made up of satiric verse? *

* The first book to be read on the Kentucky frontier, as well as the first one to be published there, was satiric in nature. Just as one would hardly expect satire to grow out of the life of the first settlers, so one would not expect the first book to be read by the explorers who preceded them to have been *Gulliver's Travels*, by Jonathan Swift. The book arrived some weeks after that day in June 1769 when Daniel Boone, along with John Findley, looked out from the top of Pilot Knob and "saw with pleasure the beautiful level of Kentucke." By pre-arrangement Boone's younger brother, Squire, and John Stewart brought fresh supplies from North Carolina through Cumberland Gap

Johnson's volume of verse bore the title *The Kentucky Miscellany*. The exact date of its publication is not known, but the volume was advertised in the Lexington *Kentucky Gazette* as early as May 2, 1789. Johnson was born in Virginia, probably in 1760, and apparently came to Danville, Kentucky, in 1785. As a boy, therefore, he grew up in a more stable and more sophisticated society than the one he found in Kentucky, and since he was a bright young man with a talent for versifying, we can speculate that his delight in satire soon led him into writing satiric verse about the frontier life he saw and the views and attitudes he discovered among the pioneers and their institutions. In time Johnson came to be known as "the drunken poet of Danville" and to be referred to as "a poet, punster, and n'er-do-well."

The subjects of Johnson's verse were as varied as the community itself: Kentucky, Danville, Presbyterians, Baptists, lawyers, judges, physicians, hypocrisy, a man who has murdered his wife, humankind generally, himself. Typical of the manner of satire in eighteenth-century England, some of what he wrote was amusing, some a bit coarse and sometimes bawdy, and some biting and even abusive. No one poem can illustrate Johnson's versatility, but "Extempore Grace" illustrates the more genial side of his humor. It was composed when Johnson, in his cups, arrived late for his usual meal in the tavern dining-room of tavernkeeper Erasmus Gill, only to find the meal over, the guests gone, and nothing left but crumbs. Looking at the table and then at his host, Johnson delivered the following:

O! Thou who blest the loaves and fishes
  Look down upon these empty dishes;
And with that power that did them fill,
  Bless each of us but d—— old Gill!

Johnson died apparently in 1820 and was buried in Danville.

---

and up the Warriors' Path to a point about four miles west of Pilot Knob where they rendezvoused with Boone and Findley and camped with them near a small stream in what is now Clark County. Here during the evenings Squire Boone read aloud from Swift's satire, reader and listeners alike, no doubt, concentrating more upon the remarkable stories than on the meanings behind them. On one occasion Stewart returned to camp and reported that he, like Gulliver, had been to Lorbrulgrud, the capital of Brobdingnag, and had killed two of the inhabitants. He had, in fact, killed two buffaloes. The name Lorbrulgrud, which these campers gave the creek, is still used today, though in the much-shortened form Lulbegrud. As a matter of interest it may be noted also that the camp site was at what is now called Oil Springs, which is near Indian Old Fields, the site of Eskippakithiki, the last Indian village in Kentucky. It was located on the Warriors' Path and was the meeting place for white traders and Indian hunters. Findley had spent a few months there in 1752–53, just before the village was pillaged and burned. Doubtless it was Findley's familiarity with the vicinity that made the place of rendezvous easy to find.

Gilbert Imlay

A literary work from the Kentucky frontier that has survived time and is regularly noted in literary histories and handbooks of American literature is Gilbert Imlay's *The Emigrants, or the History of an Expatriated Family*, published in 1793. Imlay was born in New Jersey about 1754. He was a captain in the Revolutionary War and came West by way of the Ohio River in 1784, stopping at the Falls of the Ohio (Louisville), where he worked under George May as a "commissioner for laying out lands in the back settlements." In that year he apparently owned and lived on a tract of land in Fayette County. How long he remained in Kentucky is not known. He may have gone to London as early as 1786; in any event he published *Topographical Description of the Western Territory of North America* there in 1792 and *The Emigrants* in 1793. In the latter year Imlay went to Paris and there met and formed a liaison with Mary Wollstonecraft. To them was born Fanny Imlay. In 1796 the two agreed to go their separate ways and thereafter Imlay is lost to history, though there is some evidence that he may have died in 1828. Mary Wollstonecraft later married William Godwin, and to them was born Mary Godwin, future wife of Percy Bysshe Shelley. Fanny Imlay, who also came within the Shelley Circle, committed suicide in 1816.

The Emigrants recounts the experiences of the family of a London merchant who has lost his fortune, emigrates with his family to America, arrives in Philadelphia, proceeds to Pittsburgh, and from there drifts down the Ohio River in a Kentucky flatboat to Louisville. The T——n family consists of a London merchant, his wife, three daughters, and a son. Caroline, the beautiful, sentimental heroine of the story, alternates between rapture and misery. Her lover, Captain Ar——ton, precedes the family and goes to Lexington but soon joins his sweetheart in Louisville. Caroline undergoes various trying and dangerous experiences, including capture by the Indians, but Captain Ar——ton rescues her from a captivity in which she had been treated with "the utmost delicacy and respect." The family concludes after three months, however, that they have had enough and return to London.

In addition to being a sort of novel of adventure with accurate descriptions of wilderness and frontier scenes, the book was intended to serve certain social purposes: to set forth the superior merits of the social organization of the United States, to champion the rights of women, and to support the principle of divorce. Like many novels of the time, the story is told in epistolary form through a sequence of letters that link together Louisville, Pittsburgh, Philadelphia, and London.

The Post-Frontier

Turning to post-frontier Kentucky literature requires being prepared for a world of great change that came with astonishing swiftness. A look at the years 1795–1805 reveals the suddenness of this change and the marvelous mix of attitudes and events that funneled itself into a stable and advanced society. In 1795 a treaty with the Indians settled all their claims to the land and removed them as a threat to the lives of the settlers. Then a short two years later in 1797 Henry Clay's arrival in Lexington and the departure of Daniel Boone for Missouri have great symbolic value. The region that had beckoned to the early frontiersmen was now becoming too sedate and too crowded for these restless spirits and was beckoning to a new wave of immigrants. These were the gentry—descendants mainly of the Virginia plantation aristocracy—who came in increasing numbers, built great houses on the new land, and became the first generation in a genteel tradition that would thrive until the Civil War brought it to an end.

Of course, the transition from the world of Daniel Boone to that of Henry Clay was not so simple or clear cut. Other ingredients were present, too. For example, also in 1797 Samuel Mason and his band of outlaws ensconced themselves in Cave-in-Rock on the Ohio River, and in 1798 Micajah and Wiley Harpe appeared at Crab Orchard and began a career of crime and murder that finally ended in Webster County. Another element in the sociological mix was the occurrence of the greatest religious revival that Kentucky ever witnessed, a movement that started in Logan County, reached its crescendo at Cane Ridge Meeting House in Bourbon County, August 1801, and led to the formation of the Disciples of Christ in Kentucky. At the same moment came the development of a new type of frontiersman to replace Daniel Boone and his kind: the rowdy, roistering "Kaintucks" in the Mike Fink mold that manned the keelboats, fought in the War of 1812, and moved on westward after the steamboats began plying the waters of the Ohio and the Mississippi (the first one in 1811). During this time, progress occurred in learning and the arts so that before 1820 Lexington came to be known, even in the East, as the Athens of the West. The political state became stable, and by 1820 the Commonwealth was embarked upon a period of growth and prosperity that has long been portrayed as its golden years.

CHAPTER 2

Poetry and Drama

Poetry again preceded fiction during the post-frontier period; the writing of fiction did not begin until the 1830s. During the closing years of the eighteenth century and the opening years of the nineteenth, however, American poetry was at a rather low ebb; and so in general was the first poetry about Kentucky. Just as Timothy Dwight, Joel Barlow, and John Trumbull wrote poems after the Revolutionary War that expressed faith in the destiny of the nation and celebrated great moments in the nation's war for freedom, so the first post-war Kentucky poet cited here, Stephen T. Badin (1768–1853), of Georgetown, wrote "Epicedium" (1812), an elegy upon the death of Colonel Stephen T. Daviess at the Battle of Tippecanoe. The poem was quite popular and was often reprinted.

William Littell

Of more consequence is William Littell's *Festoons of Fancy* (1816), a volume made up of both verse and prose dealing with its own times and a new society on its way to developing its own character and its own image. Littell was born in New Jersey in 1768, spent his youth in Pennsylvania, and arrived in Kentucky in 1801. Though he practiced medicine in Mount Sterling at one time, he soon turned his attention to law and in 1805 contracted with the Kentucky General Assembly to compile and edit the laws of the state from 1792 to 1809. As some evidence of how well he did his job, Transylvania University in 1810 conferred upon him an honorary LL.D. degree for his services to the Commonwealth. Littell died in 1824.

Littell prepared a number of legal works and published his satirical *Epistles of William, Surnamed Littell,* in 1806, but it is his *Festoons of Fancy* that we are concerned with here. Written in order to relieve the tedium of his more serious endeavors, the individual satirical pieces address a wide variety of topics. Most of the verses deal with love and the ladies, but unfortunately they lack the deftness, the light touch, the nicely turned phrases, and the bite of Thomas Johnson, Jr. His prose satires, in which he deals with "the servants of the people," are more effective. One of these is the "Petition of Gregory Woodcock," which satirizes the prevailing system of office-seeking. Less humorous but more biting is his satire on the divorce law, passed in 1809, which was clearly drawn in favor of men. There is no evidence that Littell's satires had much popularity or any measurable effect on public opinion, but they were noted and at least they provided some humor, though sometimes a bit embarrassing, in an age that was otherwise rather heavy-handed.

William Orlando Butler

William Orlando Butler (1791–1880) was a distinguished citizen of Kentucky, with the added distinction of having written "The Boatman's Horn" (1821), perhaps Kentucky's earliest well-loved poem. Butler was born near Nicholasville in 1791, graduated from Transylvania in 1812, studied law for a short while, and enlisted in the War of 1812. He was wounded in the Battle of the Raisin, and his gallantry at the Battle of New Orleans made him a hero and earned him a place on the staff of General Andrew Jackson. In 1817 he resigned from the military forces, returned to Kentucky, married, and lived in Carrollton the remainder of his life. During the 1830s he entered politics, served in the Kentucky legislature, was an unsuccessful candidate for governor, distinguished himself in the Mexican War as chief commander of the U.S. Forces, was nominated by the Democratic party for the vice presidency of the United States with General Lewis Cass of Michigan as the head of the ticket, but was defeated in 1851. Except for brief appointive positions, General Butler spent the rest of his life as a poet, lawyer, and citizen of Carroll County.

Though Butler published several poems in a small volume entitled *The Boatman's Horn and Other Poems*, it is the title poem that keeps his name alive. Background for the poem may be found in General Lew Wallace's *Autobiography*. Complimenting Butler and his poem, the author of *Ben Hur* gives this account of his boyhood memories of the Wabash River and of how "Nebeker, the lonely ferryman" kept his tin horn chained to a tree so that a traveler, finding no one to ferry him across the river, could blow the horn in order to attract the attention of Old Nebeker. "When the voice of the big horn on the thither side called to us," says Wallace, who as a boy often kept Old Nebeker company, "how it startled me! What music was in it! What haste I made to unship my oar."

Hew Ainslie

Born in Ayrshire, Scotland, Hew Ainslie (1792–1878) came to America when he was thirty. After farming in New York, he moved to Indiana, where he and his family participated in the New Harmony experiment of reformer Robert Owen. He moved to Louisville in 1828, and there became a successful contractor. His published writings consist of *A Pilgrimage to the Land of Burns* (1822) and *Scottish Songs, Ballads, and Poems* (1855). The former is made up of songs and ballads and an account of conversations with friends of Robert Burns. Ainslie was well known as an admirer of Burns and in 1871 served as toastmaster at a dinner of Scots assembled to celebrate Burns's birthday. Once, he confessed, he had kissed "Bonnie Jean," Burns's widow.

Theodore O'Hara

In the 1840s and 1850s three Kentuckians published lines that received attention, and in all three cases only one poem by each author has a niche in literary history. The best of the three was Theodore O'Hara (1820–67), whose "Bivouac of the Dead" has been perhaps the most celebrated and most often quoted martial elegy written in America. Though O'Hara taught Greek at St. Joseph's College in Bardstown, was a journalist in Frankfort, Louisville, and Mobile, Alabama, and died at the age of forty-seven, he also had a military career. It was as a volunteer in the Mexican War that he wrote his elegy to honor the large number of Kentuckians who died in that war and were being reinterred in the Kentucky State Cemetery in Frankfort. Since publication of the poem, it has been read and recited in every quarter of the globe and its opening lines cut into commemorative military shafts wherever fallen soldiers are honored, including the gateway of the National Cemetery at Arlington, Virginia. Written in 1847 it was published in the *Kentucky Yeoman* in 1850.

The muffled drum's sad roll has beat
   The soldier's last tattoo:
No more on life's parade shall meet
   The brave and daring few.
On Fame's eternal camping-ground
   Their silent tents are spread,

And Glory guards with solemn round
  The bivouac of the dead.

In 1850 O'Hara enlisted in the expedition led by Narcisco Lopez to fight for Cuban independence; he served in the U.S. Army, 1855–56, and enlisted in the Confederate Army, where he served under four generals, including Robert E. Lee. After the Civil War, O'Hara became a cotton planter in Georgia and Alabama.

O'Hara's first elegy was written in 1845 to honor Daniel and Rebecca Boone, whose remains were brought back from Missouri and reinterred (September 13, 1845) in the Kentucky State Cemetery on a precipice overlooking Frankfort and the Kentucky River. The ellipse where O'Hara lies buried is only a short distance from the Boone lot and monument.

Mary E.W. Betts

Mary E.W. Betts (1824–54) died young in her native Maysville but not before she published in the *Maysville Flag* a poem that was to be reprinted widely, not only at the time but half a century later as a morale booster during the Spanish-American War. "A Kentuckian Kneels to None but God" was inspired by Colonel William Logan Crittenden, who was born in Shelbyville, moved to Cloverport when he was fourteen, and was a graduate of West Point. After serving with distinction in the Mexican War he enlisted in 1851 in a force led by Narcisco Lopez, a Venezuelan, to free Cuba from the Spaniards. He and fifty of his men were captured and marched to the wharf of Castle Altares, Havana, to be executed, five at a time, kneeling with their backs to the firing squad. Colonel Crittenden refused to kneel when his turn came and spoke his now famous words, "A Kentuckian kneels to none except his God, and he always dies facing the enemy." Upon this reply Mary Betts based her four-stanza poem. Shortly after the end of the Spanish-American War almost half a century later, the Cubans erected a monument at Castle Atares to commemorate the death of Colonel Crittenden and his men, but so complete was the carnage and mutilation of bodies following the execution on August 16, 1851, that no stone marks the actual burial place.

Sarah T. Bolton

Though Sarah T. Bolton (1820–93) spent almost her entire life in Indiana, she was born in Newport and kept her friendships alive there and in Campbell County. In *Poems* (1856) she brought together the verse she had previously published in newspapers and magazines, but one of them alone secures her a place among the writers of American Victorian verse. This is "Paddle Your Own Canoe"; the last of its seven stanzas is representative:

> Nothing great is lightly won,
>   Nothing won is lost;
> Every good deed, nobly done,
>   Will repay the cost.
> Leave to heaven, in humble trust,
>   All you will to do;
> But if you succeed, you must
>   Paddle your own canoe.

Amelia B. Welby

Amelia B. Welby (1819–52), the best known of Kentucky's female poets of the mid-century, was the central figure in a curious little eddy in Kentucky literary history. Her verse was uniformly rhapsodical, heavily didactic, and sentimental; her favorite subjects were nature, children, religion, romanticized peasants, and disappointed lovers. Welby's fame and popularity extended well beyond Kentucky, for she was singled out for favorable attention by Edgar Allan Poe and Rufus W. Griswold, the latter giving her a place in his *Female Poets of America* (1856). Of particular interest is the fact that her poetry was published in George D. Prentice's *Louisville Journal*, which, according to Griswold, had been the medium for the original appearance of much of the best poetry of the West. For several years Prentice's home was the center of the literary life of Louisville. A man of unusual intellectual brilliance, he was for forty years (1830–1870) the stalwart editor of the *Journal* (merged with the *Courier* in 1868), where he lashed out at his adversaries with wit and cleverness in his editorials and was one of the forces that kept Kentucky in the Union during the Civil War. But Prentice also wrote sentimental, moralistic verse (published posthumously as *The Poems of George D. Prentice* in 1878) and had a knack for attracting ladies with poetic aspirations, women whom he and his gracious and talented wife encouraged and whose verses he published in his *Journal*. Welby was one of his favorite "discoveries," though he heaped indiscriminate praise upon others. Like Prentice's own verse, Welby's does not rise above sentimental mediocrity, but it was in such demand that in 1845 she collected it together and published it as *Poems by Amelia*. A second edition was published the following year, and by 1860 the volume had apparently reached its seventeenth edition. Welby, who came from Maryland to

Lexington with her family and later moved to Louisville, died in 1852 at the age of thirty-three and was buried in Cave Hill Cemetery.

Thomas Holley Chivers

Thomas Holley Chivers (1807–58) is best known because of his connections with Edgar Allan Poe and especially for the controversy over which one plagiarized the other. He was born in Georgia and died there, but he had Kentucky connections inasmuch as he studied medicine at Transylvania University and received his medical degree there in March 1830. Soon, however, he abandoned the practice of medicine in order to devote himself to literature. Some of the poems in *Nachoochee* (1837) were written while he was a medical student, but of more importance is his *Conrad and Eudora* (1834), a play that was the first of several literary works to deal with the sensational Kentucky murder commonly called "The Kentucky Tragedy."

The beginnings of the "Tragedy" came when Ann Cook of Bowling Green claimed that she had given birth to a child, dead, whose father was Solomon P. Sharp, a prominent Kentucky lawyer and politician. Not far from Ann lived Jereboan O. Beauchamp, an attorney, who later courted and married her in 1824, agreeing in the process to kill Sharp in order to avenge the dishonor that Sharp had brought upon Beauchamp's wife-to-be. A period of time passed during which Sharp refused to fight Beauchamp, and some plans to murder Sharp went awry. Then, on the eve of the opening of the legislature of 1825 and Sharp's being sworn into political office, Beauchamp arrived in Frankfort. That night Sharp was stabbed to death at his home. A long trial marked by corruption and perjury on both sides followed, and Beauchamp was finally convicted and sentenced to be hanged. On the night before the execution, Ann was permitted to join her husband in his cell, and there the two entered into a suicide pact. First they took the laudanum that Ann brought with her, and when that merely made them ill, they stabbed themselves with the knife she also brought. Ann died of her wounds, but Beauchamp survived and was carried to the gallows and hanged later that day. The two were buried in a double coffin in the old cemetery in Bloomfield, Nelson County.

Naturally such a tale—involving passion, the avenging of a woman's dishonor, a murder, a suicide pact, and the gallows—gained national attention and became the subject of numerous literary works and folk songs. Best known among other plays and novels about "The Kentucky Tragedy" are *Politian* (1835) by Poe, never completed; *Beauchampe; or the Kentucky Tragedy* (1842) and *Charlemonte* (1856), by William Gilmore Simms; and, a hundred years later, *World Enough and Time* (1956), by Robert Penn Warren.

Chivers continued to write almost to the end of his life, but as the years passed he became an increasingly pitiable figure. He was skilled in handling verse forms, but his later volumes were full of sentimentality, lacked critical judgment, and finally began to reveal his unbalanced mind. Chivers's best work may be found in *Lost Pleiad: And Other Poems* (1845).

CHAPTER 3

Historical Fiction

The time would come when the Kentucky frontier as well as the Revolutionary War would be among the favorite subjects of historical novelists, but in the 1790s when the frontier was coming to an end, the genre had not yet been born. In 1814, however, Sir Walter Scott published *Waverley* and therewith established the historical romance as a genre and a vogue that was to last for many years. By 1821 James Fenimore Cooper in *The Spy* succeeded in adapting American subjects to the new mode, and so pleased was he with the form that he projected a series of historical novels. Meanwhile around 1818–19 Washington Irving began using American subjects in the short fiction form at which he excelled. Imitations that exploited national subjects and themes sprang up immediately, and by the 1830s writers of historical romances turned to local history and to specific geographical regions. It is at this time that the Kentucky frontier entered the stream of historical fiction.

John Alexander McClung

Historians had begun to look back on the frontier era, but only one of them calls for attention here, for he was a historian with a difference. This was John Alexander McClung (1804–59), who came close to qualifying as Kentucky's first historical novelist and writer of fiction about the frontier. McClung, who was born in Washington, Mason County, prepared himself for the ministry, but he early gave up the church for a career in writing. In 1830 he published an undistinguished novel called *Camden*, which dealt with the Revolutionary War in the South, but in *Sketches of Western Adventure* (1832) he rose above the level of a run-of-the-mill writer. His *Sketches* is normally classified under "History," but it is history with a special flair, for though McClung got his "facts" from John Bradford's "Notes" in the *Kentucky Gazette*, he drew heavily upon firsthand sources and legends and employed his own fertile imagination by reporting interesting incidents that never occurred. McClung understood the heroic character of the frontier and knew how to embroider the basic material for dramatic effect while being careful not to tamper with what may be called the essential truth of history.

In *Sketches*, for example, McClung's most notable invention was having the women of Bryant's Station, in Fayette County, carrying water from the spring for the defense of the Station. Historians prior to McClung report the occurrence of the three-day siege basically as McClung does but make no mention of the heroic women; early historians who follow McClung label his description of their indomitable spirit and courage as "interesting." Yet this episode above all else makes the siege as McClung tells it memorable. During the night preceding the attack British Captain William Caldwell led a strong force of Indians and British soldiers to a point near the spring at Bryant's Station, ready to attack when the men should emerge the next morning. So much is history. At this point McClung invents the stuff of literature. Thus he heightens interest in the siege by stressing the presence of the treacherous white renegade Simon Girty as a leader among the Indians, and by adding the water-carrying device. When the defenders discover the attackers, they also discover that their supply of water is dangerously low. This leads to a parley at which a daring course of action is decided upon: the women will go down the hill to the spring with their water vessels just as they have done every other morning, hoping that the attackers waiting for the men to appear will believe that they have not been discovered. As reported by McClung, the plan worked perfectly, a courier was dispatched to the fort at Lexington for reinforcements, and the siege was lifted after three days with little damage to either side.

In order to appreciate the effectiveness of McClung's fiction, one must realize that in real life two days later on August 19, 1782, Colonel Caldwell with his nine hundred troops set an ambush on the northern bank of the Licking River at Blue Licks in order to entrap the pursuing Kentuckians. There followed the worst massacre to grow out of the war with the British and the Indians, rivaled only by the earlier carnage at Ruddle's Station near Cynthiana. Because of this massacre at the Battle of Blue Licks, General George Rogers Clark conducted a punitive campaign against the Ohio tribes that had participated in the British/Indian raids into Kentucky. In the popular mind, however, it is not the Battle of Blue Licks that is remembered when Indian sieges and battles are mentioned, but the siege at Bryant's Station with its heroic women.

Robert Montgomery Bird

The best novel before 1860 dealing with the Kentucky frontier was *Nick of the Woods: or, the Jibbenainosey: A Tale of Kentucky* (1837), by Robert Montgomery Bird (1803–54). It is not clear whether Bird, a Pennsylvanian, ever considered himself a resident of Kentucky, but apparently he spent a good deal of time in the state as he explored Mammoth Cave extensively, studied Kentucky's geography and terrain, and gathered facts and data for a series of novels about Kentucky that he projected but never completed. *Nick of the Woods* is a story of Indian warfare during the late summer and early fall of 1782, the time of the turning point in the war with the British and Indians. After reading, among other things, McClung's *Sketches of Western Adventure* and making use of the massacre at Blue Licks and other sieges and battles, Bird reveals his conviction that the Indian was destined to give way before a superior race. In doing so, of course, he contradicts the romantic notion of Chateaubriand and others that the Indians were gentle and noble beings who lived close to nature. Instead, he portrays them as skulking, treacherous, and heartless.

Providing a love interest in *Nick of the Woods* are Captain Roland Forrester and his beloved Edith, but more interesting by far is Bloody Nathan, a Quaker who is Nick of the Woods and greatly feared by the Indians. Though declaring himself the only man in Kentucky who will not fight, Bloody Nathan goes about systematically annihilating Indians in revenge for their massacre of his wife and children. This duality of his nature Bird keeps secret till late in the story. Big Colonel Bruce, with his Salt River dialect is reminiscent of frontier scouts and Indian fighters such as Simon Kenton and Roaring Ralph Stackpole, and of roistering keelboatmen such as Mike Fink. General George Rogers Clark is one of the real-life characters in the story. *Nick of the Woods* has some of the markings of a picaresque novel, and in combining history with thrilling adventures it may be said to have helped pave the way for the adventure thrillers and dime novels that flowed from the printing presses later in the century.

James Weir

James Weir (1821–1906) was a Kentucky writer whose first and best novel, *Lonz Powers, or the Regulators* (1850), deals with outlawry on the frontier in Western Kentucky. Based on a real-life situation that developed around 1820 in what was then a wilderness area where Muhlenberg, Todd, and Christian counties adjoin, it tells how into this community there came a number of undesirable settlers who because of their thievery, dishonesty, and general lawlessness became a scourge to law-abiding citizens. Law enforcement officials failed to deal adequately with the situation, with the result that the best citizens of the community organized a citizen group of "Regulators" to enforce the laws. Lonz Powers, leader of the outlaws, it is to be noted, is also a member of a good family and leads a double existence. Like Weir's other novels, this one is full of villainy and blood and death, and doubtless also helped prepare the way for later dime novels.

Weir wrote two more pieces of historical fiction dealing with the frontier: *Simon Kenton; or, the Scout's Revenge* (1852) and *The Winter Lodge; or, Vow Fulfilled* (1854). The former focuses on well-known frontiersman and Indian fighter Simon Kenton, who in his own day rivaled Daniel Boone. He was a scout under Boone, served in the Kaskaskia and Vincennes campaigns under George Rogers Clark, was a major under Anthony Wayne, fought in many battles against the Indians, and served with the Kentucky volunteers in the War of 1812. He is a part of many legends of the frontier and of many novels, among them Winston Churchill's *The Crossing* and Maurice Thompson's *Alice of Old Vincennes*. In Weir's novel Kenton has the nobility of Boone but lacks his gentleness; he is something of a blend of Boone and Mike Fink, boastful and violent but always noble. *The Winter Lodge* also deals with Kenton and the frontier, but this time the scene is principally in Western Kentucky. The story is full of sensationalism as it records the migration of the Duffes and the Heads from North Carolina and the relentless pursuit of them by Indians and the white renegade Simon Girty. Ultimately the heads of both families are slain.

Weir was born in Greenville, graduated from Centre College, and studied law at Transylvania University. He spent his adult life in Owensboro, where he engaged in a legal and business career as well as in writing.

Charles Wilkins Webber

Of lesser note is Charles Wilkins Webber (1819–56), of Russellville, whose short stories were published in 1852 as *The Hunter-Naturalist; or, Wild Scenes and Wild Hunters*. In the volume appear sketches of Boone, Harrod, and Audubon; "The Dark Fiddler and the Wolves," which was reprinted in early school readers all over the country; and "Bill Smith, the Silent Hunter," a story which portrays the later life of an old Revolutionary War soldier. *The Hunter-Naturalist* contains bits of frontier folklore, ranging from the remarkable marksmanship of the frontiersman to the gradual transformation of Daniel Boone the backwoodsman into Boone the heroic agent of progress.

CHAPTER 4

Literature of Life in the Grand Manner

With the Revolutionary War over and the Indian no longer a serious threat to safety, the flow of settlers across the mountains and down the Ohio River increased dramatically. The white population, numbered in the hundreds in 1780, reached 73,677 by the census of 1790, 220,655 by 1800, 406,511 by 1810, and 564,317 by 1820. A land grab was on, and among those trekking across the mountains for the first time were the second and third sons of prominent Virginia families who because of primogeniture were unable to develop great plantations of their own in Virginia. Like the first settlers, this young gentry envisioned a new Eden, though their entrance into it introduced a threat to those who had gone before, for these first settlers held possession of the land only on the basis of their prior occupancy, and, unfortunately for many of them, the land had never been surveyed nor boundary lines established. Thus the stage was set for endless litigation as the rush for land accelerated; and the incoming aristocratic gentry, aided by able lawyers, manipulated the situation to their advantage. Thus during the period of less than twenty years between the mid-1790s and 1815 they acquired land, made fortunes, built great houses, intermarried, gained influence, and quietly began making that influence felt. On their estates, in addition to the "big house," satellite cabins housed field hands, cooks, chambermaids, gardeners, coachmen, seamstresses, and nurses. Other structures included a coach house, stables, a dairy, a washhouse, a smokehouse, blacksmith and carpentry shops, and often a kitchen separated from the house to lessen the likelihood of a fire.

The Bluegrass gentry enjoyed a life of comfort and ease on estates ranging from a few hundred to thousands of acres. Visiting back and forth, even for two weeks at a time, was common, and regular visits to the spas at Olympia Springs, Blue Licks, Crab Orchard, Graham Springs, and Drennon Springs were a part of the summer season. Dining was elegant, equipages were costly, and the arts as a source of entertainment were well supported. Slavery was not universal, but it was general.

At the geographical center of this life in the grand manner was Lexington, transformed from a small frontier community into a thriving town of 2400 and by 1820 known as the Athens of the West. As more and more migrants streamed westward, most roads in Kentucky led to Lexington. Inns and taverns sprang up to meet the needs of travelers, and those who dealt in goods and supplies found their services in great demand. Though not located on a navigable river, Lexington was destined to become a thriving market center, but even more importantly it became a cultural and professional center.

In the 1780s Transylvania College and John Bradford's *The Kentucky Gazette* were established. In the 1790s a library came into being, Transylvania founded a medical school, inns and taverns began to provide entertainment, a Jockey Club was organized and a race course built. At the turn of the century the first "permanent" theater was built, and by 1820 six hundred performances had been produced in Lexington as against fifty-four in Cincinnati and thirty-two in St. Louis; and in the early 1800s stagecoach runs were started, the first to Olympia Springs at Owingsville. By 1820 Lexington had not only silversmiths, cabinetmakers, and watchmakers, but also dancing masters and a dancing school, musical organizations and public concerts, and a distinguished painter, Matthew Jouett. There were bookstores, academies for both sexes, printing offices, three newspapers and a literary magazine, a sculptor, nine physicians, a Lyceum, and a circulating library. Great houses arose, and social life was lavish. Prominent residents were businessmen like John Wesley Hunt and Benjamin Gratz, physicians like Dr. Samuel Brown and Dr. Frederick Ridgeley, and jurists like John Breckinridge, Humphrey Marshall, George Robertson, and Henry Clay. And just as the second decade ended two young people who would play crucial roles in the nation's history were in school only a short block apart: Jefferson Davis at Transylvania University and Mary Todd in a girl's school on the southeast corner of the campus.

The success of the gentry was not, of course, matched by the small farmers, who were commonly reduced to becoming renters or migrating elsewhere. Interestingly enough, however, the loss of land and station does not appear to have engendered significant anger or enmity on the part of the dispossessed yeomen. A stratified society was not a new concept to them. They might aspire to a high place in the scheme of things, but apparently it was enough that all could have the opportunity to improve upon their lot. In a well-ordered eighteenth-century view of life some were born to rule and some to serve, and there was a role and a place for everybody. In such a society, slavery, as well as a landlord-tenant relationship, was mainly an accepted way of life, but so also was something resembling the principle of *noblesse oblige*. At its best, it was a world in which rich and poor, strong and weak, were mutually supportive. Man or woman, worker or slave—all were expected to do their best for their masters, and the master was expected to safeguard the best interests of those who were responsible to him, for from the one who had most, most was expected. No doubt there was abuse of the sytem, and no doubt life was never as ideal as time and distance might make it appear to have been, but to those who produced it, it must have seemed the Garden Myth come full bloom. James Lane Allen and others at the end of the century would lament the passing of the genteel tradition as a result of the Civil War and Recontruction, for it was with a deep sense of loss that they saw the metaphor of the Garden replaced by one of Paradise Lost. But two authors, at least, wrote of this world while it was still intact.

Mary Jane Holmes

Mary Jane Holmes (1828–1907) was the first novelist to write of this idealized world. She and her husband came to Versailles from their native New York after their marriage in 1849 and taught school, first in Versailles and then in the nearby district school at Glen's Creek. In 1852 they gave up teaching to return to New York, where Mr. Holmes could practice law. Except for a visit to the Bluegrass in 1857, this was the extent of Mrs. Holmes's acquaintance with Kentucky; but for at least a dozen years she continued to draw upon her Woodford County experience, and in 1865 she published the last of her five "Kentucky" novels. The world out of which these novels grew was the heart of the affluent Bluegrass region and the lushly green, prosperous antebellum farms that operated mainly with the assistance of slave labor. The homes were aristocratic, and their occupants provided the ingredients for domestic conflict and the essential elements of plot.

Holmes's novels about the aristocratic families of the Bluegrass are tailored to fit this background, but all of her plots, characters, and plot resolutions have much in common. Her protagonists are all noble heroes and beautiful, virtuous heroines who must contend with others who are unscrupulous, dishonest or designing, or have disagreeable or overbearing personal qualities. Since Holmes's ethical system recognizes only black and white so far as conduct is concerned, virtue is always rewarded, evil punished, and no intermediate gray is allowed to confuse the reader or lead to compromise. Such an over-simplified system of values handled in a sentimental, hackneyed style would satisfy few readers today, but such was Holmes's appeal in her day that she had only one or two peers in popularity. In all, she wrote thirty-odd novels between 1854 and 1905, and over two million copies were sold by her official publisher. How many more copies were published in unauthorized paperback folio and octavo editions cannot be estimated.

Most popular of Holmes's novels was her first, *Tempest and Sunshine; or, Life in Kentucky* (1854). It is the story of two Woodford County sisters who are very different in character and behavior: Julia Middleton ("Tempest") has an unpleasant disposition and is haughty and overbearing; and Susan ("Sunshine"), with a sweet and sunny temperament, is gentle and noble. Sunshine's virtue triumphs as she makes a happy marriage, while Tempest, who has almost brought tragedy down upon herself and her sister, must repent and see the error of her ways. *Lena Rivers* (1856), almost as popular as *Tempest and Sunshine*, has its setting in an aristocratic Kentucky home just before the Civil War. It also rewards good and punishes evil, as beautiful and virtuous Lena Rivers is snubbed by the haughty kinsfolk with whom she lives and, in Cinderella fashion, turns out to be an heiress and wins an adoring and wealthy husband.

Both of these novels were adapted for stage presentation, and both became standard fare on showboats, first as melodrama played straight for unsophisticated audiences looking for drama in which good is rewarded and evil punished in uncomplicated fashion. *Lena Rivers*, however, the more sentimental and melodramatic of the two, outlasted *Tempest and Sunshine* and became a favorite "melerdrama" on Billy Bryant's showboat during the 1920's and even became a veteran on the *Goldenrod* after she was tied up at St. Louis in 1937 as a dinner theater. Here more than two million people went to hiss the villain and cheer virtue triumphant.

Other novels of Mary Jane Holmes with a Bluegrass setting are *The Homestead on the Hill, and Other Tales* (1856), *Marian Grey* (1863), and *Hugh Worthington* (1865), but only the last of the three approached *Tempest and Sunshine* and *Lena Rivers* in popularity. It is a Civil War story in which the master of a Bluegrass farm opposes slavery and fights in the Union army.

Stephen Collins Foster

Stephen Collins Foster (1825–64) was a visitor to Kentucky rather than a legal resident and a writer of lyrics for the songs he composed rather than a writer of belles-lettres. So closely associated with Kentucky is Foster's name, however, and so great has been the influence of "My Old Kentucky Home" (1852) in making the Commonwealth appear a special sort of place, that it seems appropriate to take brief note of Foster's song, whose words and music create a myth of life in the grand manner. Whatever the faults of that life and of slavery or its practice in the Commonwealth may have been, Kentucky is made to seem (as Harriet Beecher Stowe herself confirmed) a Camelot sort of place where the relationship between the master and the slave was about as ideal as such a system could allow. And to a listener today the words "my old Kentucky home far away" invite an extension of the myth to the point where the poem (or song) becomes a statement about mutability and a nostalgic reminder of an earlier day when life was simpler and the world free of hurry and confusion, of a time when life was gentler and people—the black and white alike—were a bit kinder and a bit more generous.

In view of the uncertainty about Foster's knowledge of Kentucky, it seems appropriate to cite a few of the known facts. Between 1846 and 1850 Foster worked as a bookkeeper for a steamboat agency in Cincinnati of which his brother, Dunning, was a part owner. This was at the time when Harriet Beecher Stowe was engaged in her abolitionist activities, and like her Foster must have had some knowledge of Northern Kentucky plantations and of the Underground Railroad that funneled slaves into Covington and across the river to Cincinnati. We know, too, that he was "an occasional visitor" in the home of his kinsman, Judge John Rowan, at Federal Hill in Bardstown and there doubtless saw a plantation in operation. In the Foster Hall Collection, in Indianapolis, is a letter from Gilbert L. Eberhart, dated August 29, 1900, to Foster's brother, Morrison, inquiring about the extent to which Foster was a protégé of Judge Rowan, to what extent he made his home there, and how much writing he did there. Morrison's reply apparently no longer exists, but in the upper-right corner of the Eberhart letter is a penciled note in Morrison's hand: "Ans. Oct.3/ He was not a protégé of/Judge Rowan but only an oc-/casional visitor at Federal/Hill. Judge Rowan was his/father's cousin" (John Tasker Howard, *Stephen Foster, America's Troubadour*, 175).

CHAPTER 5

Literature of Slavery

By the 1790 census in Kentucky, there were 12,430 blacks, or about 17 percent, out of a total population of 74,000. The rate of increase among blacks exceeded that of whites after 1790, but at no time before the Civil War did the number of blacks exceed 24 percent. By 1860 there were 225,483 blacks. Slavery in Kentucky was always a particularly "peculiar institution," for Kentucky's climate, soil, and terrain simply were not suited to big-scale, year-round use of slave labor as was the case in the Deep South where great cotton and sugar cane plantations flourished. There were a few plantations in both the Bluegrass area and in Western Kentucky, but by and large slavery in Kentucky was not so much a commercial, profit-making institution as it was a domestic, personal-service relationship, with one to three slaves being the commonest number on a farm.

In another way, too, Kentucky was in a peculiar position in relation to slavery in that it was the northernmost slave state, with the Ohio River constituting almost seven hundred miles of its northern boundary. As early as 1818 slaves began escaping across the Ohio River, headed for Canada; and escape from the Deep South became so common that by 1830 the Underground Railroad was organized and functioning. With support and guidance from abolitionists, "lines" (escape routes) and "stations" (stopping places for food and rest) were set up, and "conductors" (those who aided slaves along the escape routes) guided escapees to their destinations. Success depended upon the "conductors" (disguised as peddlers, census-takers, etc.), who went throughout the South making arrangements with prospective escapees, establishing "stations" twenty-five to thirty miles apart in the houses or on the property of sympathizers. At the stations escapees could get sleep, food, clothes, and general information about hiding places in hayricks and along riverbanks and about dense thickets that could provide emergency refuge. Nowhere was there a more effective line than the Kentucky-Ohio routes, where the chief organizer was Levi Coffin and his wife in Cincinnati, just as John Brown and Harriet Tubman were celebrated leaders in the East. The most efficient line was the one that led into Cincinnati through Covington and Kenton County, but there were fifteen stations on the northern bank of the Ohio, reaching from Cairo, Illinois, in the west to Ironton, Ohio, in the east. Once slaves were across the river, they might still have trouble, especially after the Fugitive Slave Act of 1850, but the worst of the journey to Canada and freedom was over.

Harriet Beecher Stowe

Although Harriet Beecher Stowe (1811–96) was never a resident of Kentucky, she lived for eighteen years across the river in Cincinnati, was familiar with the Underground Railroad Movement in Cincinnati and Northern Kentucky, and made fairly lengthy visits in Mason, Boyle, and Garrard counties, where she witnessed slave auctions and saw a large plantation operated by slave labor. During one of these visits in 1833 in the house of Marshall Key in Washington, then the county seat of Mason County, Stowe observed slaves at work, saw slave quarters, and witnessed two slaves being sold on the block in front of the Old Mason County Court House. What further exposure to the institution of slavery she experienced in Boyle County is not known, but certainly some. Here she became engaged to Calvin E. Stowe at the home of John C. Young, president of Centre College and a friend of her father.

Stowe's acquaintance with slavery on a large plantation came apparently in 1840 when she visited in what appears to have been the Spillman home at Paint Lick, near the plantation of Thomas Kennedy, Jr. Here she saw at first hand the mansion on such an estate and the slave cabins, mill, blacksmith shop, carriage house, storage buildings, and so on, that were necessary parts of the operation of a seven-thousand-acre estate with two hundred slaves. Apparently, however, Stowe's visit in Garrard County also gave her ideas for some of the characters in *Uncle Tom's Cabin*. Mr. Kennedy and his wife, for example, are believed to have been the prototypes of Mr. and Mrs. Shelby, and Little Eva is supposed to have been suggested by Kennedy's daughter, Nancy, though it has been claimed that Elizabeth Key, of Washington, was the prototype. And Lewis Clarke, a Kennedy slave, is thought to have been the inspiration for George Harris.

One other Kentucky slave is believed to have been the principal model for a character in *Uncle Tom's Cabin*. Josiah Henson, born in Maryland in 1789, was bought by Isaac Riley, whose brother Amos owned a plantation in Daviess County, Kentucky. In 1825 Henson's master placed Henson in charge of twenty-one other slaves he was sending to his brother's plantation. Despite the temptation to escape, Henson delivered his charges to Amos Riley and was soon made overseer of his lands. Three years later Isaac Riley ordered all his slaves sold "down the river" except Henson and his family. In 1829 Henson returned to Maryland and purchased his freedom, only to be tricked by Isaac Riley and returned to Daviess County still in bondage. Thereupon Henson escaped with his family and made his way to Dresden, Canada, and freedom. In 1829 Stowe met Henson when she invited him to Andover, Massachusetts, for an interview. Later she told about him in *A Key to Uncle Tom's Cabin* (1853) and still later she wrote the introduction to *Father Henson's Story of His Own Life* (1858).

Uncle Tom's Cabin began appearing serially in 1851 and was published in book form in 1852. Immediately it became a best seller and sold 300,000 copies during its first year. By December 1852 six London theaters were producing George Aiken's stage version of the novel. Almost instantly Stowe found herself a person of national prominence and influence. In writing her novel she had followed the methods of melodrama and created in Uncle Tom, Simon Legree, Eliza, Eva, Topsy, and others, characters which by any reasonable critical standards were overdrawn and basically unbelievable. The novel was lacking in objectivity and showed signs of haste; it contained exaggerations and distortions and appealed directly to the emotions. Yet it gave a reasonably balanced picture of slavery and of antebellum society and managed to thrill sophisticated readers and theater-goers, as it did those lacking in critical and intellectual pretensions. The strength of the novel comes from the author's imagination, her descriptive power, her surging humanity, and her ability in drawing characters—especially Tom, Eva, and Liza. The dramatic escape of Liza—a real-life story told to Stowe by Levi Coffin—became the stuff of legend, created an image that revealed the plight of a people, helped polarize feeling toward slavery, and made the novel one of the greatest propaganda forces of all time.

William Wells Brown

William Wells Brown (ca. 1814–84) is of particular interest here not only because he was born a slave in or near Lexington but because he was America's first black novelist. When he was ten he was taken to St. Louis to work on a steamboat on the Ohio and Mississippi rivers and tried to escape with his mother by way of the Underground Railroad to Canada. They were caught, and his mother was sold "down the river." Brown escaped again in 1834, this time through Cincinnati and Ohio, successfully. Then followed, beginning in the 1840s, a remarkably rich and rewarding career in which, self-educated, Brown became a well-known abolitionist, novelist, playwright, historian, essayist, lecturer, and physician, using his talents to point up social injustices—especially slavery—and to work in a practical way against them. He published more than twelve books and pamphlets, was invited as a delegate to the Paris Peace Conference of 1849, and was acquainted with such eminent national leaders as William Lloyd Garrison and Wendell Phillips in the United States, Richard Cobden in England, and Victor Hugo in France.

The work for which Brown is best known is *Clotel; or, the President's Daughter: A Narrative of Slave Life in the United States* (1853). It is principally the story of Currer, a mulatto slave of Richmond, Virginia, her quadroon daughters, Clotel and Altheza, and Clotel's daughter, Mary. For several years Currer was the housekeeper and mistress of Thomas Jefferson, who was the father of her two daughters. Jefferson is called to Washington for a government appointment and Currer is left behind and is obliged to take in washing to support herself and her children. Early in the story Currer and her daughter, who is sixteen, are being sold at auction. What happens to Clotel, her daughter Mary, her mother, and her sister makes up the rest of the story, which is highly melodramatic.

Dealing with miscegenation and with Thomas Jefferson as the father of mulatto daughters, the novel was sensational, shocking stuff that no American publisher would touch. As a result it was published in England in 1853. Brown had no factual knowledge of miscegenation on the part of Jefferson, but he himself had a white father, knew that miscegenation was common, and was familiar with stories that Jefferson, as well as other men of prominence, had fathered such children and then conveniently forgotten about them. He merely knew that in Jefferson's case this could have been true and seized upon the miscegenation theme as a sensational way of producing a strong argument against slavery and illustrating how a man's practice may be out of harmony with his public principles.

After being greatly censored, the novel was published in the United States in 1864 and 1867, respectively, as *Clotelle: A Tale of the Southern States* and *Clotelle; or, the Colored Heroine: A Tale of the Southern States*. All references to Jefferson were deleted. (In 1978 Barbara Chase-Ribaud tells somewhat the same Jefferson story in *Sally Hemings*, a novel based on her own research.) Most biographers of Jefferson, including the preeminent Dumas Malone, give no credence to the story. Brown was also the author of *The Escape; or, a Leap for Freedom* (1858), a play based on his own life story. In 1848 he published *The Anti-Slavery Harp*, a collection of antislavery songs; and was the author of half a dozen volumes about blacks and their history.

Mrs. A.C. Carman

Uncle Tom's Cabin inspired ardently defensive responses, particularly in the Deep South, where slavery was generally portrayed in a favorable light and slaves like Uncle Tom were depicted as contented with their bondage and satisfied with the freedom they had. Such sentiments appear in a play by a Kentucky author and actress, Mrs. A.C. Carman, who in 1863 acted in her *Uncle Tom's Cabin in the South* in a Louisville theater. The characters are *Uncle Tom's Cabin* characters, but the life of a slave is depicted in a favorable light and the ending is a happy one.

Elizabeth Bryant Johnston

More representative in Kentucky were the antislavery novels which, like *Uncle Tom's Cabin*, portrayed the slave owner as a decent, generous, high-minded individual who was caught up in an iniquitous social and domestic system of which he did not really approve. A good example is *Christmas in Kentucky* (1862) by Elizabeth Bryant Johnston (1833–1907), who was born in Mason County. This short novel, whose locale is a plantation near Covington, tells how its owner, John Montgomery Ashley, announced with great satisfaction the Emancipation Proclamation to his slaves during the Christmas holiday season. Ashley is a high-minded slave owner and is so portrayed in some touching scenes.

PART TWO

Coming of Age
1860–1930

CHAPTER 6

The Genteel Tradition

The gentry came across the mountains, mainly from Virginia, after the Revolutionary War had ended and particularly after Kentucky had become a state in 1792. This aristocracy went about building a culture in which wealth, good breeding, quality and temper of mind, education, manners, and the cultivation of learning and the arts were of paramount importance. This was the capstone of the rather complex agrarian society that had evolved in one short half-century, for by 1825–30 the Genteel Tradition was coming into full flower and would reach its zenith between 1830 and 1860.

What, then, was this pre–Civil War Genteel Tradition as interpreted by James Lane Allen, its last champion, apart from the environment within which it flourished? As seen by one critic (Grant C. Knight, *James Lane Allen and the Genteel Tradition*) its banner was "the banner of the Tories in 1900, those who clung to older regulations for behavior and who believed that there were boundaries over which no gentleman passed in conversation, thought, deed, or writing. It held aloft a standard of manners." In Allen's words, the most highly endowed nature is "he who has genius," and such a person, "no matter what the world may do to him, no matter what ruin may work in him, is under obligations so long as he lives to do nothing mean and to do nothing meanly" (*The Emblems of Fidelity*). These nine words —"to do nothing mean and to do nothing meanly"—were the grand device of the Genteel Tradition. The central problem of life, then, is how to live it; Allen plotted situations and devised elegantly chiseled statements that highlighted such problems. Another fine challenge is expressed in *The Choir Invisible* when John Gray summarizes the

James Lane Allen. Photo courtesy of University of Kentucky Photographic Archives.

philosophy of the Genteel Tradition: "To lose faith in men, not in humanity; to see justice go down and not to believe in the triumph of injustice; for every wrong that you weakly deal another or another deals you, to love more and more the fairness and beauty of what is right."

Such ringing challenges today are likely to fall upon cringing ears. They are too romantic, too idealistic, and the style is too heightened

John Fox, Jr. Photo courtesy of University of Kentucky Photographic Archives.

and too mannered. Indeed it must be said the whole doctrine ultimately came to be little more than a manner, a mode of conduct exemplified only in literature. There were, too, those in Allen's own day —the rising school of realists and naturalists—who objected to both the matter and the manner of the literature in the Genteel Tradition. By and large, however, turn-of-the-century readers were rooted in tradition, were high minded and instinctively decent, and were ready

Annie Fellows Johnston. Photo courtesy of the *Courier-Journal*.

Alice Hegan Rice. Photo courtesy of the *Courier-Journal*.

to respond affirmatively to the finely wrought principles and language that Allen used. It was not that they were ignorant of murder, violence, rape, arson, embezzlement, and perversion. They preferred drawing rooms and garden houses to mining and mill towns. When they read, they preferred men and women in their aspiring moments to characters weighed down by trouble and futility.

James Lane Allen

No matter what precisely the life of the pre–Civil War gentry may have been, James Lane Allen (1849–1925) was its principal interpreter and last champion. He was not born into the world of the gentry but into a larger world of which the gentry was a part, and he was drawn toward it by education and reading as well as by a romantic and idealistic disposition. For the first ten years of his life the Genteel Tradition was functional; by the time he was twenty the Civil War was over, Reconstruction was under way, and the old agrarian culture was joining hands with the new, more progressive ways of the North and capitalism. The abolition of slavery had of course helped alter the way life on the large estates was carried on, and now as economic life in Kentucky fell into the corporate hands of northern industrial and commercial interests, a new kind of wealth and landed estates appeared. The world of the gentry and the old agrarian life did not totally disappear, but the texture of society was forever changed. The Camelot days of pre–Civil War Kentucky were gone except as they might be relived again in books.

James Lane Allen was born on a farm about five miles from Lexington on the Parker's Mill Road, December 21, 1849. He did not grow up as a member of the aristocracy, for after 1860 his family suffered heavy misfortunes that grew out of the Civil War and Reconstruction, and so as a young man Allen endured hardship. One winter, for example, as he earned his way through Transylvania University, he was obliged to wear an old shawl instead of an overcoat. He was an excellent student and graduated in 1872 as valedictorian of his class, after which he served in various positions as a schoolmaster and college teacher: at the Fort Springs district school where he was born, as principal of the Transylvania Academy, as master of his own school, and at Richmond College in Missouri and Bethany College in West Virginia.

Allen's mind, however, turned increasingly to writing. By the mid-1880s he was publishing regularly in the best magazines of the day: *The Critic, Atlantic Monthly, Harper's Magazine, Lippincott's*

Magazine, *Century Magazine*, and others. These magazines, he had observed, were giving much space to stories and accounts of life in the lesser-known states and regions, and local colorists such as George W. Cable, Kate Chopin, Thomas Nelson Page, and Joel Chandler Harris were much published. As early as 1883 Allen began to publish articles about Kentucky and stories with Kentucky locales. In fact, writing about Kentucky and Kentuckians became a primary aim of his life. Fourteen of his eighteen volumes were devoted almost exclusively to Kentucky; three have heroes who were born in the state but who have moved to New York City, as he himself did in 1893; and one has no characters at all. Among the articles he published are "The Blue-Grass Region of Kentucky," "Through Cumberland Gap on Horse-back," "Mrs. Stowe's Uncle Tom at Home in Kentucky," "A Home of the Silent Brotherhood." Soon Allen began to pair his articles with stories. Thus "The White Cowl" grew out of the "Silent Brotherhood" and was a story of rebellion of one of the Trappist monks at Gethsemani, near Bardstown, and "Two Gentlemen of Kentucky" out of the "Uncle Tom at Home" account. Both stories were based on real events, the latter being an account of Colonel Romulus Fields, a land-owner who could not adjust to conditions after the Civil War, and his devoted servant, Peter, formerly his slave. Prototypes of the two were Major Madison C. Johnson of Lexington and Peter Vinegar, the noted black minister. Other short stories also came out of real life: "King Solomon of Kentucky," the vagrant who became the hero of the Lexington cholera epidemic of 1833; "Sister Dolorosa," a tragic love story of a nun at the convent of Loretto and a young man of the Bluegrass; and "Flute and Violin," which gave Allen the title for his first volume and told the story of a little lame boy who stole a quarter so that he could see a traveling exhibition of wax figures that came to Lexington.

These and other stories Allen brought together from the magazines and published in 1891 as *Flute and Violin, and Other Kentucky Tales and Romances*. The following year *The Blue Grass Region of Kentucky, and Other Articles*, also collected from the magazines, was published. The latter volume was not impressive, but it achieved what it was intended to, and *Flute and Violin* launched Allen's career most successfully. As judged by modern standards for the short story, the six stories in the volume have too much natural background, move too slowly, and with insufficient dramatic force. But much in them is still excellent by today's standards. In his own day Allen was instantly popular, both in Kentucky and the nation, for he wrote well and fit nicely into the current interest in local color writing. Picturing Kentucky to the world gave Allen great satisfaction, and in portraying Kentucky's people, manners, social history, and pre–Civil War glory he aroused wide interest among his readers.

Allen, then, began as a local color writer, though he was a local color writer with a difference. As early as 1886 he had published an article in *The Critic* entitled "Local Color," in which he declared that the local colorist must not be narrow or provincial but must portray the universal in the local if he is not to be limited and handicapped by the principle under which he works. Allen's principles of art would not allow him to consider local color as an end in itself. He protested against what he saw as over-use of dialect. Local colorists, he feared, had become too much concerned with picturesque externals and too little with internals. It was his aim, therefore, to make his central concern the moral and ethical problems that character and plot depend on. For his efforts Allen was identified by one critic as "the one man in the South capable of lifting fiction above the level of negro dialect stories." Neither the state nor its people, therefore, were really indispensable to his stories. The conflict between religious vows and romantic love could have taken place almost anywhere, the faithfulness of a slave to his master could be found in other states. In this first stage of his career as a writer of fiction, his period of short stories and sketches, Allen was working on a small canvas with uncomplicated plots. In 1893, his reputation made, he moved to New York City and except for one occasion in 1898 he never visited Kentucky again.

Allen now turned to longer fiction: first a slight novel, *John Gray* (1893), later expanded into *The Choir Invisible* (1897), and then *A Kentucky Cardinal* (1894), a novelette and one of his finest and best-known works. "One of the finest things in American literature," said one critic. The scene of the novelette is Kentucky in 1850 and its principal characters are the nature-loving Adam Moss and a society girl, Georgiana Cobb. Today the book does not appeal as it once did, partly because it lacks the true-to-life quality we have come to expect in fiction. But lifelikeness was not an objective of Allen: his aim, as one critic put it, was "to write an idyl of provincial life . . . a romance in which the traditional hero and heroine [are like] costumed figures in a tiny pageant and move with some of the stateliness and grace of a minuet."

Built into *A Kentucky Cardinal* are the seeds of a sequel, for Georgiana has confronted Adam with a test by demanding that he capture one of the cardinals he loves and bring it to her in a cage as proof of his dedication to her. Adam's love for wild things is thus pitted against his love for the girl; but with misgivings he delivers the caged bird, only to have her tell him that he has erred in having done so, for one should never surrender his innermost self to anyone. A partial resolution of the problem takes place, but the way is left open for the sequel, *Aftermath* (1895), which, though worthy, was not the equal of its predecessor.

It was with *Summer in Arcady* (1896) that Allen made a transition into the second stage of his career by moving toward the realism —"the Masculine Principle," he called it—that he was to explain the following year in an article in the *Atlantic Monthly*. For twenty-five or thirty years, he maintained, the Feminine Principle, rather than the Masculine, had dominated American fiction, including his own stories. Fiction, he went on, had aimed at Refinement and Grace and had failed to enter the main current of the new age that was rising. This age was more Vigorous, more Strenuous, more Virile, and literature must keep pace with it. Examples of those who had already broken with the Genteel Tradition were Mark Twain, Hamlin Garland, and Stephen Crane. *Summer in Arcady* is a study of sex in the lives of a young man and young woman against a rural background in Bourbon County. Following the naturalists, Allen deals with the laws of nature—instincts, heredity, biological forces—that are larger than human beings and control them in ways they do not understand. Its publication was met with outcries of disapproval, but Allen stood firmly on what he regarded as safe "scientific" grounds. He felt also that he was telling the truth about human life, that he had something to say to his generation, and that he had no choice but to write as he did. Already he was thinking about *The Reign of Law*.

The Choir Invisible (1897), generally regarded as Allen's best novel, was an instant success with the reading public. It rose to second on the annual best-seller list for the year and ranked among the top ten of its decade. But it was also a success with the critics, and Allen came to be acclaimed as America's greatest living novelist. At one level it is a historical novel in that it begins with the year 1795 and deals with the Kentucky frontier, especially with what is now the Fayette County area. It is not a historical novel in the conventional sense, however. The novel does take cognizance of the perilous conditions on the frontier and the presence of Indians, but it is more concerned with the way people think, their ethics and their religion, and the manner in which frontier ways are mixing and blending with the greater gentility that is also present. Allen is interested in the inner life of people, almost to the exclusion of external incidents. John Gray, the schoolmaster, is the central character of the novel. He longs for a wife who shares his stern moral convictions but falls in love with Amy Falconer, a coquette far inferior to him in every way. Before he can make the mistake of marrying her, however, he realizes that the sort of woman he wants to marry is not Amy, but her aunt, Jessica. But Jessica is married to his friend, and though she returns Gray's feelings for her, neither he nor she, for reasons of honor, declares those thwarted feelings to the other until many years later. The theme of the story, then, is renunciation of love because of moral and ethical scruples, and Allen handles it well.

The Reign of Law (1900), Allen's second novel adhering to the Masculine Principle, is one of the first American novels to deal with religious doubt. Here the author acts on his conviction that "in the light of the great central idea of Evolution, all departments of human knowledge had to be reviewed, reconsidered, reconceived, rearranged, and rewritten." The novel begins—startlingly enough—with a twenty-three page description of the growing of hemp in Kentucky. But just as Hardy (whose influence Allen felt strongly) opened *The Return of the Native* with a long statement on how Egdon Heath affected the lives of the people who lived on it, so Allen intended to illustrate how the sowing, sprouting, and growing of hemp exemplifies a law of nature. In like manner he felt that our solar system, everything that is, is the expression of immutable laws—the reign of law. For such utterances Allen was attacked from all directions, with churches taking the lead. He had written an anti-fundamentalist novel. "Is Mr. Allen's *Reign of Law* an Infidel work?" asked the *Literary Digest*. "Nowhere," said the *New York Times*, "has the parental and filial aspect of evolution been so closely and powerfully portrayed." Such a furor could only stimulate sales, and for the second time Allen made the top-ten list of best sellers in the United States. By November the *Literary Digest* was reporting that *The Reign of Law* was the fastest-selling novel in England.

It was three years (1903) before Allen's next novel, *The Mettle of the Pasture*, appeared. It also affronted many readers because it dealt with "the double standard" and seemed to come down on the side of a single standard. It is the story of Rowan Meredith, who on the night of his being accepted by Isabel Conyers feels he must tell her that he has an illegitimate child by a woman he knew in college, that he had offered marriage to her and had been refused, and that she had enlisted his secrecy about the matter. So damaged is Isabel's feeling toward Meredith that she refuses to marry him. Ultimately she forgives him, marries him, and bears him a child; but by this time the strain of all that has gone before costs Meredith his life, thus exacting of both the man and woman a heavy penalty.

Despite the ethical and moral objections of some readers, and despite its structural flaws, *The Mettle of the Pasture* not only was in the top ten for the year, but also won critical acclaim. *The Outlook* echoes a frequent judgment: "Mr. Allen's work, as it is gradually presented to us, seems to indicate that he will take in our generation the place which Hawthorne occupied in his own." What could not be foreseen at that time was that Allen would not publish another major work for six years and that, when he did, *The Bride of the Mistletoe* (1909) would puzzle readers and critics alike, as did *The Doctor's Christmas* the following year. In fact, never again would Allen regain the prestige he once had. He would be productive. Volume after volume would appear, among them *The Heroine in Bronze* (1912), *The Last Christmas Tree* (1914), *The Sword of Youth* (1915), *A Cathedral Singer* (1916), *A Kentucky Warbler* (1918), *Emblems of Fidelity* (1919), *The Alabaster Box* (1923). But no one of them stirred critics to speak of him again as the Hawthorne of his age.

The long hiatus between *The Mettle of the Pasture* and *The Bride of the Mistletoe* (1903–1909) and the falling off in the quality of his work apparently were related to the alienation of some of Allen's reading audience, and especially his Kentucky readers. The years between 1910 and the time of his death in 1925 were the unhappiest in Allen's life, for though he tried his hand at romance and realism overlaid with symbolism, nothing any longer seemed to work for him. Public manners and literary tastes were changing around him. He considered returning to Lexington, but apparently he decided against it both because of the pain of seeing how it would be changed and because he realized that a change of location would not really end his sense of isolation. Meanwhile he continued to work at a moderate rate, and he considered writing an autobiographical, historical novel that "would recreate those years when the culture of the Old South, founded upon slavery, had given life a meaning and richness that had been lost" in the modern world. He intended to call it, apparently, *The Days of Our Fathers*. Like Henry James and William Dean Howells before him, he spent his last years out of touch with his time. In "A Cathedral Singer" (1914) Allen contemplates the theme of spiritual immortality and at the same time the immortality through fame that he had sought, come close to, and missed. His mood was close to that of Hardy. *The Alabaster Box,* written less than two years before his death, is a short novel built upon the reactions of a community to the death and funeral of a kindly, antebellum gentleman with whom Allen must have identified himself. We hear remarks of members of the funeral procession: "No man dare practice with his fellow men the whole of the virtue that is in him," says the minister; "He came too late to be understood," says another; "Once there did exist such a virtue in the American people—American kindness," says still another; "Mamma, where do they keep alabaster boxes?" asks a child. The title of the story, of course, comes from the Biblical account of the woman who broke her precious alabaster box in order to anoint the feet and the head of Jesus. Allen apparently is saying that nowadays also it is rare for an alabaster box to be broken in kindness.

In his will Allen left his small estate to the city of Lexington, with the provision that the money derived from it be spent to erect a fountain for Lexington children. The fountain, dedicated October 15, 1933, stands at the north end of Gratz Park across Third Street from Transylvania University's Morrison Chapel. Allen was buried in Lexington Cemetery, February 21, 1925. Had he but known it, he would have been pleased to think that one day the prestigious *Dictionary of American Biography* would say of him, "Without being narrow or provincial in outlook, Allen was at his best when utilizing the life and scenery of his native state; and more than any other author he made the Blue Grass Region of Kentucky known to both his countrymen and Europeans."

Today Allen is regarded as a minor writer, and some no doubt suspect he will ultimately fall into oblivion; but it is likely that he will keep a niche in the history of fiction in America and that literary historians will be unable to do without him as they study the tides of our national literary tastes. Great writers, we say, are ahead of their time and write for the future, but Allen was a traditionalist. He was looking toward the future when he advocated—and adopted for himself—what he called the Masculine Principle in literature. He foresaw that the future was to belong to the Zolas and the Flauberts of America. It is to his credit that he foresaw the shape of things to come and that he wanted to speak "realistically" to his generation on subjects that mattered; but he was a man of the Genteel Tradition and was better equipped to write of men and women in their aspiring moments rather than as they merely were. Despite any sense of promise unfulfilled in his works, however, one must remember that his failures were not commonplace ones: even the books of his later years have their flashes of power and beauty and the extraordinary. The closing thought of the *New York Times* reviewer of Grant C. Knight's *James Lane Allen and the Genteel Tradition* seems appropriate even today: "As one goes back and tries to assess Allen's place in the big scheme of things," he says, "somehow he keeps trying to emerge as a larger figure than the sterner judgment is quite willing to permit."

Other Authors

James Lane Allen was not, of course, the only Kentucky writer who chose life in the Genteel Tradition as the subject for his novels. No one else so well codified the tradition or had as much talent, but Eleanor Talbot Kinkead and Elizabeth Cherry Waltz were broadly in the same tradition. Before considering them, however, we must notice two other writers who were on the edge of the portrayal of the world that Allen wrote about, both of them better writers than Kinkead and Waltz. One of these was John Fox, Jr., who in some of his novels juxtaposes life in the mountains with life in the Bluegrass region. Stories with plots to fit this pattern had their origin in the visit that Allen paid to Fox when Fox was working with his father and his brother at a coal mine in the mountains. Here the two talked about "Through Cumberland Gap on Horseback" and "The Two Kentuckys," articles that Allen had recently published, and about how the backward mountain culture could be brought into the mainstream of the outside world. *The Trail of the Lonesome Pine* and *The Little Shepherd of Kingdom Come* are the best of the novels in which Fox incorporates the world of the Genteel Tradition. The other writer to work in the tradition was Annie Fellows Johnston, whose "Little Colonel" novels have their setting in the plantation myth of antebellum days.

Eleanor Talbot Kinkead Eleanor Talbot Kinkead, a long-time resident of Lexington whose writing span almost coincided with that of James Lane Allen, wrote of fashionable life in and around Lexington during the 1890s. Her novels lack genuine literary merit so far as plot and characterization are concerned, but they do manage to portray life as apparently it was lived at the close of the century among the old families.

No phrase occurs more frequently than "high breeding" as Kinkead writes of life among the Bluegrass aristocracy. Her novels include *'Gainst Wind and Tide* (1892), *Young Greer of Kentucky* (1895), *Florida Alexander* (1896), *The Invisible Bond* (1906), *The Courage of Blackburn Blair* (1907), and *The Spoils of the Strong* (1920).

Elizabeth Cherry Waltz *The Ancient Landmark* (1905), a minor novel by Elizabeth Cherry Waltz (1866–1903), deals with the problem of divorce in the case of a heroine whose husband is a drug addict. The story is sensational and the plot improbable, but many effective scenes reflect the agrarian Bluegrass society of the day. These scenes have sometimes been compared favorably with those in Allen's work. Waltz, a native of Ohio, along with her husband, worked for the *Courier-Journal* and was its literary editor. She published another novel and some short stories now forgotten.

CHAPTER 7

Local Color Literature

In the 1880s the writing of local color fiction had sufficient force in American literature to be called a "movement." Its practitioners were Bret Harte and Mark Twain in the West; George W. Cable, Mary N. Murfree, and Joel Chandler Harris in the South; Sarah Orne Jewett and Mary E. Wilkins Freeman in New England. Kentucky writers were interested in local color subjects to such an extent that the beginning of a substantial Kentucky literature can be said to have originated in local color fiction or at least to have developed coördinate with it. In fact, many of the writers cited elsewhere in this volume, under "Literature of the Frontier," "Literature of the Civil War," "Literature of Eastern Kentucky," and "Literature of the Genteel Tradition," for example, had some of their roots in the local color movement; and there were others whose writings have no moorings outside that movement.

Though local color writing was successful in all sections of the country, it flourished best in the South, very likely reflecting the unconscious desire of the South to recapture some of the glamor and distinction that it had enjoyed preceding the Civil War and Reconstruction. All local colorists were concerned with the distinctive character of their region: its customs, manners, dress, dialect, habits of thought, patterns of speech, and any other characteristics that may have escaped or withstood the leveling forces of change and national standardization.

Kentucky writers between 1885 and World War I wrote almost exclusively about Kentucky: James Lane Allen about the Bluegrass region; John Fox, Jr., about the mountains and Southeastern Kentucky; John Uri Lloyd about Northern Kentucky; Alice Hegan Rice about Louisville; Eliza Calvert Obenchain about Western Kentucky; Irvin S. Cobb about Paducah and the Jackson Purchase; and Cordia Greer Petrie about Barren County and the hill country.

The writings of James Lane Allen and John Fox, Jr., have been examined elsewhere; as local colorists both were quite different from the six writers whose works are discussed below. Allen not only wrote fiction in the local color tradition, he also wrote critically on the subject and established himself as a voice to be listened to at the national level. His article in *The Critic* called "Local Color" made it clear that to him local color was not an end in itself, that to have merit literature must involve ethical and moral problems, and that a writer of fiction must have skill in the portrayal of character and the development of plot. He declined to use dialect or picturesque "externals" that were the stock-in-trade of so many local colorists. Fox wrote no criticism and expressed no theories about local color writing, but he and Allen talked about how they could portray Kentucky to the outside world. Unlike Allen, Fox did use dialect, but as an integral feature of the person portrayed.

Some of Kentucky's local colorists, however, paid little heed to Allen's admonition and Fox's practice. Like many local colorists elsewhere they chose to employ—even to exploit—unusual and eccentric characters and dialect. Their portrayals did achieve a certain kind of superficial realism, a kind of physical verisimilitude, that failed to be greatly concerned with the larger aspects of life and human nature. Dialect as well as customs and behavior patterns play a conspicuous—even an exaggerated—role in the hands of these same writers when hillbilly or rural dwellers are brought up against the urban dweller. The use of dialect, of course, can be appropriate, for speech practices, like manners, remain pretty much unchanged as long as natural barriers such as mountains produce isolation or separation and as long as social barriers inhibit or prevent social contact. Exaggerating for effect, however, and exploiting or sentimentalizing the eccentric in either character or dialect are devices not found in the best local color writing. In their different ways Petrie's Angeline, Obenchain's Aunt Jane, and to a lesser extent Rice's Mrs. Wiggs suffer from such exploitive portrayals.

Alice Hegan Rice

By the end of the century the dominance of the local color movement was fading before the growing popularity of realism and naturalism, but local color short stories and novelettes, generally sentimental and in dialect, continued to be written and to have a large readership. Of the local colorists contemporary with Allen and Fox, the most talented and the most widely read was Alice Hegan Rice (1870–1942) of Louisville. She was much interested in improving the lot of the underprivileged. Her methods were very different from those of the two most notable muckrakers of the day, Lincoln Steffens and Ida Tarbell, although both of them were friends of Rice and visited in her home. Rice's talents as a writer and her genuine interest in the plight of the poor complemented each other and enabled her to have a literary career that was interesting and remarkable even if in the long run her place in Kentucky literary history is a small niche, albeit a well-situated one.

Rice was born in Shelbyville at the home of her grandfather, but she spent her life thereafter in Louisville. As a child she wrote sketches for her school paper and had a humorously satiric article published anonymously in the *Courier-Journal* when she was fifteen; but not until 1901 when she was thirty-one did Alice Hegan (she married poet Cale Young Rice in 1902) take the suggestion of some of her literary friends and begin to write about one of the philanthropies she had been associated with since she was sixteen.

Like most young ladies of the day who grew up in an urban home of some means and social standing, Miss Hegan balanced her social life with participation in philanthropic endeavors among the poor. Thus it was that she chose to do volunteer work in a slum called the Cabbage Patch. The area lay just west of Central Park (South Fourth Street and Magnolia Avenue), extended along a railroad track for several blocks, and was used as a cabbage field. At an earlier date it had been laid out as a subdivision, but when the lots did not sell, squatters made up largely of farm folk came in during the hard times following the money panic of 1873 and built shacks from the materials they salvaged from the nearby city dump. Here Miss Hegan taught in a mission Sunday School and became impressed with "the way the poor met their problems and triumphed over difficulties." Here, too, as she says in her autobiography, *The Inky Way* (1940), she learned to look for and discover "the nobility that lay hidden in even the most unpromising personality." The central character in the book she wrote was Mrs. Wiggs, "a funny old woman" from the Cabbage Patch who came to the Hegans' door for hand-outs with which to support her large and fatherless family. Mrs. Wiggs's unfailing courage, good humor, and optimism in the midst of privation, her resourcefulness and her resiliency, generated the events in *Mrs. Wiggs of the Cab-*

bage Patch (1901), a story that was to have a remarkable publishing history.

The time was right for such a novel. For one thing, the local color movement was going strong, and *Mrs. Wiggs* fit it by being "local," by dealing with the effect of environment upon characters, and by utilizing local dialect and speech patterns. For another, the brand of sentimentality it purveyed was very much in vogue. As William F. Axton wrote in his foreword to *Mrs. Wiggs of the Cabbage Patch*, Mrs. Wiggs is "solidly ensconced in the tradition of the sentimental family novel, or 'glad book,' of which perhaps the best known examples are *Little Women*, *Elsie Dinsmore*, and *Five Little Peppers and How They Grew*." The conventions of the form were well established: "a family in reduced circumstances or actual poverty because of a father dead, absent, sick, or feckless, is held together by an indomitable mother who manages her brood of bright, active children with good humor, and whose ingenuity, hard work, simple virtue, and faith . . . are finally rewarded, but only after many vicissitudes, some comic, some pathetic." The time was right also because the public was very much aware of the plight of the urban poor and inclined toward the sentimental school of social work rather than the more revolutionary cures of the muckrakers and reform novelists such as Upton Sinclair. It suited the taste of the time too that well-to-do characters be presented as kind, concerned, and generous, the poor as good-natured, submissive, appreciative, and willing to live on the bounty of the rich. Likewise, it was more than acceptable that the conditions of the poor be merely touched upon by realism, that sordidness be barely hinted at or be disguised by an aura of sweetness, and that language be strictly genteel.

Concluding that "everything comes out right if we just wait long enough," this epic of optimism was launched in 1901. Only two thousand copies were printed for the original edition, but by the next year it was No. 2 on the best-seller list; it was still No. 6 in 1903, reached its forty-seventh printing in 1912, and went on to sell more than 650,000 copies in over one hundred printings. It was translated into French, German, Dutch, Danish, Swedish, Chinese, and Japanese, and into Braille. In 1903 it made its stage debut in the Macauley Theatre in Louisville, ran seven seasons on Broadway, was popular enough to support three touring companies at one time, and continued to be a part of stock company repertory for more than thirty years. Four times it was made into a motion picture, with silent versions in 1910 and 1925, sound versions in 1934 (Pauline Lord, W.C.

Fields, Zazu Pitts, and Donald Meek played the principal roles) and in 1942 (when Fay Bainter of Louisville won an Oscar for her portrayal of Mrs. Wiggs). Finally, *Mrs. Wiggs* was presented as a successful radio serial.

It was mandatory that such a popular success be followed by a sequel. So Rice wrote *Lovey Mary* (1903), a children's story about the Cabbage Patch which, though it reached No. 4 on the best-seller list for 1903, lacks the spark of its predecessor. Lovey Mary, the central character, shares the spotlight with the three-year-old Tommy, whom Lovey Mary had rescued by abducting him from a worthless mother, and with Mrs. Wiggs, who mothers both of them. Like *Mrs. Wiggs*, *Lovey Mary* was an epic of optimism and cheerfulness as Lovey Mary and Tommy enjoyed the advantages of the Cabbage Patch; and life there, with all its oddities and failings, but surrounded by essential goodness, continued to hold the interest of Rice's wide readership.

Two years later Rice again used a child as the central figure in a story to follow up the success she had achieved with *Lovey Mary*. This time she chose a boy, Sandy, and she looked outside the Cabbage Patch for her characters. Sandy is an impetuous Scottish boy, come to America as a stowaway, who has an exciting career as he becomes a bootblack, a newsboy, and a peddler; he is adopted by kindly Judge Hollis of Clayton, Kentucky, and finally becomes Judge Clayton's law partner. Again Rice had a winner, for *Sandy* (1905) was No. 2 among the best sellers of the year.

Captain June (1907) was Rice's third story with a child as the principal character. This time it is a little American boy who is left with his Japanese nanny while his mother goes to Manila to nurse the boy's father through a fever. The story relates what the boy does to amuse himself, how he gets in and out of trouble, and how he learns of Japanese customs, of wooden shoes, jinrikishaws, and beautiful dresses of purple and gold. *Captain June* was the least successful of Rice's children's stories.

The words most often used to describe Alice Hegan Rice's children's stories are "charming," "cheerful," "amusing," "wholesome," "delightful," "simple," and "lifelike." No one has ever claimed greatness for her writings. But Rice's age was less harshly critical than ours. What to many now would be "sentimental" was then considered "full of sympathy and understanding," as well as "being undergirded with fortitude" that gave "optimism" and "cheerfulness" an acceptable demeanor.

Perhaps Rice's most serious and best novel was *Mr. Opp* (1909), for while maintaining the better qualities of her earlier work it probes more deeply into the mainsprings of a developing character instead of merely portraying a static one. Mr. Opp is a country newspaper editor who, though a failure both in love and in worldly matters, maintains his self-respect by caring for his mentally incompetent sister and choosing to regard his life as a success. Perhaps no work by Rice was more favorably received; the usual adjectives such as "charming," "delightful," "wholesome," gave way to more thoughtful judgments. To the *Bookman*, *Mr. Opp* was an "excellent study of character"; to the *Nation*, "Mr. Opp is a hero worth knowing"; and to the *Spectator* he is "more than the hero of a novel; he comes near to being truly heroic."

A few more of Rice's works should be mentioned. *A Romance of Billy-Goat Hill* (1912) was, like almost all of her novels, on the monthly best-seller lists. It is a love story set in another odd corner of Louisville. *Calvary Alley* (1917) concerns social problems, including housing conditions, and was made into a motion picture as *Sunshine Man*. *Mr. Pete & Co.* (1933) was Rice's favorite among her novels and is a story about a junk dealer she met along the Louisville waterfront. Mr. Pete is a lovable old derelict who wanders over the Orient for years but finally returns to Louisville to manage the inheritance he has fallen heir to (a dilapidated tenement house) and to carry on his real mission to help young people. Her last volume was *The Inky Way*, published in 1940, two years before her death in St. James Court.

Like many another popular "period" writer, Alice Hegan Rice's reading public is gone. Her brand of optimism and sentimentalism no longer seems as appealing and convincing as it once did. Margaret Steel Anderson, a member of the Louisville Author's Club and a close friend of Rice, wrote, "To make many nations laugh and laugh innocently—to bring entertainment to sickbed, and army-trench and throne-room and school-room—and to the million common houses of a million common people—this was the mission of her books and this their finest achievement." Not everyone, even at the time, agreed with the worthwhileness of such an achievement, however. The *Saturday Review*, for example, said of *Sandy*, "Nothing but the dreariest herbage of sentimental commonplace," and many a reader, despite the popularity of *Mrs. Wiggs*, found it full of platitudinous inconsequence. But in the main the world was younger then, less ready to find fault, and more ready to forgo the heavy ammunition that might demolish a literary work that was "charming" and "wholesome."

Eliza Calvert Obenchain

Eliza Calvert Obenchain (1856–1936), who wrote under her maiden name of Eliza Calvert Hall, was born in Bowling Green and lived there most of her life. Her first published work was "Galatea," a poem in *Scribner's* magazine, and later she wrote more poems and essays for the same magazine as well as special articles for the Woman's Page of the *New York Times* and for other newspapers and magazines. Obenchain's best single story, "Sally Ann's Experience," appeared in *Cosmopolitan* in 1898. This story deals with the woman's suffrage question and brought Obenchain favorable attention, for it was reprinted in *Cosmopolitan*, was published three times in the *Ladies' Home Journal*, appeared in other magazines, was read on Chautauqua platforms, was used by teachers of elocution, and finally was published in a deluxe edition in 1910. Obenchain was at one time president of the Equal Rights Association of Kentucky. In other stories she dealt with other matters affecting women such as divorce and property rights, and her stories were generally supported by an undercurrent of social purpose.

Obenchain's first volume, *Aunt Jane of Kentucky* (1907), was a collection of short stories. Although the manuscript contained "Sally Ann's Experience," it was rejected by several publishers, principally on the grounds that a volume of short stories in dialect would never sell, for readers of local color were tiring of dialect. Little, Brown, and Company took a chance, however, and was well repaid, for the volume went into at least thirty-three editions and was read by perhaps a million people. The stories grow out of the memories of an old lady, Aunt Jane, as she recalls people of olden times in the rural districts of the Pennyrile section of Kentucky. One critic wrote: "Where so many have made caricatures of old time country folk, Eliza Calvert Hall has caught at once the real charm, the real spirit, the real people, and the real joy of living which is there."

As might be expected, Obenchain published a follow-up volume of additional Aunt Jane stories, *The Land of Long Ago* (1909). Next came her only novel, *To Love and to Cherish* (1911), a story of domestic happiness. Though these two volumes, like *Clover and Bluegrass* (1916), won a good reading audience, neither of them rivaled *Aunt Jane of Kentucky* either in popularity or in quality. Today works such as Obenchain's are no longer in fashion, but "Sally Ann's Experience" remains a good example of a kind of writing that had a wide appeal at the beginning of the century, not only in Kentucky but throughout the country.

Cordia Greer Petrie

Bringing an unsophisticated rural dweller into an urban environment for the sake of the humor that ensues was a well-established practice among the local color writers. This is what Cordia Greer Petrie (1872–1964) does with Angeline Keaton, her husband, and her son. Her first and best-known volume was *Angeline at the Seelbach* (1922), which records the Keaton family's experiences when they make their first trip from Bear Holler, in Barren County, to Louisville and stay at its finest hotel, the Seelbach. From "Miss Seelbach's little boy in a suit all kivered with buttons," to the revolving doors, to the steam radiators "with no door nor no place to poke the ashes out," to the dining room, to the bathtub "that put you in mind of a tomb with the lid off," to the pictures of "brazen hussies" on the walls, everything was a source of wonder to Angeline. Quickly *Angeline at the Seelbach* caught on both locally and nationally and went through at least thirteen printings. *Angeline Doin' Society* followed in 1923 and was succeeded by seven more volumes before *Angeline Goes on Strike* concluded the series in 1928. These later volumes take Angeline further afield and bring her new experiences with the theater, "ratskeflers," jazz orchestras, Hawaiian dancers, idle society people, antiques, and so on.

Angeline was one of the first hillbilly characters to gain a wide reputation, not only through Petrie's books but through her lectures and readings, for which Petrie dressed up—Minnie Pearl fashion—like her heroine. Her greatest triumphs came with her appearance in New York and before the Kentucky Society of Washington, when she was introduced to the First Lady, Mrs. Calvin Coolidge. Dressed as Angeline, Petrie used the dialect she had learned in her native Barren County and in the mountain counties where she lived for ten years or so with her husband while he was the physician for a number of coal mines. Just as Thomas Nelson Page and others used black characters and dialect to add an air of authenticity to their stories, so Petrie used hill-country characters and their dialect. Certainly she knew that her humor depended upon the naive observations and the speech patterns of her characters, but Petrie resolutely held that ridicule and belittlement were no part of her purpose and that the vernacular of the hill people merited preservation in literary form as the natural, unaffected speech of simple, honest people. Still Petrie may have been exploitive in her public readings in earlier life, and when in her later years she expressed the wish that she had an agent so that she could dress up again and put Angeline on television.

During the 1920s and beyond Petrie enjoyed great popularity, both in the press and in the sale of her books, though some of the national review press did find the episodes too conventional to carry conviction and the humor "manufactured" and "too obvious" for genuine amusement. Despite Petrie's popularity half a century ago, however, her books are little read today. The "Grand Old Opry" stage and television shows are evidence that audiences still find appeal in hillbilly humor, music, and dialect, but the tone and the format have totally changed. Petrie depended for her humor on the confrontation between Angeline and the urban world and Angeline's reaction to it. Many of her observations resemble the broad-humor one-liners of modern time, but the hillbilly program depends upon a number of character roles and is more of a variety show whose sole purpose is entertainment derived from the methods of vaudeville and from variety and musical shows.

Petrie died in Louisville at the age of ninety-two. She had moved to Louisville from Barren County while a child and remained there save for the period of her attendance at Eminence Kentucky College in Henry County and the ten years or more that she and her husband spent in Eastern Kentucky.

Irvin Shrewsbury Cobb

Irvin Shrewsbury Cobb (1876–1944), newspaper reporter, short story writer, novelist, actor, script writer, and essayist, once declared that he would rather be an orphan in Kentucky than twins anywhere else. Never, apparently, did Cobb change his mind about his native state. Nor did he ever cease to write about it, especially about Paducah and the Jackson Purchase area where he was born. On the occasion of his death, his request was that a dogwood tree be planted in Lot 4-J of the Oak Grove Cemetery and his ashes used to fertilize its roots. Such a monument, he said, should be sufficient, but should surviving relatives desire to mark the spot further, he suggested a simple stone bearing a small bronze plate carrying his name, the dates of his birth and death, and the line, "I Have Come Back Home." And if, he added with characteristic humor, his fellow townspeople should insist upon a memorial service, his desire was that they "make it snappy."

Cobb's work as a journalist began with the *Paducah Daily News* when he was nineteen; took him to Louisville, where he wrote political stories and a humor column called "Sour Mash" for the *Louisville Evening Post*; and then took him back to Paducah in 1901, where for three years he was managing editor of the *Daily Democrat*. In 1904 he joined the staff of the *New York Evening Sun*, where he developed a popular syndicated daily feature, and the following year moved to Joseph Pulitzer's *World*, where he wrote a daily humor column called "Through Funny Glasses." After six years he quit newspaper work and became a staff contributor to the *Saturday Evening Post*, of which Kentuckian George Horace Lorimer was the celebrated editor. In 1922 he took a similar position with *Cosmopolitan* magazine and remained there until 1932. At this time he moved to Hollywood, where he wrote movie scripts and did some acting. His greatest success as an actor was in *Steamboat Round the Bend* by fellow Kentuckian Ben Lucien Burman, in which Cobb played the role of ship captain. Also in the cast was Will Rogers, who had previously played the title role in a movie based on the doings of Cobb's Judge Priest.

In 1909 with the publication of "The Escape of Mr. Trim" in the *Saturday Evening Post* Cobb began his career as a short story writer and immediately followed with a steady stream of stories in the *Post*, *Cosmopolitan*, and other magazines. With *Back Home: Being a Narrative of Judge Priest and His People* (1912) Cobb's stories were first published in book form and established him as probably the most widely read short story writer of his time. In the group of stories called *Back Home* the author creates his best-known character, Judge Priest, a lovable figure from a Western Kentucky community around the turn of the century. The judge, once a Confederate soldier, has aged appealingly, likes his mint juleps, and combines his duties as a circuit court judge with the everyday life he finds round about him, always ready to help some innocent who has gotten himself into trouble. The characters are very human, very ordinary citizens who belong to a generation that was passing out of existence even as Cobb wrote about it. Here life goes along quietly and pleasantly unless an amusing incident, a piece of gossip, or something else out of the ordinary alters the usual course of events.

"For my material," Cobb says, "I drew upon the life of my hometown community as I remembered it. Most of the characters that figure in the events described were copies . . . of real models; and for most of the events themselves there was in the first place a fairly substantial basis of fact." These friends and acquaintances came from no one period of Cobb's life, but many of them he got to know in his boyhood. "One or two nights a week my uncle used to take me to spend the evening with old Judge Priest. There were pretty sure to be a half dozen or more grayheads there; and if it were good outdoors weather, they would sit in a row on the low verandah. . . . I would perch on the top step of the porch, hugging my bare knees together and listening. It was worth any boy's while to listen to the company that assembled on Judge Priest's front porch." So fond of Judge Priest and these friends was Cobb that he wrote about them the rest of his life. A second series of stories, entitled *Old Judge Priest,* followed in 1916; in 1922 came Cobb's first novel, *J. Poindexter, Colored,* Poindexter being the Judge's remarkable servant; in 1932 *Down Yonder with Judge Priest* followed, and in 1937 came the last of the series, *Judge priest Turns Detective.* Judge Priest had become one of the better-known fictional characters in American literature.

Cobb had no underlying social purpose or reform motive in his writings. His purpose was to depict the sort of place his home town was when he was growing up and to entertain his readers while doing so. He was also aiming to shed some light on human nature and the human condition and to do so in a genial, gentle fashion. His tools were a gift of humor, a fund of common sense, and skill with character portrayal and the use of language. These he employed with a constantly changing panorama of events and people and on an endless variety of topics. Thus he appeals to the reader's nostalgic recollection of the golden age before World War I, a time when life seemed less regimented and less complicated. In those days, Cobb says, "You could mind your own business; indeed, strange though it may seem now you might be left with some business of your own to mind" (*Exit Laughing*). There is something warm and comforting about Cobb's observations and the world he portrays, but there are also sly digs at human vanity and pretension. For example, in "The Cater-Cornered Sex," the reader is told that Judge Priest adapts himself to either an official or a private way of conducting his life. "As His Honor, presiding," Cobb says, "his language was invariably grammatical and precise and as carefully accented as might be expected of a man whose people never had much use for the consonant 'r.' As William Pitman Priest, Esq., Citizen, taxpayer, and Confederate veteran, he mishandled the King's English as though he had small personal regard for the king or his English either."

The Judge Priest stories are Cobb's best-known humorous stories, but they were by no means the only ones. *Europe Revised* (1914) dealt a bit irreverently with some of the European tourist attractions; and *Roughing It De Luxe* (1914) recounts a trip to California via the Grand Canyon, with Cobb seeing things, again a bit irreverently, in a different light from everybody else. Even *"Speaking of Prussians . . ."* (1917) and *The Glory of the Coming* (1918), written when

Cobb was a war correspondent for the *Saturday Evening Post* during World War I, portray war in tones of humorous exaggeration that are devoid of anger and hatred. *Speaking of Operations* (1915) sold more than 100,000 copies during its first year. *Red Likker* (1929), a novel, traces the history of bourbon whiskey from post-Revolutionary times through Prohibition days and examines the role of bourbon in the great scheme of the universe. There were a dozen other volumes of humor, all of them finally capped off by Cobb's long, rambling, anecdotal, witty, shrewd, warm-hearted autobiography, *Exit Laughing* (1941).

Not all of Cobb's writings were humorous, however. One of his very best volumes is *The Escape of Mr. Trimm: His Plight and Other Plights* (1913), which is made up of grim tales of real life. The title story (and Cobb's first published short story) tells of Hobart W. Trimm's journey toward federal prison and of his escape wearing "Bean's latest model little giant handcuffs." Among other stories in the volume are "The Belled Buzzard," sometimes called Cobb's best story; "An Occurrence Up a Side Street," a horror story and one of Cobb's favorites; and "Fish-head," a horror tale of Reelfoot Lake that Cobb wrote when he was twenty-four. Some readers have found the plots and the vivid descriptions in these stories gruesome, but the volume contains some of Cobb's best writing.

The vast body of what Cobb wrote makes a systematic coverage of it impossible in a brief space. As one critic has put it, "He wrote several dozen books, more than three hundred stories, and according to his own estimate, 'anywhere between two thousand to five thousand feature articles.'" Considering the time required for such a literary output, and adding Cobb's enormous popularity as an after-dinner speaker, his lectures on the Chautauqua circuits, and the work he did in Hollywood as a script writer and actor after 1932, his shortcomings as a writer are not surprising: he wrote too much for the good of his long-run reputation. His daughter's biography of him, *My Wayward Parent* (1945), reveals Cobb as unconventional, careless, and lovable but also endlessly energetic. Yet Cobb's busy-ness may not account for his works' shortcomings. Perhaps the set of mind that made him the Richard Harding Davis of his day instilled in him also the hot-haste stereotype that is often associated with the newspaper journalist and that tends to make literature part of a day's work. Perhaps, too, it is ungenerous to complain because Cobb did not do better what he did well—or was not trying to do in the first place.

At his best, Cobb could not only make us laugh but could also portray a situation full of sentiment and tenderness and with such deftness and artistry as to avoid mawkishness while achieving delicate and sensitive insights into an intensely human situation. "Up Clay Street" is such a story. At his worst his humor could be heavy-handed, a scene of high seriousness be destroyed by a quip, or a situation be dissolved into sentimentalism or disposed of with distracting levity. Nevertheless the fact remains that Irvin Cobb created one of the important fictional characters in American literature, pictured life in a small southern town, and left the suggestion that this town is only one of the many interesting towns the country over. In doing this he has written some stories that have lived beyond their day. "The Belled Buzzard," "The Escape of Mr. Trimm," "An Occurrence Up a Side Street," and "Fish-head" have already been noted. To these may be added "Words and Music." Perhaps this is quite enough for a writer to accomplish whose purpose was to entertain and to provide some insight into human nature.

Edwin Carlile Litsey

The poetry of Edwin Carlile Litsey (1874–1970) brought the author a substantial Kentucky following during his prime, but today few readers are familiar with his verse. *Spindrift* (1915) was his first volume, but *The Filled Cup* (1935) was more widely known. Both volumes depend heavily upon poems about woodlands, the meadows, and the seasons, a kind of verse that has long since lost its appeal. Some realistic poems such as "Mountain Child" and "Hill Mother" have stood the test of time better than the romantic nature poems, but others are overlaid with a kind of sentimentalism and moralism that appeals to few, such as "Old Mule" and "To One Who Failed."

Some of Litsey's poems deal with life in South Central Kentucky, and particularly in Marion and Washington counties, in what might be called the manner of the local colorist; but his fiction does this much better and is likely to outlast the poetry. *The Man from Jericho* (1911) portrays authentic scenes of rural life, horse farms, and racing. *Shadow Shapes* (1929) has good scenes involving fox hunting and chicken fighting; *Grist* (1927) with Gethsemani in the background portrays life in a religious environment. These and other lesser novels reveal the author's interest in rural Kentucky as a background for romantic fiction, but in his last and best novel, *Stones for Bread* (1940), a realistic work, he draws upon the story of two brothers he knew in Marion County. It is a somber tale of two derelicts—paupers—who live in a tumble-down cabin and are neglected by everyone except a priest. The descriptions of their wretchedness and suffering are effectively done as first one brother dies, then their animals (a dog and a mule), and finally the other brother. The novel received some national attention as reviewers passed generally favorable judgments on a grim and unrelieved tale of loneliness where the author's "only intention is to tell their story as human beings" (*New York Times*, Jan. 14, 1940).

The Love Story of Abner Stone (1902) and *The Race of the Swift* (1905), each with its scene laid in Marion and Washington counties deserve brief mention. The former is a story of a middle-aged bachelor who falls in love with a girl from Springfield, only to see her die of typhoid; the latter tells seven stories of wild animals—among them a mother fox, a raccoon, a gray wolf, a sheep dog turned traitor, a wildcat—and the tragedy that befalls them in their quest for food. Neither is the equal of *Stones for Bread*.

John Uri Lloyd

The talents that made John Uri Lloyd (1849–1936) a distinguished pharmaceutical chemist also contributed to his becoming a Northern Kentucky local color novelist. Lloyd grew up in Boone County, where his aptitude for chemistry manifested itself early and led to his being apprenticed to a Cincinnati pharmacist when he was fourteen. In 1876 he moved to Cincinnati and became an outstanding pharmaceutical chemist and later co-founder (with his brother) of his own pharmaceutical firm. Active in plant chemistry, particularly in relation to pharmaceutical products, he was the author of hundreds of publications, including eight scientific books and eight novels. He received many honors, medals, and honorary degrees for his contributions to plant chemistry, pharmaceutical chemistry, and medicine. He founded the Lloyd Library and Museum in Cincinnati, an ongoing institution to this day.

Lloyd's writing of fiction, which began as a hobby, drew upon his interest in metaphysics, superstition, folklore, language, elixirs, and people's eccentricities. Like a good scientist, he jotted down in notebooks what he observed and heard and later incorporated it in the novels that were to achieve considerable popularity in their day. His aim, he said, was to "portray to outsiders a phase of life unknown to the world at large, and to establish a folk-lore picture" of the community in which he grew up. His interest in dialect was also basic, for he considered the geographic area about which he wrote to be a language island and consequently prepared a dialect glossary while working on

Stringtown on the Pike. This he circulated among friends for examination and improvement. Thus his dialect was largely authentic and supported his knowledge of the customs, manners, and folklore of Northern Kentucky.

Lloyd's first work of imaginative literature, *Etidorpha; or, the End of the Earth* (1895), grew out of his interest in science and tells a strange story of a trip through the center of the earth in the manner of what today we would call science fiction. The story foretells the discovery of argon and helium in the earth's atmosphere and of X-rays and atomic fission. Published privately, it was translated into seven languages, and went through at least eighteen editions.

In *The Right Side of the Road* (1897), Lloyd dealt with life in Northern Kentucky. But it was *Stringtown on the Pike* (1900) and the "Stringtown stories" which followed it that brought Lloyd a reputation as a local color writer. The subject matter he drew principally from Boone County, and especially from the town of Florence; but Campbell and Kenton counties provided him with materials also. *Stringtown on the Pike* is the story of Sammy Drew, his friends, and his enemies. The first part of the story deals with Stringtown during the Civil War, its divided loyalties, and its being alternately under the control of the Confederate and the Union armies. Red Head, Sammy's rival for the affection of a girl named Susie, is introduced into the story, as are also Cupe and Dinah, an old black couple. The plot, which is not very skillfully handled, includes a rapid succession of situations involving poison, death, court trials, mountain feuds, Susie's entering a convent, Sammy's becoming a professor of chemistry, and Red Head's escape from the gallows. Folklore, elixirs, and superstition are woven into the story. In *Stringtown*, as well as in the later novel *Red Head* (1903), Lloyd gives thoughtful attention to "the two Kentuckys." In Lloyd's case it is the culture not of the Bluegrass but of Northern Kentucky that he contrasts with that of the mountains, with particular attention to the practice of feuding. He traces feuds from England's War of the Roses down to modern times; down, in fact, to Northern Kentucky, where these "descendants" from the mountains of Kentucky come to Stringtown. Lloyd contrasts them with other characters in his novels, a comparison that generally works to the advantage of the townspeople, although in some respects Lloyd finds the mountain code—in word-of-honor, for example—more admirable.

Warwick of the Knobs (1901), though a better novel than *Stringtown* and *Red Head*, lacks character development and motivation. It is the story of a stern predestinarian Baptist preacher who alienates his children with his harsh religion and loses two sons in the Civil War. Set in the hills of Boone County, the novel portrays the avenging of wrongs done the daughter of the family and includes a considerable amount of folklore, superstition, remedies, and the like. *Red Head* followed in 1903 and *Scroggins* in 1904. By this time Lloyd had gained quite a reading audience and his writing was making heavy demands on his time. For a while he deliberated whether to continue being a pharmaceutical chemist or to become a writer. His decision was to continue with his scientific work, so that his next novel, *Felix Moses: The Beloved Jew of Stringtown on the Pike*, did not appear until 1930, and his last one, *Our Willie*, in 1934. In these last two novels Lloyd again makes use of John Hunt Morgan as a character. Earlier in *Warwick of the Knobs* two of Warwick's sons are killed as they participate in Morgan's raids, and a younger son, alienated by his father's harsh religion, joins Morgan's men. In *Our Willie*, Willie joins Morgan's Raiders and comes back home to marry his childhood sweetheart. In *Felix Moses* Lloyd takes cognizance of some sentiment against Morgan as "the King of Horse Thieves" who enjoyed "wanton thievery, arson, and looting," but Lloyd declares of him that "he never persecuted an enemy, humiliated a captive, or by intent needlessly destroyed a home . . . left behind no burned villages, no desecrated home, no wreckage other than the destroyed stores of the organized enemy." Lloyd's view of Morgan is not unlike that to be found in the *Dictionary of American Biography*, which declares that Morgan was "gentle and generous, bold in thought and action" and "may well have been chivalry's last appearance on war's sordid page."

Lloyd died in 1936 at the age of eighty-six and was buried in the Hopeful Cemetery at Petersburg, Boone County.

CHAPTER 8

Historical Fiction

When Kentucky authors wrote the state's first historical fiction in the 1830s, they had only the recent frontier to write about—the land, the settlers, the Indians, and the Revolutionary War. The genre quickly disappeared, except for a few now-forgotten melodramatic novels during the 1840s and 1850s. A few novels dealing with the Civil War appeared even as the war was winding down, but the time for the Civil War as a serious subject for fiction had not yet come. The frontier, however, was a popular subject in the dime novels that began to appear in the 1860s. Abetted by the introduction of the steam rotary printing press and the development of new techniques in marketing books, the craze for these melodramatic stories of the frontier, the Indian, and the Revolutionary War took the country by storm. For the remainder. of the century the publishing houses of Beadle and Adams, Street and Smith, and others annually released hundreds of titles that were aimed at a working-class audience but which in fact pervaded all social levels. Until about 1895, when they began to be superseded by pulp-magazine stories about Frank Merriwell, the Rover Boys, and Tom Swift, the dime novels ranged through American history—the frontier first and later the Civil War—for stories of love, adventure, violence, and war. Not one of the best-known writers of dime novels was a Kentuckian, but writers such as Edward Willett, Arthur Meserve, and Edward S. Ellis kept the Kentucky frontier before the public and helped pave the way for the revival of interest in the serious historical novel in the 1890s.

Besides the dime novel, other forces worked toward a revival of interest in historical fiction after 1860. First, the local color movement was in progress, and writers were receptive to subjects, old or new, that provided apt material. In addition, enough time had passed —including the trauma of the Civil War—to enable, even to cause, thoughtful writers to look back over the past and trace the course of events that had brought the nation to the point where it was. Finally, the spirit of nationalism was abroad because of the trouble with Spain, thereby creating interest in past American accomplishments.

Three turn-of-the-century historical novels of the frontier stand out at the national level: *The Choir Invisible* (1897), by James Lane Allen; *Alice of Old Vincennes* (1900), by Maurice Thompson; and *The Crossing* (1904), by Winston Churchill; but only the first was by a Kentuckian. Allen's novel (discussed elsewhere) was widely acclaimed by critics and readers alike and contributed to the vogue in historical fiction. Two Kentucky contemporaries of Allen wrote historical fiction of the frontier, both of them minor writers.

William Courtney Watts

The first of these was William Courtney Watts (1830–97), whose *Chronicles of a Kentucky Settlement* (1897) portrays life in Livingston and Crittenden counties between 1825 and 1867, where the frontier lingered on later than it did in Central Kentucky. Though no longer read, the novel has some significance because it is historically trustworthy and depicts well the agricultural economy and society in Western Kentucky for the period with which it deals. Also running through the novel are actual events, among them the outlaw activities emanating from Cave-in-Rock on the north bank of the Ohio River and the trail of crime left by the Harpe brothers. The volume, heavy with personal reminiscence, has a somewhat inconsequential boy-girl plot.

Watts was born in Salem, Livingston County, in 1830 and lived there and in Smithland until he went to New Orleans as a clerk in a firm of cotton brokers. In time he formed his own company with offices in New Orleans, New York, and Liverpool, England. Ultimately he came back to Smithland, and late in life, lamed by rheumatism, he wrote his novel. The King Library of the University of Kentucky has a manuscript key to the characters and events. Watts was buried in the Smithland cemetery.

Nancy Houston Banks

Nancy Houston Banks (ca. 1850–1934) also dealt with the Western Kentucky frontier. She was a native of Morganfield but left home after her marriage and had quite a colorful and successful career. For a time she worked for the *Cincinnati Enquirer*; later she published *Stairs of Sand* (1890), went to New York during the 1890s to live, and there became a member of the *Bookman* staff, where she helped bring James Lane Allen to the favorable attention of the public. Subsequently she lived in England for a time and was sent to South Africa by *Vanity Fair* to cover the Boer War. Banks died in Washington, D.C., and was buried in the Masonic cemetery in Morganfield.

Oldfield: A Kentucky Tale of the Last Century (1902), her best-known novel, gives idealized pictures of the manners and customs of rural life in Western Kentucky during frontier days and devotes a few pages to Cave-in-Rock, the Harpes, and a mysterious Spaniard suspected of being a comrade of Jean Lafitte. Her *'Round Anvil Rock* (1903) also makes use of a number of historical persons and incidents in telling the story of early days in Union County. Among them are the celebrated Methodist minister Peter Cartwright, the desperado Philip Alston, and people and events associated with the Battle of Tippecanoe. (Anvil Rock is a sandstone monolith almost sixty feet high and twenty feet wide that stands on level bottom land well removed from any other rock formation. It resembles a blacksmith's anvil tilted so that the horn points upward.) Banks's *The Little Hills* (1905) deserves mention here as a novel in the local color tradition, a tradition not entirely absent from *Oldfield* and *'Round Anvil Rock*.

Other writers wrote about the frontier also. As late as 1920 John Fox, Jr., for example, wrote *Erskine Dale, Jr., Pioneer*, but it is not one of Fox's better novels and is a sort of anomaly in that it was published two decades after the historical fiction vogue reached its peak and then died out. Joseph Alexander Altsheler, a popular writer of books for boys, wrote about the frontier, but he wrote also about the Civil War, a subject that was growing in popularity. In fact, in *Fiction Fights the War* (1957) Robert A. Lively reports fifteen Civil War novels by Kentucky writers, and in identifying what he regards as the twenty-five best Civil War novels he lists three by Kentucky writers.

Sallie Rochester Ford

The first Civil War novel by a Kentucky author Lively mentions is *Raids and Romance of Morgan and His Men*, by Sallie Rochester Ford. Written in 1864, the year of Morgan's death near Greenville, Tennessee, Ford's novel is typical of other novels in the Morgan tradition in that it is almost as much about Morgan's men as about Morgan himself. Ford succeeds in portraying the romance and excitement of the raids led by "the Thunderbolt of the Confederacy," but unfortunately this success is offset by the author's hatred of the North and her inordinately idealized conception of the Confederacy. It is noteworthy that as the myth of the Civil War began to form, the legends that grew up around Morgan comprised one of the myth's strongest elements. Of the sixty or so novels about the Civil War in Kentucky, Morgan appears in approximately half and is the main character in a dozen.

Mary Jane Holmes

Mary Jane Holmes's *Hugh Worthington* (1885) also has a Civil War background. Most of the action takes place on a lovingly described Bluegrass farm, where the master, Hugh Worthington, unlike most of his landed friends and acquaintances, is against slavery. When war comes, Worthington joins the Union army, an act which produces complications that must be resolved before the hero with his "Northern" convictions can marry the beautiful Southern-sympathizing heroine Alice.

William E. Barton

William E. Barton (1861–1930), a native of Illinois who graduated from Berea College and later taught school in Laurel County, is little remembered today, but he was the first Kentucky writer to use a Kentucky mountaineer in the Civil War as a subject for a full-length novel. John Fox, Jr.'s *The Little Shepherd of Kingdom Come* (1903), on the same subject, was to achieve a popularity that Barton never dreamed of, but Barton's *A Hero in Homespun: A Tale of the Loyal South* (1897) and *Pine Knot: A Story of Kentucky Life* (1900) preceded Fox's novel and deserve mention in any record of Kentucky Civil War literature. The former follows, battle-for-battle, the campaigns of Jack Casey in the Union army through Eastern Kentucky and Tennessee and may be the best yet published on the role of the mountaineer in the Civil War. The latter, set in Rockcastle County, Kentucky, is concerned with the needlessness of the war and with the role of Mr. Buzbee, an abolitionist with a plan to liberate all the slaves in the South. It is to be noted that John G. Fee, a leading Abolitionist in Kentucky, was the founder of Berea College and was still president when Barton graduated there.

The "three best" Civil War novels by Kentuckians, according to Robert A. Lively, are *The Little Shepherd of Kingdom Come* by

John Fox, Jr.; *Warwick of the Knobs* by John Uri Lloyd; and *The Sword of Youth* by James Lane Allen. These novels are discussed under the main entries for these authors, but we can note here that Fox's novel catches well the agony of the divided loyalties that tore families and friends apart in Kentucky. Some lines from *The Little Shepherd* on this subject are well known: "As the nation was rent apart, so was the commonwealth; as the state, so was the county; as was the county, the neighborhood; as the neighborhood, the family; and as the family, so brother and brother, father and son." Allen's *The Sword of Youth* (1914) came later, and, though historical in nature subordinates history to a phrase Allen used in *Aftermath* in 1896: "She was a of a soft-heartedness that ruled her absolutely—but only to the unyielding edge of honor." This fine phrase—"the unyielding edge of honor"—applies to Joseph Sumner, a Kentucky boy who had deserted from the Confederate army for reasons he later questions and subsequently returns to Lee's army to risk disgrace and even death. *Warwick of the Knobs* is primarily a local color novel—as are Lloyd's *Felix Moses* (1930) and *Our Willie* (1934)—in which John Hunt Morgan and his men appear.

The Civil War in general and the exploits of John Hunt Morgan were the first subjects of Civil War literature, but Abraham Lincoln, born near Hodgenville, also became increasingly important. This development was slow to come, for at the time of his death Lincoln, though loved and revered by many, was hated and reviled by many others. By the time of the centenary of his birth his place was taking its final shape, however, and by the end of the second decade of the century it was secure. The hatred he was heir to had by 1920 largely passed away, and the Lincoln who emerged from his writings and speeches, his letters and acts, was a giant of a man rich in ideas, understanding, and compassion, a man of lofty utterance who could challenge other men to be faithful to the best that was in them. In his life story is found an almost endless chain of reenactments of the myths that Americans live by: he is the ugly duckling who became fairer than all the rest, and by the same token he is the unlikely hero who achieved greatly in spite of the odds against him; he is the poor boy who makes good, the prototype of the log-cabin-to-the-White House career; he is the early failure who redeems himself, the late bloomer who finally comes into his own; he is the very soul of honesty and integrity when it would have been convenient and momentarily rewarding to be otherwise. Yet in spite of all this he emerges singularly himself. Indeed, even to those who see him as the beautiful swan, the markings of the ugly duckling never disappear. It is this fact that makes Lincoln notable among American heroes. On the one hand, he is a leader of transcendent proportions, the nearest thing to a saint that America has produced. On the other hand, near-sainthood has taken away nothing earthly; the man who delivered the Gettysburg Address is still the young man who split rails and walked miles to correct a small error in change-making. He has not been cut off from us by a barrier of time or of awe and reverence. Lincoln has remained superbly and eloquently human.

Mary R. Shipman Andrews

The first Kentucky writer of fiction to make a memorable contribution to belles-lettres dealing with Lincoln and the Civil War was Mary R. Shipman Andrews (ca. 1865–1936). Shipman wrote two Lincoln stories—*The Perfect Tribute*, published in 1906, and *The Counsel Assigned* (a story of Lincoln as a lawyer), in 1912. The former earned the author and itself immediate national fame and a lasting place in Kentucky literature. The story had its origin in the total lack of applause with which the crowd at Gettysburg received Lincoln's address. Fearful that his address had been a failure, as Andrews tells the story, the disconsolate Lincoln goes for a walk alone the next day. He wanders the streets of Washington and there collides with a boy of fifteen who is running down the street seeking a lawyer to write a will for his brother, a Confederate soldier in a Washington hospital. Lincoln goes to the hospital and prepares the will, while a young soldier, who does not see him, talks excitedly of the Gettysburg Address, which he has read in the paper. The silence after the speech he terms the "most perfect tribute that has ever been paid by any people to an orator." It is then that Lincoln realizes that his address has not been a failure. The story was first published in *Scribner's* magazine in July 1906 but was reprinted in book form, of which 600,000 copies were sold. Though strongly didactic, the story reveals the author's talent for sincerity and her instinct for drama and descriptive detail.

Andrews, who first came to Lexington at the age of one, when her father, an Episcopal clergyman, became rector of Christ Church in Lexington, was also the author of other published works. Among them are *The Enchanted Forest and Other Stories* (stories told to her sons), 1909, and *The Courage of the Commonplace* (a story of Yale University and its ways), 1911. Andrews attended Christ Church Seminary from age six to seventeen and shortly thereafter left Lexington for New York, where her father had accepted a new appointment. It was here that she began her writing career.

Two other Kentucky writers contributed to the Civil War "matter." One was Maria Thompson Daviess, whose *Matrix* (1920) puts together legend and documentary evidence and tells the story of Lincoln's parents, Thomas Lincoln and Nancy Hanks. The other was William E. Barton, already noted, who was Kentucky's first important Lincoln scholar. He was the author of a dozen books on Lincoln and was one of the four Lincoln scholars who helped expose the forged Lincoln–Ann Rutledge letters that Wilma Frances Minor prevailed upon the *Atlantic Monthly* to publish in 1928–29. Today, as a result, Lincoln biographers suggest that there was nothing more than a platonic relationship between Lincoln and Miss Rutledge.

Kentucky's contribution to Civil War literature was not major, but it was respectable, and it differed from the contribution of the Deep South in that it lacked the bitterness that was often reflected in the literature of that region. Further south, bitterness was generated by the destructiveness of the war and of Reconstruction and by the loss of a way of life that could never return without the great plantations and the slave labor that made it possible.

CHAPTER 9

Literature of Eastern Kentucky

During the 1870s and 1880s the Kentucky mountaineer (like the southern mountaineer generally) came to be regarded as "different." As late as the Civil War the mountain region of Kentucky about which John Fox, Jr., was to write throughout his life was not thought of as a discrete, coherent region with a culture all its own. By 1873, however, *Lippincott's Magazine* published an article about the Cumberland Mountains entitled, "A Strange Land and Peculiar People," and in 1878 Mary N. Murfree in East Tennessee began publishing articles and stories about the Tennessee Cumberlands, collecting them in two volumes that portrayed the mountains as "different." Even though Murfree "discovered" this differentness, it was James Lane Allen, followed by John Fox, Jr., who first brought "into sharp focus the implications of Appalachian otherness" (Shapiro, *Appalachia on Our Mind*, 29). Early in 1886 Allen embarked upon his career as an author by writing a series of articles dealing with local color. The first was entitled "The Bluegrass Region of Kentucky"; the second, written four months later, was called "Through Cumberland Gap on Horseback." This latter article crystallized attention on "the other Kentucky," for here the author declared that it could "never be too clearly understood by those who are wont to speak of 'the Kentuckian' that this state has within its boundaries two utterly distinct elements of population . . . distinct in all that goes to constitute a separate community—occupations, manners and customs, dress, views of life, civilization."

Various explanations of this anomaly have been offered, one of which is that the sad state of disrepair of the Wilderness Road in pioneer days caused the less energetic and less determined settlers to become drop-outs on their trek westward and settle down in the mountain coves and hollows and on the plateaus. Another theory is that the original mountain settlers were descendants of indentured servants from colonial times, and still another that they descended from the Tidewater poor whites. More widely accepted, however, is the view that by and large settlers in the mountains were of Scotch-Irish descent not notably different from settlers in other regions of the new land. This view further holds that various sets of circumstances led, between 1770 and 1790, to their becoming the particular people they were. One of these is that intermarriage and inbreeding affected them in adverse ways. Another explanation is that out-migrations have affected them further. The first such exodus was around 1840 after the supply of game and fish was depleted and agriculture became the means of earning a livelihood. At this time, it is believed, many of the more intelligent, more ambitious mountaineers moved to the Bluegrass or farther west to Indiana, Illinois, and Missouri. A generation later the Civil War took a heavy toll of the more energetic, more venturesome young men, and around 1880 another migration took place, though this time it was representative of the whole population. Finally, by 1890 the region began to suffer from the exploitation of the forests and the coal and other mineral resources, so that by 1910 another migration took place to the Bluegrass and Middle West as a result of industrialization. In the meantime, feuds (unknown before the Civil War) and moonshining had become common throughout the mountain region, both of them a part of the stereotype that was to prevail for years.

During the century that passed after the arrival of the sturdy, thrifty Scotch-Irish, then, there was a marked falling off as poverty, ignorance, physical degeneration, and decay of self-respect slowly replaced the resourcefulness and intelligence of the original pioneers —a process that continued through the Great Depression to World War II, by which time the destruction of the old stereotype was completed. Particularly after about 1850 the mountaineer became more and more isolated from the outside world. Bad roads, few schools, and political neglect continued to do harm, but it would be a mistake to conclude that the mountaineers became degraded. More than anything else, they were cut off from the outside world, with the result that the passing of time stopped for them; their culture, their philosophy of life, their manner of speech remained pretty much what they had been in the eighteenth century. There were various social and economic levels among them: those who lived in the towns, those who farmed the valleys, and those who lived in the more inaccessible hollows and coves. This third group—the renters, the laborers, those akin to the "poor whites"—became the mountaineers of fiction and sensational report and to the outside world, therefore, seemed the only sort of mountaineers there were. The dime novels and those who dealt in sensationalism produced this distorted picture that appeared during the last third of the nineteenth century. The aim of these writers, all now forgotten, was to portray the mountaineers not as they really were but as a stereotype for popular consumption.

During the last fifty years of this century excellent writers with the perspective that time provides have seen the mountaineer whole and have gone far in setting the picture aright. Foremost among these have been Harriette Arnow, Jesse Stuart, James Still, Henry Hornsby, and others. But two earlier writers were the first to portray the mountaineer accurately. The more important of these two was John Fox, Jr., but alongside him was William E. Barton. Barton is noted elsewhere as an authority on Lincoln and as the first Kentucky writer to use the mountaineer in the Civil War as the subject of a full-length novel. In his two Civil War novels he gave an authentic picture of mountain life and mountain character. His only other novel, *The Truth about Roundstone* (1897), is sentimental and overly didactic as it tells the story of how two lifelong friends quarreled and ultimately were brought back together, but it is worth remembering today because of its authentic portrayal of the mountaineer in his small cabin, on steep mountainsides hoeing his corn, up deep hollows where only trails or the barest of roads led.

Before turning to Fox and Charles Neville Buck, it may be useful to speak of feuding and moonshining, for Fox used both as integral parts of his novels, and to Buck they were stock ingredients, sensationalized as they had not been by Fox. No stereotypes of the Kentucky mountains were so widely disseminated at the turn of the century as those of the feudist and the moonshiner. Actually feuds took place in several states, but nowhere were they so numerous or so ferocious as in the Kentucky headwaters of the Licking, Kentucky, Big Sandy, Tug Fork, and Cumberland rivers and in the adjoining regions of West Virginia, Virginia, and Tennessee. Five hundred men, it has been estimated, were killed in this region; yet it is hard to explain the rise of feuds as a social phenomenon or to identify the causes of particular feuds. Events growing out of the Civil War and Reconstruction are sometimes cited among the causes, but more likely the causes can be found in hot tempers, gun-toting, drunken rows, arguments over card games, slow-moving or corrupt legal justice, disputes over boundary lines, love slights, and local political alliances. Moreover, during earlier days in remote regions the institutions of the state or the church were often not readily available to settle disputes, so it was a common practice to settle personal differences at the personal level rather than in the courts.

The psychology behind the clan phenomenon and the will to avenge grudges by killing is not easy to comprehend, but it is likely that in the minds of most feudists something important was perceived to be at stake, such as responsibility, integrity, or honor. Possibly some sort of light is shed on feuds by calling attention to the practice of dueling. The Bluegrass country and the outside world which abhorred and deplored feuds in the mountains seem not to have had many qualms about "affairs of honor." Gentlemen of rank took their dignity and honor seriously, resulting in hundreds of affairs of honor, some ending with serious or fatal wounds. Both feuding and dueling were equally a matter of settling disputes outside the law. Why the one should be tacitly condoned and the other deplored is not entirely clear, but it seems clear that a matter of social distinction and style was involved.

At one time or another during the last quarter of the nineteenth century feuds raged in at least a dozen counties in Eastern Kentucky, and newspapers and magazines staggered the imagination of the nation with their sensational accounts. But equally lurid were stories about shotgun battles between moonshiners and revenue agents. Moonshining has a long history dating back to 1791 when the federal government imposed an excise tax on the manufacture of all alcoholic spirits in order to help retire the Revolutionary War debt; but the tax was regarded as an abridgement of personal rights and the free enterprise system. "We owned our own land and paid our taxes," says one aggrieved still owner; "we owned our own stills and it wasn't nobody's business what we done with our own. Leastsways that's how we figured it." At the end of the Civil War, with the excise tax still higher, the supply of legal whiskey low, demand big, and prices high, more than the right to make corn whiskey for oneself and perhaps for a few neighbors was at stake; moonshining was becoming a lucrative business. Thus flourished at the same time the practice of feuding and the conflict between the moonshiner and the federal revenue agent whose job was to control the making of illegal, untaxed whiskey.

John Fox, Jr.

John Fox, Jr. was the first author of any consequence to write seriously and sympathetically of the Kentucky mountaineers in their natural habitat, though he himself was born in Bourbon County in the heart of the Bluegrass country. His works became the prototype for those who came after him. He secured his early education chiefly at home from his schoolmaster father; at fifteen he went to Transylvania University for two years, and after that to Harvard, where he graduated with high honors in 1883 as the youngest member of his class. At Harvard, he says, "I wrote nothing I did not have to write for the classroom. Yet I cannot remember a time since I was twelve years old that I did not think I would some day be a writer myself."

After graduation, Fox worked several weeks for the *New York Sun* and the *New York Times*, attended the Columbia University Law School for two months, fell ill in February 1885, went home to Kentucky, and later joined his father and brother, who were engaged in mining operations in the Cumberland Mountains near the Kentucky-Tennessee boundary line. Once before during his summer vacation Fox had worked as a bookkeeper and timekeeper for his father and thus "without knowing it . . . began gathering material for the work I was to do." So it was that Fox became familiar with mines and mining camps and got to know many mountain people, among them Uncle Tommie Brooks, his wife, and his fifteen-year-old granddaughter, to whom Fox was a "furriner," and also the family of a barefooted girl, "more picturesque than pretty," whom he first saw at sunset one day "milking a brindle cow." In the girl's family were her father, her mother, "a big sullen brother," an older sister who was "the only fat young woman I ever saw in the hills," and an uncle, simple-minded, deaf, and dumb, who would "sit under the shade of an apple tree near the porch, following that shade and whittling, so that there was a perfectly circular running track of shavings around that apple tree." One day the girl brought Fox "a villainous tin-type of herself in a store dress and store shoes and with ribbon in her hair—her picturesqueness quite all gone."

Sometimes, Fox says, he would go with a young engineer just back from Germany into the distant hills, "studying the speech, habits, customs, etc., of the mountaineer." It was not unusual, he says, "to find bulls as beasts of burden. Sometimes a girl would be seen plowing one, and a brother of mine told me that he had seen a mountain maid going to mill riding one with a sack of corn in front of her." Then for the first time, he says, an idea for a story occurred to him: "If the hero of a story met the heroine on the back of a bull and her bull charged his dog, thereby endangering him, any reader in the world, I believe, would at least turn to the next chapter to see what further happened. With just that idea and no more I started my first story, 'A Mountain Europa.'" This story, he says, "I wrote and tinkered with . . . for nearly two years . . . until James Lane Allen, with whom my brother had been in college [at Transylvania University] and whom I thought the master of the most exquisite English then being written in this country, came to the mines for a visit. He read my story—what there was of it—liked it, and encouraged me to go ahead and finish it, and send it to the *Century Magazine*." One black night about six months later, he writes, "I was wading back from the post office through rain and mud by the light of a lantern with a note of acceptance and a check for $262.00 in my pocket." Thus "A Mountain Europa," published in two parts in *Century Magazine* in September and October 1892, became the first published story in what became a very prolific and successful career. In it, as in the best of his later stories and novels, Fox showed a mastery of dialect, excellent insight into the ways and thoughts of the mountaineer, and an instinct for storytelling that seemed to be infallible.

The remainder of Fox's life was crowded with events. He continued to write and grow in fame, being five times—1903, 1904, 1908, 1909, 1913—on the annual best-seller list. He enlisted with the Rough Riders and went to Cuba but left that service to become a correspondent for *Harper's Weekly*. After the Spanish-American War he came back to the home in Big Stone Gap, Virginia, that his father had bought in 1890 during the coal boom days, just across the Kentucky-Virginia boundary line. He married and was later divorced from the celebrated Austrian comic opera star Fritzi Scheff in 1908. He was popular on the lecture circuits as he traveled about giving readings from his works. In 1919 he died of pneumonia at the age of fifty-six and was buried beside his father and other members of his family in the cemetery in Paris, Kentucky, just a few miles from where he was born.

James Lane Allen had provided the impetus that started Fox on his very successful career by turning up the troubling anomaly of "the two Kentuckys," for herein lay a problem that appealed to Fox and called for analysis, explanation, and resolution. The stereotype was that of a people whose progress into time had been arrested, whose ways had somehow ceased to change. They lacked roads, schools and churches; they had reaped none of the benefits of the industrial development of the rest of the nation. They were isolated, frozen into a pattern of life that reflected pioneer times. They were Calvinistic and full of Old World superstition. They were dependent upon the earth for their necessities, hostile toward innovation, suspicious of strangers and the outside world, and limited in outlook to the boundaries of a county. They were taciturn and self-dependent, and they settled their differences without recourse to the intricacies of the law.

Juxtaposed to this stereotype was the stereotype of the agricultural aristocracy of the Bluegrass and its very different set of cultural and social values. Its fertile, rolling land fostered the philosophy that life was intended to be leisurely and comfortable and southern in its social graces; but the Bluegrass stereotype had kept pace with change and had profited from the industrialism that came in the wake of the Civil War. Furthermore, it had within it the dynamism of change.

This theme—this juxtaposition of cultures—shapes Fox's first novel, *A Mountain Europa*. Here Fox tells the story of an ill-fated love between a mining engineer from New York and a moonshiner's daughter, who is of the tradition of the half-wild mountain beauty of quick intelligence who hides behind a taciturn impassiveness but periodically breaks into outbursts of elemental savage passion. Though not one of Fox's best novels, *A Mountain Europa* is a trustworthy portrayal of mountain life: the heaps of food, the hovering together of old women, the roistering of the men as they drink their whiskey straight; the shooting match, the mountain jigs, the pranks that are carried out at a wedding; the role of the well-intentioned Calvinistic preacher; an authentic dialect.

A Cumberland Vendetta (1895) was Fox's first novel to deal with feuding, and like *The Kentuckians* (1897), which is mainly about the Bluegrass country, it does not concern the arrested development of mountain culture and the encroachment of the outside world upon it. Next came the volume that catapulted Fox into fame: *Hell-fer-Sartin and Other Stories* (1897), the title-piece a short story that had been published in the advertising section of *Harper's Weekly*. *Crittenden* (1900) grew out of Fox's experiences as a Rough Rider and war correspondent and was followed by *Blue Grass and Rhododendron* (1901), a long, involved romance. Two years later came one of the two novels upon which Fox's reputation depends today, *The Little Shepherd of Kingdom Come* (1903). This historical romance deals with the Civil War while at the same time contrasting the backward ways of the mountains and the graceful life of the Bluegrass. The central figure is Chad, a nameless "woods-colt" left homeless when cholera wipes out the family he has lived with. Through a remarkable chain of circumstances Chad is taken in by Major Buford, near Lexington, meets the beautiful and aristocratic Margaret Dean, is stunned by his sense of inadequacy, goes back to Kingdom Come, returns still later to Lexington, acquires the requisite social graces, becomes a legitimate Buford, proposes to Margaret, and is accepted. In using the Civil War as an integral part of the story Fox adds a new dimension to his juxtaposition of two ways of life and so creates a microcosm for the entire state and thereby reveals what a divisive and destructive force the war is: between friends and neighbors, between father and son, between brother and brother, even between lovers. Thus Chad alienates his friends and Margaret, who are pro-Confederacy, by joining the Union army. After the war, however, the differences between the Northern and Southern sympathies are reconciled, and, as Chad rides away to seek his fortune, it seems safe to predict that on a not very distant day he will return to "the other Kentucky" he has become a part of.

The Little Shepherd is not a great novel, but it is a very readable one. The portrayal of mountain people is successful and honest, but sentimentality sometimes gets in the way, as excessive romanticism does when Bluegrass scenes and aristocrats are portrayed. In Chad is to be found what Fox must have regarded as the ultimate model of the way the two cultures can come together, be reconciled, and be blended into one. The ways of the outside world prevailed over those of the mountains, but these ways are enriched by the sturdiness Chad brings with him from his early environment. So successful were the portrayals and reconciliations of once-conflicting loyalties that Fox and the best-selling popularity of *The Little Shepherd* are credited with helping to heal wounds still open when the novel was published.

In 1904 Fox published a collection of stories in which appeared "Christmas Eve on Lonesome," generally regarded as second only to "Hell-fer-Sartin" among his short stories. In 1905 came *Following the Sun Flag*, a weak book based on Fox's journeying to the Far East to report on the Russo-Japanese War, and in 1906 *The Knight of the Cumberlands* appeared, perhaps the poorest of his books about the mountains. Then came what is usually regarded as his best novel, *The Trail of the Lonesome Pine* (1908). At the personal level it is the story of John Hale (like Fox a Harvard-educated Bluegrass Kentuckian) and beautiful June Tolliver, a mountain girl from Lonesome Cove. At another level it is an account of what happens to a mountain people when their static way of life is confronted by the dynamic, "progressive" ways of the outside world, of which John Hale, engineer and speculator, is the representative. At still another level is the Tolliver-Falin feud, which involves the other two levels or plots, because June Tolliver, daughter of feuding Devil Judd Tolliver, loves John Hale, who organizes a volunteer police force to rid the community of the moonshining, feuding, and Saturday night rowdiness of which June's family is a part.

The conflicts and contrasts between mountains and Bluegrass in *The Trail of the Lonesome Pine* are basically the same as in Fox's other novels, for in each case the central plot involves a boy and girl from different cultures falling in love, though the conditions and solutions differ. In *The Little Shepherd*, for example, Chad the "woods-colt" leaves the mountains and becomes a part of the Bluegrass aristocracy, to which Margaret Dean belongs; but in *The Trail* June leaves the mountains to learn the ways of the world but ultimately returns and marries John Hale, who left the Bluegrass in order to establish his life in the mountains. Chad more than any other Fox character becomes a composite of the best of both cultures. June and Hale (with less than complete success) seek to fit into each other's culture and thus decide to live in neither the Bluegrass nor the mountains but instead in the shadow of the majestic great pine, which throughout the book has been the boundary line between the mountains and the outside world. In a sense they have met each other half-way (see Alvey, "Cultural Conflicts in Kentucky Literature").

The Heart of the Hills (1913) is Fox's last novel dealing with the mountains. By this time the popularity of local color stories about dwellers in the hill country appears to have dropped off sharply, but, more important, Fox seems to have come to feel that the mountaineers had changed. They have come to be conscious of themselves as mountaineers; they are learning to live with industrialism, either as laborers and managers or as speculators; their feuds, though not dead, are moribund; they are making their way with success into the outside world. The great migration from the mountains has begun, with people of a lower economic order going out of the mountains to become farmers or to enter industry. "In Steve," says Cratis Williams, "we see the prototype of the sons of the workers that are to flood the farms and industrial centers of the Midwest and the mill-towns of the South from 1910 onward" (*The Southern Mountaineer in Fact and Fiction*, 221). Fox again used the principle of contrasting cultures, this time with two sets of lovers who, interestingly, decide that they should not separate themselves from their native cultural heritage.

Though not strictly a novel about the mountains, *Erskine Dale, Pioneer* (1920), published a year after Fox's death, tells the story of the mountaineer from colonial times down to the period to which Fox had come in *The Heart of the Hills*. The locale is primarily the Bluegrass region, but the story is of Erskine Dale, a boy from Virginia captured by the Indians and brought up by them, who ultimately becomes a drummer boy in George Rogers Clark's Kaskaskia-Vincennes campaign. The novel, not among Fox's best, belongs in the tradition of historical fiction.

Another significant aspect of Fox's fiction is his focus on the world of the feudist and to a lesser extent that of the moonshiner. *A Cumberland Vendetta* (1895) was his first novel to deal with a mountain feud and his only novel in which a feud is of such central concern. It is also his only novel in which the mountaineer is not called upon to come to terms with the outside world encroaching upon mountain life in pursuit of coal and timber, and the only one in which the mountains and the outside world are not juxtaposed. As Fox tells the story of the Stetsons and the Lewallens and their feud of fifty years standing, he limits action to mountain life in isolation from the outside world. In his novels yet to come, the locale became larger, the perspective wider, and the space given to feuds less, though the feud might still be vital to plot development. In *The Kentuckians* (1897) the real-life Martin-Tolliver feud of Rowan County supplied Fox with much of his material, just as in *A Cumberland Vendetta* some was provided by the Hatfield-McCoy feud, including the love affair of Rose Anna McCoy and Jonse Hatfield. The feud in *The Kentuckians* is known largely by report, but in *The Little Shepherd of Kingdom Come* (1903) and *The Trail of the Lonesome Pine* (1908) Fox takes the reader right into the midst of the feud as he had done in *A Cumberland Vendetta*. He was most successful in doing this and presenting fully-realized characters in *The Trail of the Lonesome Pine*, where Devil John Wright (whom Fox knew well), Marshall Taylor, and Elizabeth Morris (of

Big Stone Gap) were the models respectively for Devil Judd Tolliver; his brother, the villainous Red Fox; and his daughter, June Tolliver. In *Lonesome Pine*, too, Fox succeeded in unifying the various threads and themes that run through the novel.

In *The Little Shepherd of Kingdom Come* Fox reveals his belief that the Civil War fostered a spirit of ill will that engendered feuds. How a feud "war" can originate and perpetuate itself is shown through the events of the Dillon-Turner feud. Fox's final statement on feuds, however, is found in *The Heart of the Hills*. Here the mountaineers appear to be in a period of rapid transition as their world gives way before the new industrialism and as old ways blend with the new. This view is reflected in the fact that the long-standing Honeycutt-Hawn feud winds to an end in less than blazing fashion and that Jason Hawn, only son of a feud leader, gets educated in a Bluegrass college and finally returns to the mountains to marry his childhood sweetheart and supervise a coal mine.

Fox was not blind to the fact that the blessings brought to the mountains by the outside world were not unmixed. As early as *The Trail of the Lonesome Pine* he was aware of the effect of mining on the mountain streams. Thus we read of one such stream, ". . . its crystal depths were there no longer—floating sawdust whirled in eddies on the surface and the water was black as soot. Here and there the white belly of a fish lay upturned in the sun, for the cruel, deadly work of civilization had already begun." He sees trouble too at the human level when June Tolliver goes away to school outside the hills and comes back home very much aware of the social shortcomings of her mountain relatives. In large, though, Fox seems to have approved of the coming of law and order and, despite complications, of the effects the outside would bring to the hills.

As a writer Fox is less important, certainly, than his friend James Lane Allen, but likely to retain a modest place in literary history for a number of years to come. His portrayal of the Kentucky mountains and mountaineers from the post–Civil War period approximately to World War I is unsurpassed, not only among Kentucky writers but among the writers of what we now consider the eight-state Appalachian area. No one questions Fox's ability to tell a story well, his use of dialect is generally regarded as good, and his portrayal of mountain life interesting and trustworthy. He was also an interpreter of his times in that he sought to say something worthwhile about the two Kentuckys that Allen had identified. If Fox's fiction never rose beyond those virtues that a "popular" novel must have, we must agree nonetheless with the reviewer in the *Nation* (Nov. 12, 1908) who, summing up *The Trail of the Lonesome Pine*, said: "It is melodrama—granted; but melodrama of so high a grade, so joyous an enthusiasm, and so compelling an interest as to give its reader an hour of uncritical pleasure." Fox seemed more important in his own day than he does at present, but even yet the average reader is likely to agree that his stories are eminently readable.

Charles Neville Buck

Next to John Fox, Jr., Charles Neville Buck (1879–1930) was the most talented and most popular of the novelists and short story writers who wrote about the Kentucky mountains. He was born in Midway, Woodford County, and lived there until he was fifteen except for four years when his father served as Minister to Peru under Grover Cleveland. At fifteen he moved to Louisville, where he attended the public schools and received his A.B. and law degrees from the University of Louisville. Subsequently he passed his bar examinations but never practiced law. He also attended the Cincinnati Academy of Art, took a position as cartoonist with the *Louisville Evening Post*, and later became an editorial writer for the same paper. As early as 1909 he was publishing short stories in magazines and soon gave up journalism to devote his full time to fiction. First came *The Key to Yesterday* (1910), a story of mental aberration, and after that *The Lighted Match* (1911), an international romance. *The Portal of Dreams* (1912), though not primarily about mountain life, did come closer to what would become Buck's life's work by introducing mountaineers and a feud into the story. From this time onward Buck exploited these subjects in more than twenty novels. For some years he divided his time between Louisville (living in St. James Court) and New York City and eventually came to reside in New York except for summers on Cape Cod. He died in 1930.

Buck's novels reveal a great deal about the manners, customs, and traditions of the mountaineers, for Buck spent much of his time in the mountains and even did some writing in the home of Devil John Wright. He spent some of his time, too, at the Pine Mountain Settlement School, but whatever knowledge he gained there and in conversations with serious students of the mountains such as Lucy Furman, his books evince little sociological interest in mountain subjects. His chief concern appears to have been popular appeal, and in this he succeeded, for he was widely read and many of his novels were adapted for presentation on both the stage and the screen. His characters are standard stereotypes, his plots uncluttered and well put together, the suspense element well managed, and the story well told. His portrayals, though lacking in depth, are accurate. Even the response of the mountaineer to the coming of industry he had observed closely enough to portray it accurately.

Three of Buck's novels can be selected as his best. *The Call of the Cumberlands* (1913) is a story of how Samson South leaves his native Kentucky hills to become a painter, abandons a promising career in Greenwich Village and Europe, gives up a society girl he has met, returns home, leads the Souths to victory in their feud with the Hallmans, and marries his childhood sweetheart, Sally. Buck reveals the view (perhaps derived from *The Little Shepherd of Kingdom Come*) that the Kentucky feud families descended from fine Virginia stock and became feudists only after their migration westward was interrupted when they remained in the hills and became isolated there.

In *Battle Cry* (1914) Buck tells the story of Juanita Holland, a Bryn Mawr graduate, who gives up her sophisticated life in the outside world in order to go to the hills of Kentucky, start a school, and ultimately marry a feudist of unsavory reputation, Anse Harvey. Obviously her school on Tribulation Creek bears a similarity to the Hindman Settlement School on Troublesome Creek. Again Buck makes the point that feudists came from good stock; Bad Anse, for example, still remembers the Plutarch and the Shakespeare he read as a boy in the Revolutionary War home he left when he migrated westward to Kentucky. In *The Code of the Mountains* (1915) Buck is innovative when he introduces feud animosities into the Spanish-American War and the Philippines. He is able to portray the feudists' loyalty to country and also to introduce a feudist code of honor when a member of one clan finds a member of another clan in dire straits in the Philippines.

Though Buck is primarily interested in action, his novels are not totally devoid of "purpose" and meaning. In *The Portal of Dreams*, for example, he makes the point that mountaineers are often mountaineers by choice and for good reason. In *When 'Bear Cat' Went Dry* (1918) he shows why moonshining stands in the way of progress in the mountain counties. But, beginning with *Flight to the Hills* (1926), disappointed with the way of life that post-war America had turned to, Buck began to portray mountain life as less violent than it was in his previous works and the mountains as a place to which social change was coming and making life there more attractive to outsiders. *Iron Will* (1927) pursues this new view by having the grandson of a feud leader lead his class in the Harvard Law School, fall in love with a beautiful and wealthy young lady with social standing, and return to the mountains to rid his home county of a nest of political rascals. *Hazard of the Hills* (1932) has Adam Ballard outsmarting the Eastern gangsters who have joined forces with some corrupt politicians in order to defraud the people.

Mountain Justice (1932) was Buck's last and best mystery novel. The complex story is filled with improbabilities that involve a Louisville surgeon unjustly accused of murder who flees to the mountains, where the county attorney protects his identity until he is cleared. But since the novel was written in the midst of the Great Depression, Buck deals with coal mines that are closed, hunger, Communist agitators, privation, and mine violence. These ills he laments, but he celebrates the virtues of the mountaineers and invites comparison of their feuds with violence in the outside world, observing that in spite of the homicidal tendency of the mountaineer he at least never kills a man unless he "needs killing."

Settlement Centers and Mission Schools

The local color writers studied the mountains again and wrote about it, and teachers, missionaries, and sociologists analyzed it and sought to introduce social action programs that would bring the mountaineers into the mainstream of America. As a result, by 1900 the idea of the mountains as "Appalachia" had taken shape and uplift organizations and movements had come into being.

No county in Kentucky received more attention from "improvement" programs than Knott County. Here in 1902 the first notably successful program was introduced, the Hindman Settlement School, established by Mary Stone and Katherine Pettit to provide educational opportunity for mountain children while keeping them mindful of their heritage. This school continues to operate, as does the Carr Creek Center, founded in 1920, nine miles from Hindman. Fully as noteworthy was the educational work of Alice Lloyd, who came to Pippa Passes from Boston and established Caney Creek Community Center in 1917 and Caney Junior College in 1923 (now Alice Lloyd College). The success of these and other centers encouraged the establishment of comparable programs throughout the mountains until finally, it is estimated, there were upwards of two hundred of them, supported by religious and other philanthropic groups that brought in teachers, nurses, and doctors. Some of these groups limited their activities to fairly narrow geographical areas but some were multicounty in scope. Most notable among the latter was the development by Mary Breckinridge in 1925 of the Frontier Nursing Service, an organization that generated both national and international interest and led its founder to write her much read and well-praised *Wide Neighborhoods*. A number of these organizations continue today to render fine service, but many collapsed before or during the Great Depression or were taken over by local community agencies. It is not surprising that such activities should enter into the literature dealing with the mountains.

Lucy Furman

The most productive years of Lucy Furman's literary life (1870–1958) were the seventeen years she spent at the Hindman Settlement School, where she went when she was thirty-seven years of age. She was born in Henderson, Kentucky, in 1870, was brought up by an aunt after her mother and father died, was graduated from Sayre Institute in Lexington at sixteen, took a secretarial course and got her first job as a court stenographer when she was nineteen, had stories published in the *Century Magazine* when she was twenty-three, and in 1897 when she was twenty-seven published her first volume, *Stories of a Sanctified Town*. The "Town" was Robards, in Henderson County, the scene of a wave of religious enthusiasm Furman had witnessed.

In 1907, after ten years of ill health, Furman offered her services to a Sayre schoolmate, Katherine Pettit, who with Mary Stone founded the first settlement school in the mountains. Thus Lucy Furman became a teacher in the Hindman Settlement School on Troublesome Creek, in Knott County, and for seventeen years taught and served as housemother for small mountain boys. Furman's experiences began to find their way into print, first in the *Atlantic Monthly* and then in books: *Mothering on Perilous* (1913), *Sight to the Blind* (1914), *The Quare Women* (1923), *The Glass Window* (1925), and *The Lonesome Road* (1927). "I have charge of the gardening and outdoor work at the Settlement School," she writes, "but the happiest part of my life is my residence at the small boys' cottage, about which I have told you in the 'Perilous' stories, and in which I have found endless pleasure and entertainment."

Lucy Furman had indeed found her life's work which she delighted to write about. She wrote about the "quare women" who came from "furrin parts" (mostly the Bluegrass) to teach the young to cook and to sew, to play and to sing, to lay aside their blood feuds, and to look forward to a better life. She tells of baptisms, feuds, sudden deaths, and murder; she reports on mountain preachers with their stern creeds, and she records the humor that arises when children fostered by one culture are confronted by their teachers ("quare women") of another culture. But in depicting life as she saw it, she belittled no one, and the mountaineers remained a people with their dignity intact.

Actually Furman's books are only marginally classified as novels, for each of them grew out of what she had experienced and had some of the characteristics of a sociological treatise. As a writer of fiction, therefore, her task was to give real-life events the "feel" of fiction instead of lending verisimilitude to fictitious events. Despite their sociological purpose and generally weak plots, however, her volumes are delightfully written and interpret life in Southeastern Kentucky from about 1900 to the 1920s well. They capture the spirit of the Kentucky mountain social order at the time when the static life of generations of mountaineers is being penetrated and modified by the new industrial order.

Mothering on Perilous takes the form of a diary of Miss Loring, teacher and housemother for twelve mountain boys. It records how she is slowly drawn into the lives of the boys' families and the life of the community, and also reveals the early history of the school and its relationship to the region it serves. *The Quare Women* and its sequel *The Glass Window* continue the report on incidents in the life of the school and the community. In *The Quare Women* three girls from the Bluegrass come to the mountains to serve as social workers; *The Glass Window* contains the only romance in Furman's five volumes. Subjects and events in the volumes range from convincing Uncle Lot that he should put glass windows in his eighty-year-old log house to discussing ideas of law and order that are inconsistent with the tradition of feuds.

The Lonesome Road, stronger as a novel than the other volumes, tells of the struggles of a mountain boy, Jared Stoll, to become a medical doctor. How young Jared copes with the problem of going from a static society into the outside world tells something of the difference between Furman and the popular novelists of mountain life such as John Fox, Jr. and Charles Neville Buck. In Furman, there is, for example, no engineer or geologist or mine operator to recognize talent in a young man and encourage him to go forth into the big world; there is no wealthy distant kinsman to turn up as an aristocrat and sponsor him; there is no Bluegrass girl to prefer him to one of her own social set. There is still the conflict of cultures and the need for mountaineers to learn to cope with the outside world, but apparently the entering wedge is for education to motivate the young Stolls to venture into the world and bring back with them the traits and skills that make leaders who can cope with the complexities of the burgeoning twentieth century. There are feuds and enmities as well as most of the mountain characters that appear in other novels, but missing in Furman's novels is romantic adventure.

From the beginning Furman's books were well received by the review press, and she was cited as a faithful interpreter of the people about whom she wrote. Of *The Lonesome Road* the *New York Post* wrote, "Here is an excellent portrayal, not of the white trash of the foothills but of the real mountaineers—descendants of those English pioneers who settled there many years ago." Furman, says a *New York Times* reviewer of *The Glass Window*, "is preserving an artistic record of a life that is fast dying—and she succeeds. A life that would torment most of us to bitterness and resentment, under Miss Furman's sure and sympathetic hand, is lifted into its actual beauty."

In 1924 Furman went back to Henderson and in 1934 moved to Frankfort, where she lived until 1953. During these years she wrote a few stories, but most of her energies were directed against cruelty to animals. She took issue with the practice of selling live baby chickens and ducks at Easter time for children to play with, and she gained her name as "The Steel Trap Lady" because of her four years of campaigning against needless cruelty to animals. While she was teaching at Hindman, her children told her how trapped animals gnaw their legs off in order to escape the steel trap that holds them. The new trap which she advocated was a chain-loop device that secured the animal without hurting or maiming it, and she toured the state demonstrating the trap. In 1953 Furman moved to Cranford, New Jersey, and died there in the home of her nephew in 1958.

Genevieve May Fox

Genevieve May Fox (1888–1959), a native of Massachusetts, graduated from Smith College and engaged in an editorial career before coming to Pippa Passes and the Caney Creek Community Center.

Her first three books constitute a trilogy that tells of the struggles of Kentucky mountain girls in getting an education. *Mountain Girl* (1932), which was a Junior Literary Guild selection for February 1932, is the story of Sairy Ann Hall, who goes from a settlement school to the Bluegrass for nurse's training so that she can return and help the community in which she grew up. In *Mountain Girl Comes Home* (1934) she and her physician husband have established a clinic and manage to overcome the initial opposition to a "fotched in" physician. In *Lona of Hollybush Creek* (1935) Lona, who has been cured of her long-time lameness, revives the neglected art of quilt-making, finds a market for her products, marries a native handicraftsman, and with him establishes a crafts center that flourishes.

Fox, who spent the latter part of her life married to Raymond G. Fuller in New York City, wrote several other juvenile books on non-Kentucky subjects, the best known of which is probably *Army Surgeon*.

Ann Cobb

Ann Cobb (1885–1960) was the first Eastern Kentucky author to write a volume of verse of publishable quality. Cobb, a member of a distinguished New England family, met Mary Stone while the two were students at Wellesley College. In January 1906, after Stone and Katherine Pettit had established the Hindman Settlement School in 1902, Cobb set out for Kentucky by train in order to visit her friend and take a look at the new school. So interested did she become in the work being done there that she joined the teaching staff and remained at the school until her retirement in 1957. She thus became the third of the "fotched-on quare women" who joined the school's staff. Like Lucy Furman, who joined the three the following year, Cobb had a talent for writing and soon was publishing poetry in *Outlook, Saturday Evening Post, St. Nicholas,* and other national magazines. Finally at the urging of Furman she submitted a manuscript to the Houghton Mifflin Company, which published it in 1922 as *Kinfolks,* a volume of forty-eight dialect poems about the hill-country life.

Kinfolks: Kentucky Mountain Rhymes had a warm reception at the hands of the press and drew praise for the author's understanding and the care with which she recorded the customs and traditions and dialect of the people about whom she wrote. The judgment of *The Bookman* (July 1922) is typical of the reviews: "As homely as a patchwork quilt and as genuine as the Cumberland Mountains themselves.

The quaint old English words bring out, very simply and poignantly, the bits of happiness and tragedy, the love of their hills, and the pride and courage of these most individual of the American pioneers."

At her death in 1960 Cobb left a great many poems, plays, and sketches, a few of which have been published in *Kentucky Writing*, edited by Albert Stewart, one of Cobb's students at the Hindman Settlement School.

CHAPTER 10

Poetry

By the end of the nineteenth century America had lost its last two important poets—Emily Dickinson in 1886 and Walt Whitman in 1892. A renaissance in American poetry, however, was about to begin. In 1912 Harriet Monroe founded the notable and influential magazine *Poetry*, and beginning at almost the same moment the poems of an astonishing number of good poets began to appear regularly: poets with a sense of purpose such as Stephen Vincent Benét, Robert Frost, Edgar Lee Masters, Edwin Arlington Robinson, and Carl Sandburg; "imagists" such as John Gould Fletcher, "H.D.," Amy Lowell, and Ezra Pound; poets more primarily lyrical, such as Conrad Aiken, Adelaide Crapsey, Edna St. Vincent Millay, Alan Seeger, and Sara Teasdale; and a group in rebellion against order and tradition, both of the spirit and of poetic practice: E.E. Cummings, Hart Crane, Robinson Jeffers, Wallace Stevens, and William Carlos Williams.

In Kentucky the same period was undistinguished. It did produce some poets whose place in Kentucky literature depends entirely on one poem even though they wrote more, as had been the case with William Orlando Butler, Theodore O'Hara, Mary E.W. Betts, and Sarah T. Bolton a few years earlier. None of them rivaled the one-poem poet Edwin Markham, but two or three had national visibility. Each left a poem that has one quality or another that makes it more lively, more witty, more original, more clever, or even more corny and hence better remembered than the works of poets whose laurels rest on a larger and more formal body of writing.

Kentucky's Madison Cawein was perhaps the best nature poet in the nation and was Kentucky's first poet to win national and international fame, but his adoption of the tradition that peopled fields and forests with elves and sprites and nymphs that were invisible to naturalists and others tended to foreshorten his reputation with the public. Other Kentucky poets will be noted, but only Elizabeth Madox Roberts wrote verse—*Under the Tree*, 1922—that was to outlive its day.

Young E. Allison

Born in Henderson, Young E. Allison (1853–1932) was to move to Louisville, where he was a journalist for many years. In spite of his heavy journalistic duties, Allison found time for a short story and a novelette, which were published in *Lippincott's Magazine* and *Century Magazine*, and for a series of essays and critical pieces on novels and novel-reading called *The Delicious Vice* (two series, 1907 and 1909). But it is "On Board the Derelict," a six-stanza extension of the four famous lines in Robert Louis Stevenson's *Treasure Island*, that is known around the world. Beginning with Stevenson's four lines, the last stanza concludes,

Fifteen men on the Dead Man's chest—
  Yo-ho-ho and a bottle of rum!
Drink and the devil had done for the rest—
  Yo-ho-ho and a bottle of rum!
We wrapp'd 'em all in a mains'l tight,
With twice ten turns of a hawser's bight
And we heaved 'em over and out of sight—
  With a yo-heave-ho!
    And a fare-you-well!
  And a sudden plunge
    In the sullen swell,
Ten fathoms deep on the run to hell—
  Yo-ho-ho hum and a bottle of rum!

James Hilary Mulligan

James Hilary Mulligan (1844–1915), a native of Lexington, was the author of a number of poems in the local color tradition, such as "Over the Hill to Hustonville" and "The Bells of Old St. Joseph," both made up of easy-flowing lines. But it was "In Kentucky" that has kept Mulligan's name alive. The poem was introduced to the world in February 1902 when Judge Mulligan was invited to be one of several speakers at a dinner given by the Lexington Chamber of Commerce for the legislature at the Phoenix Hotel. According to local newspapers, Mulligan spoke wittily for about fifteen minutes on his earlier membership in the Kentucky General Assembly; then he "drew from his pocket, as if drawing a deadly weapon, a dangerous looking manuscript" and read the poem which has no doubt been more widely circulated than any other poem written in Kentucky. It was set to music and chanted, it was widely reproduced in newspapers and journals, it was quoted in the halls of Congress and read into the *Congressional Record*, additional verses were composed and publicized, at least fifty parodies in most states of the Union have been traced, and withal, it is estimated, well over a million souvenir postal cards have been sold with the verses printed on them. The first and the last stanzas follow:

IN KENTUCKY

The moonlight falls the softest
    in Kentucky;
The summer days come oftest
    in Kentucky;
Friendship is the strongest,
Love's light glows the longest,
Yet, wrong is always wrongest
    in Kentucky

. . . .

The song birds are the sweetest
    in Kentucky;
The thoroughbreds are fleetest
    in Kentucky;
Mountains tower proudest,
Thunder peals the loudest,
The landscape is the grandest—
And politics—the damndest
    in Kentucky.

Langdon "Denver" Smith

Langdon "Denver" Smith (1858–1908), who was born in Louisville and attended the public schools there, wrote poems, short stories, and novels, but his reputation depends entirely upon a poem that appeared in the midst of want ads in the *New York Journal*. This was "Evolution, a Fantasy." The poem, begun in 1895 and written over a period of at least four years, is a love song addressed to Smith's wife, Mary Antoinette, whom he married in 1894.

I

When you were a tadpole and I was a fish,
  In the Paleozoic time,
And side by side on the ebbing tide
  We sprawled through the ooze and slime,
Or skittered with many a caudal flip
  Through the depths of the Cambrian fen,
My heart was rife with the joy of life,
  For I loved you even then.

II–XIV

Mindless we lived and mindless we loved,
  And mindless at last we died,
And deep in a rift of the Caradoc drift
  We slumbered side by side.

. . . .

Then light and swift through the jungle trees
  We swung in our airy flights.

. . . .

Thus life by life, and love by love,
  We passed through the cycles strange.

. . . .

I flaked a flint to a cutting edge,
  And shaped it with brutish craft.

. . . .

And that was a million years ago,
  In a time that no man knows;
Yet here tonight in the mellow light,
  We sit at Delmonico's. . . .

Overall Smith's masterpiece is a clever poem, sometimes witty and even at times learned. Smith died in New York City in 1908.

Henry T. Stanton

Henry T. Stanton (1834–98) came from Virginia to Maysville with his parents when he was two years old, attended school in Maysville and at West Point, and served in the Confederate army during the Civil War, rising to the rank of major. After the war he practiced law for a time, served in editorial capacities on newspapers in Maysville and Frankfort, and held positions in Kentucky state government. Stanton published two volumes of verse and two novels, but today only the title poem of *The Moneyless Man and Other Poems* (1871) survives. It was written, so the story goes, at the request of a "wandering elocutionist" who came to Maysville and asked Major Stanton to write for him "a poem that would draw tears from any audience." The result was a melodramatic, sentimental poem, which mournfully explores the lack of welcome for the Moneyless Man in the banquet hall, in the church pew, in a place of business, and in the courtroom. Only in heaven, the reader learns in the last stanza, will he find a welcome.

Agnes E. Mitchell

Little is known of Mrs. Agnes E. Mitchell, but apparently she was a resident of Louisville for a number of years and wrote "When the Cows Come Home" (ca. 1870), a pleasantly lyrical poem well remembered and sung by an older generation (Townsend, *Kentucky in American Letters*, 2: 385–87). Some lines from the first and last stanzas follow:

With Klingle, Klangle, Klingle,
'Way down the dusty dingle,
The cows are coming home;
Now sweet and clear, and faint and low,
The airy tinklings come and go,
Like chimings from some far-off tower,
Or patterings of an April shower
That makes the daisies grow;
Koling, Kolang, Kolinglelingle,
'Way down the darkening dingle,
The cows come slowly home.
. . . .
Let down the bars; let in the train
Of long-gone songs, and flowers and rain,
For dear old times come back again
   When the cows come home.

Madison Cawein

Madison Cawein (1865–1914) was the first Kentucky poet to gain a national and international reputation. In 1887 William Dean Howells read Cawein's first volume of verse, *Blooms of the Berry*, and the following year in his "Editor's Study" column in *Harper's Magazine* praised him warmly and predicted bright days ahead for him in what "might almost be called a landscape school of poetry." Thus encouraged by a critic of Howells' eminence, as well as by reviewers and other critics, Cawein devoted himself single-mindedly to his Muse and turned out verses at a great rate. Despite the critical commendation he received, however, Cawein failed to gain popular favor, became discouraged, and brought the charge of materialism against his age. At about the same time Sir Edmund Gosse, with Cawein's permission, published in London a carefully selected edition of Cawein's poems under the title *Kentucky Poems* (1902), with a prefatory compliment to "a poet who seems to stand alone in his generation." Still Cawein's popularity failed to prosper.

Poetry has seldom been popular in the marketplace, but Cawein's problem in winning a reading audience was worsened by his fascination with the Ancients and with earlier English and European literature where descriptions of nature are overlaid with classical allusion and the presence of mythological beings. He was writing in a tradition well established in literary history, but not meaningful to his own generation. In 1919 Cawein's lack of appeal was made clear by Louis Untermeyer's comment in *Modern American Poetry*: "He pictures all outdoors with painstaking detail; and yet it is somehow unreal, prettified, remote . . . the reader is quickly wearied by the almost interminable procession of gnomes, elves, dryads, spirits, fays, and fauns."

Despite disappointments, however, Cawein continued to work indefatigably, with both honor and honors accruing to him. He did seek to understand the preferences of his time and tried to make adjustments, though unsuccessfully. In some of his work individual poems could be called "more realistic" or "more human" than had been Cawein's wont; but his effort failed and he died a disappointed and frustrated man.

Cawein was not an 1890s poet in a transitional period consciously abandoning old ideas and conventions in order to find and adopt new techniques but rather a poet dedicated to the tradition of the past and trying to prove the validity of both his own writing and the tradition. From his father, who gathered herbs and compounded patent medicines, he came to have an extensive knowledge of Kentucky flora and fauna and a love for the outdoors. Thus he grew up with the eye of a naturalist and came to maturity with a love of poetry and a knowledge of and fondness for mythology and of the ancient and modern classics. From this background and a feeling for the supernatural that he gained from his mother's interest in spiritualism, he fashioned his own way of seeing the world and writing about it—a style that meshed poorly with the industrial, materialistic outlook burgeoning around him. He received only a small income from his writings and thus had to earn a living in the workaday world, which he did by dabbling in real estate and the stock market. In 1912 he lost heavily in a stock market crash and, threatened with poverty, moved with his wife and son from their handsome St. James Court home to an apartment. He sold a portion of his library in order to alleviate his financial strain and in September 1914 was placed on the relief list of the Authors Club of New York City and was awarded a monthly check. In December 1914 he died at the age of forty-nine and was buried in Cave Hill Cemetery.

There is no doubt that Cawein's life and his hopes for himself went unfulfilled and that he never won the public acceptance he longed for. On the other hand, he won a great deal of critical praise and public honor that set him apart. William Dean Howells and Sir Edmund Gosse were not the only critics to speak well of him. To the London *Poetry Review* (Oct. 1912) he "appears the biggest figure among American poets." In the opinion of the *Dial* (Jan. 16, 1914), "Other poets may voice the spiritual issues of our national life with richer expression and greater authority, but none of them can surpass Mr. Cawein as an interpreter of the beauty that lies at the heart of natural things." He was called "the greatest nature poet of his time" by Joyce Kilmer in *Catholic World* (March 1917) and "the greatest nature poet his country has produced" by the *Christian Science Monitor* (Jan. 24, 1920).

Today Madison Cawein is seldom read. In publishing thirty-six volumes in twenty-eight years he published far too much, for a great deal of his poetry was completely undistinguished, and the import too slight to endure. And, of course, his use of folklore and mythological beings to animate landscape alienated the modern reader. Yet there are fine lines and sensitive short poems which have merit. Madeline Covi is bringing these together for a modern edition that may well rescue Cawein from oblivion.

Robert Burns Wilson

Madison Cawein was regarded as the foremost contemplative nature poet of his time, but Robert Burns Wilson (1850–1916) had a national reputation also. Indeed, literary historian Fred Lewis Pattee in his *A History of American Literature since 1870* (1915), calling Wilson and Cawein "the two most prominent poets of the South," compares the two by saying, "Wilson undoubtedly was the most inspired singer, as Cawein was the most careful observer of nature" (246). Even more than Cawein, however, Wilson's reputation has not stood the test of time.

Wilson came to Frankfort to live in 1875—having first arrived in Union County, Kentucky from Pennsylvania—and there seriously embarked upon the career of painter and poet he had determined upon when he was a schoolboy in Wheeling, West Virginia. Delighted with the Kentucky River and Elkhorn Creek valleys and the terrain generally, Wilson did many landscape paintings, though he did portraits and other subjects as well. His "Head of Christ" is regarded as his masterpiece.

Many of Wilson's poems seem almost as if they were written as inscriptions for his paintings. "When Evening Cometh On," one of his early poems and perhaps his best nature poem, appeared in *Harper's Magazine* in 1885 and seemed to critics "somehow to have the singing quality that may not be learned, that may not be taught." Despite an undoubted gift, however, Wilson failed to develop into the poet that his early talent seemed to promise. His published volumes include *Life and Love* (1887), *Chant of a Woodland Spirit* (1894), and *The Shadows of the Trees* (1898). Wilson voiced little of the concerns of his time, but many of his contemporaries regarded him as a highly gifted, brooding man whose graphic power to please the eye was equaled by his lyric talent.

Wilson's greatest moment of triumph came when his "Battle Song," written after the sinking of the United States battleship *The Maine* in Havana Harbor, was published as a full-page spread in the *New York Herald*, April 17, 1898. *The Maine* had been sunk on February 15, and American sentiment, already in favor of the Cuban insurrection against Spain, was inflamed by the decision of a naval court of inquiry that the ship had been destroyed by a submarine mine. Wilson's poem, employing the already popular slogan "Remember the *Maine*" as a refrain, brought the author instant fame, was set to music immediately, and became the battle song of the Spanish-American War, which in effect was authorized by Congress on April 19, 1898. The first stanza is typical:

> When the vengeance wakes, when the battle breaks,
>   And the ships sweep out to sea;
> When the foe is neared, when the decks are cleared,
>   And the colors floating free;
> When the squadrons meet, when it's fleet to fleet
>   And front to front with Spain,
> From ship to ship, from lip to lip,
>   Pass on the quick refrain,
> "Remember, remember the *Maine*."

Wilson's last published volume was a novel, *Until the Day Break* (1900), a not very successful Gothic story mostly set in Frankfort. The following year, Wilson—who had remained a bachelor until this time—married; and marriage, along with the birth of a daughter, placed a heavy strain upon the small income he had previously managed on. In the spring of 1904 the Wilsons moved to Brooklyn in the hope that in a metropolitan area his creative talent in painting and poetry might fare better and produce a better income. The change, however, brought no financial improvement. Wilson died in Brooklyn in the spring of 1916, following a heart attack some months earlier. His body was shipped back to Frankfort and was interred in the Frankfort Cemetery.

Joseph Seamon Cotter

Joseph Seamon Cotter (1861–1949) has been called Kentucky's "first Negro poet with real creative ability." According to Cotter's own handwritten sketch of his life, "I was born in Nelson County, Kentucky, February 2, 1861, on a farm owned by my great grandfather, Daniel Stapp. He was a tanner. In 1829 he bought himself and a part of his master's farm. Later he bought his daughter, Lucinda, my mother's mother. . . . Prior to my birth [my mother, Martha] lived in Bardstown and was a servant at "My Old Kentucky Home." When he was only a few weeks old, Cotter moved to Louisville with his family, learned to read by the time he was four, attended a private school, dropped out at the end of the third grade, worked at various jobs, entered Louisville's first night school for blacks at twenty-two, received a high school diploma after two five-month sessions, later taught in several black high schools, served as principal, and founded the Paul Laurence Dunbar School. Cotter was entirely self-taught in English and American literature and in poetic composition.

Cotter's published volumes were eight in number, including five volumes of verse, one of drama, one of fiction, and one a collection of tales, poems, short plays, and other pieces. *A Rhyming* (1895) was his first volume, containing some poems not without merit, but on the whole the volume was conventional, bookish, and sometimes artificial. *Links of Friendship* (1898), a collection of lyric verses, attracted the attention of William Dean Howells and increased the interest of Paul Laurence Dunbar, who had visited in Cotter's home in 1894. "Sequel to 'The Pied Piper of Hamelin'" was Cotter's favorite poem in the volume and he reprinted it in three other collections of his poems. Robert T. Kerlin said of it in 1921 (*South Atlantic Quar-*

terly) that "it surpasses the original—Browning's—that is, in rushing rhythms and ingenious rhymes. It is an incredible success." (For more details, see A. Russell Brooks, "Joseph Seamon Cotter," *Dictionary of Literary Biography*, vol. 50: 62–69).

Caleb the Degenerate (1903), a four-act poetic drama, like Cotter's early verse, advocated friendly relations between blacks and whites and advised against blacks' participating in politics. *A White Song and a Black One* (1909) and *Negro Tales* (1912) proved Cotter a disciple of Dunbar, but except for a few poems that relate to children the number that is noteworthy is small and is generally ignored by black literary scholars. In 1938 Cotter, having completed fifty years of service to the Louisville public schools, published *Collected Poems* and dedicated it to those "who have made this long service possible." The new poems in the volume seldom deal with the subject of race, though Cotter is still engrossed in the relationships between blacks and whites and advocates hard work for his people.

In 1939 *Sequel to "The Pied Piper of Hamelin" and Other Poems* appeared and included not only Cotter's favorite *Sequel* but three other favorites of earlier years, "Mr. Goody's Goat," "Six in Deportment," and "Johnny's Dream of Santa Claus" and what was perhaps his most popular poem, "The Tragedy of Pete." He was to publish one more miscellaneous volume, *Negroes and Others at Work and Play*, two years before his death in 1947. During his long life of eighty-eight years he had won a place of esteem in the world and served in important positions with such organizations as the National Association for the Advancement of Colored People, became a member of the Authors League of America, and was included in *Who's Who in America*. His writings have never won him high recognition, but he has been anthologized in Afro-American anthologies of poetry, and has fared rather well at the hands of black literary historians. The following is a sample of his verse:

THE TRYST

The moon hangs limp in a lusty sky
  And trysts with the evening star,
Which flingeth back a golden smile,
  And they straightway lovers are.

The rich man trinkets the wares of life
  And mocks at the poor man's plea,
Which flingeth back a dagger-thought
  That trysts with anarchy.

Joseph Seamon Cotter, Jr.

Heretofore Joseph Seamon Cotter, Jr. (1895–1919), has gone unnoted in volumes dealing with Kentucky literature. After graduating second in his class at Louisville's Central High School, young Cotter entered Fisk University but was forced to withdraw during his sophomore year because of tuberculosis. He died four years later. During only one and a half years did he write poetry, but in *The Band of Gideon and Other Lyrics* (1918), as well as some poems published posthumously in *The Zion Quarterly* in 1920 and 1921, he established himself as a young poet of promise.

Versatility in subject matter and poetic techniques are characteristic of Cotter's verse. One of his constant concerns was the problem of identity for blacks. In "The Mulatto and the Critics," for example, he identifies himself with the Afro-American community, and in one of his poems he writes of the bravery of blacks as soldiers in World War I and reflects the commonly held view that they were often shabbily treated. Though a poet of restraint, Cotter was not without his note of protest and was a harbinger of the voice of blacks in the role of protest and the search for a new identity:

> The band of Gideon roam the sky,
> The howling wind is their war-cry,
> The thunder's roll in their trump's peal
> And the lightning flash their vengeful steel.

Young Cotter had made a good start at achieving critical recognition with the volume he published, but at twenty-three he was dead. (For further discussion see James Robert Payne's "Joseph Seamon Cotter, Jr." *Dictionary of Biographical Dictionary*, vol. 50: 70–73.)

Will S. Hays

William Shakespeare Hays (1837–1907), who lived in Louisville all his life, had a widely varied career. He was a war correspondent for the *Louisville Democrat* during the Civil War, commanded the river transport "Grey Eagle" for a time, became marine editor of the *Courier-Journal*, was a river captain between Pittsburgh and New Orleans, had a steamboat named after him, wrote the words and music for some 350 songs, and composed countless other poems and ballads that were never set to music.

Hays often chose nostalgic subjects, some joy or pleasure that could be no more, but his writing generally lacked depth of feeling and was too topical to achieve universal quality. Whatever Hays's shortcomings may have been, however, his popularity was phenomenal.

It is known, for example, that up to 1873 J.L. Peters and Sons sold 2,688,000 copies of his songs, and it is estimated that during his lifetime the number reached more than 6 million. Hays's songs, which were simple in harmony and easy to sing or perform, were popular among the minstrel companies and played before full houses in theaters, on showboats, and at various community celebrations and entertainments.

"Mollie Darling" (1866) was doubtless Hays's best and most popular poem and song. Some 2 million copies of it were sold. Among others of his popular songs are "Sweet Bess o' Bonnie Doon," "Shamus O'Brien," "Down in De Co'n Field," and "Roll out! Heave Dat Cotton." But most famous of all—if indeed it was his—is "Dixie," perhaps the most stirring of the musical legacies left by the Civil War. Dan Emmett, a well-established minstrel who traveled with the famous Bryant Minstrels, is generally credited with writing the song, for when he arrived in New York in 1859 after a southern tour, he had the song published by the Firth, Pond Company. Hays, however, contended that the Buckner Guards on their way South in 1857 asked him to write a "glee song" for them and that they popularized it. Incontrovertible evidence of the authorship, however, may never be found.

Hays's published volumes of verse include *The Modern Meetin' House and Other Poems* (1874), *Will S. Hays Songs and Poems* (1886), and *Poems and Songs* (1895).

Daniel Henry Holmes

Daniel Henry Holmes (1851–1908) was born in New York City. Later his family lived in New Orleans, but in 1852 his father bought a colonial house near Covington, Kentucky, as a summer home in order to escape the heat. As a result, Holmes from the age of one spent his summers in what came to be called Holmesdale, returning to New Orleans for the winter. Later Holmes adopted Holmesdale as his year-round residence and practiced law in a desultory fashion. Being a man of wealth, he traveled a great deal, but spent parts of at least forty years at Holmesdale.

Holmes's first and best volume of poetry was *Under a Fool's Cap: Songs* (1884), a most unusual volume in that Holmes took twenty-four familiar nursery rhymes—printed in blackface type just above his own lyrics—and amplified or otherwise elaborated or continued the originals. With one exception ("Margery Daw") he employed the metrical patterns of the originals. A few of the thirteen stanzas of "My Lady's Garden" exemplify Holmes's method:

How does my Lady's garden grow?
How does my Lady's garden grow?
With silver bells, and cockle-shells,
And pretty girls all in a row.
. . . .

They all have crowns and all have wings,
Pale silver crowns and faint green wings,
And each has a wand within her hand,
And raiment about her that cleaves and clings.
. . . .

But what have my Lady's girls to do?
What maiden toil or spinning to do?
They swing and sway the live-long day
While beams and dreams shift to and fro.
. . . .

They deck themselves in their bells and shells,
Their silver bells and their cockle-shells,
Like pilgrim elves, they deck themselves
And chaunting Runic hymns and spells.
. . . .

And this is why my Lady grows,
My own sweet Lady daily grows,
In sorcery such, that at her touch,
Sweet laughter blossoms and songs unclose. . . .

Holmes lived in Europe for seven years but returned to Holmesdale in 1901 and made it his principal residence the remainder of his life. In 1906 he published *A Pedlar's Pack*, a collection of witty and often clever verses. Of the collection the *Literary Digest* (Nov. 22, 1906) says, "Ninety clever short poems which the author declares are intended to help 'a tired man to kill a Sunday,' but they are really better than their mission implies."

J.T. Cotton Noe

James Thomas Cotton Noe (1869–1953) has the honor of having been Kentucky's first official poet laureate (1926–53), and doubtless at the time was a good choice as a poet of the people. On the one hand, he was a fine-looking man and made a good public appearance, he had been a lecturer on the Redpath Chautauqua circuit, he had been a teacher and administrator in the public schools, and he was then a professor in the Commonwealth's state university. On the other hand, he had an eye for the simple, the commonplace in the lives of ordinary people, a love for the land, and a respect for the dignity of the individual. As an editorial writer in the *Lexington Leader* put it, in his works "there runs a profound and refreshing philosophy of human kindness, recognition of the romantic and the commonplace, generous interpretations of the lives of lowly people, devotion to the simple and fundamental virtues and belief in the grandeur and worth of the human spirit." Furthermore, he had a regional reputation and was a voice for sanity in the postwar jazz age of the 1920s. He had a sense of humor and a talent for gentle satire but used neither in ridicule; his writings had a moralistic bent.

Noe had a feel for rhyme and especially for the anapestic measure that makes a line swing along at a rattling good clip. Some lines from "Tip Sams," Noe's best-known poem, illustrate his talent:

> Tip Sams had twins and a razor-back-sow,
> Five dogs and a mule, and an old roan cow;
> A bone-spavined filly and a one-room house,
> And a little wrinkled woman just as meek as a mouse.
> Old Tip raised tobacco and trafficked in skins;
> For he had seven sons in addition to the twins. . . .

Noe's principal works include *The Blood of Rachel* (1916), a dramatization of the book of Esther; *Tip Sams of Kentucky and Other Poems* (1926), poems about life in the hill country; *The Valleys of Parnassus* (1935), satire and humor; *Tip Sams Again* (1947), selected poems by the author. In a sense, Cotton Noe was the James Whitcomb Riley of Kentucky.

Cale Young Rice

Although Cale Young Rice (1872–1943) never won the fame that his wife, Alice Hegan Rice, did, he had a good though not unmixed reputation in both the United States and England. Rice was the author of two novels, a number of short stories published in three volumes in collaboration with his wife (*Turnabout Tales*, 1920; *Winners and Losers*, 1925; *Passionate Follies*, 1936), and an essay on his theory of poetic inspiration, "Poetry's Genii," which was appended to his autobiography, *Bridging the Years* (1939). But he was best known for his poetry and his poetic dramas. Rice was very prolific and between *Dusk to Dusk* (1898) and *High Perils* (1933) published twenty-one volumes of verse and ten volumes of verse drama.

Like Cawein, Rice was a traditionalist in both the form and content of his poetry and resisted the *fin de siècle* clamor for change that existed elsewhere in the nation. Like the other traditionalists of his day he wrote many nature poems and much philosophical and meditative verse, as well as dramatic lyrics such as "Mary at Nazareth," "A Japanese Mother," and "On the Moor." He wrote many love poems, among them *Songs to A.H.R.* [Alice Hegan Rice] (1918), and other poems that deal with places he had visited. The latter include lines about Japanese life, religion, and art in *Nirvana Days* (1909), as well as poems about other lands in *Many Gods* (1910), *At the World's Heart* (1914), and *Pilgrim's Scrip* (1924). The sea was another favorite subject, as in *Sea Poems* (1921) and *A Sea Lover's Scrip* (1925).

At his best Rice was a poet of respectable talent who attracted favorable attention from such critics as Gilbert Murray, who declared that "his books open up a most varied world of emotion and romance." In "Night in Avignon," says academic critic Fred Lewis Pattee, Rice "bursts upon one in the tropic beauty of a night-blooming cereus. An anthology from his poems, a thin volume, would possess surprisingly high merit" (*The New American Literature, 1890–1930* [1930], 393). And a similar enthusiasm was sometimes registered by reviewers. *Wraiths and Realities* (1918), says the *Bookman,* "contains many fine poems and one bit of sheer magic, 'The Chanson of the Bells of Osenèy' " (May 1918).

Such judgments are not the modern view of Rice's poetry, nor the typical view in Rice's own day, for not only could Rice be uneven and uncritical—even banal—he lacked genuine poetic inspiration and depth. He was an able craftsman, he wrote at ease in whatever poetic form he chose, and he was capable of musical, satisfying lines; but he failed to be provocative or insightful. *The* [London] *Times Literary Supplement* near the end of Rice's poetic career sized up his poetic talent and achievement well in its review of *High Perils* (1933): "It lacks the concentration of feeling and form which makes poetry memorable. There is seldom an image or a phrase in it which surprises us into a recognition of life at a new depth or which haunt us by their magic. But he who runs may read it and in the reading enjoy its author's lucid perceptions and the rippling current upon which he launches his thoughts and memories" (Sept. 21, 1933).

Isaac Joseph Schwartz

Isaac Jacob Schwartz (1885–1971), born in Lithuania, has been hailed as "Kentucky's Yiddish Poet" and his volume of poetry called *Kentucky* (1925) as the "first important work of Yiddish literature in America." Schwartz came to New York in 1906, learned English, and between 1911 and 1918 translated into Yiddish *Hamlet* and *Julius Caesar* and parts of *Paradise Lost,* while at the same time writing Yiddish verse. In 1918 he arrived in Lexington and opened a millinery store. Though he had left behind him in New York the intellectual life he relished and a reputation as a poet and translator, he was soon writing verse that has been described as "a Yiddish poet's love song to America." His *Kentucky* reveals enthusiastic appreciation for the Bluegrass countryside with its undulating land, the green carpet of "blue-green" grass, the white fences, and the peaceful serenity of the countryside. But *Kentucky* was also the record of an immigrant in a new land and of the forging of a new culture from its disparate parts.

In fact, the memorable thing about Schwartz's volume is the way he reminds us that everyone in America—Christians, whites, Jews, and blacks—are immigrants and have shared the trauma of separation and deprivation and suffering. It is this realization that is brought home in the nine poems which make up the volume. Three poems, for example, are about blacks in a fictional town (strongly resembling Lexington), "a little world of good natured people, living in shanties, doing unskilled work for the whites," often pilfering and scrounging, with "sex, emotional religion, and drink" their consolations. (See Joseph R. Jones, *Kentucky Review*, 3, no. 1 [1981].)

The longest poem of the nine is "New Earth," which records the experiences of a Lithuanian immigrant peddler who comes to America after the Civil War by way of New York and settles in the Bluegrass, selling housewares and trinkets from a backpack. In time he starts a hides and scrap-iron business that thrives, sends for his wife, buries his child in a Christian cemetery, helps establish a synagogue, expands his business, finally declines into senility, and ultimately dies in his garden dreaming of his first days in Kentucky. Another long narrative poem is "John," the story of a "moonshiner from the hills, a descendant of pioneers, who is lured into the city by the cinema, dance halls, and the racetrack," all of them parts of what is to him a hostile urban environment. He marries, settles down, has a child, but occasionally disappears for a night on the town. On one of these occasions he is killed. "Joe" (another immigrant peddler) and "The End of Thomas" (another black) are concerned with the dark side of life in Kentucky; both end in violence, the latter with a lynching.

CHAPTER 11

Drama and Theater

Early Theater in Kentucky

As early as 1790—even before Indian raids had ceased—there were dramatic performances in Lexington, and by 1820 Kentucky audiences had witnessed more than six hundred performances, four hundred of them in Lexington. The plays of George Colman, the Younger, were most often produced; those of Shakespeare were a respectable second, followed by the plays of R.B. Sheridan. During this period only fifty-four plays are known to have been produced in Cincinnati and thirty-two in St. Louis. The earliest known performance of a play was an unnamed tragedy and a farce by the students of the Transylvania Seminary on April 10, 1790. During the years ahead Transylvania students and other amateurs in the community gave plays in the courthouse, in the "new exhibition room" adjoining Colman's Tavern, and perhaps in Henry Clay's Traveller's Hall Hotel. Apparently there was a "permanent" theater by 1801, but its location is not known. Between 1802 and 1807 no plays were given, perhaps because of religious opposition to the "sinful nature" of the theater. In October 1808 came an important theatrical event: Luke Usher fitted out the second story of his brand-new brewery at the corner of Spring and High streets as Lexington's first real theater and called it the New Theatre.

From Usher's New Theatre developed the first theatrical circuit in the West. As early as 1807 plays were being produced at Frankfort in taverns, and by 1811 there was a theater there. Thereupon Usher inaugurated a Lexington-Frankfort circuit. In the fall of 1814 Usher sent his son to Albany, New York, to recruit a strolling company to come west and perform in the Kentucky playhouses. This recruiting trip brought a capable, ambitious British actor-manager by the name of Samuel Drake, his family of six talented actors, and Noah Ludlow. In May 1815 this troupe set out for Kentucky, putting on performances in the river towns as they floated down the Allegheny and Ohio rivers on a "kentucky ark" or "broadhorn" until they reached Limestone (Maysville). From there they traveled overland in wagons to Frankfort, where the legislature was in session, and opened their season. In March 1816 they moved to Louisville, where as early as 1808 there had been amateur performances and by 1814 a "season" of plays. By May 20, Drake's players were in Lexington, the principal town on the circuit. In the summer of 1817 Noah Ludlow and others withdrew from Drake's company and founded a company called the "Kentucky Comedians." They played in Elizabethtown, Russellville, Hopkinsville, and other towns and hamlets. Meanwhile Usher's New Theatre in Lexington gave plays in nearby towns such as Harrodsburg, Danville, and Paris, though not on a regular circuit basis. (See West T. Hill, Jr., *The Theatre in Early Kentucky, 1790–1820*, for a full and authoritative account of these years.)

By 1820 Lexington had lost much of its prestige as a theater town due to the coming of the steamboat and the flowering of river towns such as Cincinnati, Louisville, and St. Louis. In that year Drake dropped Lexington from his regular Kentucky circuit. In 1840 Louisville had a flourishing playhouse on almost a year-round basis. Prior to 1843, City Theatre on Jefferson between Third and Fourth streets served as the town's principal theater until it burned in that year. It was replaced in 1846 by the Louisville Theatre at Fourth and Green (Liberty) streets, which for twenty years dominated the theatrical scene.

It was after the Civil War that the heyday of drama in Louisville and Lexington arrived—first in Louisville when Macauley's Theatre opened in 1873 at Fourth and Walnut. Here the opening night on October 4 inaugurated more than half a century of distinguished theatrical productions until the theater closed in 1925. In Lexington the new Opera House on Broadway opened in 1887, replacing the Odd Fellows Hall theater, built in 1856, which had burned in 1886. The Opera House apparently kindled a new interest in drama, for soon many show people regarded Lexington as "the best one-night stand in the country."

Prior to the Macauley, Louisville patrons saw many of the most celebrated actors of the day at the Louisville Theatre, among them William Charles Macready, Joseph Jefferson, John Wilkes Booth, John

Drew, Laura Keene, Charlotte Cushman, and Julia Dean. The list was no less impressive at both the Macauley and the Opera House in Lexington, where performers included Sarah Bernhardt, Joseph Jefferson, Sir Henry Irving, Edwin Booth, Minnie Maddern Fiske, Thomas Keene, Julia Marlowe, Ellen Terry, Frances Kemble, Lily Langtry, Helena Modjeska, Richard Mansfield, and Robert Mantell; and just a little later Walter Hampton, Maude Adams, Otis Skinner, Helen Hayes, the Barrymores, and many others. On the stage audiences saw *Macbeth, Hamlet, Othello, Richard III, Romeo and Juliet, The Rivals, She Stoops to Conquer, School for Scandal, Love à la Mode, Our American Cousin,* and many other plays that through the years had tested the mettle of the great actors of the world.

Lest citing such an impressive list of world famous actors and plays mislead a reader about the theatrical taste of the time and the plays that audiences witnessed and enjoyed, it should be noted that these actors and these plays were only a small portion of the total seen on stage and reveal nothing of the small audiences that attended many of them. Perhaps the experience of the Opera House will tell us something about Lexington but also about the Macauley in Louisville, or, for that matter, about theaters in Cincinnati, Nashville, and elsewhere, for the Klaw and Erlanger syndicate managed bookings throughout the country. An analysis of the offerings of the Opera House for the years 1887–1900 reveals the following: 24 percent were sensational and sentimental melodramas, 15 percent comic and light operas, 15 percent comedies, 9 percent minstrels, 8 percent farces, 4 percent musical comedies, 4 percent Shakespearean tragedies and comedies; the remainder were grand operas, vaudeville numbers, spectacles, bands, magicians, and so on (see Arnold, "A History of the Lexington Theatre from 1887 to 1900."). Putting it another way, one quarter of the offerings were productions such as *The Stowaway, In Old Kentucky,* and *Ten Nights in a Barroom.* Some 40 percent were comedies that were mainly farcical, and it was not unusual that farces played to full audiences while Julia Marlowe played Viola to an almost empty house. Then as now, the largest audience segment simply had a preference for sensational melodrama, broad comedy, and musicals.

In the 1890s one segment of the theatrical audience patronized the plays based on historical fiction and those in the romantic tradition. This preference for Dumas's *The Count of Monte Cristo,* Hugo's *The Hunchback of Notre Dame,* and Rostand's *Cyrano de Bergerac* grew out of the same intellectual climate that explains the growth of the historical novel and the romantic tradition of poetry. Equally interesting is the resistance to and absence of productions of the realistic, naturalistic "problem" plays that we have come to associate with modern drama, paralleling resistance to the realistic and naturalistic fiction and poetry that began to appear just before the turn of the century. It is true that in 1883, at the Macauley Theatre, Helena Modjeska starred in the first production of Ibsen—*A Doll's House*—ever given in America and perhaps the first in English in the world. Its performance provoked little stir, however, though its presentation of the troubling problem of divorce had caused it to close in Paris. *A Doll's House* was not produced again in the United States until it was staged in New York in 1894 and in San Francisco in 1898. *Ghosts* and *Hedda Gabler* had to wait until 1903 and 1904 respectively. Pinero's *The Second Mrs. Tanqueray* fared a bit better, as did Oscar Wilde's *Lady Windermere's Fan*, but Europeans such as Hauptman, Strindberg, Sudermann, and even Brieux and Maeterlinck, like Ibsen, had to wait till the new century was under way. The day of the theater of ideas had simply not come.

Both Macauley's Theatre and the Opera House continued to flourish after the turn of the century, but both would become victims of a new technology, the motion picture, a development that Kentuckian David Wark Griffith had much to do with. The last season at Macauley's ended on August 25, 1925, and the building was demolished soon thereafter. The Brown Theatre on Broadway took its place, but its days were numbered too, for first it became a motion picture theater and finally on October 5, 1972, after a major renovation, gave up its name and the proud name of Macauley's replaced it. The fate of the Lexington Opera House was different in that the building was never torn down, though it survived only because it became a theater in which "B Grade" movies were shown. Better days were ahead, however, for through the efforts of public-spirited citizens the building underwent extensive renovation and was re-dedicated on May 7, 1976, as a proper theater where a full range of dramatic events could be staged.

Playwrights

On a national level, the writing of plays fared poorly during the early days of the republic, nor was the situation much improved between the Civil War and 1900. Drama continued to be the weakest of the literary genres. As the new century got under way, there was no substantial amount of drama that could be called characteristically American, nor was the quality anything to be proud of. At one level, it was still a period of literary colonialism with heavy dependence on British and European drama. At another level, the dominant literary form was historical fiction, and the stage was pretty well monopolized by plays based upon historical novels. During the season of 1900–1901, for example, John Drew was playing in *Richard Carvel*, Julia Marlowe in *When Knighthood Was in Flower*, E.H. Sothern in *If I Were King*, Richard Mansfield in *Monsieur Beaucaire*, and Kentucky's own Mrs. Leslie Carter in *Du Barry*. The list could be expanded to include *Quo Vadis*, *Ben Hur*, *Barbara Frietschie*, *Under Two Flags*, *Alice of Old Vincennes*, and others. The realists and the naturalists were inching their literary way along, but except for them few writers were concerned with contemporary problems or with strictly American subjects.

Bronson Howard was a pioneer in the drama of contemporary manners with *Saratoga* (1870) and social criticism in *Young Mrs. Winthrop* (1882). Clyde Fitch wrote some social problem plays, including *The Climbers* (1901), but his best play was *The Girl with the Green Eyes* (1902), a psychological study of jealousy. Langdon Mitchell's *The New York Idea* (1906) dealt with marriage and divorce; Augustus Thomas's *The Witching Hour* (1907) was a study of hypnotism and psychological domination in hampering individual freedom. These plays looked toward the future, but they would have to wait for full recognition. The "new" drama would not come full center stage until the third decade of the century was well advanced.

Perhaps the force that was most inimical to good drama and good production was the Theatrical Syndicate, founded in 1895. The syndicate was a group of theater owners that controlled most of the theaters across the country. They were anxious to give audiences their money's worth, but since they also had to be concerned with turning a profit, they were more likely to select a play with certain audience appeal than one more innovative and even more meritorious. The syndicate brought order into scheduling, guaranteed appealing programs, and helped theater owners to prosper financially, but it did nothing to encourage new and challenging drama. Actresses such as Sarah Bernhardt and Minnie Maddern Fiske rebelled against the syndicate and, along with others among the country's best actors, performed in makeshift theaters and even in skating rinks and circus tents. Such a rebellion was not enough, but other forces of opposition were forming. One was George Pierce Baker's course in playwriting at Harvard (later to be called 47 Workshop). Another was the formation and development of two outstanding theater groups, the Provincetown Players and the Washington Square Players (later the Theatre Guild). By 1915 their combined force came to be felt, and before 1930 they had won the victory they sought.

In the meantime, Kentucky, like the rest of the country, was only moderately active in drama and dramatic production. The quality was not outstanding compared with what was to come in the 1930s, but it was no doubt reasonably representative of the drama that led up to "Modern Drama."

Charles T. Dazey

Arthur Hobson Quinn, in his monumental two-volume *A History of the American Drama* (1927), introduces chapter 17, "The Height of Melodrama," by citing and analyzing Charles T. Dazey's *In Old Kentucky* as an outstanding example of nineteenth-century "older melodrama." Dazey (1855–1938) was born in Illinois, but his parents were Kentuckians and Dazey visited at length with his grandparents in Bourbon County when he was a boy. He also attended Transylvania College in 1872 until forced to withdraw because of ill health. In 1877 he entered Harvard and graduated in 1881 as class poet, but more importantly he had tried his hand at dramatic composition and after graduation developed into a full-fledged playwright. Most of his plays were acted on the stage, among them *Love Finds a Way* and *The Old Flute-Player*. More successful were *The Stranger*, which ran for two seasons, and *An American King*, with James O'Neill (Eugene O'Neill's father) playing the principal role, which had a long tour on the road. To the extent that Dazey is remembered today, however, it is because of *In Old Kentucky*, which he wrote in 1892 at a time of utter discouragement over his ever being able to earn a living as a playwright.

The main action of the play is the running of the great horse race, the Ashland Oaks, which comes as the culmination of a succession of fights and accusations of murder. Leading up to this event is a story centered around Madge Brierly,a mountain lass, and Frank Layson, a Bluegrass patrician; in supporting roles are a black-hearted villain, a brave moonshiner, stableboys, bookmakers, touts, and others, including Colonel Sandusky Doolittle, a great speculator and horseman, and Aunt Althea, a memorable speculator. A mountain feud is thrown in for good measure. The happy climax of the play comes when the brave little heroine, risking her reputation, dons the hero's colors and rides the horse, Queen Bess, to victory in place of the regular jockey, whom the villain has made hopelessly drunk.

Always the play was staged in lavish fashion, but the most spectacular production of all was that reported in the *Courier-Journal* on September 20, 1933, as having just taken place at Quincy, Illinois. Ordinarily, the *Courier* reported, the victory of speedy Bess had been only a behind-the-scenes simulation of hoofbeats. But for the Quincy production, the seventy six-year-old Dazey came out of retirement to direct a performance in which a half-mile race track was a part of the stage and the heroine rode her horse, "coming from behind in the stretch to win the race, confound the villain who doped the regular jockey, and nestle in her sweetheart's arms at the final curtain."

In Old Kentucky was first performed in St. Paul in 1892, went on tour in 1893, and ran for twenty-six more seasons in the United States, sometimes with several tour companies on the road at the same time, and for twenty years in England. It has been estimated that the play was seen by over seven million people during this period. In addition to a silent screen version around 1920, there was also the well-known version of 1936 in which Will Rogers played the leading role. According to Dazey in 1937, some thirty million people saw *In Old Kentucky* as a play or as a movie. Next to *Uncle Tom's Cabin* it has been the most performed play in American theatrical history.

Ann Crawford Flexner

More representative of the plays of the day than Dazey's spectacular melodrama were those of Anne Crawford Flexner (1874–1955). Flexner was one of four Kentuckians before 1930 to write plays that were successfully produced on the legitimate stage in New York or other theatrical centers. She was born in Georgetown in 1874, graduated from Vassar College in 1895, married Abraham Flexner of Louisville, lived in Louisville until 1905, and spent most of her life thereafter in New York City. Her first drama, *Miranda of the Balcony*, was the play with which Harrison Grey Fiske opened his Manhattan Theatre in 1901, and even more notably the distinguished actress Minnie Maddern Fiske played the title role.

With such a success to her credit Flexner obtained the rights to dramatize Alice Hegan Rice's *Mrs. Wiggs of the Cabbage Patch* in 1904. This dramatization, the plot altered enough to accommodate it to a three-act play structure, preserved the flavor, the dialogue, and the characterizations of Rice's novel and retained its essential sprightliness. It premiered at the Macauley Theatre in Louisville, had a prolonged tour, including an engagement in Chicago, and ran on Broadway for what was then a phenomenal 150 performances, with Madge

Carr Cook in the title role. Subsequently the play was produced in London, on the Continent, and in Asia and Africa. As one commentator put it, "Mrs. Wiggs has held the 'boards' for eight years, and it seems destined to go on forever." The play was revived later and was adapted a number of times for motion pictures.

Anne Crawford Flexner wrote at least seven other plays, but only three of them need be noted here. *The Marriage Game* (1913) portrays a farcical situation in which three married couples on a three-day cruise have their problems because a misunderstanding has led one of the husbands to invite "an other" woman to accompany him. *All Soul's Eve* (1919) is concerned with spiritualism. *Aged 26* (1936) deals with the love affair of John Keats and Fanny Brawne. More than was usual at the time, Flexner portrayed Fanny sympathetically and as being more sensitive and more in love with Keats than had been traditional. Here as elsewhere Flexner displayed her ability to handle dialogue, her skill in characterization, and her capacity for variety and breadth in subject matter.

Thompson Buchanan

Thompson Buchanan (1877–1937) came into writing social comedy and social drama by way of journalism. After coming to Louisville with his family when he was thirteen, graduating from Male High School, and attending the University of the South (Sewanee), he became a reporter for the *Louisville Commercial* in 1897 and for the *Courier-Journal* in 1900, after which he became dramatic critic for the *Louisville Herald*. In 1903 he went to New York City and was on the staff of the *Evening Journal* for four years, during which time he wrote two novels (*The Castle Comedy*, 1904, and *Judith Triumphant*, 1905). He then turned exclusively to playwriting and succeeded in getting *The Intruder* (1908) staged in Boston, only to see it close after one night. Then came his great success, *A Woman's Day* (1909), a play about a young wife who wins her husband's affection by fighting for it against a sophisticated rival. For this play Buchanan secured the backing of New York producer William A. Brady, who agreed to star his wife, Grace George, in it. Buchanan's clever talent as a playwright, Grace George's skill as an actress, and Brady's lavish production fused instantly and theatrical history was made, for *A Woman's Day* set a record for consecutive performances in New York that stood for several years. The play had comparable successes in Chicago, Los Angeles, and elsewhere.

Throughout his life Buchanan continued to write social comedies, some reasonably successful on the stage, but none matched *A Woman's Day*. *The Cub* (1910), a newspaper play, starred Douglas Fairbanks and met with some success; *Civilian Clothes*, dealing with the snobbishness of women toward demobilized soldiers after World War I, was aptly characterized by Alexander Woollcott as "a piece which threatened at first to be a penetrating and rather embarassing comedy on the return of the soldiers, but which soon relapsed into the broad carelessness and cheerfulness of farce" (*New York Times*, Sept. 13, 1919).

After serving in World War I Buchanan became head of the editorial staff of Goldwyn Pictures in New York and then went to Hollywood, where he organized and was the first president of the Screen Writers' Guild. After 1922 Buchanan again began writing plays for the legitimate stage, but never again did he equal his earlier success. He died suddenly of a heart attack in Louisville in 1937 and was buried in the family cemetery off Brownsboro Road near Louisville.

Cleves Kinkead

Cleves Kinkead (1882–1955) won considerable renown for one play that he wrote, but he was never able to achieve such success again. He was born in Louisville, attended Centre College for a time, and received a law degree from the University of Louisville. After this he followed a journalistic career that took him to St. Louis, New York, and finally back to Louisville and the *Evening Post*. He began the practice of law in his father's law firm, became interested in politics, and was elected to the house of representatives of the Kentucky General Assembly in 1908. In 1913 he gave up politics and law and went to New York to try his hand at playwriting, something he had wanted to do since his days as a journalist. During a visit to Boston he heard there was a vacancy in George Pierce Baker's famous 47 Workshop, applied for admission, and was accepted a few weeks later.

In the Baker workshop at Harvard Kinkead wrote *Common Clay*, a play that won him a strong reputation. It was first produced by the Harvard Players and won the Craig Prize in Drama, after which it moved to the Castle Square Theatre in Boston, where it ran an unprecedented twenty-two weeks. The play then moved again to the Republic Theatre in New York, with Jane Cowl in the leading role. After a year's run in New York, four companies took the play on the road. It ultimately played in London and became a favorite of stock companies. It was twice made into a movie, the second time in 1930 with Constance Bennett playing the role of Ellen Neal, the leading character. *Common Clay* is a sociological play about the problems of a young girl who is unprotected by a social background and is forced to accept domestic service.

Poetic Drama: Cale Young Rice and Olive Dargan

The writings of Cale Young Rice and Olive Dargan did not establish a new form but, rather, revived an older one: poetic drama. William Vaughn Moody, in revolt against the realists and the naturalists, was a leader in this mode; his objective was to produce drama that showed the way out of a plagued and confused world by depicting an idealistic belief in the greatness of human destiny. His first verse play was *The Masque of Judgment* (1900), followed by *The Fire Bringer* (1904) and the never-completed *The Death of Eve*, which was to have rounded out the trilogy. Importantly, Moody passed his torch on to his student Josephine Peabody at Radcliffe. *Marlowe* (1901) and especially *The Piper* (1910) are examples of her very successful verse dramas. Percy Mackaye was another writer of poetic dramas, *The Canterbury Pilgrims* (1903) and *Joan of Arc* (1906) among them. Cale Young Rice and Olive Dargan sought to follow the lead of writers such as these.

In their day the poetic dramas of Cale Young Rice (1872–1942) received some national attention and mixed reviews. His own statement in his autobiography, *Bridging the Years* (1939), seems a fairly accurate assessment of his intended role in the romantic drama movement. Late nineteenth-century romanticism, he says, had become sterile by the time his writing career began. As a result it became his aim in poetry to contribute "new reality" to it through "a more natural, less literary speech and a truer account of experience." When his *Charles di Tocca* (1903), *David* (1904), *A Night in Avignon* (1907), and *Yolanda of Cypress* (1906) were published, he says, and were "widely praised as modern stage productions, popular success and a livelihood from poetry seemed near—and sweet." This promise of success was not to materialize, though *A Night in Avignon* was produced, *Yolanda of Cypress* had some success as an opera, and Charles Loomis wrote grand opera scores for *David* and *A Night in Avignon*. Poetic drama, Rice declared, was eclipsed by "commercial" theater, though a longer perspective suggests that the causes for its lack of success lay deeper.

When Olive Tilford Dargan (1869–1968) turned novelist in the early 1930s under the pseudonym of Fielding Burke, she was superior to Cale Young Rice as a writer. Her earlier poetic dramas, however, despite certain merits, were not successful either on the stage or with the critics. *The Mortal Gods* (1912), a not very effective study of the oppression of the working class in an industrialized society, is interesting in light of the left-wing novels Dargan was to write twenty years later. Her *Flutter of the Gold Leaf* (1922) also embodies sociological and scientific thought as she explores conflicting emotional and intellectual loyalties and the nature of public and personal roles. As this and her later work shows, Dargan had an interest in the literature of ideas. The poetry she was soon to write earned her a better reputation than did her poetic dramas, but in her proletarian fiction after she left Kentucky for North Carolina she succeeded best of all.

Theater Arts

A literary history of Kentucky does not call for a detailed survey of the contributions of Kentuckians to the theater arts, but noteworthy as they have been they deserve at least brief mention. For example, three actresses won places of eminence for themselves on the legitimate stage. First was Mary Anderson (1859–1940), of Louisville, who after her debut at the Macauley Theatre in 1875 toured the Midwest and South and made her New York debut at the Fifth Avenue Theater in November 1877. Here she was acclaimed by the critics and therewith established as a star. Her success later in England matched her success in America. Mrs. Leslie Carter (1853–1937), born in Lexington, rose to stardom under the aegis of David Belasco, playwright and celebrated producer at the Belasco Theatre in New York City. For sixteen years she was Belasco's favorite and played starring roles until she and Belasco severed relations. Elizabeth Robins (1862–1952), was born in Louisville. After winning a place on the American stage, she won even greater fame in England, where she introduced Ibsen to the London stage and in succeeding years triumphed in a long list of Ibsen plays.

Three other Kentuckians made significant contributions to the world of the theater. One was William Thompson Price (1846–1920), a native of Louisville, whose contribution to American drama was declared by the celebrated actress Minnie Maddern Fiske to "exceed in value those of any man thus far identified with the stage." His teaching in the American School of Playwriting (which he founded), his criticism as dramatic critic for the New York *Star*, his contributions to the magazine *The American Playwright*, and his books (*The Technique of the Drama*, 1892; *Analysis of Play Construction and Dramatic Principle*, 1905; *The Philosophy of Dramatic Principle and Method*, his unpublished textbook) caused him, says the prestigious *Dictionary of American Biography*, "within the dramatic Profession [to be] looked upon as the highest authority." On the fringes of the legitimate theater was David Wark Griffith (1875–1948), born in Oldham County, who for ten years in Boston and elsewhere engaged in acting and writing plays for the stage. In New York just after the turn of the century he began the career of film-making that led to his developing techniques that succeeded in "revolutionizing Motion Picture drama and founding the modern technique of the Art." Griffith's innovations and his *Birth of a Nation* and *Intolerance* are doubtless among the most important and most influential contributions ever made in the history of motion pictures. Finally, Stuart Walker (1888–1941), born in Bracken County, is remembered for the Portmanteau plays he wrote and the Portmanteau Theatre he originated and directed in a repertory of fourteen plays, first on Broadway and then on tour. A Portmanteau Theater includes a small stage that can be boxed, loaded on a truck, and shipped anywhere. Containing its own lighting system and simple scenery, it can be set up in a garden, a ballroom, or an auditorium. Walker had remarkable success in converting the simple stage into the world he wanted his audience to believe in. One of Walker's influences was the encouragement he gave throughout the country to the little theater movement.

CHAPTER 12

Children's Literature

The remarkable increase in the number of Kentucky authors and the popularity of fiction by Kentucky authors around the turn of the century has already been commented on. Best-remembered among those responsible were James Lane Allen, John Fox, Jr., Annie Fellows Johnston, and Alice Hegan Rice. Four authors more unlike in subject matter are hard to imagine, but the books they wrote captured the imagination of the country and enabled Kentucky writers for more than a decade to dominate the annual best-seller lists as no other state has ever done. Works by Allen, Fox, and Rice were among the top ten annual best sellers twelve times, and though Annie Fellows Johnston never won this distinction, it has been estimated that two million copies of her novels were sold by the middle of the century.

Of these four writers, Johnston and Rice are known for their children's books; Allen also wrote a book for boys near the end of his career, and one of Fox's novels often appears on reading lists for boys. But there were also other authors of children's books. Joseph Alexander Altsheler was an extremely popular author of boys' books and influenced children's literature during his lifetime and beyond. Others, such as Mary Finley Leonard, Henry S. Spalding, and Frances Barton Fox, never achieved the reputation of the authors just cited, but they were not without merit. The period closes with Elizabeth Madox Roberts, an author who wrote little for juveniles, but the quality of the volume she did write gives it a place as a classic in children's literature. (For further information about children's literature before 1930, see the sections on Alice Hegan Rice, Frances Barton Fox, and James Lane Allen.)

Annie Fellows Johnston

The first Kentuckian to gain fame as an author of children's stories was Annie Fellows Johnston (1863–1931). Born in Evansville, Indiana, the daughter of a Methodist minister, she became an avid reader of the *Youth's Companion, Godey's Lady's Book, St. Nicholas,* and the books she found in her father's library. In 1888 she married William L. Johnston, a widower with three children, and during the four years her husband lived published stories in the *Youth's Companion.* After his death she began writing in greater earnest in the hope of being able to support herself and her three step-children, who were living with their aunt in Peewee Valley, Oldham County, near Louisville. By 1895 when she went to Peewee Valley to visit the children she had published two novels: *Big Brother* (1894) and *Joel, a Boy of Galilee* (1895).

It was this visit to Peewee Valley that changed the life of Annie Fellows Johnston and started her on a writing career that was to produce a remarkable series of children's books. It was, first of all, the community that seized her interest and imagination. She felt, she said, as if she had stepped back into an antebellum time "where people had leisure to make hospitality their chief business in life, and could afford for every day to be a holiday." But perhaps best of all she came to know a spirited little girl named Hattie Cochran, who was visiting her grandfather, Confederate Colonel George Weissinger, at his home called "The Locusts." The two were inseparable, and Hattie, a child of considerable charm, amused people by imitating her grandfather's fiery temper and sometimes imperious manner. From this companionship came the notion of the "Little" Colonel, Lloyd Sherman, and from Peewee Valley came Lloydsboro Valley.

When Johnston returned to Evansville from her visit, she was so full of the new world she had found, both real and imagined, that she immediately wrote *The Little Colonel* (1896), first of the twelve volumes that make up the *Little Colonel* series. Three years later in 1898 she moved to Peewee Valley, where she and her stepchildren moved into a house she named "The Beeches." The following year her stepdaughter Rena died and her stepson's health failed. In 1901 she interrupted her life in Peewee Valley and spent the next nine years in Arizona, California, and Texas trying to find a climate that would be beneficial to the boy's health. In 1910, however, he died, and in 1911 she returned to Peewee Valley and "The Beeches" with her remaining stepdaughter, Mary, who illustrated some of her mother's books, and lived there the remainder of her life. She was back home again, for Peewee Valley and Kentucky were her chief inspiration.

From first to last the novels tell the story of Lloyd Sherman, five years old, who is taken to Lloydsboro, Kentucky, by her mother, where her widowed grandfather lives. The old Colonel has been saddened by the death of his son in the Civil War and by the marriage of his daughter, whom he has disowned because she has married a "Yankee." But the little granddaughter wins her grandfather back to joy in life, and thus their lives are bonded together. In the years that follow, the Little Colonel goes to school, entertains her friends in the Colonel's mansion, flirts with the boys, takes vacations, and does other things that a growing girl does, until finally the day comes when her "knight comes riding." With the Little Colonel married, Johnston brings the story to an end, leaving her young lovers in a sort of never-never land where forever they will be young and time and age will take no toll.

For two generations the *Little Colonel* books served as both practical and inspirational guides for girls. Says one critic, writing some time ago, "On the subject of today's bobby-soxer we profess abysmal ignorance. We only know that our generation pulled through 'that trying period' with no conduct manual at its side. . . . We are convinced that the Little Colonel taught us more about 'Junior Prom glamor' and how 'to handle the last half hour of a date' than a shelf full of 'how-to' books." This must have been Annie Fellows Johnston's opinion too, for she wrote, "I contend that a girl's book of fiction should help her meet her problems. . . . For over twenty years I have been receiving letters from the girls of America." As a matter of fact, Johnston became a sort of Dorothea Dix to girls, sometimes receiving as many as fifty letters in one mail, many asking for help and advice. In her answers to letters and in her books Johnston insisted upon integrity of character and the simple virtues to see her readers through their problems. There is no doubt that though Johnston lacked a superior imagination and psychological acuteness she was able through precept and the example of her characters to exert a tremendous influence upon her time. This fact is attested to not only by the letters she received and answered but by the fact that she motivated the formation of "The Order of Hildegarde" clubs and the wearing of "Tusitala rings" all over America. Even the departments of education of Kentucky and Indiana put the *Little Colonel* books on their approved lists of readings. For more than half a century they flourished in remarkable fashion. By 1910 eighteen printings had been necessary to meet the demand; by the time of Johnston's death in 1931 more than a million copies had been sold; 1948 saw a twenty-eighth printing, and by the 1950s it is estimated that almost two million copies had been published. In 1934 *The Little Colonel* novels were made into a movie with Shirley Temple in the starring role and Lionel Barrymore as her grandfather, ably supported by a cast that included Bill "Bojangles" Robinson.

Despite the hundreds of thousands of avid readers they had won, *The Little Colonel* novels held within themselves the seeds of their own undoing. A more sophisticated age was to find them dated, their particular brand of sentimentality and their naive simplicity no longer appealing. The world moved on to the Bobbsey Twins and Nancy Drew and still later to other heroes and heroines with still different perceptions. There were twelve of the *Little Colonel* novels: *The Little Colonel* (1896), *The Gate of the Giant Scissors* (1898), *Two Little Knights of Kentucky* (1898), *The Little Colonel's House Party* (1900), *The Little Colonel's Holidays* (1901), *The Little Colonel's Hero* (1902), *The Little Colonel at Boarding School* (1903), *The Little Colonel in Arizona* (1904), *The Little Colonel's Christmas Vacation* (1905), *The Little Colonel: Maid of Honor* (1906), *The Little Colonel's Knight Comes Riding* (1907), and *Mary Ware's Promised Land* (1912).

Among Johnston's more than thirty novels there were other children's stories, many of them originating in particular events. Among the better ones are *Mary Ware* (1908) and *Mary Ware in Texas* (1910), both growing out of her residence in the Southwest, as did also *The Desert in Waiting* (1905), an allegory of the Camelback Mountain in Arizona that was translated into Spanish (for use in the schools of Mexico) and also into Japanese. *Georgina of the Rainbows* (1916) and *Georgina's Service Stripes* (1918) grew out of summers spent on Cape Cod. There were other children's stories as well as a volume of poetry and some books for adults; but not one of them was equal to those already named. *The Land of the Little Colonel* Johnson began in 1920 and finished in 1929, a book of reminiscences and photographs related to the persons and places that inspired the *Little Colonel* stories. Johnston died at "The Beeches" in 1931 and was buried in her native Evansville; her stepdaughter, Mary Lee, lived on in the house for many years, maintaining it much as it had been during her mother's lifetime.

The *Little Colonel* stories owed their popularity to a number of circumstances, not the least of which, of course, was Johnston's ability to do so well the thing she set out to do. Her talent fit well the upsurge of interest in the historical novel during the 1890s and even better the requirements of the local color movement, which was still very much alive. It also fit the nostalgia for antebellum days and the Genteel Tradition that James Lane Allen had fostered, a nostalgia not only southern but also in considerable measure northern.

Mary Finley Leonard

Mary Finley Leonard (1862–?) was the author of at least thirteen children's stories, of which the best known was *Everyday Susan* (1912). Her first published volume was *The Story of the Big Front Door* (1898), a story with a great deal of moralizing. It was not till she had published nine more volumes—including *Everyday Susan*—that Leonard began to receive some national attention. The attention began with *The Christmas Tree House* (1913), a sequel to *Susan*, using the same group of young people and adding spice to the story with the addition of a villain. *The Little Red Chimney* (1914), with its surprise ending, came the following year, and *The Ways of Jane* (1917), which introduced a problem of class distinction into the story, came three years later.

Henry S. Spalding

Henry S. Spalding (1865–1934), of Bardstown, was the author of a dozen or so boys' books, four of which have a Kentucky setting in or near Spalding's home town. None of these nor Spalding's other books received wide attention, but they were not without their readers. *The Cave by the Beech Fork* (1901), set in Bardstown, portrays the trials of pioneer missionaries in Kentucky; *The Sheriff of the Beech Fork* (1903) and *The Old Mill on the Withrose* (1910) both are set in Nelson County; and *Sugar Camp and After* (1912) deals with the adventures of a Chicago boy in Kentucky. Typical of Spalding's other books is *Race for Copper Island* (1905), a story of a Quebec lad who ventured into Indian country in search of the copper mines in the region of the Great Lakes.

Mrs. George Madden Martin

Mrs. George Madden Martin (1866–1946), like Alice Hegan Rice and Annie Felllows Johnston, was a member of the Authors Club of

Louisville and shared their interest in writing stories and novels that served a useful purpose. During the last third of her life, Mrs. Martin played an active role in public affairs and was involved in reform activities, but it is principally for her Emmy Lou stories that she is remembered today. These stories appeared serially in *McClure's Magazine* during 1900–1901 and were subsequently published in book form as *Emmy Lou, Her Book and Heart*.

The stories had been widely read in serial form, of course, but as a volume they were an even greater success and went into frequent reprintings and ultimately sold well above two hundred thousand copies. The reason for this popularity was in part Martin's skill as an author, but it was due also to the fresh and different subject matter. She dealt with the problems of a charming, born-to-be-loved little girl who is slow to learn in school but is always faithful and always tries. By implication Martin is saying that current methods of teaching are not designed for such children, with the result that their road is difficult and life frustrating. Since counterparts to Emmy Lou were to be found in all schools and many homes, the book appealed to a wide audience and remained a steady seller for forty years or more, was never out of print, and is credited with motivating change in teaching methods.

It was natural that Martin should follow up the success of *Emmy Lou* with other books dealing with children. *Abbie Ann* and *Laetitia: Nursery Corps, U.S.A.* were both published in 1907. They deal with attractive little girls who have problems in making headway in the world, one because of being brought up with only a father's care, the other by being reared in an army camp by unhelpful parents. *Selina* (1914) portrays a girl being brought up in a southern city (presumably Louisville), where she is supposed to follow in the traditional footsteps of her elders but instead questions the infallibility of the standards set before her. Without quite realizing it, Selina stands on the threshold of a world of revolt that will blaze a trail for a new order of things. In *Emmy Lou's Road to Grace* (1916) Martin returns to her first child character and this time portrays the home as a place where she must face—without adequate help—problems that she does not understand. Each of these four volumes won a large reading audience, but no one of them quite equaled the original *Emmy Lou* in either quality or the number of readers it attracted. *Abbie Ann* is the only children's story Martin wrote from a child's point of view. In the others the perspective is that of an adult. *A Warwickshire Lad* (1916)—a story of Shakespeare's boyhood—concludes Martin's writings about children and childhood. After this she became involved in public affairs and social problems both in her activities and in her writing.

Selina: Her Hopeful Efforts and Her Livelier Failures (1914) can be cited as the novel in which Martin was turning to the problems of adult society, for here there is some exploration of the emerging role of the "new woman"; and *Emmy Lou's Road to Grace* (1916) deals with the home and its responsibility in preparing girls for adult life. *Children in the Mist* (1920) is Martin's first volume to deal with public affairs. It is a series of sketches dealing with the southern black, her aim being to portray blacks realistically. It is implicit in what she says that the white majority has been too little concerned with providing justice and opportunity for blacks. *March On* (1921), the last of her better novels on matters of social concern, is set in an old Kentucky town with fine old homesteads. It focuses on several social issues, including the role of blacks, but principally its concern is with the "new woman," with the lively octogenarian Lucy Wing, a militant feminist, in the limelight as she brings up her namesake great-granddaughter to follow in her footsteps—and succeeds. The novel is broad enough in scope to encompass many matters that involve the "new woman." *Made in America* (1935), Martin's last novel, is the story of Sheridan McNeill, a poor Irish boy who rises to a position of power and wealth. The story reflects the growth and development of America as the events in McNeill's life are chronicled.

Except for *Made in America* Martin's writing career almost came to a halt with *March On*. She did publish a series of articles in the *Atlantic Monthly* (1924–25) that set forth her views on women in politics, but in general she spent her energies on matters of public concern. She was a board member of the Committee on Interracial Cooperation, which she helped to found, 1920–34; and in the 1930s she was chairwoman of the Association of Southern Women for the Prevention of Lynching. As might be presumed, her views on racial questions, including her advocating the teaching of Negro history in Kentucky schools, seemed quite advanced in her day. Martin's works on social reform were usually reviewed favorably when they were published, and she was not without influence on her times. Martin and her good friend Alice Hegan Rice were friends of Ida M. Tarbell and Lincoln Steffens, the celebrated muckrakers, and Tarbell was sometimes a guest in their homes in Louisville. Martin and, to a greater extent, Rice were far more moderate in their views than was this sturdy reformer and leader of the muckraker school.

Joseph Alexander Altsheler

Joseph Alexander Altsheler (1862–1919) had a remarkable career that gave him prominence at the national level. He was one of the most prolific historical novelists the country has produced. More importantly, in 1918 the public libraries of the United States voted him the most popular writer of boys' stories in the country. From the late 1890s to the 1920s Altsheler had a large following that remained loyal to him well after his death in 1919. As recently as 1976 Altsheler was honored again. During the national bicentennial, the Lighthouse Press reissued four of his juvenile novels as a tribute to his genuine interest in American history, the pains he took to be factually accurate, his natural gift for writing, and, at his best, his talent for telling a good story.

Altsheler was born in Three Springs, Kentucky, and attended first Liberty College in Glasgow and then Vanderbilt University. Compelled to drop out of school because of his father's death, he took a job in Louisville with the *Evening Post* and after a year joined the *Courier-Journal* staff in 1885. In 1892 he went to New York as a feature-writer for the *World*, and before the turn of the century he became the editor of its triweekly magazine edition. In this role somewhat by chance he began to write the sort of stories that were to change the course of juvenile fiction. Like other newspapers of the day, the *World* published fiction, and when a need developed for more fiction than was being submitted, Altsheler began writing stories to fill the space. From short stories he turned to novels, and with his novels of excitement and adventure he eclipsed none other than Horatio Alger and his formula of poverty and hard work leading a boy to fame and prosperity. Henceforth the trend was toward adventure and mystery. It was inevitable, however, that one day Altsheler's appeal should fade—his Henry Ware and Paul Cotter were succeeded by the Hardy boys and Nancy Drew—but not before Altsheler was voted the most popular writer of boys' fiction in America in 1918.

Altsheler wrote forty or so novels; brief notes on his several series give some idea of his scope and variety. The Young Trailer series of eight novels (1907–17) is perhaps the best and the best known. Three of the four novels reissued by the Lighthouse Press were selected from this series: *The Young Trailers* (1907), *The Forest Runners* (1909), and *The Border Watch* (1912). The series deals with the fortunes of two boys, Henry Ware and Paul Cotter, and their friends, who with their families had come to Kentucky about the time of the Revolutionary War. The novels depict frontier life, the taming of the wilderness, conflict with the Indians, encounter with wild animals, and the rigors and dangers the settlers faced. The series collectively gives a good picture of pioneer life, but each volume also stands alone.

The fourth of the Lighthouse Press reprints is *The Scouts of Stonewall* (1915), the third in a series of seven volumes dealing with the Civil War. The scope of the series is suggested by the fact the titles of five of the six remaining volumes contain these names: Bull Run, Shiloh, Antietam, Gettysburg, and Appomatox. *The Guns of Bull Run* (1914) portrays how the passions of the South and the North were fomented long before Fort Sumter was fired upon. The story opens in Kentucky by following young Harry Kenton into action and ends with the Battle of Bull Run. *Shades of the Wilderness: a Story of Lee's Great Stand* (1916) closes the series, with Harry Kenton on a dangerous spy mission to Richmond and Lee retreating from Gettysburg. The final chapters are given over to the battle of the Wilderness. Each story is told from a southern perspective.

The other series include the West, with such titles as *Last of the Chiefs* (1909), *Horsemen of the Plains* (1911), *Apache Gold* (1914), *The Great Sioux Trail* (1918), *Lost Hunters* (1918); the French and Indian Wars, with *Rulers of the Lakes* (1917), *Masters of the Peaks* (1918), and *Sun of Quebec* (1919) among the titles; a trilogy on Texas in 1912-13 dealing with its struggle for independence from Mexico; and a series on World War I in 1915 before America's entry into the war.

Altsheler also tried his hand at nonhistorical and adult fiction, of which *The Candidate* (1905), a political novel, and *Guthrie of the Times* (1905), a novel of contemporary journalism and politics, are the best examples. Neither, however, succeeded as did his series of historical novels for boys. Altsheler died in New York in 1919 at the age of fifty-seven, having been in ill health for five years as a result of hardships sustained in 1914 when he and his wife were caught in Germany at the outbreak of World War I.

Maria Thompson Daviess

Maria Thompson Daviess (1872–1924), born into a prominent and talented Harrodsburg family, wrote fiction for both juveniles and adults, but she was best known for the former. She had what one critic called "the best-seller touch," which in Miss Daviess's day and for her reading audience meant that she had a deft style, a quick and lively mind, and a sunny disposition that dispelled gloom and brought good cheer. And, as one might expect, her plots were thin and sentimental.

Miss Selina Lue and the Soap-box Babies (1909) brought the author to the attention of readers, adult as well as juvenile. Miss Selina is a sort of Mrs. Wiggs who runs a grocery store and has a free day nursery where she tucks babies into a row of soap-boxes. *The Treasure Babies* (1911), almost as successful as *Miss Selina Lue*, according to the *New York Times*, is "such a dear little story" of the children of Cloverbend, who sit at the Captain's feet under a big apple tree and listen over and over again to the story of how the battery plunged across the creek and up the hill and how the man carrying the flag fell and the Captain seized the staff from his hand and held it high.

It was *The Melting of Molly* (1912), however, that attracted more attention than any other of the fifteen books Daviess wrote. For eight months it was the best-selling book in America and later was produced as a play and a motion picture. Molly is a young widow, twenty-five pounds too heavy, who must get rid of the weight in two months, for an old sweetheart returning from a distant country has asked her to wear again the blue muslin dress she wore at their parting years ago. Molly's regimen—her diets, her exercises and her tribulations—is recounted and leads up to an O. Henry ending when her old sweetheart turns out to be almost a giant and excessively fat. "Dr. John," however, helps Molly solve her problems.

Other successful novels for juveniles by Daviess include *Phyllis* (1914), *Golden Bird* (1918), and *Broadway and Blue-grass* (1919), each, like its predecessors, well received by reviewers and readers alike. Despite her contemporary fame, Daviess's name and her writings are unknown today except to the literary historian.

Daviess's books for adults won less attention than her juvenile stories. Among them are *The Tinderbox* (1913) and *Over Paradise Ridge* (1915), the first seeking to advance the cause of woman suffrage and the second to slow the exodus of people from rural areas to the cities. *Matrix* (1920), though not a critical success, tells the story of Thomas Lincoln and Nancy Hanks and tries to show the indebtedness the nation owes the mother of Abraham Lincoln.

Venita Seibert

Another member of the Louisville Authors Club, Venita Seibert (1878–?), a native of Louisville, wrote a serial story called "The Different World" for the *American Magazine* in 1907–1908. In 1910 Seibert brought these stories together as "the chronicles of Velleda, who understood about 'the different world' " and entitled the volume *The Gossamer Thread*. Velleda is a little German-American girl, a dreamy, sensitive child who in her doings and imaginings reveals the world that makes up her life, including her German home.

The volume—the only one Seibert has left us—did not achieve the fame books by some of her fellow Authors Club members did, but it did receive favorable national attention. *Catholic World* (Sept. 1910) spoke of the volume as an "exceptional piece of child portraiture" and the *New York Times* (July 23, 1910) judged that Velleda "is one of those rare children for whom 'the different world' . . . is a somewhat topsy-turvy region all bedight with illusion and alluring with wonderful imaginings, is quite as real as the actual world in which she lives." The world of childhood with its "incongruous mixture of dreams and faiths and visions and realities," the reviewer says in appraisal, "is realized with understanding and much skill by Venita Seibert." Seibert subsequently resigned from the Authors Club when she married and moved West.

Emma Speed Sampson

A prolific and popular writer of children's stories, Emma Speed Sampson (1868–1947), was a member of the Speed family of Louisville and a great-granddaughter of George Keats, brother of the English poet John Keats and a successful business man who had immigrated to Louisville. She studied at the Art Students' League in New York City, 1888–92, and later in Paris. In 1896 she married Henry Aylett Sampson and subsequently moved to Virginia, where for a time she was a feature writer for the *Richmond Times-Dispatch*.

Sampson's juvenile fiction earned her a reputation that peaked during the early 1920s, though she had been writing as early as 1915 and continued to write until the early 1940s. During her early years under the pseudonym of Nell Steed she wrote the "Tucker Twins" series and the "Carter Girls" series, and, as Edith Van Dyne, two detective stories for girls. She also wrote the "Miss Minerva" books, beginning in 1920, nine years after the death of the original author, Frances Boyd Calhoun (1867–1909). There were at least six volumes in this series. It was, however, *Molly Brown of Kentucky* that more significantly brought Sampson to the attention of the public and led to two sequels: *Molly Brown's Freshman Days* and *Molly Brown's Sophomore Days*.

Sampson's *The Comings of Cousin Ann* (1923) and *Masquerading Mary* (1924) received substantial national attention. The following extract from the *Saturday Review of Literature* review of the latter represents both the nature of Sampson's work and the critical judgment of it: "It is good comedy material neatly handled. The chief values, however, as in her preceding books, lie in the presentation of negro character, especially in the case of the women. They are done very well indeed; without any caricaturing and with a friendly understanding of their humors and their amiabilities but without any undue sentimentalizing over them. It is a pleasantly amusing tale" (October 25, 1924).

CHAPTER 13

Other Writers

The four other authors discussed here simply do not fit neatly under any other subject heading in this literary history. Nor do they resemble each other. Virginia Cary Hudson was a schoolgirl when she wrote the gay, witty, sparkling little volume that made her famous years later; George Horace Lorimer achieved the unlikely when he wrote a "business" novel that became No. 8 on the nation's best-seller list for 1903; and Frances Caldwell Macaulay achieved even more fame when the letters she wrote home from the mission school where she taught in Japan were converted into a story that became the No. 1 best seller in 1907. Foxhall Daingerfield is here because he turned aside from the not-too-successful mystery stories he liked to write and ended his career with an unpretentious but effective novel about the tragic struggles of the mother of a poor white family in the Bluegrass.

Virginia Cary Hudson

Since almost sixty years passed between the writing and the posthumous publication of Virginia Cary Hudson's best-known volume, one must be arbitrary about what period to assign it to. The spiritedness and wit of the contents make the volume sound more "modern" than 1904, when it was written, but the fact remains that it emerged out of a turn-of-the-century context. Literary fame came to Virginia Cary Hudson (1894–1954) after she had been dead for eight years, for it was only then that her family published the essays she had written when she was a schoolgirl of ten. The setting is Versailles, where Hudson spent most of her childhood and attended the Episcopal school for girls, Margaret Hall. Here she is said to have written the collection of essays that was to become a best seller under the title of *O Ye Jigs and Juleps* (1962). During the interval between 1904 and her death fifty years later, Hudson had married Kirtley S. Cleveland of Louisville, reared a son and two daughters, and lived an active life, often as a sort of gadfly who made sharp and perceptive observations on the world, religion, and human behavior. She privately committed her observations to paper and stored them away in a trunk in the attic of her home at 1453 St. James Court. These papers were "discovered" before Mrs. Cleveland's death when she and her daughter, Mrs. Lewis Mayne, were "going through some things." "I begged my mother to have them published," her daughter says, and "She was always going to call somebody who was going to call somebody who was going to call somebody. But she never did."

Finally, though, the girlhood essays—written and graded as English assignments—were published as *O Ye Jigs and Juleps* (1962) and won immediate fame for the author. The book, which was on the best-seller list for almost thirty weeks, sold 400,000 copies, and many, many more have been sold since that time. No one would claim greatness for the little volume, but many would characterize the author's remarks on school, church etiquette, the sacraments, everlasting life, libraries, personal appearance, gardening, and other subjects as "delightful," "funny," or "charming." But the "charm" is of a particular sort. Says the *New York Times*, "Virginia was a combination of brat and acute observer of the human scene . . . as though Machiavelli had rewritten Emily Post—to the greater good and glory of all concerned." Perhaps the words of another reviewer (*Library*) sum up well: "Recommended" for all libraries that believe in "pleasure reading." Some of the choice bits and observations follow:

> Education is what you learn in books, and nobody knows you know but your teacher.
>
> Do not hop, skip, jump, or slide in the church vestibule. Tip. Tip all the way to your seat. Be sure and don't sit in other people's pews. Jesus wouldn't care, but other people would.
>
> Sacraments are what you do in church. What you do at home is something else.
>
> Gardening is growing things. First you find somebody to dig up the ground, and when he tells you what he charges, you say "Too much" and get another somebody. After he digs and rakes, you start planting. . . . Then you pray for rain to come and if too much comes, you pray for it to stop. It keeps you busy all summer praying and hoeing.

> In the library there are three kinds of books. Books people like to read. Books people do not like to read, and books people never will read. . . . [Our] library is a memorial. A memorial is something that somebody gives or builds after you are dead and can't hear it or get it or see it.

Two volumes of Virginia Cary Hudson's later writings were published. *Credos and Quips* (1964) came first. It is made up of four essays on the church and human nature that were first given before the Guild at Calvary Episcopal Church in Louisville. *Flapdoodle, Trust, and Obey* (1966) is a series of letters to her children on subjects ranging from "Old Beaus" to life in a boarding house. Both volumes contain humor and hardheaded sense, both reveal the foibles of human nature and are even capable of giving a fillip to one's thinking; but the sparkle, the gay spontaneity, and the incisiveness that set the first volume apart as rather special just aren't there.

George Horace Lorimer

George Horace Lorimer (1867–1937), born in Louisville, is included here partly because of the novels he wrote but also because of his work as a literary editor and his influence on literary taste. As editor for thirty-nine years of the *Saturday Evening Post*, Lorimer exercised a profound influence on writers, on the artistic form and moral tone of what he accepted, and on his readership. Before Lorimer joined the *Saturday Evening Post* he had been in business for ten years, but his career with the *Post* began in 1898 when he was a reporter for the *Boston Herald* and applied for a job with the *Post*, then a small magazine in Philadelphia with a circulation of eighteen hundred. Lorimer was hired as literary editor, became editor-in-chief the following spring, and before he stepped down from this position in 1937 had made the *Post* one of the most successful and significant magazines in the history of American letters.

The *Post* reflected some of Lorimer's fascination with business, not only in its contents and some of Lorimer's editorials but in the "business fiction" which he himself pioneered. First in serial form (1901–1902) and then in book form (1902), he published his *Letters from a Self-made Merchant to His Son*. In 1903 this novel of unpromising title and content was No. 8 on the nation's list of best sellers and for forty years appeared in various editions in several countries of the world. Following this came *Old Gorgon Graham* (1904), which was a sequel to the "Merchant" letters and was widely read. Of a different sort, but still containing the worldly-wise philosophy of Lorimer's first volumes, are *False Gods* (1906), a stirring adventure novel full of Egyptian mysteries, black cats, and statues with human power, and *Jack Spurlock, Prodigal* (1907), a funny story of a young man in the last act of sowing his wild oats. Neither novel was up to the level of Lorimer's "business fiction," but today no one of his books is of more than historical interest.

Within a decade of Lorimer's taking charge of the *Post*, his aggressive policies began attracting big-name authors, for he paid well and he had adopted the practically unknown policy of accepting or rejecting manuscripts within seventy-two hours and paying for them as soon as they were accepted. Important, too, was the fact that by 1908 circulation was up to one million (three million by the time he retired in 1937). Willa Cather and Mary Roberts Rinehart were among the early ones to publish with the *Post*, but others followed: Joseph Conrad, Stephen Crane, Sinclair Lewis, Ring Lardner, Theodore Dreiser, John Galsworthy, O. Henry, F. Scott Fitzgerald, and Ellen Glasgow, to name only a few. Among those to whom Lorimer made a more personal contribution through his editing were Joseph Hergesheimer, Rupert Hughes, Peter B. Kyne, Booth Tarkington, Clarence Buddington Kelland, and Kenneth Roberts. Among the well-known works to make their original appearance in the *Post* were Jack London's *The Call of the Wild*, Frank Norris's *The Pit*, Stephen Vincent Benét's *The Devil and Daniel Webster*, and J.P. Marquand's *The Late George Apley*. Seldom in the history of publishing has one man had such phenomenal success, for from first to last the *Post* was Lorimer's creation. His incisive, sensitive mind and his firm hand were behind every department.

Fannie Caldwell Macaulay

The Lady of the Decoration (1906), by Frances Little (pseudonym for Fannie Caldwell Macaulay), achieved an honor that no other book by a Kentuckian ever achieved: it was No. 1 on the annual best-seller fiction list (1907). Macaulay was born in Shelbyville in 1863, was a kindergarten teacher in Louisville, 1899–1902, and in the latter year went to Hiroshima, Japan, where for five years she taught in a mission school kindergarten and wore off the memory of an unhappy marriage to James Macaulay. While in Japan she wrote many letters to her friends, including her niece Alice Hegan Rice. Rice was so impressed with the quality of the writing and the content of the letters that, according to her autobiography, *The Inky Way*, she "cut out the more personal parts, provided the thread of a love story," and (apparently) sent the manuscript off to the publisher. The "thread of a love story" that Rice contributed was the love "the lady of the decoration" held for the man she had supposed to be lost to her. This appellation came from the fact that each time Fannie Macaulay pinned on her little enameled watch her Japanese children called her their "Lady of the Decoration." The letters were, of course, made up principally of what Macaulay observed about Japanese life and customs, her school and her pupils, and what she saw and felt and learned.

In 1907 Mrs. Macaulay wrote *The Lady and Sada San* as a sequel to *The Lady of the Decoration*. Here she takes "the Lady" back to Japan from Kentucky to be as close as possible to her husband, who has been sent on a medical mission to China. Excitement and suspense are added to the story as the Lady's husband becomes chaperone to Sada San, a charming American-Japanese girl whom he saves from a cruel fate. *Little Sister Snow* (1909) is a story about a Japanese girl who in early childhood is about to drown a naughty cat but is interrupted by an American boy. Later when she has grown up and is committed by parental agreement to marrying a Japanese officer, the American boy returns and she falls in love with him. The struggles of the girl to conquer this impossible love constitute the remainder of the story. *The House of Misty Star* (1912) and *Jack and I in Lotus Land* (1922) are also set primarily in Japan.

Perhaps the word most often used to describe Mrs. Macaulay's books was "charming," but there were other recurring words and phrases too, such as "graceful," "an eye for picturesque detail," "good use of atmosphere," "clever combinations of tears and laughter, wit and wisdom." Her bookes received almost no harsh criticism, but also none that claimed excellence for the volumes. One reviewer, with something of an air of resignation, called them "sweet and harmless for young and old," and there was fairly frequent apprehension about the author's ability to discriminate between tenderness and sentimentality. Another reviewer speculated that Macaulay's last volume would be a success "unless it be that the taste of the reading public has changed again." But every reviewer found the volumes appealing, and certainly the public seemed to like them, for they were frequently on best-seller lists, though never again at the top.

Fannie Caldwell Macaulay died in 1941, four years before her beloved Hiroshima became the first city in the world to be hit by an atomic blast. She was buried in Cave Hill Cemetery, Louisville.

Foxhall Daingerfield

Since his early death at forty-six, Foxhall Daingerfield (1887–1933) has not received the attention he deserves from those who have written about Kentucky authors. Daingerfield was born in Virginia but came to Fayette County in 1893 after his parents' divorce. He was reared by his grandparents at Castleton Farm, the dominant racing stable in the Bluegrass just after the turn of the century, where his grandfather was the farm manager and James H. Keene was owner. Later the racing environment entered into Daingerfield's stories, particularly in *The Silver Urn* (1927), a mystery novel in which the annual race-week dance given by Ellen Chandler is brought to a sudden end by a double murder.

Daingerfield's first literary and creative interests, however, expressed themselves in drama and the theater and may have grown out of his student days at Transylvania University. He looked back into Central Kentucky history and wrote a four-act play called *Bryan Station*, which was produced at the Lexington Opera House in the fall of 1908. In the spring of 1909 another of his plays was produced at the Opera House—*The Southern Cross*, "produced for the Benefit of the [John Hunt] Morgan Monument." Subsequently he was an actor in the touring company of the celebrated actress Minnie Maddern Fiske and did some acting in early movies when the center of the movie industry was on Long Island. A bit later but prior to America's entry into World War I he enlisted in the Red Cross, where he was organizer and director of a group called The Liberty Theatre at Camp Taylor, near Louisville, a sort of forerunner of the USO shows of World War II.

Around 1920 Daingerfield took up residence in Washington and later became a friend and sort of protégé of the well-known mystery story writer Mary Roberts Rinehart. *Ghost House* (1926) was his first volume, followed by *The Silver Urn* (1927), a story based loosely on the once-famous Harper murders in Woodford County. Others of his mystery stories using a Kentucky background include *White and Gold Lady* (1927), a story of double intrigue in the 1880s, and *The Gay Nineties Murder* (1928). *Linden Walk Tragedy* (1928), his last murder mystery, was perhaps his most successful novel with the critics. All of Daingerfield's stories were regularly noticed widely by the review press, including the *New York Times*, the *New York Herald-Tribune*, the *Boston Transcript*, the *New York Evening Post*, the *Saturday Review of Literature*, the *New Republic*, and the *Times Literary Supplement*. Occasionally there was a warm commendation, such as that of the *Linden Walk Tragedy* in the *Boston Transcript* (March 30, 1929), but more generally the reviews were mixed and the reviewers of the opinion that though Daingerfield's faults were not notable, neither were his merits.

The reason for including Daingerfield here, however, is *Mrs. Haney* (1933), written four years after his last mystery novel and representing a distinct departure from the type of novel he had been writing. The novel, dealing as one reviewer says, with "a tragedy so humble that it could have been only of casual interest to the sheriff," won Daingerfield entirely favorable reviews, though its author died before he could read them. Living on the edge of the John Carroll Bluegrass estate, Mrs. Haney struggles to hold up her head and salvage the lives of her family. The remarks of the reviewer in the *Saturday Review of Literature* (November 25, 1933) typify the praise the novel enjoyed:

> Told with skill and delicacy far beyond the ordinary, this haunting novel of a southern poor-white family cannot fail to bring to its readers a renewed sense of loss at the recent death of its author, who after devoting most of his writing career to detective stories, proved himself with this book an important writer of serious fiction. It is essentially a study of character, a complete and rounded portrait of a woman who, with every handicap life could impose upon her, held fast to her courage and defiantly saved something from the wreckage. It is most unusual to find in contemporary fiction anyone done with so much genuine understanding as is this Mrs. Haney; she is very far removed from the poor-white stereotype common to Southern fiction. . . . The book makes no pretense to large significance except in its careful and honest revelation of the way human beings act in certain circumstances, but it will linger entire in the memory when many more pretentious novels are forgotten.

CHAPTER 14

Retrospect

In tracing the fortunes of Kentucky literature between 1860 and 1930, we have referred to the frequency with which the books of Kentucky authors appeared among the top ten on the nation's best-seller lists; we have also mentioned the Authors Club of Louisville. It seems appropriate here to say more about these two phenomena, not only because they merit more detailed discussion but also because they provide a desirable perspective from which to view the period. Before 1885 there was nothing that resembled a Kentucky literature: there was no deceased Kentucky author that could be referred to with pride; there was no Kentucky writer who was known outside the state. Twelve years later, in 1897, James Lane Allen published *The Choir Invisible* and became the first Kentuckian to write a novel that appeared among the top ten on the national annual best-seller list; and in 1913 when *The Heart of the Hills* by John Fox, Jr., appeared among the top ten for the year it was the fourteenth time that a book by a Kentuckian had done so. In ten of those seventeen years one or more titles appeared there; four times they appeared as No. 1 or No. 2; and in one year no fewer than five of the top ten were by Kentuckians:

1897 *The Choir Invisible*, by James Lane Allen, No. 2.
1900 *The Reign of Law*, by James Lane Allen, No. 4.
1902 *Mrs. Wiggs of the Cabbage Patch*, by Alice Hegan Rice, No. 2.
1903 *Lovey Mary*, by Alice Hegan Rice, No. 4.
Mrs. Wiggs of the Cabbage Patch, by Alice Hegan Rice, No. 6.
The Mettle of the Pasture, by James Lane Allen, No. 7.

Letters of a Self-Made Man to His Son, by George Horace Lorimer, No. 8.

The Little Shepherd of Kingdom Come, by John Fox, Jr., No. 10.

1904 *The Little Shepherd of Kingdom Come*, by John Fox, Jr., No. 7.

1905 *Sandy*, by Alice Hegan Rice, No. 2.

1907 *The Lady of the Decoration*, by Frances Caldwell Macaulay, No. 1.

1908 *The Trail of the Lonesome Pine*, by John Fox, Jr., No. 3.

1909 *The Trail of the Lonesome Pine*, by John Fox, Jr., No. 5.

1913 *The Heart of the Hills*, by John Fox, Jr., No. 5.

Remarkable though such a list is, it by no means tells the whole story, for it takes no cognizance of the books just below the top ten or those on the monthly or weekly best-selling lists. The sale of Annie Fellows Johnston's *Little Colonel* series (1896–1912), for example, reached one million before her death in 1931 and two million before the middle of the century, and Eliza Calvert Obenchain's *Aunt Jane of Kentucky* (1907) also found a million readers; yet neither was among the top ten any single year. Much the same is true of Mrs. George Madden Martin's *Emmy Lou* (1902), Irvin Cobb's Judge Priest stories, and such of his collections as *Speaking of Operations* (1915), though the numbers drop to the hundreds of thousands. To cite one more example, Joseph A. Altsheler's "The Young Trailers" series of historical novels for juveniles (1907–12) were the most popular stories for young people in their day. None of these novels or collections of short stories can really be said to be read today, nor any of the authors to be among America's better writers of fiction. Yet the fact remains that the sudden productivity of Kentucky writers and their domination of the best-seller lists between 1897 and 1913 to an extent never equaled before or since by any other state are still remarkable phenomena.

Another phenomenon—the Authors Club of Louisville—came into being at the same time. The club, which was organized just before the turn of the century, perhaps in 1898, first had eight members but later expanded to twelve. Several of the members—Evelyn Snead Barnett, Alice Hegan Rice, Annie Fellows Johnston, Frances Caldwell Macaulay, Mrs. George Madden Martin, Mary Finley Leonard, and Venita Seibert—are discussed elsewhere. The other five deserve our acquaintance.

Margaret Steel Anderson (1869–1921) was a poet and art critic. She was the book review editor of the *Louisville Evening Post* and a "reader" for *McClure's Magazine*; she lectured widely on literature and art, including engagements in New York, Philadelphia, Pittsburgh, and Memphis; and she contributed verse regularly to the *Atlantic Monthly, McClure's Magazine*, and the *American Magazine*. She published one volume of verse, *The Flame in the Wind* (1913), which was enthusiastically reviewed locally, and *A Study of Modern Painting* (1913), which enjoyed a favorable national reception.

Eva Madden (1863–1958), Mrs. George Madden Martin's sister and a pioneer newspaperwoman, was one of the original members of the Club but joined the *New York Herald* staff and became a foreign correspondent in Florence, Italy. She was the author of several children's stories, the best known of which is a historical novel entitled *Two Royal Foes*. The volume had a limited but favorable reception at the hands of the review press.

Abby Meguire Roach (1876–1968) published poetry and short stories in *Harper's Monthly, Century Magazine, Cosmopolitan*, and *Criterion*. Some of these stories and Roach's novel, *Some Successful Marriages* (1906), dealt with marital problems. The volume received generally favorable but limited national attention.

Evelyn Snead Barnett (1861–1921), founder of the Authors Club, was the author of a collection of short stories, *Mrs. Delire's Euchre Party and Other Stories* (1895), and of *The Dragnet* (1909), the first murder mystery worth noting by a Kentuckian. She became famous because of her reviews in the *Courier-Journal* and introduced a new form of lecture into the Redpath Chautauqua program—the oral book review.

Ellen Churchill Semple (1863–1932) was an internationally known anthropogeographer, lectured at Oxford, and was adviser to Woodrow Wilson on territorial boundaries for the Treaty of Versailles. A *Nation* reviewer of her *Influences of Geographical Environment* says that the book "places Miss Semple among a handful of women over the world who are the peers of the foremost men of science."

Margaret Womack Vandercook (1868–1936), who wrote both verse and fiction, was one of the authors of the Ranch Girls series:

Ranch Girls at Rainbow (1911) and *Ranch Girls' Pot of Gold* (1912). She was also the author of *Loves of Ambrose* (1911). All three of these novels received generally favorable, though limited, national review attention.

Before the club was disbanded its members had published seventy books in addition to many articles, stories, and poems that appeared only in magazines. Five times between 1902 and 1907 their novels appeared on the nation's top-ten best-seller list, once as No. 1, twice as No. 2, and once each as No. 4 and No. 6. In addition, as noted above, Annie Fellows Johnston's *The Little Colonel* novels sold two million copies, even though they never once made the annual best-seller list; and *Emmy Lou*, by Mrs. George Madden Martin, sold a quarter of a million copies. As evidence of the prestige of the group, seven of them were listed in *Who's Who in America* in 1909.

Though not officially or unofficially connected with the Authors Club, the St. James Court and Belgravia Court neighborhood must be noted as a part of the Louisville literary scene of the day. This neighborhood, open only to pedestrians, had its origins in 1883 when the Victoria Land Company purchased a forty-acre tract of land that had been used by the Louisville Southern Exposition and subsequently developed it—in the manner of residential parks in London—into a quiet, secluded, tree-lined, fashionable community. Soon the area became a favorite place of residence—as it still is—of authors, artists, musicians, and others interested in and supportive of the arts. Among the writers who lived in the Courts at the turn of the century and during the life of the Authors Club were Cale Young Rice (husband of Alice Hegan Rice and an author himself), Madison Cawein, Fannie Macaulay, Charles Neville Buck, Eleanor Mercein Kelly, Virginia Cary Hudson, Elizabeth Robins, and Abbie Carter Goodloe, all but the last noted elsewhere in this volume. Goodloe (1867–60), besides contributing to the best magazines of the day, published a blank verse tragedy, *Antinous* (1891); *College Girls* (1895), a collection of short stories; *Calvert of Strathore* (1903), a novel with a French setting; *The Rockies* (1905), another collection of short stories; *The Star-Gazer* (1910), a novel that grew out of a winter spent in Mexico. She did her best work as a writer of short stories and in 1924 won the O. Henry Prize Award for "Claustrophobia," first published in *Scribner's Magazine*. In 1935 the story was made into a movie by Metro-Goldwyn-Mayer and was called *I Live My Life*.

By the time of World War I the writers of the Louisville literary renaissance, as well as those of the rest of the state, had had their day in the sun. A few continued to write on into the twenties and even beyond, but the national taste had changed. No single volume that they wrote is still read today, but to a remarkable degree their writings had seemed to fit the national taste for more than a decade. Despite the growing influence of the realists and the naturalists, the country had been in a mood for literature in the friendly, homespun, sentimental tradition, and Kentucky did its share to satisfy the demand.

If, however, Kentucky literature had come of age during the first two decades of the century, it had yet to achieve maturity. And that maturity would come, just as it already had begun elsewhere in the nation. Stephen Crane published *The Red Badge of Courage* in 1895; Theodore Dreiser published *Sister Carrie* in 1900; Ellen Glasgow, *Battle-Ground* in 1902; and Upton Sinclair, *The Jungle* in 1906. Succeeding years brought more new names that were to occupy high places in American literary history, among them Willa Cather, Edith Wharton, Robert Frost, Edgar Lee Masters, Carl Sandburg, Edna St. Vincent Millay, Amy Lowell, Sherwood Anderson, Eugene O'Neill, T.S. Eliot, Ezra Pound, F. Scott Fitzgerald.

By comparison with these, Kentucky's literature during the first quarter of the century was lightweight, but the years of maturity lay just ahead. Elizabeth Madox Roberts led the way with *Under the Tree*, a volume of verse, in 1922, and with *The Time of Man* in 1926. Less than a decade later Caroline Gordon, Harriette Arnow, Jesse Stuart, James Still, Allen Tate, and Robert Penn Warren served notice that a great age was dawning in Kentucky literature. If between 1860 and 1930 the literature of the Commonwealth came of age, then it is safe to say that between 1930 and 1980 it achieved maturity. In contrast to the previous era, no single book by a Kentuckian during these years would be among the top ten on the best-seller list. But six of them would win Pulitzer Prizes.

PART THREE

Maturity: 1930–1980

CHAPTER 15

Kentucky Literary Renascence

During the late 1920s and the 1930s a notable group of Kentucky writers came on the scene: Elizabeth Madox Roberts, Allen Tate, Robert Penn Warren, Caroline Gordon, Jesse Stuart, Harriette Arnow, and James Still, all of whom belonged to the distinguished era of writing in the South called the "Southern Literary Renascence." Between World War I and World War II literature throughout the South flourished as never before and, in the view of many students of literature, surpassed the writing of any other section of the country.

The terms "regionalism" and "regionalist" have often been applied to the writers of the Southern Literary Renascence, for, just as did the late nineteenth-century local colorists, each has written about a region. The regionalism of the Southern Literary Renascence, however, was a far more complex concept than that of the nineteenth century, a fact that must be kept in mind whenever either term is used. Certainly there is no suggestion that such writers are "provincial" or "narrow" in their attainment or are limited per se by the fact that they have used the places they know best. No one speaks of Thomas Hardy and Arnold Bennett being provincial or limited in their portrayal of human beings merely because they wrote of life in Wessex and "the Five Towns" in England.

No matter what collective term is applied to them, some of Kentucky's finest and best-known authors were writing during the middle third of the twentieth century. All writers are individuals, however, and develop themes and ideas peculiar to their own make-up. Thus Jesse Stuart, Harriette Arnow, and James Still have written almost ex-

Elizabeth Madox Roberts. Photo courtesy of W. H. Slavick.

Allen Tate. Photo courtesy of Mrs. Allen Tate.

Robert Penn Warren. Photo courtesy of University of Kentucky Photographic Services.

clusively of Eastern Kentucky and along with other lesser writers will be examined in a chapter on the literature of that region. Caroline Gordon wrote in great part about Agrarianism and along with other writers will be included under "Agrarianism," a movement which in the 1930s was a powerful shaping force in the thinking of a number of literary figures of the South. Elizabeth Madox Roberts was never self-

Caroline Gordon. Photo courtesy of the *Courier-Journal*.

consciously a member of any group and in a sense was a precursor of the notable literary figures of the Kentucky literary renascence. Allen Tate was one of the original Nashville" Fugitives "in the 1920s and one of the Agrarians, but, perhaps as much as any American writer, he can be considered "cosmopolitan." Warren had the same affiliations but was perhaps the least "Agrarian" of the Agrarians and has the greatest breadth of attainment among them.

Elizabeth Madox Roberts

The main lines of the literary career of Elizabeth Madox Roberts (1881–1941) are fairly simple. She was born in Perryville in 1881 and in 1884 moved with her family to Springfield, which she would regard as home the rest of her life, despite temporary absences. The first of these was in 1896–1900, when she went to high school in Covington and, in the fall of 1900, enrolled at the University of Kentucky until she was obliged to withdraw because of ill health. Back in Springfield she taught in public and private schools until 1910, when tuberculosis and other respiratory ailments sent her to live with her sister in Colorado. Here she wrote some poetry that has been characterized as "written for the tourist trade" and intended to be accompanied by drawings of alpine flowers. The results were published in 1915 as *In the Great Steep's Garden*.

Then came the watershed years of Roberts's life. When she reached thirty-six in 1917, James T. Cotton Noe of the University of Kentucky, a regional poet and a long-time friend, wrote a letter in her behalf to Robert Morss Lovett of the University of Chicago. As a result, in January 1917 began four great formative years in Roberts's life through her work with faculty members such as Lovett and the medievalist Edith Rickert and through her experience in the University Poetry Club, of which she was president in her senior year and in which she was associated with other student-writers such as Glenway Wescott, Monroe Wheeler, and Yvor Winters. She also came to know Harriet Monroe, editor of *Poetry* magazine and, through limited access to Monroe's salon, Carl Sandburg, Vachel Lindsay, Edgar Lee Masters, and other writers of the Chicago "renaissance," which provided perhaps the most stimulating literary atmosphere in America at the time. During this period Roberts won the McLaughlin Prize in the essay and the Fiske Prize in poetry, published poetry in the *Atlantic Monthly*, *Poetry*, and elsewhere. But doubtless the greatest benefits she gained from her Chicago years were the opportunities for liberating experiences and aesthetic explorations, and the increase in intellectual self-confidence that her associations with other poets and writers afforded her.

In 1921 she returned to Springfield and dedicated her life to writing. In 1922, many of the poems she had written in Chicago appeared in her first volume of serious verse, *Under the Tree*, which views the world from the perspective of a child. More important was her turning to the novel as a literary form, for in 1926 she published *The Time of Man* and in 1930 *The Great Meadow*, two novels that for years to come are likely to be known as classics in American literature. Between these came *My Heart and My Flesh* (1927), which tended to consolidate her reputation as an important writer. After *The Great Meadow* she published *A Buried Treasure* (1931) and *The Haunted Mirror* (1932), a collection of short stories, but neither of them strengthened her reputation. During these years, however, she won critical acclaim and received honors and awards. *The Time of Man* was a Book-of-the-Month selection and *The Great Meadow* a Literary Guild selection. In 1928 she was awarded the John Reed Memorial Prize by *Poetry* magazine and a comparable prize in 1931 by the Poetry Society of South Carolina; in 1932 "The Sacrifice of the Maidens," a short story, won the O. Henry Second Prize. Meanwhile Roberts's health was causing her trouble and continued to do so the remainder of her life. *He Sent Forth a Raven* (1935) recouped some of her old fire but received mixed reviews; and *Black Is My True Love's Hair*, though very favorably received, showed reduced scope and failed to win back the towering acclaim she once enjoyed. By the end of the decade her health was failing rapidly because of Hodgkin's disease, but in 1940 she published another volume of poems, *Song in the Meadow*, and in 1941 she was able to read proofs of *Not By Strange Gods*, her second collection of short stories, before she died in the spring. In all, her career was a notable one even though she did not come to the form—the novel—in which she would excel until she was forty-five and would write her last one only twelve years later.

When Elizabeth Madox Roberts published *The Time of Man* in 1926, she had only a handful of poems in print to recommend her, but when she set to work on the novel in the summer of 1922 the idea was not new to her. As early as 1919, she says, she began to think of the life of a "wandering tenant-farmer" as an example of man's odyssey through life. The experience of a tenant farmer she knew well from having grown up in a farming community of South-Central Kentucky and from her association with the children and the parents she came to know while teaching in the schools of Washington County for ten years.

The story she settled upon was that of Ellen Chesser, the daughter of a tenant-farmer family that moves from farm to farm and asks for little more from life than food to eat, clothes to wear, and a roof over their heads. Ellen, however, differs from most share-croppers in that she yearns for something better—maybe not just a parlor to sit in but a book to read. In due course she marries a luckless young farm hand, Jasper Kent, and moves about from farm to farm as other share-croppers do. There are moments when it seems some of her dreams may come true, but eventually her husband proves unfaithful to her and is beaten by a band of hooded men as a suspected barn burner. The novel comes full circle, with Ellen on the road again, seeking a place where she can have a roof over her head, some clothes to wear, and food to eat.

Such a description fits the external events in the lives of the people with whom the novel is concerned, but to Roberts the important thing is not what happens to people but how they respond to what happens. It is clear that the story is intended to be archetypal, a tale of a human being's journey through life, and that the heroine's life is to be seen at two levels: the physical and the spiritual. At one level, like her mother and father, Ellen has won no single material success; yet her life has been a triumph. She has triumphed, not merely because she has survived the physical passage to maturity with five children, but because she has been engaged in a spiritual, existential search for identity, and has found it. She has become an individual who can cope with whatever world she is destined to be a part of—and even transcend it. Thus, in spite of all that has happened to her, she is glad to be in the world and a part of life; she can even say in a moment of ecstasy, "I'm Ellen Chesser and I'm lovely."

My Heart and My Flesh (1927) is an equally serious inquiry into the meaning of life. In it Theodosia Bell, unlike Ellen Chesser, has grown up accustomed to wealth, family position, and social prestige; she has education, the social graces, and a cultivated musical talent. Then in Job-like fashion, one by one, these things and more are taken away from Theodosia, as Roberts probes the depth of human character. The security that comes from family pride and respectability is the first to go as Theodosia learns that her father has sired three Negro children. Her grandfather dies, the young man she was to marry deserts her, and another suitor dies in a burning building. She learns that her hand is not broad enough to permit her to realize her potential as a violinist. She loses her wealth; members of her family die; she becomes irrationally and tragically involved in the lives of her mulatto half-brother and half-sisters. Her degradation is complete when she becomes the mistress of a young lawyer in Anneville.

Of Theodosia's descent into hopelessness and despair Earl H. Rovit (*Herald to Chaos*, 42) says:

> The time-span is approximately eighteen months—eighteen months of a long gray convalescence, in which Theodosia moves to the very edge of suicide, halts, and begins her return to life. The setting and

> atmosphere are surrealistic, the house . . . the characters, Theodosia's state of mind, the wild dogs—all are blurred into indistinct but insistent shapes which howl at the fringes of consciousness. The setting is thus a perfect projection of the hysteria which marks Theodosia's descent into the living veins of her soul.

But resources within her rally and she begins a new life.

Not surprisingly, the novel met differing critical responses. For one thing, there is much that is unpleasant about it. Faulkner and others in the 1940s would explore miscegenation and abnormal states of mind as subjects for literature, but in 1927 such subject matter was new and far from popular. In its way the novel was the antithesis of *The Time of Man*. In the former, Ellen Chesser grows spiritually as the novel develops; Theodosia, by contrast, seems to diminish as the novel explores "the darkest areas of the human soul, the area where morality and order have their genesis" (Rovit, 47). Despite her appearance of security in wealth, position, and public approval, Theodosia lacks the solid core of self-identity and self-mastery that Ellen Chesser built and is unable to cope with the ills that befell her. Full self-identity could come only after her odyssey had taken her into a harrowing experience and she had won her way to a peace deeper and more secure than she had known when she was younger and had only the peace of protected innocence.

Next to *The Time of Man* in excellence was *The Great Meadow* (1930), Miss Roberts's historical novel of the Kentucky frontier and perhaps the greatest novel ever written on the subject. The action begins in 1774 and ends in 1781, roughly the Revolutionary War era. At the narrative level the reader learns of the emigration of Berk Jervis and his wife Diony from her tidewater Virginia home to Harrod's Fort in Kentucky, how the Kentucky settlements were affected by the way the British supplied arms, men, and leadership to the Indians as they sought to drive the settlers back across the mountains, and how the settlers experienced hardships, loneliness, and hunger and endured Indian attacks, torture, and death.

Roberts is most concerned with the mental and spiritual responses that characters make to their environment and to each other, for she writes a historical novel as if she were writing poetry. We see the opening of the West in its epic proportions, but less of subduing Indians and canebrakes and more of the heroic dimensions of the migration of a people. This portrayal requires characters of epic stature and a sense of the grandeur of places and events. "There were giants in the earth in those days," we are told. There was James Harrod, for example, "a big man that never tires, and a heart in him like pure gold"; there was Benjamin Logan, "his body made big to hold his big heart," a man who once traveled for a week through the wilderness to get ammunition for his beleagured fort—"a great man, a giant, a hero, walked out of a half-mythical land, striding down an unbroken way to get ammunition for his people." And there was Daniel Boone, to whom Diony observes one day that there are places in the Kentucky wilderness where "a body could get lost and never find himself again." Boone replies, "I don't reckon I'd get lost in e'er one. Not to say lost. I never was lost. I was bewildered right bad once for as much as a week, but not lost. I never felt lost the whole enduren time."

These were the leaders, the trailblazers, but there were other heroes too—those who came with them and established order in the wilderness. Diony was one of these. One day, reflecting on Boone's remarks to her, she muses: "It's curious . . . I'm not the Boone kind. I never was. . . . I'd be more at home somewheres else. . . . I don't know where." Rovit puts it well: "The Boone strength is that which leaps outward into the wilderness, blazing the pioneer trail into the wilderness without substantially altering the wilderness. The Diony strength . . . is that which follows the trail after it is blazed, setting things in order, establishing a routine and a familiarity in the areas barely wrested out of the grip of chaos" (59).

All were endowed with an epic inner strength that the hero, Berk Jervis, well describes when he relates the words he cried out in the faces of the Ojibways when they would have eaten his flesh in order to gain his strength: " 'When life goes outen me,' I says, 'the strong part goes too, and I take it wherever I go when I go from here. . . . You couldn't eat ne'er a bit of it. Whe'r I go to heaven or whe'r I go to hell or whe'r I go no place at all, whenever I go from here my strength goes along with me.' " Indeed, this speech of Berk's may be said to contain the meaning of the whole book, just as it is the theme of *The Time of Man* and *My Heart and My Flesh*. Strength is from within.

Roberts's first novel after *The Great Meadow* was *A Buried Treasure* (1931). It is a gently humorous story of the finding of a pot of gold and silver by an old Kentucky farmer and his wife, who give a party at which they announce their good fortune. The story tells what happens as a consequence. There are flashes of excellence in the volume, the poetic style of the author has not deserted her, but substance—in comparison with the three great novels—is lacking. Structurally, the parts do not fuse well, and the symbolism is complex and at times confusing.

The Haunted Mirror, her first collection of short stories, appeared in 1932 but seems not to have enhanced her reputation generally. The volume was well received, but there appears to have been a growing apprehension that Roberts's style (her poetic language, her symbolism, and her "oblique technique") was becoming "a bit trying" and was sometimes allowed to overbalance "the effects of characterization." Still, the usual praise was there. *The Bookman* (Dec. 1932), for example, prefers her short stories to her novels and the *New York Times Book Review* (Nov. 20, 1932) thinks that "Three perhaps four, of [the stories] stand apart as work of the highest order, stories which a Tchekhov could have been proud to sign."

During this period Roberts's health appears to have been what one might call normal for her, but a turn for the worse came apparently around 1932. A constantly annoying skin irritation worsened, and by 1935 her periods of weakness and anemia sent her to Louisville to specialists who early in 1936 diagnosed her illness as Hodgkin's disease. At that time such an illness had no cure, but Roberts was told that its progress would be slow and that she would have a few years in which she could continue to write. At the time she was fifty-five. The diagnosis and prediction were accurate enough, for she was to write one more novel (*Black Is My True Love's Hair*, 1938), was able to write some verse and bring together her second volume of poetry (*Song in the Meadow*, 1940), and read proofs on her second volume of short stories (*Not by Strange Gods*, 1941) before she died in Orlando, Florida, in the spring of 1941 and was brought back home for burial in the cemetery at Springfield.

As her health worsened, Roberts worked on *He Sent Forth a Raven*, which was published in 1935. A consensus on the merits of this novel has not yet been reached. Willard Thorp in the *Dictionary of American Biography* calls it "her most baffling work," and Frederick P.W. McDowell (*Elizabeth Madox Roberts*, 27) writes, "*He Sent Forth a Raven* . . . brought little praise or understanding from reviewers. Thereafter, Miss Roberts' reputation with the public declined sharply." Such views seem to overstate the case. The novel has indeed continued to be regarded as "baffling," but Earl H. Rovit, perhaps the most perceptive of those who have written full-length studies of Roberts, taking his lead from Grant C. Knight (*Saturday Review*, Jan. 6, 1945), has declared that in the novel Roberts returns "to the epic scale" and then analyzes the three lines of action in the novel in order to show that "this novel [is] the culminating achievement of Miss Roberts' developing thought and artistry. . . . I believe [it] is one of the finest achievements in modern American letters" (68, 88).

The novel is about Stoner Drake, who in angry defiance against the immutable laws of nature vows that if his second wife (then ill) should die, as his first has done, he will never "set his foot on God's earth again." She does die and Stoner reiterates his vow:

> I know every field and know how far each goes, up and down, and what limestone is on the under side. God knows I know. But so help me God, I'll never set foot on earth again. No man will persuade me. I'll stay here and if God so desires he can rot me of my whole flesh. He can put thistles in my mouth for food and he can sink my acres into the bottomless pits of weeds and hell.

In Grant Knight's view, more than any other of her novels *He Sent Forth a Raven* reveals Miss Roberts's "exquisite sense of reality, her bewilderment with things as they are, her lyric anger, her slight vein of madness, her faith in man's redemption."

Roberts's next, and last, novel, was published three years later. This was *Black Is My True Love's Hair* (1938), which is more limited in scope and far more serene than *He Sent Forth a Raven*. It is set in pastoral Pigeon River country, has a female protagonist, and employs the familiar archetypal pattern of spiritual death and rebirth. The novel opens with Dena Janes returning from a six-day sexual escapade into which she has been lured by Will Langtry. The plot centers upon the "ruined" woman's gaining the community's and her own reacceptance of herself and upon her ultimate marriage to Cam Elliot, the miller's son. The threads of symbolism and the subtleties involved in Dena's gaining a new sense of herself led to the very favorable critical reception of the novel. Some reviews were rather extravagant: "[One feels] gratitude---there is no other word for it—for the spell she weaves with her language" (*New York Herald-Tribune*), "[the novel] needs no comment or criticism. It needs only to be read" (*Nation*); "a memorable piece of fiction" (*New York Times Book Review*); "Elizabeth Madox Roberts has taught us to expect complete magic from her deep, modulated prose" (*Saturday Review of Literature*). Despite the excellence of the novel, however, those who criticized it knew—and some said so—that Roberts had not reached the level of greatness, or near-greatness, she had achieved in *The Time of Man* and *The Great Meadow*. Still it was, as no one could have known at the time, an immensely satisfying way for her in ailing health to end her career as a novelist.

Song in the Meadow added no luster to Roberts's reputation, though the volume was well received. *Not by Strange Gods*, her second collection of short stories, appeared shortly after her death in 1941, which motivated some reviewers to look back through the years and remark on the change that came about in Roberts's work during the latter half of her writing career. Clifton Fadiman's essay in the *New Yorker* (March 29, 1941) is a good example. He, as well as others, finds these latest stories baffling and some of them incomprehensible.

Roberts's poetry requires further comment, for poetry lies at the heart of her writing. Over and over again critics and readers alike have exclaimed over the poetic quality of her prose. It is a rare review that failed to speak of her lyricism, of her control of words, of the magic of her language. If she had been less a poet, she would have been less a novelist. Of a different sort is the observation made above about *The Great Meadow*: that she wrote her historical novel as if it were poetry, by which is meant that to her the facts and events of history have meaning only as they are clothed in human actions and feelings. In her own words, "Poetry is forever trying to make clear obscure relations in the worlds and systems of things and ideas." Such a view, of course, is applicable not only to history but to any social or intellectual concept.

Roberts's first serious publication was a volume of poems about childhood, *Under the Tree*, in 1922; *Song in the Meadow* (1940) contained ballads and poems in the folk tradition, but most of the poems were about childhood, a sub-genre in which Roberts had a great deal of talent. "The most delightful book of children's verse I have ever seen," was the ecstatic appraisal of a *New York Herald-Tribune* reviewer of *Under the Tree* (Jan. 28, 1923); "The best book of poetry dealing with children that has been produced in recent years. . . . an American classic," says the *Saturday Review* of the enlarged edition of 1930 (Nov. 15, 1930), and the reviewer proceeds to put the volume on the same shelf as *Alice in Wonderland* and *Water Babies*. Not every critic wrote with such uninhibited enthusiasm, but none failed to find excellence of the first order even though there was "some chaff."

The success of the volume resides in the author's talent for writing of the joys, the interests, the thoughts, the reveries of childhood with the simplicity with which a child views them, while at the same time coloring the poetry with the knowledge and wisdom and experience of adults. In general, the poems can be read at two levels, the child's and the adult's, the latter appearing in the overtones. In "August Night," for example, the speaker is first of all a child but it is also an adult awed and frightened by the immensity of the universe. Naturally the poems do not pretend to fathom the philosophical depths of life, but at times they are almost startling as the reader comes to see the world with the unsophisticated, or candid, or unconventional, or untutored vision of a perceptive child.

Sixty poems that range from four to forty lines each make up the original volume of *Under the Tree*. The subjects range from "sticktights" that cling to clothes, to a child's fears, to Christmas morning, to "The Sky"—which follows:

> I saw a shadow on the ground
> And heard a bluejay going by;
> A shadow went across the ground,
> And I looked up and saw the sky.
>
> It hung up on the poplar tree,
> But while I looked it did not stay;
> It gave a tiny sort of jerk
> And moved a little bit away.
>
> And farther on and farther on
> It moved and never seemed to stop.
> I think it must be tied with chains
> And something pulls it from the top.
>
> It never has come down again,
> And every time I look to see,
> The sky is always slippin back
> And getting far away from me.

Interestingly enough, though Roberts began writing poetry while she was in Chicago at the time Sandburg and others were leading the revolt against conventional forms of verse, she chose to use the stanzaic forms, the rhyme schemes, and the metrical patterns of traditional poetry. Above all else, poetry to Elizabeth Madox Roberts was song.

The final judgment on the place of Roberts in American literature lies ahead. Those who know her writings predict a revival that will increase her stature, but except for sporadic praise from a reader or a critic who "discovers" her, she has remained relatively little read since her death. She left no school and she has had no "influence" in the conventional sense. Her probing the inner life of her characters precedes similar undertakings in the work of Thomas Wolfe, William Faulkner, Katherine Ann Porter, Eudora Welty, and others; but here she was no more than a forerunner. So far as reputation and popularity are concerned, she labors under the disadvantages of having left only two volumes that can lay claim to excellence and two others that seem to confirm the talent these two revealed. It has been to her disadvantage too that the decline in the quality of her work came during the last of the two decades she wrote, so that her reputation suffered even while she still lived. In 1981, the one hundredth anniversary of Miss Roberts's birth, a national conference of Roberts scholars was held in Springfield for the purpose of focussing attention on her. Whether the work that is being done now as a result of this conference will hasten a revival of interest in her remains to be seen. In the meantime, *The Time of Man* and *The Great Meadow* are greatly admired by those who have read them and are thought to be worthy of being called classics. Lesser classics, perhaps, as the masterpieces of literature go, but still classics.

Allen Tate

Perhaps as much as any American author Allen Tate (1899–1979), born near Winchester, was cosmopolitan in taste. Such a statement may seem to conflict with our identification of him as a regionalist, but both characterizations are accurate enough. When Tate entered Vanderbilt University in 1918, he had attended the Cross School in Louisville (1909–12) and Ashland High School (1912–14), but otherwise his education had been haphazard because of the way his family had moved about. It concluded with a year in the Georgetown University Preparatory School in Washington (1917–18) to ready him to follow his brothers at Vanderbilt. Whatever ill effects Tate's erratic early education may have had, his brilliance of mind was evident to John Crowe Ransom, with whom he took advanced composition. "He wrote essays," says Ransom later, "about the literary imagination, with corollary excursions into linguistics and metaphysics; they were slightly bewildering to me in more ways than one. But I would not have stopped him if I could." Elsewhere Ransom adds that Tate wrote "in the consciousness of a body of literature which was unknown to his fellow students, and to my faculty associates and myself, unless it was by purest hearsay. A new literature had made its brilliant beginning." By this Ransom meant the poetry of William Butler Yeats and presumably that of T.S. Eliot, for Tate is credited with being one of the earliest Americans to "discover Eliot." "I began an impertinent campaign in Eliot's behalf in the South," says Tate.

When Tate entered Vanderbilt, America was experiencing a notable upsurge in the quantity and quality of the poetry that was being published. Among the new poets were Amy Lowell and the Imagists as well as Robert Frost, Edna St. Vincent Millay, and others in New England; Carl Sandburg, Edgar Lee Masters, Vachel Lindsay, and others in the Midwest; and Robinson Jeffers in the West. By 1920 only the South was not involved in the poetic revival. "Down there," says H.L. Mencken in *The Smart Set*, "a poet is as rare as an oboe player." This deficiency was to be remedied in part by the formation in Nashville of a group of academicians, businessmen, bankers, and others that called themselves "The Fugitives" and met together weekly to talk about literature and philosophy and particularly about the poetry they submitted for discussion. The success of the group and the establishment of its magazine, *The Fugitive* (1922–25) would have a far-reaching influence, not merely because some of the members were to become major American writers and critics—Andrew Lytle, Merrill Moore, John Crowe Ransom, Donald Davidson, Allen Tate, and Robert Penn Warren—but because they came to influence literature both in the region and in the nation.

Tate was the first of the major Fugitives to leave Nashville, when he set out for New York in June 1924 and started his rise to fame. In New York he began work on his biography of Stonewall Jackson, but more importantly he began publishing poetry in magazines and reviewing books for *The New Republic*, *The Nation*, the *New York Herald-Tribune*, and elsewhere. These reviews served two important purposes: they sharpened Tate's critical faculties, and they provided him with an income. Before the summer was over, Tate took time off to visit Robert Penn Warren in Guthrie and while there met Caroline Gordon, who had earlier written enthusiastically about the Fugitives in the *Nashville Tennesseean* and at the moment was back in Todd County, where she had grown up near Warren. Gordon and Tate were married in November. At first they were so hard-pressed for money that Tate took a part-time job as a janitor; but they soon began making their way up in the literary world. Among their friends in Greenwich Village were Hart Crane, Malcolm Cowley, Edmund Wilson, and Louise Bogan, as well as Mark Van Doren, who was a young teacher at Columbia University. In 1928 Tate published his biography of Stonewall Jackson as well as his first volume of verse, *Mr. Pope and Other Poems*.

Tate's accomplishments during his New York days were recognized with a Guggenheim fellowship that enabled him, with his wife and daughter, to go first to England, where he met Eliot, and then for a longer period to France during 1928 and 1929. There the Tates joined a celebrated group of expatriates that included John Peale Bishop, Ford Madox Ford, Ernest Hemingway, F. Scott Fitzgerald, Archibald MacLeish, and others whom Tate came to know in the literary conclaves that took place at the teas of Gertrude Stein. This was perhaps the high point of Tate's cosmopolitanism, and when, at twenty-nine, he joined the expatriates in Paris, he wrote, "This was the place we were headed for—our spiritual home." But Tate was never really happy there. As early as November 6, 1928, he wished in a letter to Mark Van Doren that he were back in the United States; in another letter to Van Doren, January 29, 1929, he declared, "I didn't really like Miss Stein and I have never been able to read her works with either pleasure or edification."

The Tates were back in Tennessee by February 1930 and by June were living in an antebellum house that Tate's brother Ben had bought overlooking the Cumberland River. Here Tate was back near the friends and in the milieu he cherished. Ransom and Davidson were still teaching at Vanderbilt; Warren was back from Oxford and was teaching at Southwestern University in Memphis; and Andrew Lytle was at Monteagle. While Tate and Warren had been out of the country, Ransom and Davidson had been involved in "the defense of the South" by writing essays for the *Sewanee Review* and the *Forum* that attacked northern industrialism and urbanization and sought to avoid the spread of both into the South. *God Without Thunder* (1930) brought Ransom's essays on the subject together. By the end of the summer of 1930, with some of the Fugitives forming the nucleus of what came to be called the "Agrarian Movement," twelve "Agrarians" had each written an essay for *I'll Take My Stand*, the manifesto that set forth the Agrarian principles.

Tate was one of the twelve. Already in his biography of of Stonewall Jackson (1928) and his biography of Jefferson Davis (1929) he had set forth his view that southern culture was more humanistic than northern industrialism. Between 1930 and 1936 he published *Poems: 1928–1931*, some of which reveal his dedication to the southern cause; and he worked on a biography of Robert E. Lee and a novel perhaps to have been called *The Ancestors*. Neither of these volumes was ever finished, but in 1938 he published his novel, *The Fathers*, and in it utilized some of the background material he had thus brought together. Tate's earliest important work to reflect his Agrarianism, however, was his "Ode to the Confederate Dead," which he started in 1925, published in 1927, and continued to revise for a decade.

In the "Ode" Tate portrays his age as lacking in belief and purpose —as cut off from the past and the tradition of which that past was a part. As Tate conceives it, it is a fallen world of spiritual and social disorder, a disorder due to the industrial, commercial, materialistic mentality which had superseded religion and tradition and order as the Old South had known it. Such people, including the watcher at the gate of the cemetery are unable to comprehend and feel the heroism, the courage, the commitment of the Confederate dead whose graves he sees. All they see in the cemetery are the leaves that blow among the tombstones. The poem, therefore, is not a celebration of the Confederate dead but a statement of humankind's inability to celebrate.

The Fathers also deals with the Civil War and reflects Tate's Agrarianism. Here Tate goes back to 1860–61 and to Fairfax County, Virginia, the ancestral seat of his mother. The story is told by Lacy Buchan, an old man who was a boy of fifteen when the events he describes take place. Major Buchan, Lacy's father, is the exemplar of the Old South and of the values to which the old order was committed. George Posey, the protagonist, is modern man in a transitional society, rootless and ruthless in spite of his charm. Though neither a rebel nor a reformer, he unwittingly brings inward destruction to the Buchan family into which he has married just as the war brought outward destruction.

The fable is concerned with the individual in relation to his world and the myth he lives by. Thus Major Buchan is rooted in custom and tradition and order, whereas Posey prefigures the new South and lacks the Major's inborn sense of guidance. The fable comes dramatically alive at the very beginning of the novel when the Major's wife dies. The Buchans know their roles in the ceremony of grief and play them out. George Posey, the son-in-law, bright, attractive, sensitive, and upset, violates decorum by riding away from the funeral and declining to attend. Major Buchan's sense of tradition and propriety causes him to leave his place in his wife's funeral procession, take "the brown hand" of his wife's maid, and "lead her into the line and make a place just behind the body of her mistress."

Many such tensions are to be found throughout the novel that throw into sharp focus the contrast between the old way of life and the new. To cite one more instance, George Posey hates money as such, thinks of Yellow Jim, his slave and half-brother, as "liquid capital" and sells him. Such an attitude toward slavery shocks Major Buchan, who though he uses the slaves he has inherited will have nothing to do with buying or selling them. When he disposes of a slave, he gives him his liberty and sends him off to Pennsylvania. Posey is generous and honest, but he does not live within the framework of established custom and must therefore improvise and invent on the spur of the moment the code he lives by, a fact that leaves him unprotected from what is outside him as well as what is within him. Deterioration and disintegration are inevitable. He reflects the new order of things.

Insofar as *The Fathers* contains Tate's views on Agrarianism, one must remember Tate's reply to the charge that Agrarianism was naive and worse: "I never thought of Agrarianism as a *restoration* of anything in the Old South. I saw it as something to be created . . . not only in the South . . . but . . . in the moral and religious outlook of western man." Such a view may still seem naive, but with half a century of perspective now, the Agrarian movement takes its place alongside other movements of the 1920s and 1930s which sought to warn the world away from the dangers towards which many people saw the post–World War I years headed. From the time of its publication to the present *The Fathers* has been regarded as a perplexing work. (Those who would examine it further may wish to supplement their own reading with the criticism to be found in such volumes as Radcliffe Squires's *Allen Tate and His Work: Critical Evaluations*—as the present writer has done, freely.)

Ever since Tate had returned from France he had continued to write criticism and reviews and to establish himself as one of the English-speaking world's leading critics, while at the same time writing his best poetry. The formation of his aesthetic creed goes back as far as 1925 when he published in *The Nation* the essay "Last Days of the Charming Lady," in which he noted the absence of a vigorous literary tradition in the South, not only before the Civil War but up to the very present, and he and Ransom called for a new poetry and criticism with a greater intellectual content that could serve the needs of the post-war world. By 1927 he was increasingly freeing himself from earlier influences. He now called for a school of critics concerned not with moral, historical, sociological, and philosophical criteria but "exclusively" with "the properties of poetry as a fine art." Such a view, of course, prefigures the New Poetry and the New Criticism.

Tate's first volume of criticism—and also the first by any of the Fugitives—was *Reactionary Essays on Poetry and Ideas* (1936). Here Tate is close to the view that Ransom expresses best in *The World's Body* (1938): namely, that the sciences can merely analyze and strip the world closer to its constituent parts, whereas poetry synthesizes, sees interrelationships, and sets these forth as "the world's body." Here poetry is close to religion but is more disinterested than religion and hence more objective, less polemical. *Reactionary Essays* grew out of the fact that during the Great Depression leftist-leaning proletarian writers used literature as propaganda to argue the plight of the working man. Tate takes his stand against this kind of writing or against any literature that is dominated by a "practical" purpose, elevating instead what he called "pure" poetry—poetry without contemporary moral, political, religious, or sociological ramifications. A poem, therefore, should be a complete entity, a self-contained structure, that must be examined without reference to the author or the age that produced it—a view that clashed with the teachings and methods of the literary historians. The critical principles that evolved into the New Criticism as a result of this approach to literature are too complex to set forth here, but the titles of some of the volumes and essays can be mentioned. First, as noted above, came Tate's *Reactionary Essays* (1936), followed by another important collection by him five years later, *Reason in Madness* (1941). To be noted also are three important volumes by Tate's friends: Ransom's *The World's Body* (1938) and *The New Criticism* (1941) and Cleanth Brooks's *Modern Poetry and the Tradition* (1939). These volumes constitute a fine statement of the critical theory and practice of the New Critics. Nor should one neglect the enormously influential volume *Understanding Poetry* (1938) by Brooks and Warren.

Not all of Tate's criticism was intended to instruct the reader in how to read and understand the literature that he admired and championed. As a look at Tate's *Essays of Four Decades* (1968) will make clear, the essays are of many sorts. There are, for example, essays that make a contribution to literary theory ("Tension in Poetry," "The Angelic Imagination"); essays on the function of literature ("Literature as Knowledge," "The Man of Letters in the Modern World," "To Whom Is the Poet Responsible?" "The Present Function of Criticism"); essays on individual writers (including Hart Crane, Ezra Pound, Thomas Hardy, Edgar Allen Poe, Emily Dickinson); essays in poetic interpretation (none better than "Narcissus as Narcissus"). During the late 1940s and the early 1950s Tate continued to write criticism: *On the Criticism of Poetry* (1948), *The Hovering Fly* (1949), and *The Forlorn Demon* (1953). The quality of this later writing continued at a high level, but it added little to Tate's prestige.

At the time that Tate and Ransom were laying the groundwork for the New Criticism they were also trying to formulate a historical myth that would fit their view of the fortunes of southern life and culture. Tate accepted T.S. Eliot's "waste land" metaphor as describing the plight of humanity in the twentieth century—impotent and powerless to find commitment in a sterile age. The sentimental local color stories and the exaggerated pictures of the plantations with their white-columned mansions he could only reject; but beyond this view he had a sense of something that could be the core of a powerful myth. Ingredients of this myth included a love of the land and a love of place, a sense of the interrelationship of the past and the present, and a respect for gracious living and good manners. Such qualities are, of course, reminiscent of Agrarianism, but the application of the myth was broader than that, for it ran through much southern literature and offered a possible way out of the waste land.

As already noted, it was "pure" poetry that Tate came to champion and for which he helped construct a method of reading and understanding. As anyone who has read criticism of Tate's poetry knows, the two words most frequently applied to it are "difficult" and "obscure." Even the reviewers often found themselves grasping for meaning. This is not because it lacks a recognizable structure or logical imagery, but because it is notably intellectual and greatly compressed, even to the point sometimes of seeming to be elliptical. Furthermore, Tate liked bold and startling imagery, often accentuated by the presence of unusual or unexpected adjectives. Thus in Tate's best known poem, "Ode to the Confederate Dead," we have "ambitious November," "The brute curiosity of an angel's stare," "the immoderate past," "malignant purity," to cite only a few. There is, too, a great deal of allusion, often esoteric; wit and irony are characteristic of his poetry. Collectively such characteristics impose almost constant intellectual demands upon the reader and discourage all but a limited audience. Tate's poetry, consequently, has never been popular; yet it has stayed in print.

We will here probe further into only one other poem, "The Swimmers." The student who wishes to read further in Tate's poetry is advised to turn to such poems as "The Mediterranean," "Aeneas in Washington," "To the Lacedemonians," "Seasons of the Soul," and "Winter Mask," and may wish to supplement such reading with commentary by Tate scholars such as Radcliffe Squires, R.K. Meiners, Ferman Bishop, John M. Bradbury, and Louis D. Rubin, Jr. "The Swimmers," the scene of which is identified as "Montgomery County, Kentucky, July 1911," was published in the *Hudson Review* in 1952 and was intended to be included in a never-completed long poem, of which "The Maimed Man" (1952) and "The Buried Lake" (1953) were also to have been parts. It is reprinted in *The Swimmers and Other Selected Poems* (1970) and by common consent is regarded as one of Tate's best poems. In fact, the poet Robert Lowell wrote to Tate (March 15, 1954) to say that it was the finest poem that Tate had ever written and its use of terza rima the finest in English, surpassing even Shelley's use of the form. *The* [London] *Times Literary Supplement* (March 19, 1971) in its review of *The Swimmers and Other Selected Poems* also singles it out for particular attention: "Few poems entice one to a second reading, possibly only 'The Swimmers': that does demand reading again, and then again, with the peremptoriness which is inflicted on one by the real thing." "The Swimmers," along with the other two poems that were intended to be parts of a long poem reflect a different sort of Tate and a poetry that is more personal, more confessional, than most of his work.

At the narrative level the poem is a childhood recollection of an event that actually took place. Five boys whose names are given, including Tate's, are on their way during the hot, sultry, "Dog-days" of July to go swimming in a creek swimming-hole. "No more'n a mile," Layne said, when suddenly, at a noise, "all five stood still";

> Peering, I heard the hooves come down the hill.
> The posse passed, twelve horse.
> . . . .
> We scuttled down the bank below a ledge
> And marched stiff-legged in our common fright.
> . . . .
> Dropped the dull hooves again; the horsemen came
> Again, all but the leader [leaving eleven in the posse].

Then the boys see the sheriff beneath "a giant sycamore" looking at the corpse of a black man, the victim of a lynching. "We come too late" the sheriff says. Then the narrator, his companions now having deserted him, sees the sheriff joined by "A single horseman [who] came at a slow lope." Together the two men with a rope, one end "noosed" around the dead man's feet, the other "slip-knot" to the pommel of the stranger's saddle, prepare to drag the body "towards our town" and the court house square, while the boy follows.

> Alone in the public clearing
> This private thing was owned by all the town,
> Though never claimed by us within my hearing.

And with that the poem at the narrative level ends; but other meanings are implicit. At one level of meaning the poem is about social injustice, though it is not primarily a study of lynching. Rather, it is a poem about the human condition, about how people are made what they are by the moment of time they live in. Religious overtones are also present. Thus there are parallels with the crucifixion, some equation between the body of the black man and the body of

Christ, between the disappearance of the leader of the posse and that of Judas, who went out and hanged himself, leaving the eleven Disciples, and between the sheriff and the unnamed horseman and Joseph of Arimathea and Nicodemus, who claimed the body of Christ and prepared it for burial.

Considering that he wrote for almost sixty years, the quantity of Allen Tate's literary output was not great. His contribution to humane letters, however, is greater than the sum of his writings. He was a teacher during much of his life, including stints at Southwestern University at Memphis and the University of North Carolina at Greensboro, as well as lectureships at Princeton and Oxford; but his tenure at the University of Minnesota from 1951 until he retired in 1968 was of longest duration. He gave lectures at countless universities and participated in writing workshops all over the country; he held the Chair of Poetry at the Library of Congress; and he was a panelist on the CBS "Invitation to Learning" program alongside Mark Van Doren, Katherine Anne Porter, John Peale Bishop, Jacques Barzun, and others. He was ever an ambassador of culture, and whatever role he played he showed himself to be a man of almost impeccable taste who was unwilling to compromise with mediocrity. By the 1960s a new generation of poets and critics came along and Tate's influence waned, though honor after honor continued to come to him as they had done during the 1950s. Some felt the esteem in which he was held was overblown, and some of those who disagreed with him or had felt the lash of his critical ire spoke out against him. Perhaps a fair epitaph is to be found in the *New York Times Book Review* assessment (Oct. 12, 1975) of Tate's *Memoirs and Opinions, 1926–1974*: " "One looks on the shape of Allen Tate's career through the refracted medium of these superb essays. If the projected image wavers in the glass of time, it will not be because the author flinched in his commitment to art."

Robert Penn Warren

Robert Penn Warren (1905–   ) was born in Guthrie, in Todd County. In the fall of 1921 he enrolled in Vanderbilt University intending to study science, but like Allen Tate before him he had the good fortune of having his freshman composition with John Crowe Ransom and deciding to become a writer. Tate has left this account of the first time he saw Warren: "He was tall and thin, and when he walked across the room he made a sliding shuffle, as if his bones did not belong to one another. . . . This remarkable young man was "Red," Robert Penn Warren, the most gifted person I have ever known" (*Princeton University Library Chronicle* 3 [April 1942], 81–82). This view Tate later supplemented in a letter to Donald Davidson: "That boy's a wonder—has more genius than any of us; watch him: his work . . . will have what none of us can achieve—power" (Cowan, *The Fugitive Group: A Literary History*, 150).

It was the three men just mentioned—Ransom, Davidson, and Tate—who had an important role in nourishing Warren's early promise, including his being invited to become a member of the Fugitives. Beginning in his junior year, Warren participated in the weekly discussions that took place when the members submitted poems for criticism, and the group gave a great deal of attention to poetic structure. Thus Warren participated in the sort of textual analysis he would later advocate in textbooks written jointly with Cleanth Brooks.

Warren went on to the University of California at Berkeley, where he received his M.A. in English in 1927 and subsequently did advanced study at Yale before receiving a Rhodes Scholarship that took him to Oxford for two years. Thus Warren was too far away from Nashville to be meaningfully associated with the development of Agrarianism, but he did write an essay for *I'll Take My Stand* entitled "The Briar Patch," in which he discussed the race question and advocated gradualism as the best way to improve the lot of blacks. For northern industrialism to try to pull blacks quickly into the work force, he argued, would only worsen the plight of blacks, for their experience and skills were agricultural.

Warren began to be a seriously productive man of letters in the mid-1930s. He had published *John Brown: The Making of a Martyr*, in 1929; but his next volume, *Thirty-Six Poems*, was not to be published until 1935, the year after he became an assistant professor at Louisiana State University. Here he joined Cleanth Brooks, whom he already had known at Vanderbilt and Oxford, and along with Charles W. Pipkin they founded the *Southern Review*. The journal was almost instantly successful and continued so until it ceased publication in 1942, the year Warren joined the faculty at the University of Minnesota. In 1936, with Cleanth Brooks and John T. Purser, Warren published *An Approach to Literature*, the first of several highly influential textbooks that centered attention upon the text and away from biography and the social and cultural context out of which a literary work grows—the approach of the New Criticism as it was soon to be called. In 1938 came *Understanding Poetry* by Warren and Brooks, a volume that virtually wrought a revolution in the teaching of poetry in American colleges and universities. *Night Rider*, Warren's first novel, was published in 1939, followed by *Eleven Poems on the Same Theme* in 1942. *At Heaven's Gate*, along with *Understanding Fiction* (with Brooks), came in 1943; *Selected Poems, 1923–1943*, was next in 1944; then in 1946 came *All the King's Men*, which won Warren's first Pulitzer Prize and the recognition that had escaped him thus far.

Warren's first piece of fiction was "Prime Leaf" (1931), a well-told short story about a boy who watches his father get involved in the Black Patch Tobacco War, the same subject he dealt with later in *Night Rider*. During the first three years of Warren's life the Tobacco Wars raged in Western Kentucky, and Night Riders struck fear into the farmers who refused to join the Planters' Protective Association that had been organized to force manufacturers and exporters to pay the planter a high price for his tobacco. Some planters refused to withhold their tobacco from the market, however, and were paid more money per pound than those who joined the association. As a result many members of the association aligned themselves against the non-members, even to the point of destroying their plant beds and farm equipment or, at the worst, subjecting them to physical violence and burning their tobacco barns. These men were called Night Riders. Guthrie, Warren's birthplace, was the center of the trouble and the place where the Planters' Protective Association was organized in 1903.

At the narrative level *Night Rider* is a fictional account of events in the Black Patch Tobacco War, but, typical of Warren, the central concern of the novel is the truth of human nature. The main character is Percy Munn, a lawyer, who is drawn step by step into the leadership of the Association and away from his peaceful, ordered life. Thus at the core of the novel lies a favorite theme of Warren's—the quest for selfhood, something that Munn never achieves. In the beginning, Munn seeks high prices for tobacco growers but has little interest in anything that does not relate to himself. He is, however, aware of his own emptiness, of being a hollow man. He joins the association and begins to enjoy the involvement. As he becomes a leader, even more he enjoys the decision-making, the mob aspect of his activities, and ultimately the violence. Still, however, he does not find fulfillment as a person, and ultimately as his nighttime activities spill over into his daytime life he loses his wife and home, is accused of a murder he did not commit, goes into hiding, and in the end is shot by soldiers. Munn, in short, dies without achieving a redeeming vision of selfhood. He never even senses himself as adrift or on the wrong course, an essential preliminary to beginning the painful journey to self-knowledge.

Warren was an Agrarian but not a dedicated one, and such Agrarian views as appear in *Night Rider* are incidental to the larger purposes of the novel. One such view may be found in the depiction of the evils of cash-crop farming, a practice that put the tobacco farmer at the mercy of the tobacco corporations. As a result the former were forced to join together in an association in which, eventually, hotheads took matters into their own hands. An Agrarian outlook is also evident in that the hollow men of the novel—Percy Munn and Senator Tolliver—have abandoned the land for other endeavors, thereby losing their bearings. Captain Todd and Willie Proudfit, on the other hand, both men of unfailing honor and integrity, have remained close to the land. But to focus on Agrarian doctrines as central to the novel is to miss its paramount meaning.

Warren's second novel, *At Heaven's Gate* (1943), also has its origins in real people and events. The story is based on the Tennessee business tycoon and securities manipulator, Luke Lea, a former U.S. Senator who went to prison for his financial dealings. The time is the 1920s in an industrialized, urban area of the "New South," where the surrounding rural countryside is seen as potentially yielding up quarries and mines which, under a smooth public relations banner, can be ravaged in the name of "progress," "development," and "expansion." In the novel all this takes place under the aegis of big business and respectable society, of which the center is Bogan Murdock, whose ruthless, unscrupulous methods and manipulations exploit the functionaries who do his bidding. The resolution includes the disintegration and collapse of Murdock's empire and with it the fall of those who participated in its rise.

Like *Night Rider*, *At Heaven's Gate* can be said to reflect Agrarian views and to accurately depict conditions in the post–World War I era. Though there is an absence of the positive features of an Agrarian society, the portrayal of the sickness and emptiness of the age, as well as of the destruction that take place in the collapse of Murdock's empire, can be said to grow out of Warren's Agrarian sympathies and the predicted destructiveness of industrialization and urbanization.

Almost all those associated with Murdock are hollow people who are part of a rootless society, but two in particular fit this description and are central to the progress of the novel. One is Jerry Calhoun, a farm boy and a football hero who became an All-American success in the financial world and is high up in Murdock's financial empire. The other is Murdock's daughter, Sue, likewise a sort of All-American girl who, while despising her father and all that he symbolizes, is a sportswoman and a dabbler in art, and thus like her father lives off the efforts of others. Despite all their advantages, however, both of these characters feel the emptiness of their lives. For a short time Jerry and Sue seek to find their identity in having an affair with each other, but their sensuous indulgence is joyless and they drift apart and further lose their sense of direction. Subsequently Sue becomes involved sexually with two other men, both of whom despise her father just as she does: Slim Sarrett, an intellectual, a poet, and a boxer whose sexual ambivalence is symptomatic of other troubles, and Jason Sweetwater, a Marxist organizer and strike promoter who seeks to find a sense of purpose in "righting economic wrongs." Sue, who comes to a violent end because of her amours, never finds herself. In a sense she is the precursor of Samantha Starr of *Band of Angels* with her cry of "O, who am I?" just as Percy Munn and Bogan Murdock are forerunners of Willie Stark in *All the King's Men*. There are other confused people in the novel, but among them only Jerry Calhoun finds partial redemption when at last he recognizes Murdock for what he is and returns to the home of his dirt-farmer father to begin to discover himself.

Warren's leap from apprenticeship in *Night Rider* and *At Heaven's Gate* to mastery in *All the King's Men* (1946) was not really foretold in the earlier novels. *All the King's Men* was one of those rare novels that are both a critical and a popular success. This verdict was not unanimous, but many reviewers and readers saw it as "a great and enduring novel," a judgment that has not been negated to this day, for it still holds an exalted position among the novels of the middle third of the century. At least two reviewers correctly predicted that it would win a Pulitzer Prize, and others spoke words of praise that ranged from comment on the overall force and power of the novel to enthusiastic commendation of the way Warren uses "the full resources of the American language." The *New Republic* (Sept. 2, 1946) compares *All the King's Men* with *Moby Dick*, *Huckleberry Finn*, *The Sun Also Rises*, and *The Great Gatsby*. A few reviews were unfavorable and found faults ranging from "the language would shame a pagan hottentot" to "the novel seems to justify [Huey] Long and the intellectuals who played ball with him." In the main, however, those who found defects saw them merely as blemishes on a work of great excellence.

The forty years since *All the King's Men* was written have wrought changes in critical perspectives. When it appeared in 1946, most critics and readers thought of it as a political novel in which Willie Stark was a thinly disguised version of Huey Long, Louisiana's assassinated dictatorlike governor. Today, younger readers who did not read of "The Kingfish" in the daily press are more likely to think the novel has moral import and an informed, strong political base. Time and a more thoughtful reading of the novel have also reduced the centrality of the role of the demagogue Willie Stark. The action may center around Willie, but the narrator, Jack Burden, provides the windows through which the various characters, including Willie, are viewed and understood. It may be said, in fact, that Warren's happy use of a narrator such as Burden does much to give the novel its excellence.

Burden is a newspaper reporter when he first meets Willie, then a struggling, idealistic young lawyer from Mason City pushed into a losing gubernatorial race by a political faction in order to split the opposition vote. Later when Willie runs for governor again, Jack Burden leaves his newspaper job, goes to work for him, becomes his right-hand man in politics, and remains with him until the very last, when Willie is mortally wounded by an assassin in the foyer of the state capitol.

Burden, descended of a patrician family of Burden's Landing, went to college and then to law school, but abandoned a legal career for the study of history and the editing of the journal of Cass Mastern, a kinsman, for his doctoral dissertation. Then, beset with a sense of purposelessness, Jack turns his back upon his aristocratic background and professional goals and turns to the upstart, "poor white" Willie Stark, who has promised to fight against entrenched political power and obtain a fairer share of the benefits of government for the poor and others who have been all but disenfranchised. As the pace quickens, Willie's need and desire for power blinds him to his earlier idealism. Burden is troubled, but he tells himself that the objectives are good and that this neutralizes the disregard that Willie has developed for law and excuses the blackmail and the corrupt practices that he fosters in order to gain his ends. He carries out whatever assignments Willie gives him, including research into the lives of Willie's enemies, and accepts Willie's contention that all men are incurably evil and that in every man's past there is a blemish that reveals his hidden flaw. One such investigation, in fact, leads Burden to realize that he has in effect killed his own father and has been in part responsible for Willie's death. With Willie dead and himself finally free of his Burden's Landing past, Jack has found his own identity and will go back into politics, this time with his friend Hugh Miller, a man of principle and integrity.

A commentary on *All the King's Men* might best conclude by quoting one of the finest passages in the book. Jack Burden is discussing the subject of his dissertation, but his analysis is applicable to anyone's life and the interconnectedness of all of life:

> Cass Mastern lived for a few years and in that time he learned that the world is all of one piece. He learned that the world is like an enormous spider web and if you touch it, however lightly, at any point, the vibration ripples to the remotest perimeter and the drowsy spider feels the tingle and is drowsy no more but springs out to fling the gossamer coils about you who have touched the web and then injects the black, numbing poison under your hide. It does not matter whether or not you meant to brush the web of things. Your happy foot or your gay wing may have brushed it ever so lightly, but what happens always happens and there is the spider, bearded black and with his great faceted eyes glittering like mirrors in the sun, or like God's eye, and the fangs dripping.

This statement is perhaps the central metaphor that controls the whole book.

World Enough and Time (1950), the novel that many regard as Warren's second best, grew out of actual events widely known as "The Kentucky Tragedy," which were detailed in the section on Thomas Holley Chivers. To repeat briefly, Jereboam O. Beauchamp, a young attorney, hears the story of how Solomon P. Sharp, solicitor-general of Kentucky, seduced and abandoned Ann Cook, whereupon Beauchamp impetuously seeks Ann out and proposes marriage. Ann accepts on the condition that Beauchamp kill Sharp. This is done in Frankfort on the night of November 6, 1825, and in due course Beauchamp is arrested, tried, and found guilty of murder. Ann joins him in the cell where he awaits execution, and the night before the date of the execution the two try unsuccessfully to commit suicide by taking laudanum. When the attempt fails, Beauchamp stabs Ann to death and wounds himself but lives long enough to be hanged the next day. By their own request the two were placed in a single coffin and buried in the cemetery at Bloomfield.

Among Warren's predecessors—besides Chivers—who made use of these melodramatic events are Edgar Allan Poe, Charlotte Barnes, Charles F. Hoffman, and William Gilmore Simms. Warren reworks the tale, giving the events universal moral significance that is applicable to the present. The proper names and details of the plot are changed. Jereboam Beauchamp becomes Jeremiah Beaumont, Ann Cook becomes Rachel Jordan, Colonel Solomon P. Sharp becomes Colonel Cassius Fort, and other characters are added, dropped, or given new names. Warren reduces the melodramatic sensationalism and lurid romance by inventing an unnamed historian who has ferreted out the details of the story and tells it in objective fashion. In addition, Warren shifts the focus of the story from the sentimental, revenge-minded Rachel Jordan to the idealistic but confused Jeremiah Beaumont. Beaumont is another Warren character in search of self-knowledge. To Warren the most important thing is not Jeremiah's legal punishment but the growth of his personal insights that lead him to accept responsibility not only for his own deeds but for the events produced by them.

No subjects have held Warren's interest longer than slavery, the Civil War, and the attainment of rights by blacks. Beginning in 1929 with *John Brown, the Making of a Martyr*, Warren published no fewer than seven volumes on these subjects, together with a well-known essay, "The Briar Patch." The focus continues in four other nonfiction volumes—*Segregation: The Inner Conflict in the South* (1956); *The Legacy of the Civil War: Meditations on the Centennial* (1961); *Who Speaks for the Negro?* (1965); *Jefferson Davis Gets His Citizenship Back* (1980)—and two novels, *Band of Angels* (1955) and *Wilderness: A Tale of the Civil War* (1961). To Warren the Civil War was the nation's greatest and most intense struggle in its search for a national identity, a theme that parallels the individual's search for personal identity. Indeed, in *Band of Angels* the search at the personal and national levels may be said to merge.

The central figure of *Band of Angels* is Amantha Starr, the only child of a "widowed" plantation owner in Kentucky. Just before the Civil War "Mandy" is suddenly called home from her college studies because of her father's death, and soon she learns that her mother was a slave, that she therefore is of Negro blood and a chattel possession, and that as such she will be "sold" into slavery in the settlement of her father's estate. The remainder of the novel concerns Mandy's search for an answer to the question she utters in the opening sentence of the novel, "O, who am I?" Amantha's discovery of a new identity is long, painful, and subtle. She must get beyond thinking of herself as "poor little Mandy" or saying to herself that her plight is not really her fault or hoping that she can find someone who will somehow "save me." She must cease to confuse freedom with not being a slave, must abandon the notion that self-discovery and self-sufficiency can come through other people, must come to see that only she can free herself and come to terms with the world and herself.

A lesser-known Civil War novel by Warren is *Wilderness: A Tale of the Civil War* (1961). It is the story of a Bavarian ghetto Jew, Adam Rosenzweig, who in 1863, inspired by European revolutionary zeal, comes to the United States to help free the slaves. This he does by joining the Union cause, though in a civilian capacity because of his deformity—a twisted foot. Like *Band of Angels, Wilderness* has much to say about the nature of freedom, but the plot revolves around a search for identity—Adam Rosenzweig's search for "what a man must know to be a man." It is not, as one might expect, a typical war novel with cavalry charges or plantation scenes; rather, it is heavily weighted with ideas.

To anyone familiar with the exalted position that Warren holds as a writer but unfamiliar with the critical evaluation his novels have received, it must come as a surprise to learn that much of it has been negative. Even *All the King's Men* had its detractors, and *World Enough and Time* received a substantial share of adverse criticism as well as praise. Even the reviewers who praise Warren's work often qualify their praise. Of the major novels, *The Cave* (1959) met with the most adverse criticism, though it must be noted that it also received enthusiastic commendation from some of our most distinguished writers and critics: "This is one of the country's finest novels in years" (Paul Engle in the *Chicago Sunday Tribune*, Aug. 23, 1959); "Warren at his best, and they don't come much better than that" (Arthur Mizener in the *New York Times*, Aug. 23, 1959); "There is nowhere a point at which one can willingly put the book down" (Granville Hicks in the *Saturday Review*, Aug. 22, 1959). But these judgments are matched by others in a different key: ". . . he throws in incidents and data that are largely, if not wholly, irrelevant. His style runs to overwriting and to a stagy intensity" (Charles Rolo in *Atlantic*, Oct. 1959); ". . . his instinct for melodrama has unhappily run wild" (*London Times Literary Supplement*, Nov. 27, 1959); ". . . cheap shock effects. . . . Trash-novel episodes . . . seamily detailed personal histories" (Melvin Madocks in *Christian Science Monitor*, Sept. 24, 1959).

The Cave grew out of events associated with the attempt to rescue Floyd Collins, a real-life Kentucky cave explorer, from a crawl-passage where he had been trapped when a dislodged rock pinned his foot. He could be freed only by sinking a shaft to the point where he lay, and when he was reached, after eighteen days, he was dead. In the meantime the event captured national headlines, and a tent city sprang up near the cave mouth. "Thousands of people . . . had come. They had wept, and prayed, and boozed, and sung and fought, and fornicated, and in all ways possible had striven to break through to the heart of the mystery which was themselves." The action traces three days in the lives of a dozen or so people in the nearby town, called Johnstown. Both major and minor characters are caught up in the crisis situation, look into themselves as grievers and searchers, and seek a meaning and purpose for their lives. Jasper Herrick, the cave-crawler based on Collins, never appears in the action, but through him the Collins story becomes a variation on Plato's allegory of the cave. Jasper is trapped in a literal cave, but each of the other characters is trapped within the figurative cave of his or her nature, each mistaking shadows for reality. Each must find his own true self, just as Jasper, ironically, had found himself in being a compulsive caver. His mother remembers his saying, ". . . in the ground at least a fellow has a chance of knowing who he is." With its symbolism and search for identity the novel stretches the mind and the patience of many readers, but as in other Warren novels its purpose is beyond the narrative level.

The Cave was the last of what some would call Warren's major novels. He was to write four more—*Wilderness* (1961), *Flood* (1964), *Meet Me in the Green Glen* (1971), and *A Place to Come To* (1977)—but no one of them gained much critical or popular approval. From this point onward Warren's poetry would greatly overshadow his fiction.

Though *Circus in the Attic and Other Stories* (1948), Warren's only collection of short stories, contains one story—"Blackberry Winter"—that some critics regard as one of the great stories of American literature, neither Warren nor his critics consider the short story the genre to which the author's talents are best suited. His gift in fiction has been for sustained narrative and invention, a fact that makes the short story form seem cramped for him.

"Blackberry Winter" is a story told by a man of around forty years who looks back to a day in his life when he was nine years old and to a great rain—"a gully washer"—that has brought devastation into the life of the community. It is an unseasonably cool day in June, a "blackberry winter" day, when blackberries are ripe, and the boy is pestering his mother to let him go barefoot in spite of the cold. The narrator conducts us through the events and sights of the day: the drowned chickens; a dead cow floating down a swollen creek; the trash washed out from under Dellie's neat cabin; the consternation when Dellie, suffering from "woman mizry," uncharacteristically slaps her son, Little Jebb. Questions form and half-form about the world the boy sees and is puzzled by, and he feels secure when his father lifts him onto the horse and into the comfort of his arms as they watch the rushing, swirling stream. Later he asks Old Jebb what Dellie's "woman mizry" is:

> "Hit is the change," he said, "Hit is the change of life and time."
> "What change?"
> "You too young to know."
> "Tell me."
> "Time come and you find out everything."

But most striking of all is the stranger, the sullen tramp with a menacing knife, who appears as if washed up by the storm or out of the woods. The boy asks, "Where did you come from" and "Where are you going?" to which the man replies, cursing him, "You don't stop following me and I cut yore throat, you little-son-of-a-bitch." Then after a brief retrospect by the narrator over the thirty-five years since the tramp leaned his face down at him, he concludes, "That was what he said, for me not to follow him. But I did follow him all the years." The story, then, is the progress of a boy who wanted to stay barefooted but is in the process of making his transition into manhood; an initiation into the adult world as the boy-now-man remembers some of the things that puzzled him when he was nine.

Though Warren had published three volumes of verse by 1944—*Thirty-Six Poems* (1935), *Eleven Poems on the Same Theme* (1943), and *Selected Poems, 1923–1943* (1944)—and had won a place as a poet of respectable promise, it was not until 1953 that he published another volume, followed by another in 1957. Until this time his fiction had overshadowed his poetry, but with the appearance of *Brother to Dragons* (1953) and *Promises* (1957) the long dry spell was at an end and he was fully launched upon the career that was to become "my central and obsessive concern." He won the 1957 Pulitzer Prize in Poetry for *Promises* and therewith became the first writer to win the honor in both poetry and prose. Even so, his best years still lay ahead, for he would grow in stature as a poet and would win yet another Pulitzer Prize for *Now and Then: Poems, 1978–1979*. Warren had become regarded by many as the foremost man of letters in the country.

During his years of poetic drought, says Warren in an interview with Marshall Walker on September 11, 1975, "I got so I could not finish a short poem. I wrote, started many over that period of years. I never finished one. . . . I'd write five lines, ten lines, twenty lines—it would die on me." It was in the summer of 1954 that he regained his talent for lyric verse and a "new sense of poetry," following his divorce from his first wife in 1951, his marriage to Eleanor Clark in 1952, and the birth of his two children. The renewal came while he was living with his family in a ruined fortress on the Italian coast about one hundred miles north of Rome. From this renewal three years later was to come *Promises: Poems, 1954–1956*, and the beginning of the most distinguished stage of Warren's career.

Here we must first look back to *Selected Poems, 1923–1943* and two earlier poems, and note the development of Warren's "new sense of poetry." In *Selected Poems* there was one poem of consequence that had not appeared in either of the two earlier volumes. This was "The Ballad of Billie Potts." It was unlike the compressed, intricately wrought lyrics such as "Bearded Oaks," which had their origins in Warren's Fugitive days and showed the influence of the seventeenth-century English Metaphysical Poets. It was a benchmark poem in Warren's poetic and artistic development. Billie Potts runs a frontier inn in that area of Western Kentucky between the Tennessee and Cumberland rivers known as "the land between the rivers" (now "between the lakes"). There he offers hospitality to travelers and he and an accomplice rob and often murder guests at or on their way to the inn. One day Billie's son, Little Billie, sent to apprise an accomplice of the approach of an affluent traveler, attempts to kill the man himself, only to fail and be wounded in the effort. Little Billie quarrels with his parents, sets out for the West, and after ten years returns, wealthy and well pleased with himself. He withholds his identity when he goes to the inn, however, in order "to tease 'em and fun 'em." His plan works, but not alas for his own good, for his father takes him for a real stranger and kills him for the money he thinks he has.

One evidence of Warren's development in this poem is the free, relaxed manner in which the author handles the archetypal themes of loss of innocence and the undiscovered self. Warren's earlier verse was full of the passage of childhood into the tainted world of adults, but here there is a development in freedom and depth with the "land between the rivers" setting, for there are echoes of the traditional Garden of Eden in Mesopotamia, which also was "between the rivers," and of the Adam and Eve theme. More significant artistically, however, is the device that may have come to Warren from his study of

Coleridge's *Rime of the Ancient Mariner*. In his celebrated essay on that poem ("A Poem of Pure Imagination") Warren notes that the tale is concerned with the problem of "crime and punishment and repentance and reconciliation" and that Coleridge uses the glosses on the margins so that the author can enter the story as a sort of stage manager and thus be able to comment on the action and call the reader's attention to avenues of thought that he might miss or not understand. Warren gains a comparable effect by interspersing through "The Ballad of Billie Potts" commentary by a twentieth-century man who calls attention to the larger implications of the story. This commentary is at a rather formal level and contrasts with the vernacular, sometimes coarsely comic, level of the ballad-like narrative. Through this device Warren arrives at the universal "you" that he would use over and over during the years ahead. This device he would use in *Brother to Dragons* in 1953 by having "R.P.W." play a role in the long narrative poem. He had, in short, found a means of moving in and out of such a poem as he had already learned to do in fiction. This was important for the years ahead and the lyric poetry he would soon begin writing, not only because of the universal "you" effect but because of the ways of injecting into his poetry a more personal and more meditative quality, a greater sense of honesty and sincerity. He would come, for example, to see, as one critic put it, that a "certain rawboned vigor (both of attitude and word)" could serve him well, and he learned to cultivate with good effect the use of vernacular and a more formal style. In *Promises* Warren would first fully employ the new manner that led to his increasing mastery, making the years after he was sixty the most distinguished period of his life. But here we must first note *Brother to Dragons* (1953) as marking the beginning, or at least the transition, to Warren's progress into the period of his greatest mastery.

Brother to Dragons was a tale of violence also out of Kentucky history, albeit not in ballad form. In 1807 Lilburn and Randolph Lewis, nephews of Thomas Jefferson and cousins of the celebrated explorer of the Northwest, Meriwether Lewis, migrated from Virginia to Livingston County, Kentucky, and bought separate tracts of land near the frontier town of Smithland. Among other members of the family and farm retinue were another brother, Isham, and a slave named George, a teenager and a sort of body-servant to Lilburn. During the four years following the arrival of the Lewises, Lilburn's mother Lucy died, as also did his wife. Lilburn's personal and business affairs deteriorated and the master who had been known as firm but fair became erratic and unreasonable and began to drink too much. On Sunday evening, December 15, 1811, Lilburn, drinking heavily, ordered George to bring water from the spring in a pitcher that had belonged to Lilburn's mother. Somehow George broke the pitcher and Lilburn in a drunken rage, with Isham's help, dragged George into the kitchen cabin adjoining the house and bound him carefully. Then he and Isham assembled the slaves, locked the door, and told the slaves that they were going to be given a lesson about disobeying orders. Apparently Lilburn took a swing at George with the axe and almost decapitated him, after which he forced another slave to dismember George's body and place the dismembered parts on the fire and burn them so that no evidence would remain. This dismemberment and burning, coupled with Lilburn's ranting, continued past the midnight hour. At 2:00 a.m., the orgy still not over, the earth began to shake and the cabin to rumble. What was perhaps the worst earthquake ever to hit the North American continent had just started.

The epicenter of the quake was at New Madrid, Missouri, just across the Mississippi River from Fulton County, Kentucky. The land in both Kentucky and Missouri became as rolling waves not unlike a long swell of the sea. As the swells undulated, trees tilted until their branches became entangled. The river beds heaved and sank, and for one short while the Mississippi flowed northward. Thousands of acres of land sank twenty-five feet or more and filled with water, forming great lakes, of which Reelfoot Lake, twenty miles long and from one to five miles across, is the best known but not the largest. Two counties away in Lilburn's cabin a sense of terror and awe seized the occupants as the chimney collapsed upon the fire and George's sizzling remains. Other quakes followed, and when daylight came Lilburn rebuilt the fireplace and chimney, hiding pieces of bone and unburned flesh as best he could in the masonry. Subsequently Lilburn either killed himself or was killed in an intended double-suicide. Isham was tried and was sentenced to be hanged but escaped and, by report, was killed three years later in the Battle of New Orleans.

The murder itself and the coincidence of a devastating earthquake on the same night clearly fascinated Warren, but even more fascinating to him were the philosophical and moral implications of the fact that the two nephews of Thomas Jefferson—sons of his sister—should have been the principals in the crime and that the whole set of events should have gone unrecorded in Jefferson's papers.

As the creative process got under way, Warren first considered writing a novel on the subject, then a drama, and finally a literary work that "contains some of the features of a narrative poem, a poetic drama, and a philosophical dialogue, with a commentator," who is, as noted earlier, Warren himself. Thus the poem, which carries forward the technique that Warren first employed in "The Ballad of Billie Potts," has eleven characters who are directly or peripherally involved in the murder or its backgrounds, among them "R.P.W." Through dialogue that pushes beyond the sordid facts of the murder itself, the poem becomes a study of good and evil as these characters meditate upon the crime and the irrational mixture of good and evil in the world. The arguments are too extensive to be followed here, but meaning does emerge as the implications of the crime are clarified and two questions answered: Why did Lilburn do it? Can Jefferson reconcile his optimistic confidence in the natural goodness of man, his belief in perfectibility, with the evil done by his own kin? To this end the questions of "R.P.W." challenge Jefferson's doctrine of innate goodness and his belief that because man is a reasoning creature he is also a reasonable one. Jefferson's sister Lucy, the mother of the killers, reflecting the understandings of the heart, drives home the point that the very best of us are compounded of good and evil and that even Jefferson himself is capable of great violence and evil. Seeing in Lilburn's crime a negation of his beliefs, Jefferson, the creature of reason, comes to the acknowledgment of his own dark side and his likeness to Job, who after a just and upright life is obliged to acknowledge himself to be "a brother to dragons." All men, in short—not just Lilburn and Isham Lewis—are capable of evil.

Promises: Poems, 1954–1956, appeared thirteen years after Warren had published his last volume of lyric verse. It is at once apparent that the author's "new poetry" differs from his earlier verse in ways already noted: the language is less "literary" and more colloquial, the manner more direct and personal, more reflective and meditative; the focus is on the poet's thoughts and feelings; the tone is more optimistic, though at no time can Warren be called a cheerful optimist. The subjects are his children, Rosanna and Gabriel, and his own childhood, which becomes the link between the generations. Though the poet is in Italy, Kentucky is often the subject about which he writes. There is "Country Burying," for example, and a vivid recollection of a threshing day in "Boy's Will, Joyful Labor without Pay, and Harvest Home," and "Summer Storm and God's Grace," which is reminiscent of "Blackberry Winter." Not all, however, is pleasant or cheerful or warm. In "Infant Boy at Midcentury" he writes, "You come in the world when promises are broken . . . When the young expect little. . . ." There are two lullabies to his son and the lovely "The Flower" and other poems to his daughter; there is a change of pace to the vernacular in "Go It, Granny—Go It, Hog"; and there is the darker view of "Dark Night of the Soul," which suggests that humankind at the mercy of itself. The topics are almost as many as the poems themselves, and the tone and mood as varied.

Between *Promises* and *New and Selected Poems, 1923–1985*, published in April 1985 on his eightieth birthday, Warren brought out twelve more volumes of verse and year by year grew in stature and reputation. As he continued to write it began to be perceived that he was perhaps becoming a major poet. In a review of *You, Emperors and Others* (1961) the *Yale Review* (March 1961) declares: "Warren may come to be remembered as a poet who also wrote novels." Five years later the *New York Times Book Review* (Oct. 9, 1966) says of *Selected Poems: New and Old, 1923–1966*: "Some of the best poetry of our day." The *New Republic* (Sept. 30, 1978) writes in more august tones of the volume that was soon to win Warren's second Pulitzer Prize in poetry, *Now and Then: Poems, 1976–1978*: "Like Hardy, Yeats, and Stevens, Warren is at his strongest past 70. He is achieving the height in verse that Faulkner did in prose." *Newsweek* (Aug. 25, 1980) says of *Being There: Poetry, 1977–1980*: "Warren's poetry keeps getting better and better . . . profound simplicity that marks the best autumnal poetry." The *Atlantic* (Dec. 1981) says of *Rumor Verified: Poems: 1979–1980*, "Staying Power is rarely a feature of genius . . . but Robert Penn Warren has gained strength with the years," and the (London) *Times Literary Supplement* (Jan. 29, 1982) says of the same volume, ". . . he has taken on the mantle of the vatic poet and turned his own life into an exemplar. The lyric 'I' in these poems is simply man at his best: simple, learned, loving, and completely human."

How can one in brief space here give an adequate notion of the twelve volumes of verse that Warren wrote between 1957 and 1985 and that have elicited such judgments? It serves only a slight purpose to say of volumes not already mentioned that *Incarnations: Poems, 1966–1968* (1968) is a collection of poems written since *Selected Poems: Old and New, 1923–1966*; or that *Audubon: A Vision* (1969) is a series of poems individual but related that, taken together, constitute a single, unified poem about the great naturalist who lived in Kentucky much of his life; or that the title of *Rumor Verified: Poems, 1974–1980*, suggests that no one can escape the limitations of the human condition. Nor is it enough to provide commentary on a representative poem or two in each of the volumes, with here and there an excerpt to exemplify contents and style.

Perhaps a clue to an overview of Warren's poetry may be found in an article that Warren published in the *New York Times Book Review* (May 12, 1985) called "Poetry Is a Kind of Unconscious Autobiography." Here Warren, who has steadfastly said that he would never write his autobiography or give assistance to a biographer, writes: "Not long back at a cocktail party, a lady, being polite, asked me if I was going to write an autobiography. I was startled, never having thought of such a thing, and I seemed to hear my rude answer so clearly that, for a fraction of a second, I thought I had uttered it: 'Hell no—I've done that already. . . . For poetry is a kind of unconscious autobiography.' " If this is correct, the answer to the question of what to say about Warren is to be found in his verse. Not in any single volume but in all of them collectively. Ideas and themes naturally appear and reappear as they take on new shape or are reinforced and enriched as the passing of time brings maturity to the poet and provides new dimensions to what he has to say. Victor Strandberg (*The Poetic Vision of Robert Penn Warren*, 22) estimates, for example, that "roughly half of the poems Warren has written over a fifty-five-year career as a poet" have dealt with the passage from innocence into a tainted or fallen world and the consequent search for a new footing.

In amplifying his statement that "poetry is a kind of unconscious autobiography," Warren ponders the question of why "you are drawn to write about certain things" and in the process suggests the contents of his poetry: "Certain characters. Problems. Situations. Landscapes. Birds. Certain long-forgotten events"—and why the mind returns to them after many years. One is reminded of one's own experience with the passing of the years and how events long since forgotten (remembering Wordsworth) undergo "tranquil restoration" and how "feelings too of unremembered pleasure . . . little, nameless, unremembered acts" are recollected, fit themselves slowly into patterns, and take on meanings that help to shed light on "this unintelligible world."

In two separate places Warren speaks of how the subjects of poetry come to him. First, he mentions "something coming out of my country summers at my bookish old grandfather's remote farm —the sound of some tenant farmer picking his box, at night, in the distance, and singing a ballad, a lantern-lit revival (white or black) and the wail of a hardened sinner struck down by God A-mighty in the 'straw pen,' a lynching, or the sound of a 'holler,' musical in the distance, from some Negro man cabin-bound after a day in the tobacco field." Then later in the essay he writes, "The recollection might be that of the sudden blood-blur on your windshield when, long years back, you were headed west at seventy miles an hour, and a pheasant, lifting from the brush, smacked the glass with a bloody explosion, cutting off your first magical glimpse of a snow-range at utmost distance. But now in the random recollection, the event seemed to be telling me something, something about history—and the title of the poem becomes suddenly 'Going West'—a beautiful land blurred with blood. Or the golden-headed baby's hand grasping for a hedge-bloom at always the same spot while being carried home from the beach. Or the vision of a hawk at sunset, years back, above the Tetons. Or simply the wondering what, some thirty-odd years before, had made you swim west, and west, in the moonlit Pacific, enslaved by your rhythm until exhaustion told you it was now or never. Or the memory of standing, alone, in the middle of the great circle of the desert with your eyes lifted to the moon."

But not only are there strikingly individual subjects and moments in Warren's work but also subjects that he has used often enough with variations that they may be called thematic and sometimes mythic. We noted above his frequent evocation of the rites of passage, the loss of innocence in a world of experience, and the trial of new beginnings. Here obviously the passage of time is a vital theme—a matter of unending concern to Warren as he tries to understand himself and the world he lives in. His perspective on time is both individual and collective, for it is not only the poet's own personal past that interests him, but the pasts of family and friends and the community and world of which these are a part, for all flesh is interrelated. And as he remembers father and grandfather he remembers too the close friend of his youth, "a woodsman who knew the track of every animal (even that of a field mouse in mud or dirt) and, sitting on a log, could whistle almost any bird up." And he remembers and writes about Todd County and the tobacco wars in *Night Rider*; the Kentucky frontier and the immediate post-frontier in "The Ballad of Billie Potts," *Brother to Dragons*, and *World Enough and Time*; and slavery in *Band of Angels*.

Warren, in short, is concerned with the basic spiritual problems of people, with the human condition and often with violence where the moral order is involved. It is a confused and troubled world that he sees, where the old verities and belief in God have faded; and he counsels, not despair, but the need for each individual to work out the code by which he will interpret the world he lives in. In a sense, then, Warren is a philosophical poet, but he is the first to say that for "a man like me" philosophy is not "a finished product. . . . It's a way of thinking about your life as you live." Self-knowledge is the end in view and that is a process of continuous and never-completed becoming, for the self is forever becoming a new self as one's relationship to others and the world changes; it never becomes a fixed, knowable object or thing. Almost everything Warren has written is concerned ultimately with self-knowledge and the world he lives in, including the perverseness of man himself. He is alarmed because of the decline in the understanding of history and of things past, because of the rootlessness of people, the absence of a sense of belonging, and a lack of a sense of place. Humanity is faced with a grim plight, but the world is not a cheerless place and not a place to be afraid of. Should we look back over our shoulder for the "creak of the wing-joint gigantic in the distance?" he asks. The answer is a resounding "No!": "I beg you not to look back, in God's name." As for himself,

> . . . I love the world even in my anger,
> And love is a hard thing to outgrow.

Such views reflect the Warren of the later years: *Now and Then* (1978) and *Being There* (1980), even *New and Selected Poems, 1923–1985*, which in a sense constitute a summing up, though these are the themes and the thoughts that have long been the benchmarks of Warren's philosophy. One can only regret that there is not space enough to quote lines that adequately exemplify both the poet's views and his ways of expressing them. The range is great: there is the Warren of beauty, the Warren of anger, and the Warren of sentiment and gentleness and love; the Warren of coarse comedy and explicit earthy shock, of shimmering gossamer and of sudden explosiveness and violence.

Such are the main features of the literary career of one who many would agree to be the most distinguished author that Kentucky has produced and perhaps also the most distinguished American writer living today. Yet we have not even alluded to his volumes devoted to Theodore Dreiser, William Faulkner, Randall Jarrell, Herman Melville, and John Greenleaf Whittier in which he provides criticism and analysis and a selection from their writings. There are those who have said that the fifty-odd volumes he has written or edited have been too many and that some of them are not up to the level they should be; but the criticism of detractors has never seemed to bother Warren, who has kept his productive level high, has been the recipient of almost every award a writer can receive, and has been hailed as one of the great American writers of all time. The most recent recognition is his being appointed the nation's first Poet Laureate.

Though Warren has been adept as a poet and as a novelist and highly skilled as a practical critic, it seems likely that he will live longest as a poet—though *All the King's Men* shows no signs of yielding up its place of eminence. Nothing has distinguished Warren's long career so much as the late flowering of his poetic powers, during which he became both a more prolific and steadily better poet. His *New and Selected Poems, 1923–1985*, presumably well represents the poetry he is willing to trust his reputation to; and indeed it reflects well the informal, personal, and meditative poem that has become the trademark of the work that traces back to *Promises* and even to "The Ballad of Billy Potts."

One cannot reduce the essence of Warren's poetry or fiction to some thesis about human life. A "moral statement" can be said to be central to each of his major works and to all of his poetry collectively, but no single statement can be large enough to encompass what they say. We have noted some meanings in passing and have seen how some of the views have been present from his earliest work to his last. As adequate as any other statement, perhaps, is one that says he is constantly concerned with the meaning of the past and the need to understand and accept the past if one is to live meaningfully in the present. He takes a rather dim view of the human condition, and he offers no short-cuts or any easy solutions; but he does see the possibility of ultimate triumph, and he does not counsel despair as the individual works out a faith to live by.

CHAPTER 16

"Agrarians" and Agrarians

Introduction

Agrarianism has been a part of the literature of every nation and every age, but here we are concerned with the word in a particularized as well as in the generic sense. In the first sense we are concerned with the Agrarian Movement that grew out of the Nashville "Fugitive" group. Early in the 1920s a group of individuals—mostly students and teachers at Vanderbilt University—began meeting weekly to discuss their own poetry. Chief among them were Tennesseans John Crowe Ransom, Donald Davidson, and Merrill Moore, and Kentuckians Allen Tate and Robert Penn Warren. Soon the group was publishing *The Fugitive* (1922–25), a "little magazine" of poetry and criticism that anticipated the agrarianism that was to receive full expression in the symposium *I'll Take My Stand: The South and the Agrarian Tradition* five years after *The Fugitive* had ceased publication. Here "Twelve Southerners" took their stand against the industrialization and urbanization that was transforming the South following World War I and was, they believed, leading to community break-up by undermining the individual's self-identity and sense of having a personal relationship to the world.

Between World War I and *I'll Take My Stand* the South was very rural. In 1919 approximately half of its population made a living from farming, and most of the non-farming population lived in small towns and villages; only 4 percent lived in cities of 100,000 or more. Family ties were strong, and family reunions and community homecomings were important events that brought kinsfolk home from great distances. A strong strain of puritanism was reflected in religious conservatism and fundamentalist interpretation of the Bible. The South was the stronghold of Prohibition, though there was hard drinking and the ever-present brown paper bag at social gatherings. And there was a mellow view of the Old South, of which the Lost Cause of the Confederacy was an important ingredient.

Simultaneously, however, there were advocates of the New South who deplored the economic dependence of the South on the North for manufactured goods; and there were textile mills in the Carolinas, steel mills in Alabama, oil and chemical industries in Louisiana and Texas. In general, commerce and industry were beginning to flourish and the skylines of tall buildings to rise in Atlanta and other large cities. The national image of the Old South continued to be one of moonlight and magnolias, a notion gained in part from the turn-of-the-century local colorists, who were read as avidly by northerners as by southerners. But what most caught the attention of northern social critics, editors, politicians, and preachers was the South as the home of racial discrimination, religious fundamentalism, political conservatism, and a backward economy. Most flamboyant and best known among these critics was Henry L. Mencken, whose characterization of the South as "the Bible Belt" has not even yet disappeared.

Such was the world and the setting out of which the 1930 manifesto of the Agrarians grew. In part, this world was still the "Old South" and in part the "New South," and in both instances it was behind the rest of the nation when judged by the usual national measurements of "progress." *I'll Take My Stand* was, of course, an intellectual response, but it was also a "southern" response and doubtless was written with a sense of the South's having been "aggrieved," as Donald Davidson put it, as "a region full of little else but lynchings, shootings, chain gangs, poor whites, Ku Klux-ers, hookworms, pellagra, and a few decayed patricians. . . ." Thus *I'll Take My Stand* was intended to set the facts aright, to identify and portray what the "Twelve Southerners" regarded as the southern tradition, and to delineate a course for the future that would be in harmony with the agrarian past and avoid the menace of industrialization.

Naturally the Agrarians looked back to the historical South as they sought for a role model that would enable them to avoid the mistakes they saw the "impersonal," "soulless," industrialized urban Northeast as having made. They saw the Old South—pre–World War I and antebellum—as a more leisurely world where there were happy, meaningful relationships and the individual had a sense of identity with the world. The good life was seen as based on nonmaterialistic values. Such a culture—a proven regional culture—they regarded as adequate to meet economic needs and satisfy the intellectual, religious, social, and aesthetic needs of a people. Thus for the Agrarians the South of the past came to serve as a metaphor for the good life.

The agrarians (not capitalized) were never organized as a group as the Fugitives had been, and only Ransom, Davidson, Tate, and Warren among them ever became Agrarians (capitalized). There was not even uniformity of belief among the Agrarians: each spoke for himself. Nevertheless, something resembling a united front emerged and pointed the way for an individual to achieve a meaningful relationship with the universe. The fate of the Agrarian movement was not unlike that of the proletarian and leftist groups of the 1930s. Members of each group, dissatisfied with the direction in which America was going, found their identity by giving themselves to a cause larger than themselves. The Agrarians rejected "the old high-caste Brahmins of the Old South" and the sentimentality of the earlier local color writers, but they did reconstruct what they regarded as the best features and virtues of the agrarian past by comparing life in this earlier time with life in the industrial present. Today, some understanding of Agrarian principles can not only guide readers to a better comprehension of Robert Penn Warren, Allen Tate, Caroline Gordon, and others, but also provide insight into one of the many well-intentioned movements that sought to protest against the dehumanization of society.

Caroline Gordon

Caroline Gordon (1895–1981), novelist, short story writer, and critic, was never a Fugitive or a signer of Agrarian manifestoes, but the place where she was born and brought up gave her familiarity with a way of life that most Fugitives and all Agrarians would have held dear. This was at Merry Mount Farm, in Todd County, close to the Tennessee line and not far from Guthrie, where Robert Penn Warren was born. Her mother, Nancy Meriwether, was a Kentuckian; her father, James Morris Gordon, was a Virginian who came to Kentucky in the 1880s as a tutor to the Meriwether family and other households. When Gordon began to write her novels, the Meriwethers at Merry Mount became the model for the Llewellyns in *Penhally*, the Fayerlees in *Aleck Maury, Sportsman*, and the Allards in *None Shall Look Back*.

Gordon graduated from Bethany College, West Virginia, in 1916, taught school until 1920, took a job as a reporter for the *Chattanooga News*, and made her first acquaintance with Fugitives and Agrarians while doing commentary on *The Fugitive*. Because of her articles and reviews Gordon met Allen Tate, whom she married in 1924 (divorced in 1959). Other members of the Fugitive group whom she met were Warren, Ransom, and Donald Davidson, all of whom, like Tate, became Agrarians and were among the twelve contributors to *I'll Take My Stand* (1930).

Like Allen Tate, Gordon held conservative views and was opposed to the spread of industrial "progress" and "modernism" to the South. As a result, four of her first five novels explore her heritage, beginning in Virginia and working towards the present as she examines the agrarian pattern and its decay in the South. Gordon was first among the Agrarians to turn to fiction—short stories in 1930 and a novel in 1931. The latter, *Penhally*, was an excellent book that found favor with the reviewers. *Penhally* is about a Kentucky manor house and estate and the Llewellyn family that lived on it, loved it, and quarreled over it for three generations through a hundred-year period from 1826 to the 1920s. These generations correspond roughly to antebellum days when the way of life in the Old South was intact, the Civil War and Reconstruction period when the old way of life changed and the attitude toward the land deteriorated, and the period of the New South when the ills of an increasingly industrialized, urbanized world slowly dehumanized the lives of those who loved the land that was to go into the hands of strangers. At the beginning of the story Nicholas Llewellyn, the eldest son, presides over the estate along the Kentucky-Tennessee boundary line that his father has willed to him under the old laws of primogeniture and entail. Despite the best that Nicholas and his successors can do, however, the lands are finally entailed to a Llewellyn who defects from traditional agrarianism and sells to a hunt club the land whereon his forebears had lived for generations. The destruction is complete, for the land has been sold for mere money and used to make way for a new wealth based on industry.

Aleck Maury, Sportsman (1934), Gordon's second novel, written in autobiographical fashion, tells the story of Aleck Maury, tutor to the Fayerlee family, who marries Molly Fayerlee and subsequently follows a career of teaching the classics in small colleges. Details of his role as teacher, husband, and father, however, are secondary to the consuming passion of his life: fulfilling his never-ending desire to go hunting or fishing.

After Maury's wife's death and his retirement from teaching, his daughter Sally invites him to make his home with her and her husband, Steve, in the Potter house, which she plans to buy. When

Maury points out that the nearby river "looks as if it would be muddy about half of every year," Sally continues her search for a place to live. Finally one day as she, Steve, and Maury continue the search, they stop for drinks at a bus station, and when the conversation turns once again to buying and remodeling the Potter house, Maury, seeing himself all but trapped and remembering the river he had seen earlier that day, slips out of the restaurant, takes his bags from Steve's car, places them in the bus, and in answer to the bus driver's query about his destination, replies, "Caney's Fork," a place he had seen earlier and fallen in love with.

The light tone of irony and the amusing resolution of the story make it clear that Gordon knows that from the point of view of the practical world Maury's single-minded dedication to fishing is somewhat frivolous. At the same time, she knows—and the reader knows—that it is not merely fishing that provides Maury pleasure; instead, his satisfaction comes from living his life as he feels it should be lived. This leads the reader to the underlying Agrarian views that the novel expresses. Maury is a sort of prototype of the gentle spirit of the Old South, of the affinity between men and the earth, a relationship that can only be weakened by industrialization with its emphasis on "progress" and profits. Maury, too, is the antithesis of the money-minded, success-oriented man; a rebuff to a world that regards Latin and Greek and fishing as wastes of time. Written no doubt out of love for her father and a way of life she cherished, it is not surprising that this novel became Gordon's most popular novel or that *The Nation* (Jan. 9, 1935) said of it, "This is clearly one of the most distinguished and beautiful novels to come out of the South in recent years, and as a document supporting the Southern idea—if it is that at all—it is worth tons of polemical literature."

None Shall Look Back (1937) is both a historical and an Agrarian novel. In fact, it is commonly acclaimed as one of the half-dozen best Civil War novels of its time. The story centers upon the battles of Donelson and Chickamaugua and the remarkable exploits of Nathan Bedford Forrest, major general of the Confederate cavalry, in the region near the Allard estate on the Kentucky-Tennessee line. General Forrest is one of the three principal characters in the novel, along with Lucy Churchill and Rives Allard. He is not merely a historical personage but a real character; the reader identifies with him and gets caught up in the drama of his life and the selflessness and dedication to the cause for which he fights.

But like *Penhally*, where the war is less central to the story, the novel is more than a novel of war. It begins, like Tolstoy's *War and Peace*, with the effects of war on the lives and culture of the aristocrats, for just as *Penhally* traces the fortunes of the Llewellyns for a hundred years, *None Shall Look Back* examines the part played in the war by the members of a wealthy Kentucky family, the Allards. Thus the novel becomes not just a historical novel but a record of how a way of life—the agrarian way—was destroyed and the way left open for industrialism and urbanization.

As the old order falters and finally fails, only one member of the Allard family survives untouched, Jim Allard, the man of commerce. Another who prospers even during the war is Joe Bradley, a storekeeper who takes no sides and shrewdly continues to make money. Despite the odds against them, however, the Allards never cease their aversion to the principles upon which the new order rests. In the short run, they see, it is their lives and their lands that are at stake; in the long run it is a way of life indigenous to the South—the special relationship between people and this land—that is being lost. But despite their commitment, time runs out for them, and the image in the novel that lingers longest is the burning of the home as the war rages—not only the outlines of the manor house but the silhouette of the original cabin that marked the beginnings of the Allard tutelage of the land. The loss is deep and irrevocable.

Gordon's next two novels carry her study of Agrarianism both forward and backward in time. *The Garden of Adonis* (1937) has a contemporary setting during the Great Depression; *Green Centuries* (1941) reaches back to pioneer days. In the former we have the Allards again, a family whose members have been planters for generations and know the ills that befell agriculture as a result of the Civil War, Reconstruction, and industrialization. Now they are contending with the ills of economic depression and a series of severe summer droughts. Four families are central to the plot: the Allards and the Mortimers, tenant farmers who, like their landlords, love the land; and in contrast with them the shiftless, no-account Sheelers, also tenant farmers, and the Camps, northerners who have moved their factories to the South in order to avail themselves of the cheap labor there. Alas, however, destruction of the old order comes from within as well as from without, for Letty Allard and her brother have abandoned the principles of their forbears.

Green Centuries reaches back further in time in order to portray life on the Tennessee-Kentucky frontier about the time of the Revolutionary War. The chief characters are two brothers, the younger of whom has been captured during an Indian raid and been adopted into the tribe; the older, a settler who cannot settle down, becomes a hunter and Indian fighter. To him and the other westward-bound frontiersmen the forests are something to be conquered; to the Indian both the forests and the land are a legacy to be protected. Herein, of course, resides an Agrarian point of view that precedes even the early settlers.

The Women on the Porch (1944) can be said to be a transitional novel in Gordon's development. This time the setting is Swan Quarter, Tennessee, where people are rooted in the land; but it also deals with New York City, which is the very symbol of a rootless people and becomes a second focal point and the other end of the axis. Catherine Chapman, thirty-five years old—the character with roots—is married to Jim Chapman, a brilliant scholar and professor of history and a man without roots. Thus the stage is set for a marriage that goes wrong. Catherine goes back to Swan Quarter, where on land settled by pioneer forebears live Catherine's grandmother, her aunt, and her cousin. Here Catherine hopes to rediscover values that will settle her.

The action of the novel becomes increasingly symbolic as Swan Quarter turns out to be an isolated place that is reached through brambles and bushes and where on the porch, sitting and waiting, the women—Catherine's three kinsfolk—resemble the Three Fates. After her initial shock Catherine settles into the place, and for a time it appears she may reestablish her roots, get a divorce, marry her childhood sweetheart, and settle down with someone whose heritage is similar to her own. Before this happens, however, Jim realizes that Catherine provides the only sense of security he has and sets out for Swan Quarter, where he and Catherine reach a reconciliation of sorts and return to New York. Such a resolution seems to say that in Catherine occurs the struggle between two ways of life, that Swan Quarter and the women on the porch symbolize the deterioration of the old agrarian order, and that Catherine's decision to leave Swan Quarter symbolizes the capitulation of the old order to the new. Gordon does not again return to the subject.

With *The Strange Children* (1951) Gordon continues the psychological probing of her characters; but a new ingredient is introduced—a religious interest found in the concern with spiritual regeneration through suffering, a concern no doubt related to Gordon's conversion to Catholicism in 1947. The "strange children," with the exception of the protagonist, a bright, curious nine-year-old girl, are a group of adults who were once friends and have come together in a sort of chance reunion. The details of what happens to the child and the "strange children" are too complex to be told here; but it can be said that they are self-destructive intellectuals in a confused and restless world who are in need of putting down roots by finding a faith to live by.

The *Malefactors* (1956) deserts Kentucky and Tennessee for a Pennsylvania locale. It carries the religious theme further and is an artistic success, but its multilevel movement and the curious and esoteric learning with which it abounds limit its appeal. The novel on which Gordon was working at the time of her death was never finished, of course, but insofar as it was finished it too must be characterized as baffling.

Though Caroline Gordon saw herself primarily as a novelist, some critics point to a half-dozen or so of her short stories as her greatest achievements. Her first volume of stories was *The Forest of the South* (1945), her second, *Old Red and Other Stories* (1963). In 1981, the year of her death, *The Collected Stories of Caroline Gordon*—more than forty of them—were brought together in one volume. Speaking of "The Forest of the South," "Old Red," and "The Brilliant Leaves," John M. Bradbury (*Renaissance in the South*, 63) declares that Gordon's "most complete successes" are "in the short stories where her impeccable technique and command of symbol can operate freely with characters sketched in rather than presented in their true complexity . . . she employs unobtrusively natural symbols: a deserted house, a fox, and blood-tinted leaves. Each involves, without forcing or melodramatic action, a significant revelation."

The themes and subjects of Gordon's stories are similar to those in her novels, though in general the tone and technique are very different, the stories being more tightly structured, more dramatic, and more symbolic. The stories deal with the rural South, reflect Gordon's Agrarian views, depict the special relationship that exists between a people and their land, and set forth the role of the family as a cohesive factor in maintaining social stability. Some focus on the Civil War. "The Forest of the South" shows how certain values indispensable to life, all associated with the family and the Agrarian way of life, are disappearing from the world. "Hear the Nightingale" and "The Ice House" both depict the defeat of the Confederacy, but in each is portrayed a loss in human values more important than the loss represented by military defeat.

Not all of Gordon's best stories are grounded in Agrarian philosophy. "The Brilliant Leaves" is a skillfully constructed love story of how a boy and a girl, separated by the space of a summer, are reunited in a woods where the brilliant red leaves of autumn cover the ground and where the pair find death instead of the joy they sought. "The Petrified Woman" is another somber and strange story of love, this time between mature adults. Very different from tales such as these is the longer story called "The Captive," a vivid account of Jennie Wiley, the Kentucky frontier woman who was taken captive by Indians and underwent extreme physical hardship and mental suffering.

Perhaps best known of all of Gordon's short stories is "Old Red," one of six stories about Aleck Maury that combine with *Aleck Maury, Sportsman,* to round out the author's most fully developed and best-loved character. In "Old Red," Maury, who is beginning to age, feels himself pursued and increasingly hemmed in by the approaching years and thwarted by those about him, including his own daughter. Even if he lived to the Biblical three-score-and-ten, he tells himself, it is the month of May and he would have "only nine more Mays out of all eternity and they wanted him to waste one of them sitting on the front porch at Merry Point." It is then that he feels his identity merge with that of Old Red, the hunted fox. He is much like the fox, he has come to realize, and must struggle to the end to escape whatever would destroy him. Before Maury goes to sleep that night, he is planning how he can escape the next morning to Elk River, one of his favorite fishing haunts.

To sum up Gordon's career, one can say that from the beginning she enjoyed the respect and admiration of serious critics and had a loyal band of readers. Her following was never large, however, and she was never a popular success. Her techniques were admired, as were her clarity of style, her accuracy of observation, and her detachment. She was ever an artist. Yet herein may reside a clue to her lack of a more general appeal. Her commitment to technique, her artistic integrity, her refusal to play to the gallery, the degree of her detachment earned her more respect than readers. That is to say, one senses an austerity in her writing, an absence of warmth towards her characters and a lack of involvement in their condition or plight. Not that the characters are automatons, but such detachment does tend to keep the reader from fully empathizing with them. Yet one may well ask, "But how about Aleck Maury?" The answer is, of course, that she does care about him and that he is her most fully realized character. Saying this, however, but confirms the point, for *Aleck Maury, Sportsman,* has been her most popular novel and some of her short stories about him among her most admired.

Still Caroline Gordon must be reckoned with as a writer of national importance, not just as a "southern" or a "Kentucky" writer. She began as a southern writer and won a solid place in the literature that grew out of the Fugitive and Agrarian movements in the 1920s and 1930s, but like Tate and Warren she went on to themes that reach well beyond the South and Agrarianism. Her first novels were concerned with the land and the agrarian way of life as a means of grace, but as American life and her novels grew more complex, she moved in her stories from the depiction of a sort of primitive innocence to a more sophisticated and ever more restless, confused world where salvation can be found in a spiritual and religious sense of order. Her journey from lamenting the passing of the Old South to a sense of certitude in religion was not, however, a great distance, nor was it illogical.

During the years ahead one can well expect Gordon to hold a minor place in American literature but a more important one in Kentucky literature. Some views she held and espoused have lost their timeliness, but basically she was concerned with values that are timeless. One can only regret that she created so few memorable characters, that in wrestling with the big problems that trouble the world she could not rise to the level of true tragedy, and that the increasing complexity of her story-telling techniques left all but a few readers behind. She was, however, blessed with great skill and seriousness, and she engaged the interest of some of the best critics of her time.

Frances Barton Fox

Frances Barton Fox (1887–1967) began her writing career as the author of a novel for juveniles, *The Heart of Aresthusa* (1918). Described by the *New York Times* as "a gay, amusing, and interesting book from beginning to end," it tells the story of a girl of eighteen who joins her father abroad, becomes infatuated with a young man she meets, but grows hungry for the life she left behind on a farm in Kentucky and hurries back to the farm and young Timothy.

Sixteen years later, writing under the pseudonym of Frances Renard, Fox published *Ridgeways* (1934), a novel which though generally acclaimed nationally by reviewers has received less attention since that time than it deserved. It is the story of the ups and downs of a fictitious Kentucky homestead through five generations beginning before the Civil War and ending in 1927. The story is told historically, but the novel is far more than a historical novel designed to make an entertaining and lively evening's reading; it tells of a family's love for the land. At the same time, it is the story of the South after the Civil War and is reminiscent of the novels of the Agrarians.

Joel Hardison had acquired his land after moving from Virginia to Kentucky and has built a fine home called Ridgeways. The story begins in antebellum days when life was lived in a comfortable and gracious fashion, and Joel Hardison relishes the thought that the tradition of which he was a part will be perpetuated by generations of Hardisons not yet born. Even before the war, however, untoward events occurred. Joel's son William had no interest in land and turned to law as a profession, and his favorite grandson, named for him, died, leaving his second grandson, Ben, as the one to carry on the tradition.

Then comes the Civil War. Ben at sixteen joins John Hunt Morgan's Raiders. At war's end he returns to Ridgeways permanently crippled by a severe wound, finds his father dead and his home looted and deserted, the slaves gone, and the family money worthless with the loss of the Confederate cause. Physically unable to farm the land profitably and beaten in spirit, Ben is forced to sell the estate in order to pay his debts. In the meantime, he has married Ellen, who had formerly been a devoted serving girl in the home of the Hardisons. Ben dies and Ellen becomes obsessed with the notion that it will be her mission in life to own Ridgeways and through herself and Ben's daughter Noncie to bring the land back into the possession of the Hardisons. Despite her heroic effort to achieve what proved to have been an unattainable goal for her lifetime, the victory is finally won, just as Ellen dreamed it would be, by her daughter and her daughter's daughter, the second Noncie.

All in all, it is a moving story, told simply and straightforwardly and with a fine sense and sweep of history that leaves the reader with the tragic realization that what happened to Ridgeways also happened throughout the South but not always with a courageous Ellen to put the pieces together again. The similarity of *Ridgeways* to such a novel as Caroline Gordon's *Penhally* is apparent, but so too are the differences, for the author of *Ridgeways* is not committed to the doctrinaire acceptance of Agrarian principles. Indeed, the novel is more an affirmation of the strength of human will and courage and determination. A reviewer in the *New York Times* wrote, "*Ridgeways* is a novel of amazing scope and vitality: it seems hardly too much to say that it is one of the best novels the South has yet given us. . . . Ellen Hardison . . . is a fictitious character in the same vital sense that Maggie Tolliver and Becky Sharp are" (March 4, 1934).

Frances Barton Fox was born at Gap-in-the-Knobs, near Shepherdsville, Bullitt County, in 1887 and lived there and in Louisville until 1928, when she moved to New York City. Her brother, Fontaine Fox, was the author of the nationally syndicated "Toonerville Trolley," 1915–54.

Wallace McElroy Kelly

Wallace McElroy Kelly (1910–), a native of Lebanon, Marion County, was awarded the first Alfred A. Knopf fiction fellowship in 1940 and in 1941 completed *Days Are as Grass*, a novel which is set in the post–Civil War era and covers three decades that tell of the social and economic decay of plantation life in a rural community in Kentucky. The central figure is Florrie Evans, who began life as a Kentucky plantation beauty and life's darling. Then after the Civil War hardship befalls, and heartbreak comes as the new era of "progress" produces a new breed of people with wealth and power, along with chambers of commerce that set new goals supplanting those of the past. Gone is the love of land to which Florrie Evans and Pick Hayden and their families have been dedicated for generations. Florrie, seeing her world crumbling around her, crumbles also as the old order changes, the members of her family die one by one, and the family wealth erodes. Pride goes first, and after that her degeneration becomes almost complete as she turns to drink.

Pick Hayden, the poor and illiterate caretaker on the Evans land, helps halt the progress of Florrie's degeneration. He has long admired and loved Florrie from a distance, even when she was young, and has done so unswervingly through her period of deterioration. Florrie, in turn, has always been kind to Pick, though their stations in life have been far apart; but in desperation she turns to him for strength and help. Pick becomes not only her friend but her companion and protector, and ultimately her lover. Gossip has its way, but this somber ending is manifestly an affirmation of life.

In many ways *Days Are As Grass* is a work of excellence. It is well written and, as one reviewer put it, the story has "the substance and feel of a major novel." Yet it is not wholly convincing. Perhaps it would have fared better had the author been able—even though the postbellum decay of the genteel tradition is well known—to show the processes of decay at work, and especially had he been able to show why Florrie's degeneration was so much more complete than that of others in comparable circumstances. Nevertheless, the novel was acclaimed by many readers and critics alike. Even the more tepid readers predicted a bright future for its author, but he wrote no more.

Wendell Berry

In 1934 when Wendell Berry was born, some of the Nashville Agrarians were still voicing their Agrarian views, but others were in the process of abandoning them or modifying them. By the 1950s when Berry was in college and evolving an agrarian view of his own, it was clear that the Agrarian Movement was a practical failure. Indeed, no Agrarian had moved back to the land, and the industrialization and urbanization of the South and the nation were continuing unabated. On the other hand, *I'll Take My Stand* had achieved a landmark status and had taken on an oracular quality as a warning against what the doctrine of progress and materialism can do to the quality of life of a people.

While he was growing into maturity, Berry became aware of the Agrarians and their views, just as he did of Thomas Jefferson's distrust of cities and industrialism and Henry David Thoreau's radical experiment in living. At the same time he was having the experience of growing up in agricultural Henry County, where his family had lived since the first decade of the nineteenth century. But the catalyst that began to bring Berry's somewhat amorphous agrarian views into meaningful focus was witnessing the technological revolution that followed World War II and the constantly accelerating pace at which change took place. Concomitant with this—though not fully recognized at the time—was the emergence of increasingly severe ecological and conservationist problems that the nation had not experienced before. And in human terms there were the effects of these developments on the agricultural, economic, and cultural life of communities such as the one in which Berry grew up. All of these concerns have been the subjects of his writings.

Berry's first published volume came in 1960, and during almost three decades of a prolific writing career since then he has written almost exclusively on agrarian matters, with increasing attention to environmental concerns. He has been a versatile writer of fiction, poetry, essays, and polemical prose for readerships as disparate as those of the *Hudson Review* and *Organic Gardening*. Berry has been and still is one of the strongest and most persistent agrarian voices in America. How his ideas developed requires some amplification.

Noteworthy in his development was the period of his Guggenheim Fellowship in 1961–62, following his A.B. and M.A. degrees in English at the University of Kentucky and two years as a student and lecturer in the Wallace Stegner writing program at Stanford University. Six months of his fellowship period he spent in Italy and there observed how generation after generation of Italians used the land with great skill, keeping it productive and making it beautiful at the same time. It was an object lesson in what the right relationship between a people and their land can produce and a living example of the "continuous harmony" he was to dwell on later.

The next two years Berry spent in New York City, where he taught in the writing program of New York University. This was an important opportunity for a young agrarian to reflect and to engage in self-examination. He then accepted an appointment in the writing program of his alma mater and returned to Kentucky against the advice of some of his friends and colleagues, who told him his interest in Kentucky as the compelling subject matter of his writing could best be served by remaining at a distance. Back in Lexington, Berry began to think of buying the small farm near Port Royal where he now lives in Henry County. In 1965, he moved there; and for twelve years as he commuted to work he grew more and more convinced of the importance of his working out his life on a small farm of "marginal" land. His sense of urgency increased as the technological revolution progressed and the plight of the small farmer worsened in the face of the growing power of corporate agribusiness and the dictum of secretaries of agriculture Ezra Taft Benson and Earl Butz to "get big or get out." To this declared war on the traditional small farmer were added other ills stemming from agribusiness and the industrial age: the depletion of the land through bad soil practices growing out of the emphasis on maximum production; the contamination of the soil and natural underground water systems by pesticides; and the pollution of air and earth by industry and automobiles.

In 1977 Berry resigned his university professorship in order to devote himself exclusively to farming—"to live out a possibility that I believe in"—and writing. The farming he still carries on with a pair of draft horses as he does the usual farm labors of clearing fields, breaking ground, growing crops, mending fences, milking cows, and the rest. His poetry and his essays continue, but in general his nonfiction prose has become more polemicized and more "practical." *The Unsettling of America* appeared in 1977, and since that time he has been a contributor to the Robert Rodale Press and its *New Farm* and *Organic Gardening and Farming* magazines. Here he reports on his experiences and thoughts as the operator of a small farm.*

More than most writers whose works are likely to live beyond their day, Wendell Berry has devoted himself to one subject: human

*Berry returned to teaching at the University of Kentucky in 1987.

beings and their relationship to the land. All his writings are complementary and could be studied collectively in chronological order. Perhaps, however, a better approach is to begin with his three novels —*Nathan Coulter*, *A Place on Earth*, and *The Memory of Old Jack*. In them we can not only find some of his premises but also gain some insight into the point at which he started his writing.

First of all, Berry is concerned in his novels with the history of our relationship to the land, although he voices no ideas from what could be called the neo-Confederate outlook of the earlier Agrarians. This historical perspective is gained through seven generations of three families in particular—the Coulters, the Feltners, and the Beechums—all distantly related, interlocked through marriage, and identified with a place called Port William. Here since the early 1800s succeeding generations have performed their work as "dirt" farmers whose lands and operations bear no resemblance to the Deep South plantations reflected in *I'll Take My Stand*. The actual historic period portrayed in some detail by Berry's novels is from the early decades of the present century to the early 1950s. Thus the period under close scrutiny begins with the final years of the traditional farm of pre–World War I America and traces the changes that come about through the years, including the period at the end of World War II when technology and economics begin to alter the very nature of farming. In *Nathan Coulter* (1960), farming is done by hand, using mule-drawn equipment; in *The Memory of Old Jack* (1974), when Old Jack dies in 1952, advanced technological change is under way.

The three novels present different ways of regarding the land. In the first, Jarrat Coulter, father of the central character, is a man of strong will whose method is to dominate and control the land as something he owns. Counterbalancing Jarrat is Nathan's uncle and surrogate father, Burley, who lacks the acquisitive, dominating nature of Jarrat but who also lacks a full commitment to the land. Under the influence of these two men young Nathan comes to learn farming. In Berry's second novel, *A Place on Earth* (1967; rev. ed. 1983), Mat Feltner, the central character, is in contrast to Jarrat. Mat thinks of himself as holding the land in trust and wants desperately to leave it—better land and a better farm than when it became his—to his only son, Virgil, when he dies. Ironically, the son is killed in World War II, a tragic turn of events that leads almost to Mat's undoing but at the same time underscores the fact that the land is the only immutable thing and that we who tend the land must be responsible for our stewardship of it.

In *A Place on Earth* stories are told of various people in or near

Port William. Old Jack Beechum is the subject of one of these, and seven years later he becomes the central figure in *The Memory of Old Jack*. This novel, as one critic points out, "is the embodiment of Berry's agrarian ideals and is at once elegiac, didactic, and exhortatory" (Gary Tolliver, *Dictionary of Literary Biography*, vol. 6:12). The action takes place during one day in September 1952, and since Old Jack is ninety-two years old, his memory goes back through much of Kentucky's history as an agricultural state. Thus through his recollections during the last day of his life can be seen the long history of small farms in America and in his life and death the prefiguring of the death of a way of life. As a young man Old Jack had married a woman of the mercantile class and for a time sought to satisfy her desire for acquisition of land as a commodity. From this near-fatal error he recovers, but his only child, a daughter, married to a banker, is also of the mercantile turn of mind. She and her husband have a sentimental view of farming but no sense of the hard work that goes into being a good steward of the land. Thus is raised the grim specter of what will come when men like Old Jack have no one to whom they can leave their land in the expectation of its being cared for as they have done. Such an eventuality is avoided as Old Jack's farm passes into the hands of Andy Catlett, Old Jack's tenant, who has already proved himself a responsible steward; but despite this reprieve, one can only feel that the time cannot be far off when the long tradition of the small farm will come to an end and the land fall into a stranger's hand.

Berry's poetry supplements his fiction and creates a richer texture for the totality of his writings. In *Openings: Poems* (1969), for example, one passage amplifies Berry's hatred of war, a hatred already noted in *A Place on Earth* in the suffering of the families who have lost loved ones. Burley Coulter experiences that suffering upon the death of his nephew Tom in World War II, but more than anyone else it is Mat Feltner, that good steward of the land, who suffers when his only son is killed and he sees his lifelong intention of passing his land on to the next generation thwarted. In "Window Poems" Berry employs the sublimer manner of poetry to explore the subject, as when he has his narrator speak:

> He said: If man, who had killed
> his brothers and hated himself,
> is made in the image of God,
> then surely the bloodroot,
> wild phlox, trilium, and May apple

are more truly made
in God's image, for they have desired
to be no more than they are,
and they have spared each other.
Their future
is undiminished by their past.
Let me, he said in his dream,
become always less a soldier
and more a man. . . .
When he woke and went out
A flock of wild ducks that had fed
on the river while he slept
Flew off in fear of him.
And he walked, manly, into the new day.

Berry's works are imbued with a strong sense of place, commonly in conjunction with the continuity of generations of families. Thus, in "The House," from *Findings*:

In a back upstairs room
a gallery of portraits
without names, quilt pieces,
bank notes, canceled mortgages,
hymns and oaths, broken books,
colorless dusks and shambles,
letters from the dead
to the dead:
  the hands
that laid them by never
took them up again.

This is what my mind owes
for its life. . . .

A passage from *Openings* amplifies Berry's recurrent idea that, unless we cease to pollute the earth and the air, and unless we do begin to build up instead of deplete the soil, the earth will become uninhabitable for human beings.

He had imagined animals
grazing at nightfall
on the place where his house stands.
. . . .
hearing the grass
quietly tearing as they graze.
. . . .

There will be
a resurrection of the wild.
Already it stands in wait
at the pasture fences.
It is rising up
in the waste places of the cities.
When the fools of the Capitols
have devoured each other
in righteousness,
and the machines have eaten
the rest of us, then
there will be the second coming
of the trees. They will come
straggling over the fences
slowly, but soon enough.
The highways will sound
with the feet of the wild herds,
returning. Beaver will ascend
the streams as the trees
close over them.
The wolf and the panther
will find their old ways
through the nights. . . .

Berry published seven volumes of verse between 1964 and 1980, each devoted to agrarian subjects and themes. The central concern of *The Broken Ground* (1964) is death, though it is not death as an enemy but as a part of a whole and without which there can be no seed to fall into "the broken ground," sprout, and carry on the endless cycle of life and death. *Openings* (1968) is not unlike *The Broken Ground* in general content and introspective nature. The "Window Poems," perhaps the best in the volume, are "openings" which constitute a sort of fugue in which Berry's favorite themes are brought together. *Findings* (1969) continues the themes of the preceding volumes. "The House" and "The Handing Down"—the two main parts of the volume—examine the roots of the individual and a community and present an intensified look at the importance of place in the life of a people as generation succeeds generation.

In *Farming: A Handbook* (1970) Berry becomes the poet-farmer even more than he has been before. The poems are lyrical and reflective, but there is some shift in theme and content towards matters pertaining to farming: the pleasing fatigue that comes from physical labor, the renewing of earth by rain, man's abuse of the soil, farming in a technological age, and so on. *The Country of Marriage* (1973) elaborates a metaphor introduced in *Farming*. The metaphor has its origin in the marriage of a man to a woman and in widening concentric circles expands to include "marriage" to a place, to a community, and to the world, to the land, and to the universe. Each of the thirty-four poems in the volume relates in one way or another to this metaphor.

The remaining two volumes of verse that Berry wrote by 1980 pose a problem, for they seem to foretell a change in him as poet and writer. Both deal with agrarian matters: farming, the seasons, the earth and its fullness, the ravaging of the land. The quality of the collections is good, but the number of memorable poems and lines is fewer; and in the first—*Clearing* (1977)—Berry is obviously questioning his attitude toward his work and his future as a poet. In "Work Song," under the heading of "Passion," he writes:

> I am curious and afraid
> one day my poems may pass
> through my mind unwritten
> . . . .
>   I am afraid,
> some days, that only vanity
> keeps me at my words . . .
> Some days I wait here
> empty as a tree
> whose birds and leaves
> have gone. . . .

In the last stanza of "Reverdure," the final poem in the volume, he addresses the subject again:

> It is time again I made an end to words
> for a while—for this time,
> or for all time. Any end may last.

In 1980 Berry published *Part*, whose subject matter is still mainly pastoral, but whose tone is different. Despite the seriousness of most of the verses, there is often a lilt in the lines, a playfulness, a greater use of rhyme, and a faster, lighter movement than characterized the earlier volumes. There are more poems whose primary reason for being is humor; there is more playing with words.

What does all this signify? Is the author changing directions? Has his creative passion waned? Has his subject been mined out or his relationship to it changed? It is worth pointing out that though Berry has revised *A Place on Earth* recently, his last novel was published in 1974. He has continued to write nonfiction prose, but as the 1970s passed there was less of the personal essay and more of the prose of persuasion.

During the period of our survey Berry published four volumes of essays: *The Long-Legged House* (1969), *The Hidden Wound* (1970), *A Continuous Harmony* (1972), and *The Unsettling of America* (1977). At the time of the publication of the first of these, Berry had written four principal volumes: two novels and two volumes of poetry. In his first book of essays his subject matter, his themes, and his point of view are much the same as those already set forth in his fiction and verse. From his "heron-like house" on stilts overlooking the Kentucky River Berry contemplates a world in which man and nature are no longer in harmony and seeks to point the way to a just and liveable world. In seven essays in the first two parts of the volume he deals with specific ills that he regards as threatening life on earth. The final section is made up of three excellent autobiographical essays, the longest being "The Long-Legged House." All three are especially well written and show how the skills of a poet can enhance his prose.

A Continuous Harmony, made up of eight essays, examines the relationship of humankind to the earth. Between "A Secular Pilgrimage," the first essay, and "Mayhem in the Industrial Paradise," the last, Berry explores such subjects as consumerism, exploitation of the land, the ravages of strip-mining, and various other ways in which the earth is being devastated. Rarely, he says, except among so-called primitive peoples has there ever been a "continuous harmony" between man and the land. *The Hidden Wound* analyzes the damage —"the wound"—left by slavery and racism on both black people and white. In doing so Berry recounts his family's history in relation to slavery and tells of his childhood friendships with Nick and Aunt Georgie, two blacks who spent their lives on his grandfather's farm.

The capstone of Berry's nonfiction prose, the most outspoken and the most controversial of his books, is *The Unsettling of America*. In a way it is the culmination of everything else he has written and the point to which, as a reformer, his essays, novels, and poems had been leading him and for which they had been preliminary studies. The form, however, is different and the scope and conclusions more sweeping. Berry believes that small farmers have been victimized by a coalition of corporate interests, government agencies, and land-grant agricultural experiment stations, all advocating the economic principle that bigger is better. Productivity and profit—their chief concerns

—have been achieved with heavy machines that compact the soil and with pesticides, fertilizers, and soil practices that contaminate the environment, deplete the humus in the soil, and ultimately make the soil sterile. Furthermore, in the pursuit of profit, mechanized agribusiness has constantly reduced the number of farms and has driven farmers and farm workers off the land and into the cities, while at the same time making it all but impossible for young men to buy the land and the equipment necessary to becoming farmers. To complete the dismal picture, Berry says, traditional farming has ceased to be a way of life and farms have come to be looked upon as mere units of production. In the wake of the destruction of traditional farming has come the breakdown and demoralization of rural communities. Berry calls for an immediate reversal of the trend and for a return of the role of the traditional farm in American life and economy. As a beginning, he argues, government can discourage large land holdings, can give attention to the technology of small-scale farming, and can reduce the emphasis on operations devoted to heavy production of a few crops. And above all, people should again be encouraged to become good stewards of the land. Furthermore, steps must be taken swiftly before those who have a knowledge of farming, a sense of seasons, and a sensitive responsiveness to the earth learned from generations of living close to it have died or have left farming for other occupations.

Berry has done well by his subject. *The Unsettling of America* has received national attention and has been required reading in college courses. It was, however, two or three years following its publication, as already noted above, that Berry began raising questions about his creative imagination and his future as a poet, as if there had been a change in his sense of aesthetic distance from the subjects about which he had been writing from the beginning. Since that time, however, Berry has continued to write both poetry and fiction and in 1985 published *Collected Poems: 1957–1982*. In this collection, the author has deleted some of the earlier poems that he regarded "least good," shortened others, and deleted portions of still others. Among the lines deleted are those quoted above from *Clearing*. "Reverdure" is no longer included, and gone are sections 3 and 4 of "Work Song," each of which reflected the author's apprehension about himself as a writer, and particularly as a poet. Such deletions seem to suggest that there had indeed been some sort of crisis as the 1970s came to a close, but that it has passed or is no longer a matter of concern.

Berry's new writings during the earlier 1980s bear out such a conclusion, for during these years he published three more volumes, all of which reassert his commitment to the mission that has been his for twenty-five years. The first of these is *The Wheel* (1982), his eighth volume of verse. Like much of his poetry it is in the elegiac vein and has as its themes stewardship of the land, the cycles of the seasons, sowing, cultivating, and reaping, all touched with mysticism. As the title suggests, "The Wheel" is "the wheel of life," and the structure is one of death, decay, and rebirth. *Standing by Words: Essays* (1983), Berry's third such collection, was next. Most of the essays are about poetry, the subject of which is the world; and the author's viewpoint is that of the regionalist and the poet of place. *The Wild Birds: Six Stories of the Port William Membership* (1986) is a set of short stories which fit loosely together and exemplify Berry's moral vision of how people can responsibly take their place in the world. Not much happens in the stories, but ultimately each is concerned with the relationship of the characters to the larger world. An old man walks the boundary-line fence of his farm for the last time, a farm is auctioned off, a will is drawn up, and so on; and in each is to be found a sense of human responsibility—to oneself, to one's fellows, and to the world. It's all vintage Berry. He is still the traditionalist, a latter-day romantic celebrating the importance of the individual, the need for a sense of community in the natural and social order, and the centrality of our relationship to the land and through it to the universe. These are the matters he writes about, and perhaps no one today does it better.

CHAPTER 17

Literature of Eastern Kentucky

When one thinks of the economic plight of the mountaineer during the 1920s and the 1930s, it is coal that first comes to mind. But actually lumbering preceded coal mining as a threat to the environment and the way of life of the mountaineer. As early as the 1780s settlers had forged their way into the wilderness all along the Big Sandy River and its Tug and Levisa forks, even as far south as Pike County; and before long the rivers that carried the settlers inland were transporting produce down to Catlettsburg and from there up and down the Ohio River to an ever-expanding market. First furs by the thousands went to France and other domestic and foreign markets, and ultimately timbermen floated logs down the rivers. By the 1870s the railroads were working their way through the rough terrain after coal, but logs continued to reach the outside world by water. In 1880 Kentucky produced approximately 300 million board feet of lumber, most of it coming from the Big Sandy region. It was this lumbering that Harlan Hatcher wrote about in the 1930s. Comparable operations were also taking place in the mountains and in the Knobs region westward, and logs were being floated down the Cumberland and Green rivers. Eva Wilder Broadhead wrote about logging operations in the 1890s. Her *Earthly Paragon* (1892) has Yosemite in Casey County as its background and *Bound in Shallows* (1897) centers upon Burnside in Pulaski County.

There was some writing too about coal around the turn of the century, but neither coal nor lumber was to become a cause célèbre until the 1930s. John Fox, Jr., wrote about the conflict that ensued when the mountain people came into contact with the outside world, but he retained the conviction that this contact was the best way to bring the backward "other Kentucky" into the mainstream of the Commonwealth. Such "conflict" as there was in Fox's novels, therefore, took place in a context of optimism for the future and the expectation of better things to come. When *The Heart of the Hills* was published in 1913 Fox had apparently come to feel that the mountaineers were changing rapidly, that they were learning to live with industrialism and were often migrating into the outside world, sometimes as small farmers in the foothills, sometimes into the industrialized cities of the North and the Midwest. Fox had no way of knowing it, but when in 1911 he saw the first coal mine opened and the first railroad track laid in Harlan County, he was seeing the beginning of what was to happen all through the mountains. Indeed, Fox had learned what was being lost to "progress" on the day in the 1880s when the mountain girl he first saw milking a brindle cow brought him a "tin-type" of herself in a store dress and store shoes and with ribbons in her hair —"her picturesqueness all gone." Maybe, too, in *The Heart of the Hills* (1913) he foresaw, albeit dimly, the shape of things to come, for after using again the formula of the conflict of contrasting cultures, he had both sets of lovers decide not to separate themselves from their cultural heritage. Both the author and his "quare" women had come to believe that mountain children needed to be steeped in their own heritage and traditions as well as in books and learning.

Harlan County can be singled out from among the forty or so Kentucky mining counties as the prototype of what happened in the coal fields. The county was all mountainous, had an assessed value of $10,000 in 1880, was found to be rich in coal, had its first mine opened and the first railroad tracks laid in 1911, and by the same year was largely owned by outside corporations—Andrew Mellon, Samuel Insull, Henry Ford, U.S. Steel, International Harvester, and the rest. Almost overnight everything began changing, but the real boom came with World War I as coal came to be needed by the steel mills to make munitions. The price of coal soared, wages in the coal mines rose to heights never before dreamed of, and miners began to receive more cash in a month than they had formerly received in a year. Then suddenly the war was over and the coal boom ended, even before the miners had learned to manage the money they were so little accustomed to. Many had uprooted themselves and moved into the operators' hastily built barracks and shacks, and now when they lost their jobs they could not pay their rent or their bills at the company store. A few older people had never left their cabins and continued to raise their own hogs, harvest their own corn and beans, and in general garner their foodstuffs for winter as well as summer. But this was the exception, not the rule.

When the Great Depression closed in on Harlan County in 1930, the county had a population of 65,000, some 85 percent of which were miners and their families. As the Depression worsened, wages were lowered, workdays were shortened, and more and more miners were laid off. The tapering off of the boom in the 1920s became a collapse in the 1930s. Unions, some with Communist infiltration, sought to organize the mines; operators fired those who joined. The company stores on which miners had come to depend had to curtail credit and often developed a peonage system. Disagreement and strife developed and finally violence flared. On May 5, 1931, the "Battle of Evarts," nine miles east of Harlan, took place, and in the following months there were pitched battles in the coal camps of Harlan County and in surrounding counties. Newspapers carried lurid accounts of the events throughout the nation, and Harlan County came to be the very symbol of disorder and labor unrest. All sorts of people, most of them well meaning, flocked to Harlan County, among them a series of literary men: Theodore Dreiser first, and after him Edmund Wilson, John Dos Passos, Malcolm Cowley, Heywood Broun, Waldo Frank, and others. But despite the miners' need for help and guidance, even the best-intentioned of the outsiders departed ingloriously. Sometimes their ignorance of the people and their customs led to failure, sometimes a lack of practical common sense or some other deficiency. Whatever the cause, they often seemed like "meddlers" even to the people they sought to help.

John L. Lewis and his United Mine Workers were able to bring some order into the coal fields, build hospitals, and generally bring improvements from which miners profited. Finally on September 1, 1938, despite the distrust and bitter feelings of many operators, a contract was signed by the Harlan County Coal Operators Association with the United Mine Workers. Many problems, however, still lay ahead.

Another development during the 1930s was to have far-reaching and long-lasting effects. This was the institution of relief measures by the New Deal. As early as the 1920s the traditional mountain pride and individualism had been dealt heavy blows as the boom faded and unemployment developed, but in the 1930s with state, federal, and

Harriette Arnow. Photo courtesy of University of Kentucky Photographic Archives.

semi-private organizations trying to find solutions to Appalachia's problems, women and children as well as men became sociological and political pawns. Harry Caudill in *Night Comes to the Cumberlands* gives a vivid picture of how personal pride and family honor gave way in the face of poverty and how poverty and the urge to survive

James Still. Photo courtesy of Dean Cadle and the University of Kentucky Photographic Archives.

have produced a social and economic system—the welfare state—that perpetuates both the welfare and those who need it.

This mountaineer world, of course, is very different from the one that John Fox, Jr., and his followers knew. Fox, who died in 1920, did live long enough to see the results of the coal boom that came with World War I but not long enough to see the slackening off in the 1920s and the disaster of the 1930s. No doubt he was pleased to see benefits accruing to the mountaineers as the demand of the nation's industrial system called for more and more coal, but he would have drawn back in horror had he been able to see the pace at which the journey into industrialization would take place, including the migration to the Midwest and North, how strong the pull of materialism would be, and how devastating the mountaineer's collision with the outside world would be, with even their very self-image as a proud, separate people swallowed up.

Jesse Stuart. Photo courtesy of the Jesse Stuart Foundation.

In perspective it is apparent that the writer of belles-lettres about the region has had something of a moving target to aim at, for the welfare recipient of more recent years has been a very different figure from the mountaineer working in the mine or in the industrial complex of the North during the 1920s and 1930s or during the 1940s and 1950s after the Depression had loosened its grip. At the earlier time, writers had the dramatic opportunity to witness the moun-

Janice Holt Giles. Photo courtesy of the *Courier-Journal*.

taineer caught between the old world and the new, ready to embark upon a course from which there would be no returning. For some the crossover was complete and satisfactory; others would be absorbed by the new world but would be little more than ciphers, though reconciled after a fashion; but for some the journey would end in a sad and tragic suspension between two worlds, the old still cherished in memory but no longer a viable alternative, the new powerless to be born. Late every Friday afternoon Old U.S.-25 (later I-75) would be crowded with cars headed south toward Appalachia from Cincinnati and Middletown and Dayton and even Detroit, and busy again on Sunday afternoon as the same cars headed north to the jobs from whence they came two days earlier. It was clearly a matter of an identity in transition that was involved. This migration still goes on, and both the novelist and the sociologist still have a moving target.

Harriette Simpson Arnow

The Kentucky mountain people have been blessed in having so many talented writers to portray them with so much understanding —John Fox, Jr., Lucy Furman, Harriette Arnow, Jesse Stuart, James Still, Henry Hornsby, and Janice Holt Giles among others. Only Harriette Arnow (1908–86), however, has portrayed in a succession of three novels mountaineer life as it traditionally was (*Mountain Path*, 1936), as it was during the Great Depression (*Hunter's Horn*, 1949), and as it was during the World War II years in the industrial North while the mountaineer gained a livelihood but became a social nonentity and disappeared as a unique, identifiable American type (*The Dollmaker*, 1954). Arnow was well equipped to do the job she set for herself. Born in Wayne County, Kentucky, she attended Berea College for two years, taught in a one-room school in Pulaski County for two years, received her A.B. degree from the University of Louisville, and went to Cincinnati, where she worked and began her writing career by publishing some short stories and her first novel, *Mountain Path*. In 1939 she married Harold B. Arnow, a newspaper reporter, and moved with him to a farm on the Big South Fork of the Cumberland River, where for five years they wrote and farmed. In 1944 she went to Detroit, where her husband took a position with the *Detroit Times*. Subsequently they moved to Ann Arbor, where they still lived at the time of her death in 1986.

Mountain Path broke with the sentimental tradition of mountain fiction and sought to portray life as it actually was. At the time the traditional way of life was pretty well gone except in some of the more remote valleys and hollows, but Arnow achieved her objective of reporting it realistically by having Louisa Sheridan, a young lady from Lexington, take her first teaching job at "a kind of lost place in a bend" on the Cumberland River. Here she portrays the traditional mountain people in accurate detail: their customs and traditions, their daily lives, the work they do, the tools they work with, the insides of their houses, their clothes and food and drink, their ethics and their moral values. It all has the ring of authenticity gained through the author's own experience as a child and through the knowledge she acquired through hill-country pioneer ancestors and her own careful research.

The plot of *Mountain Path* is negligible and is secondary to the portrayal of life and character. Such plot as there is has Louisa slowly gaining an understanding of the life around her, falling in love with Chris Bledsoe, a young feudist wanted by the law but a person who perceives the world much as she herself does. In the end, Chris is killed and Louisa leaves the community a much wiser person than when she came, for during her seven months in the valley she was a learner as well as a teacher. She has learned, for example, what life can be like uncluttered by the complexities of the outside world. Brought up never to be quite content with the present but to work always toward a future goal, she has learned to live for the present, the only life of which she can be sure. She has learned how Chris, a hunted man, loves life and lives each day for the joy that is in it. He ought, she thinks to herself, "to be insensitive and stupid and un-thinking"; instead, he loves the same things she does: "beauty, and long silences, and the play of rain and light and mist over the hills." And from Corie she learns of the anguish and pain a mountain woman experiences as she waits alone for word of her husband after report of a disaster comes: "Women has th' hardest work 'uv all, and that's th' waitin'. 'Pears like all my life I've been a waitin'."

Though *Mountain Path* was well received by both the critics and the reading public, it was *Hunter's Horn* (1944) that brought Arnow recognition as an important American novelist. At one level the novel tells the story of a subsistence white mountain farmer who seeks to destroy a fox that has been killing his chickens and his lambs and with whose pursuit he has become so obsessed that he almost brings his family and his farm to ruin during the two-and-a-half-year period covered by the novel. By the time the story is under way, his pursuit has gotten beyond being a traditional, ritualistic fox hunt. Neither is it just a case of a farmer trying to protect his livestock and his chickens, nor of a typical hill-country man bringing pleasure into an otherwise dull and tedious existence. Nunnelly Ballew has become progressively a man driven by a demon within, and the fox is far more than an ordinary fox. By common report he is an unusually large red fox gifted with such wiliness and speed that he not only eludes the hounds but even leads them to their deaths as they chase him over a rugged, forbidding terrain. He is King Devil, and Nunn and his neighbors spend many a night listening to the baying of their hounds pursuing him. One night Nunn glows with excitement as he listens to the voice of Zing, a favorite hound, pursuing King Devil at close range. Suddenly the baying and the sounds of the chase change and Nunn knows that another hound—his—has been led to his death. But despite Nunn's reasons for hating the fox, he also has respect for him. Even after Zing's death he cannot use the gun that was offered him to kill King Devil, for fair play and the rules of the chase require that only the hounds can bring the fox to his final end. Nunn does sell some of the livestock his family stands in need of in order to buy two pedigreed hound pups. These he trains and nurtures, and finally they run down and kill King Devil, who in a stunning irony turns out to be not a huge red fox at all but a mere vixen about ready to give birth to a litter that has slowed down her usual speed and agility and made her fall victim to the hounds she has eluded so often.

But nailing King Devil's hide to the wall is a hollow victory for Nunn. On the one hand he has neglected his crops and his farm and property; he has neglected his wife, and his daughter is pregnant by a young man who has left for Detroit. Nunn has awakened too late to recover most of what he has lost. And he has lost in other ways: he has given up fox-hunting and with it has gone his relief from the tedium of life; with King Devil dead he has lost the thing that made him come alive and that gave form and point to his life just as much as if larger principles were at stake.

But there is far more to the story. There is Milly, Nunn's wife, who accepts uncomplainingly whatever life brings her. When Nunn sells the chickens, the pigs, and the cows in order to buy the pedigreed pups, she covers her head with a pillow at night so that her sobs won't be heard. There is Suse, who longs to escape her dreary life and envies King Devil because he is free to "run and run forever," and Sue Anne, who sees no use in educating girls, for it is more important "to know how to diaper a baby than to spell diaper." And there is also the Great Depression that adds to the Ballew family's miseries; there are those who leave Little Smokey Creek and go to Cincinnati and Dayton and Detroit, hoping for a better life. Arnow is portraying the last phases of the old social pattern that constituted the way of life of an earlier generation but is now decaying.

When Harriet Arnow wrote her masterwork, *The Dollmaker* (1954), she was breaking new ground. Most post–World War II novelists who wrote of the mountain people wrote historical fiction, tales of adventure, thrillers of one sort or another, or juvenile fiction. A few dealt with contemporary problems, but only Arnow depicted the uprooting of a mountain family and followed them into the midst of a northern industrial city ghetto, portraying each member's search for a new identity. As in her earlier novels, Arnow is concerned with character first, situation second, and hence has left a memorable picture of a family—and particularly of the wife and mother, Gertie Nevels—as it tries to adapt to a new culture and a strange environment.

The story begins on a piece of rented land in the Kentucky mountains, where the Nevels struggle to extract a living from the poor land. Gertie dreams of owning a little farm where she can rear her five children in peace and security. Clovis, her husband, a mechanic of sorts and a part-time coal hauler, wants to go to Detroit and make big money. After Clovis goes to Cincinnati to take his World War II military service examination, fails it, and then goes to Detroit and gets a factory job, Gertie with great misgivings uproots her children and joins the stream of mountain migrants to the North.

In Detroit the family moves into a crowded government housing project, a melting-pot of nationalities, religions, and social classes, where there is quarreling and jangled nerves, and people are "niggers and kikes and Poles and hillbillies." Everywhere the advice is to "adjust—learn to get along, like it—be like others." And indeed Clovis does adjust, as do two of the children. With Gertie and Cassie and Reuben, though, adjustment does not work so well. The family that was close-knit in Kentucky is now splintered. Gertie forces herself to make the best of her new life, but she understands when Reuben resolves to preserve his individuality by returning to Kentucky: "he cain't hep th way he's made." Little Cassie, however, fares less well. Her active imagination creates Callie Lou, an imaginary companion who is always with her and helps her make her world tolerable; but one day, as Cassie searches for a place for herself and Callie Lou, she is run over and killed by a box car that is being switched.

Gertie, the central figure of the novel, is a big raw-boned woman cast in a heroic mold. She still longs for the peace and comfort of the hills—and for the Tipton Place she once almost owned; but with

Reuben gone and Cassie dead, and Clovis and the other children readily adjusting to the new environment, she turns her resourceful energies to finding meaning in the crowded alley where she lives. She realizes that her only source of spiritual sustenance is where she is. She grows to meet the demands made upon her, and she discovers that others in this place also once had their dreams. That she succeeds is suggested one day when a woman who is leaving the housing complex says to her, "I wish you'd been my kin."

In a way Gertie has had her Callie Lou in both Kentucky and Detroit—a sharp-bladed pocketknife that she carries in her apron. With it she once whittled handles for the farm tools and carved dolls with jointed legs and arms; but she has also a great block of cherry wood from which she is carving a bust of Jesus. She works on this bust throughout the book, but never has she been able to carve the face, for the features simply will not come clear. She wants nothing to do with the forbidding Christ of the fundamentalists, however, or with the defeated Christ on the cross that her neighbors want her to carve. She comes to work on it less and less as her creative talent fades in the dehumanizing society which manipulates people and robs them of their spiritual independence. As the novel ends, Gertie is having her treasured block of wood cut into pieces from which she can carve crucifixes and other small objects that will sell.

Most readers see Gertie's final act as not only her own capitulation but the surrender and final swallowing up of an American way of life. Some critics, in fact, are disturbed by the grimness of the portrayal. Of *The Dollmaker*, for example, the *New Yorker* (May 1, 1954) says, "It remains a depressing picture of human defeat and bewilderment"; and *Canadian Forum* (July 1954) declares, "This is a harrowing tale completely unrelieved by one positively joyous occasion or a single scrap of humor." Indeed, as Mrs. Arnow pursues her deterministic course, no alternatives seem to have occurred to her. Writing in the 1930s, 1940s, and 1950s, she has a clear perspective as she looks back over the history of the Kentucky mountaineer: the lingering on in the mountains of some of the early settlers on their trek westward, the development of a differentiated type insulated from the outside world after the Civil War, the first signals by the turn of the century that incursions of the industrial world might make the mountaineer an endangered species, and the hastening of the whole process by the Great Depression. At this point in the relentless sequence of events Arnow wrote *Mountain Path* (1936). By the time she had written *Hunter's Horn* (1944), World War II and a wartime economy had lured a steady stream of migrant mountaineers to the industrial centers of the North, where soon they become social nonentities and so cut their ties with the past that they can never really go home again. The cause-and-effect relationship seemed all too clear to Arnow; hence the last volume of the trilogy, where without blinking an eye she carried the story down to the inevitable, inescapable ending. There is, of course, tragedy and pathos aplenty, but the author stops short of disavowing moral choices for her characters. Like Louisa Sheridan and Nunnelly Ballew, Gertie Nevels meets defeat, but before she accedes to it, she has been a strong contender even though it may have been an unequal battle.

Arnow tells her story with loving care and sympathy, for the people about whom she writes are important to her. Gertie Nevels is a far more towering, more heroic figure than were mountaineers generally, but only in such a person—preferably a strong woman, for women are the greatest continuity factor in the value system of a mountain family—can the dramatic tension be brought about and final capitulation be dramatically and adequately represented. In such a character, too, tragedy can be translated into some sort of affirmation of life, for Gertie is an indomitable spirit. Perhaps it was such a point as this that a reviewer in the *Chicago Sunday Tribune* (April 18, 1954) had in mind when she said, "Some will find it [*The Dollmaker*] a bitter tale of man's inhumanity to man. . . . Some will find [it] a story of the strength of the human heart against the bitterest odds."

After completing her trilogy on the Kentucky mountains and the mountaineer, Arnow continued during the 1960s and 1970s to write about Southeastern Kentucky in four more volumes. Three of these were personal and social histories of the country in which she grew up: *Seedtime on the Cumberland* (1960), *Flowering of the Cumberland* (1963), and *Old Burnside* (1977). Of the first, one reviewer (*Library Journal*, June 15, 1960) says, "No detail [of pioneer life] is overlooked, not an item of clothing nor frontier recipe. Neither the loading of a long rifle nor the treatment of a scalped head." In the second, she is "concerned with the pioneer as a member of society engaged in those activities which could not be performed by a lone man." The last tells of the growth of a Pulaski County town from stage-coach days to motor-coach days. Taken collectively these volumes constitute a vast store of information about ordinary people during the westward movement in Kentucky and are of inestimable value to anyone who wants to know what life was like at this time.

The fourth novel after *The Dollmaker* that deals with Kentucky is

The Kentucky Trace: A Novel of the American Revolution (1975). Its scene is far away from the battles and other events of the war. The place is Southeastern Kentucky, and the characters are the hill people who have been left behind as the men have gone away in service to the rebel cause. On this scene arrives Leslie Collins, a surveyor, or what the Indians call a "land stealer," who has come home from active service with the colonists, only to discover that his farm has been deserted and his family is gone. Following a clue as to what has happened, Collins sets out down the Kentucky Trace and finds an encampment of men, women, and children trying to survive the ills that have befallen them. They are banded together in the struggle of everyday life trying to live through a traumatic time in an untamed frontier land.

In working out the action of the novel through the characters, Arnow reveals her views on a variety of subjects that are still of concern. One is the futility of war, and closely associated is the acquisitiveness of the white man operating under the banner of Manifest Destiny. The Indians, Collins is made to say, are dying "not for their sins but for the land that belonged to them"; and a farmer speculates, "Supposen the rebels lose. They'll try again. Supposen they win. . . . They'll be jarren and fighten around over slavery trade and a lot of other things. . . . Supposen they kill every Indian, plow up every acre a ground from the Atlantic to the Pacific. They'll still have their wars." Arnow, like Caroline Gordon in *Green Centuries* thirty-odd years earlier, also raises the ecological questions that trouble us today. Thus Collins the surveyor expresses his concern over the timberland being cut away and burned into charcoal with which to run iron furnaces and over the flight of the buffalo as the wilderness is laid waste because of destructive land practices.

Despite the timely concerns and the warm appeal of some of the matters with which the novel deals, it is not among Arnow's best. Sometimes it is beset with a sentimentality that cancels out the objectivity usually present in an Arnow novel and that will irritate more sophisticated readers. The tough-mindedness of the author of *Hunter's Horn* and *The Dollmaker* is too often lacking. Though Arnow's social history volumes were well praised for their thoroughness and accuracy, neither they nor her last two novels added to the excellent reputation her first three novels had achieved. These social histories are about as definitive as such volumes can be, but Arnow's place in literary history will rest on *Hunter's Horn* and *The Dollmaker*. So unpretentious are these novels that one is in danger of underrating them and failing to include them among the finest regional novels the country has produced. Time almost certainly will select *The Dollmaker* as her masterwork; it has a lasting quality and is one of the finest novels in recent American literature.

James Still

Unlike Harriette Arnow and Jesse Stuart, whose novels have appeared on best-seller lists, James Still (1906–) has never won a popular audience. He has, however, won many honors and has been well praised by a small but select band of supporters. Still was born in Lafayette, Alabama, got his A.B. from Lincoln Memorial University (where he knew Jesse Stuart), his M.A. from Vanderbilt University, and his B.S. in library science at the University of Illinois. When he was finishing his library science degree, jobs were scarce because of the Great Depression, and Still wandered over much of the East-Central United States doing odd jobs. While working with boys' clubs in Knott County, Kentucky, he was offered a library job at the Hindman Settlement School in 1932. There he stayed for six years, and in his zeal to get books to people in the surrounding countryside he operated a library-on-foot service, carrying books across his shoulders or on a pack-horse to one-room schools without libraries.

During this period Still was becoming well acquainted with mountain landscapes and the people who lived in them. He carefully observed their ways, their customs, their stories, and their manner of speaking, and he stored them away in notebooks and in memory for later use in the poetry and fiction he began writing in 1935. His first volume was *Hounds on the Mountains,* a collection of poems that was well received by the critics in 1937. His career as a writer thus established, Still resigned as librarian at the Hindman Settlement School and moved into "an ancient cabin" on Little Carr Creek near Wolfpen, in Knott County. Here, isolated by dirt and creekbed roads, Still began to work on his novel *River of Earth.*

In fairly quick succession Still published three rather small volumes: *Hounds on the Mountains* (1937), *River of Earth* (1940), and *On Troublesome Creek* (1941), a collection of short stories—490 pages in all. For thirty-five years Still's reputation depended on this rather slender output, save for the poems and short stories he published in the magazines. Then in 1976 he published *Pattern of a Man and Other Stories* and in 1980 *The Run for the Elbertas,* both volumes being selections of stories he had published in magazines, plus new versions of three stories previously published in *On Troublesome Creek.* Still's reputation still rests heavily on his first three volumes, but his last two not only make his writings more readily accessible but also contain some of his best short stories, the genre in which he excels.

The area Still writes about is Knott County, and the time is just following the coal boom that faded in the mid-1920s and forced the mines to operate on part-time schedules. Well before Still arrived in Knott County in 1932 poverty was widespread and full-time employment was nonexistent. What Still saw in the people and their plight seized his interest. First he tried to render practical, visible assistance and later to write about them. He chose not to follow the mountaineers who migrated to the outside world of Detroit and elsewhere but rather to portray what happens to miners and their families who remain behind and try to ply the only trade they know.

The key to Still's works lies in *River of Earth*. At the simplest level the novel traces the fortunes of a coal digger's family—the Baldridges—as they move from one coal camp to another. As the novel opens, the family is living on a small farm which it owns and on which the father, Brack, works while the Blackjack coal camp is closed. At the end of the first section, the mines are reopened, and in the second section the Baldridges move into the coal camp. In the third and final section the family is living on a small rented farm that it leaves as soon as the mines open again. But again Blackjack closes down, and at the end of the novel the family is preparing for yet another move, this time to Grundy and a new mine three days' journey away. "Hit's a far piece to Grundy," Brack says; "can't haul all our belongings. We'll sell and give away. We've got to begin over again. We've got to start from scratch." Brack keeps hoping each move will be his last, but no mine or camp is ever open more than a few months during a year; and as the Baldridges prepare to go to Grundy, it is clear that they are not headed for a better land but for another coal camp and that between camps they will have to find other ways to earn a living. Thus the constant opening, closing, and reopening of mines becomes the controlling factor in the life of a family who were lured away from their mountain plots and small farms by the attraction of high wages in the mines.

On Troublesome Creek (1941) and other stories written in later years also tell of miners and their search for intermittent work in the mines, but the scope is widened as we learn of the lives and experiences of mountaineers both inside the mines and out. Thus "The Moving" records the actual departure from a coal camp and reveals not only a miner's fear of losing a job but also his faith that somehow things are going to get better. In "The Proud Walkers" we read, ". . . all she feared was true. The building stood windowless, board ends of walls were unsawn, and the chimney pot barely cleared the hiproof." In "I Love My Rooster" the young narrator tells of how his family has been lured away from the land to the mines but is determined to farm again and put down roots. Sooner or later, in fact, mountaineers are seen in almost every aspect of their lives. Thus in "Quicksand Creek" the narrator is swindled, and in "Locust Summer" his mother becomes ill. "The Stir-Off" tells of the making of sorghum molasses; "The Fun Fox" tells of the experience of an eighteen-year-old schoolteacher in an unruly community. Everything is there: being born, growing up, and growing old; celebrations and funerals and weddings; the weather, the coal market, fights, politics, and fire-and-brimstone sermons. The whole culture of one place during a brief period has been recorded. "As the past withdraws," says Still in the "Afterword" of *The Run for the Elbertas* (1980), "it may be that the stories . . . amount to a social diagram of a folk society such as hardly exists today and may even include some of the uncharted aspects of the Appalachian experience."

But this sociological record is no more than a serendipitous fringe benefit as Still focuses on the people and the eternal verities. No one else has said it so well as did Dean Cadle, who in the *Yale Review* (Winter 1968) addressed Still's "concern with love, loyalty, hunger, death, and with the reactions of the individual when he is cornered, when he reaches the breaking point. . . . His is not a socio-economist's collection of figures, causes, and possible cures, but the dramatized plight of human beings accepting poverty without accusations or judgments and without rantings against ephemeral institutions. Acceptance of life as it is and refusals to admit defeat aptly describe the philosophy of most of Still's characters. They are always on the move in search of better living conditions. Like migrating birds, they move with the seasons back and forth from coal camps to hillside farms, always confident that this is the last move, that a life of plenty is ahead."

More than most writers of fiction Still keeps himself out of what he writes. He takes no sides, preaches no social doctrine, and offers no propaganda; nor is he writing proletarian fiction that deals with broad labor movements. Indeed, there are no labor disputes, unions are not involved, and the coal companies are small ones without undue industrial power. Yet "meaning" does emerge. There is, for example, the familiar metaphor of the machine engaged in a struggle against "the garden," the encroachment of industry upon the agrarian life. In *River of Earth* Brack Baldridge is the example of those who have "learned a trade," have no other way to make a living, and thus have become a cog in an industrial system which is dependent upon the demand for coal to keep the mines open. Juxtaposed throughout the novel is the image of the traditional mountaineer on a plot of hillside land. In particular, Alpha Baldridge—Brack's wife—dreads "being driv from one coal camp to another" and longs for "a lonesome place" where she can plant a garden, raise her children, and put down roots. Still treats Brack's need to follow the mines with the same understanding that he does Alpha's need for permanence and stability, but the debilitating effects of unemployment and poverty upon people and the contrast between the ugly terrain of the mines and the beauty of the earth do imply preferences. So likewise does Uncle Jolly Middleton's sizing up of the increasing neglect of the land: "Hain't many folks know how to tend dirt proper. . . . Land a-wasting and a-washing. Up and down Troublesome Creek it's the same. Timber cut off and hills eating down. Hit's alike all over. . . . What's folks going to live on when these hills wear down to a nub?"

A word must be said here of Still's narrator device and other metaphors of meaning. In *River of Earth* the narrator, Brack Baldridge's son, is seven years of age at the beginning of the novel, nine by the end of it. In other stories the narrator is sometimes older, sometimes younger. In any case, he determines the point of view in each of the stories and poems of which he is a part. Always he is unnamed, perhaps because by remaining so he is less a fixed personality, for without a name he remains a boy still in process of discovering his identity. Being but a boy, he comprehends less than adults do from the vantage point of their experience; at the same time, his innocence has not dulled his sense of wonder at the world, at spring and autumn, at birth and death. Sometimes in recording what he sees he gives a special quality to it because he does not understand; at the same time, his uncomprehending mind leaves him free to perceive things that the comprehending mind can no longer perceive because the impedimenta of time and experience have impaired the vision of innocence. Such a device is, of course, an old one, but it is still useful, for it gives the author the opportunity to be a sort of stage manager and to be center-stage even while seeming not to be there at all. If sometimes the young narrator seems more precocious and more perceptive than most boys his age, the author is exercising a bit of poetic license in order to provide an insight.

One more point about the narrator. In being young and in growing older as *River of Earth* progresses (as well as being older or younger in some of the stories and poems) we find in him the familiar metaphor of innocence giving way to experience, the age-old metaphor of the journey into life in search of meaning and purpose. Indeed, though the narrator is not the only quester, his search for meaning is central to Still's novel. He loves growing things, he wants to go to school, and he hopes to become a "horse doctor." The big question to him is "how fellers git growed," for he has observed that "some never git growed up. They git killed down." Elsewhere he declares, "I don't know how fellers git growed," for he is confronted with the reality that heredity and environment may already have shaped the outcome for him. "You can't git above your raising," he observes; "Hit's like metal agin lode-stone. Can't tear loose." He will, he senses, end up "snagging jackrock."

It is apparent that *River of Earth* is more than an account of the trials of one family in search of work and that, like other of Still's stories and poems, it has meaning beyond the narrative level. This is apparent, for example, in the sermon preached by Brother Sim Mobberly and in what is said not only by the narrator but also by other characters. "Oh, my children," intones Mobberly, "where are we going on this mighty river of earth, a-borning, begetting, and a-dying—the living and the dead riding the waters? Where air it sweeping us?" It is, of course, Brack Baldridge and his family to whom the metaphor of the journey of humankind through life is applied, but it is clear also that the scope of the metaphor applies to all human beings, including the author himself. Each person is in search of personal meaning; and each person is in search of an ideal world of being; and for each it is a different search. The kind of peace and sense of security that each seeks varies according to the scope of his or her own experience, or the need, or the vision. Brack Baldridge's dream is to have permanent work in a coal mine; Alpha's vision is to have a place where she can put down her roots, have a garden. Her quest—her journey—is nothing more than a return from the mining camps to the land whence she came. She says, "Walking John Gay traipsing and trafficking, looking the world over. Walked all the days of his life; seen more of creation than any other living creature. A lifetime of going and he's got nowhere, found no peace." Even more succinctly she says elsewhere, "Moving hain't nothing but leaving things behind." And Uncle Jolly Middleton exclaims, "Looky here, John Walkabout, where are ye forever going? What air ye expecting to see you've never saw before?" Then there is the point of view of John Gay himself. "I'm a-mind," he says, "to see every living hill against I die." For him, perhaps, the journey itself is the worthwhile thing, an end sufficient unto itself.

Although Still's works contain no allusion to books and to other matters outside the situation the author has created, there are metaphors that invoke archetypal patterns in the mind of the reader, repeated patterns that Jungian psychologists tell us have become apart of the racial memory and inheritance. These patterns, therefore, embody in myth form some of the deepest truths of the human race and are the possession of all men and women. We respond, we are told, when an author employs images or patterns of thought that correspond to the elements of the racial memory. One of these is man's alienation from the garden of plenty by the forces of evil, here present in the form of the destruction of the agrarian life by the machine of industry. Equally universal is the myth of man's odyssey, his journey through life and his search for purpose and meaning. These and other metaphors of meaning may be found in Still's stories and poems; they undergird and lend significance to the narrative level, though he does not weight these meanings heavily or dwell upon them.

Since Still is a regional writer, a word about his use of dialect is in order. He is totally free of the faults of the local colorists of the turn-of-the-century era, when the typical writer played up the quaint and outlandish dialect and behavior of his or her characters—and even exploited them. In Still's works, however, the behavior and speech patterns are authentic. Completely absent are dialect spellings and typographical symbols that suggest elisions. Still does not even drop the letter *g* from present tense participial forms. One could say correctly that in real life his characters speak of *doin'* things and *goin'* places, but Still has chosen to give the flavor of dialect by using a limited number of authentic dialect words and expressions. Thus with characteristic words of hill country speech he achieves his purpose without forcing his reader to decipher words that are typographically strange to him. Words such as "hain't," "boughten," "airy and nary," "poke," "air (for "are"), "fit" (for "fought"), "hit" (for "it"), "seed" (for "saw") are regularly in their proper places and in combination with the syntax of oral language achieve the status of authentic dialect. Language is one of the most important means through which a culture can be portrayed sensitively and convincingly. Still knows how to do this.

Still's style contains rhythms and poetic qualities in general as well as in particular when he describes a scene, makes a transition, portrays a reverie, creates a mood:

> The lamp was smothered; we crawled between covers. Once the light died the window hole turned gray. You could see the shoulders of the hills through it. Fern and Lark hushed and slept. I lay quiet, listening, and my ears were large and dark, catching midges of sound. The shuck mattress ticked, ticked, ticked. A rooster crowed. Night wore.

Such passages do not readily yield the secrets of their artistry. One can, however, speak of the simple spareness of the words, their exactness, and their tonal quality, and of the syntax and the ability of the words to create images. Still hears, sees, and writes prose as a poet; such passages open the way for the reader to "experience" what is being said rather than merely read it.

Since 1975 Still has published six volumes, all of them rounding out his "social diagram of a folk society." *Pattern of a Man* (1976) and *The Run for the Elbertas* (1980) were collected editions of short stories, but four other volumes were of a very different character, as the titles suggest adequately: *Way Down Yonder on Troublesome Creek: Appalachian Riddles and Rusties* (1974); *The Wolfpen Rusties: Appalachian Riddles and Gee-Haw Whimmy-Diddles* (1975); *Jack and the Wonder Bean* (1977); and *Sporty Creek: A Novel about an Appalachian Boyhood* (1977).

These four children's books were drawn from the "notebooks" and "steel cabinets filled with hundreds of manila folders" that Dean Cadle spoke of in his "Man on Troublesome." These files, apparently, are a "mixture of fact and imagination" and contain "a thirty-year history of the people in and around Knott County—their culture, their relationships with each other and with the land in all seasons" (*Yale Review* [Winter 1968]). All of them relate to Knott County or the nearby area, and while they are a contribution to children's literature, they are at the same time an in-depth record and reflection of the culture—customs, folklore, amusements, linguistic practices, and so on—of a people whose lives remained pretty much insulated from the outside world from pioneer days until well into the twentieth century.

Way Down Yonder on Troublesome Creek: Appalachian Riddles and Rusties (1974) refers again to Troublesome Creek, a sixty-seven mile-long stream that flows through three counties of Eastern Kentucky. In these stories Still writes of the lives and experiences of mountaineers both inside and outside the mines, reflecting a cross-section of the life of the region. He records the "riddles and rusties" he has collected in the area. By "rusties" he means "turns of wit, tricks of words, or common pranks" that have been a part of Appalachian oral tradition for generations. These stories provide a cultural study of a region that as late as World War II was still isolated from the world outside. Still's method, however, is humanistic rather than statistical or sociological.

Quite apart from being "a social diagram," the volume stands on its own as a collection of "riddles and rusties" designed to entertain both the young and the old. It is generally classified as "juvenile literature," and the *Library Journal* recommends it for "grades three to six," declaring that "except for a few selections in Ray Wood's *American Mother Goose*, this joke collection presents a fine assortment of riddles and rusties (wise cracks or pranks) that are unavailable elsewhere" (March 15, 1974). By their very nature riddles and rusties are often "corny," but children throughout time have shared the irresistible attraction of trying them out on their friends: "My pappy gave it to me, though it belonged to my grandpaw . . . and proud as I am to have it other people use it more than I do." Answer: "My name." "There is a toe that will never suffer a corn or be pinched by a tight shoe." Answer: "Mistletoe." Janet McCaffery's woodcuts are excellent and enhance the folksy, sometimes earthy, contents.

The Wolfpen Rusties: Appalachian Riddles and Hee-Haw Whimmy-Diddles (1975) has its origins in a valley two miles long and about one hundred-fifty yards wide that was cut by Wolfpen Creek. This volume, also based on Still's own observations and investigations, records riddles, rusties, and pranks, and contains descriptions of celebrations, customs, and the whittling of wooden toys called Hee-Haws and Whimmy-Diddles. A page contains several riddles whose answers are printed upside down. Thus: "How many dead folk in Bald Point graveyard?" Answer (upside down): "All of them." The volume is a record of folk humor and again is well illustrated by Janet McCaffery's woodcuts, which as one reviewer puts it, picture "the smiles, chortles, and horse-laughs" which the rusties and the descriptions provoke.

A different sort of volume for children is Still's *Sporty Creek* (1977), subtitled "A novel about an Appalachian boyhood." The story comprises ten chapters—or separate stories—which tell of life in the Kentucky hills during the Great Depression. The narrator is a nine-year-old boy whose family, with work almost nonexistent in the mines, moves from place to place, eking out a living as best they can. The novel is not, however, a saga of downtrodden vagrants but of a robust people with courage, a sense of humor, and a zest for life. Like Still's adult novels, this one tells a compelling story about people who as they struggle to survive also love, get angry, laugh, and are aware of themselves and of the beauty and the ugliness alike of the world they live in.

In *Jack and the Wonder Bean* (1977) Still has written an Appalachian version of the old fairy tale *Jack and the Beanstalk*. The Wolfpen additions to and variations on the traditional story and the language are often startling and amusing, not only in content but in the dialect and the colloquialisms employed. Thus the giant says, "Fee, fie, chew tobacco, I smell the toes of a tadwhacker," and Jack's mother chides her son with, "You couldn't be trusted to pack slop to a sick bear." The volume, which was illustrated by Margot Tomes, was a Library of Congress Children's Book of the Year and a *New York Times Book Review* Best Illustrated Children's Book of the Year.

Although the fiction and poetry of Still and Arnow cover overlapping time periods, the differences between the two are greater than their similarities. They differ, in fact, in their focuses, purposes, and methods. Whereas Arnow's expository volumes are all rooted in history, Still's record, is more exclusively contemporary and personal, as well as more limited in geographical area and time covered. Writing of two areas only a few miles apart, these two have left a remarkable gift to posterity, not only in their fiction but in the storehouse of "information" they have collected and published with remarkable care.

Still is a writer's writer, and his audience has been small. Writing in 1980 about his earlier years as an author, he says, "Although my stories and poems were appearing in *The Atlantic Monthly*, *The Yale Review*, *The Virginia Quarterly Review*, and a variety of other publications and I had three published books, I do not recall encountering anybody during these years who had read them. I wrote in an isolation which was virtually total." Nevertheless, in 1941 he was awarded a Guggenheim Fellowship and another in 1946 after he got out of the army. Other recognitions that came through the years include awards from the American Academy of Arts and Letters and the National Institute of Arts and Letters, inclusion of three stories in *Best American Short Stories* and four in the O. Henry Memorial Award Prize Stories (1937, 1938, 1939, 1941); and in 1940 his *River of Earth* enabled him to share the Southern Author's Award with Thomas Wolfe (for *You Can't Go Home Again*). There have also been awards from Kentucky organizations and honorary degrees from Kentucky universities; and, notably, fellowships have been established in his name, including those funded by the Mellon Foundation for Advanced Study in the Humanities and Social Studies and by the University of Kentucky in Appalachian Studies.

Jesse Stuart

It is not easy to write about Jesse Stuart (1907–1984) within the space limitations imposed by a volume such as this. Stuart not only wrote in no fewer than five literary genres, but was one of Kentucky's most prolific authors; and his place in the literary world is decidedly controversial. There can, however, be no question about where one should begin a discussion of Stuart:

> I didn't have any choice as to where I was born,
> But if I had had my choice,
> I would have chosen Kentucky.
> . . . .
> If I could have chosen the spot in Kentucky,
> I would have chosen W-Hollow,
> The place where I was born.

These lines from *Kentucky Is My Land* express the central fact in Jesse Stuart's life and works. Not only was he born at W-Hollow, but its past and its present, its land and its people, its seasons and its crops, its plants, its flowers, and its trees, as well as the social and political structures that hold it together—these constitute the subject he wrote about throughout his life.

W-Hollow is first of all a geographical place among the Plum Grove Hills, but it is also a place at the imaginative level. Not only was it there waiting for Stuart with subjects to be written about when he was born, but in time Stuart came to see that he was living in and writing about a time and a place that was changing in the face of the technological advances that were opening up W-Hollow to the world and the world to W-Hollow even as he wrote. Soon, he saw, the place as he knew it would cease to be, and he felt that he must record it in his writings. What he found to write about was almost unending in its variety, but as he was to learn, there were dangers in the abundance, for it was inevitable that particular subjects, themes, and character types would occupy his attention and sometimes lead to complaints about repetitiveness.

Stuart began writing about his world during the Great Depression; yet the W-Hollow he portrays has no sociological implications.

Some of the characters are strange and have their psychological problems and phobias, but he takes no sort of pathological interest in their doings. Uncle Jeff is "worn out" from working hard for the railroad, and the hill people generally are hard put to avoid poverty, but Stuart shows no proletarian interest in their situation. Nowhere is a character portrayed who might be likely to get involved in a labor dispute. Stuart was writing his best fiction and poetry during the 1930s, 1940s, and 1950s just as Harriette Arnow and James Still were, but the worlds they portray and the relationship of their characters to the outside world are wholly different. Stuart does make use of the welfare state in *Taps for Private Tussie*, but he does so largely for the sake of the extravagantly humorous situations it provides. Any concern about a welfare system that perpetuates both itself and those who need it is present only obliquely.

The fact is that Stuart dealt with the people of W-Hollow as individuals or small groups rather than in a collective or sociological sense. We know them as they are given life in his stories and poems, as they are revealed in vignettes. Many of them are his friends and acquaintances, and often they, like Stuart himself, are revealed with biographical accuracy, though both they and he move back and forth between biography and fiction so easily that it is not always possible to distinguish between the two. The people as well as the place have actual physical shape and geographical boundaries, but both exist at another level also because of the coloring of the imagination that has played over them; some are not native to W-Hollow but are drawn there from the community that lies just outside its perimeter.

When Stuart began his literary career by publishing his first volume of verse privately in 1930 as *Harvest of Youth*, he was almost entirely ignored, but four years later when he published *Man with a Bull-Tongue Plow* (1934) he suddenly found himself famous. What was it that happened during this interval that made such a difference? Most of all, no doubt, it was his experience at Vanderbilt University while working on his M.A. in 1931–32. Harry Harrison Kroll at Lincoln Memorial University, where Stuart had received his A.B. in 1929, had encouraged him to write verse and he had done so at a great rate. This verse made up the contents of *Harvest of Youth*. At Vanderbilt he came under the influence of Edwin Mims and Donald Davidson. When (according to Stuart) in the former's Victorian poetry class Stuart had submitted a three-hundred page autobiographical typescript instead of the much shorter assigned account, Mims scolded him sharply. Then a few days later he handed the paper back to Stuart, declaring, "I have been teaching school for forty years. I have never read anything so crudely written and yet beautiful, tremendous and powerful as that term paper you've written." What Mims had just read was the first draft of *Beyond Dark Hills*, written in just eleven days while Stuart carried on his duties of being a janitor as well as a graduate student. But Donald Davidson exerted the greatest influence of all, for it was he who worked with Stuart, advised him to avoid "arty" poems, and admonished him instead to write about the land and the people he knew and loved.

By the fall of 1932, his native agrarianism no doubt reinforced by the Vanderbilt Agrarians, Stuart was back in W-Hollow declaring to his brother, "I am going to write poetry to suit myself from now on. . . . I'm going to be myself and write to suit myself and the way I damn well please. I can't do any worse than I have done." Within less than a year he had written more than seven hundred "sonnets" that ranged from twelve to seventeen lines and reflected no concern about adhering to the usual sonnet conventions. Many of these poems appeared in magazines with a national circulation; then in October 1934 they were published as *Man with a Bull-Tongue Plow* and Stuart was at once a national literary figure. It was perhaps the best volume of verse Stuart ever published. It was also vintage Stuart with its headlong flow of words, intense emotion, strong subjectivity, and careless attention to form. Much of the criticism of the volume was harsh but much was also warmly favorable; hardly any was neutral. To some reviewers Stuart had written entirely too much for his own good or the reader's; half the time, said another, he had been careless, trite, and perfunctory; he had, according to others, tossed the poems at the reader helter-skelter, had been glib and careless with words, had said everything twice. But there was praise too: some of the poems were said to have the freshness of medieval ballads; some of them, though rough, were declared to have great beauty. Generally Stuart was seen as a true original and as a poet of great honesty. Stuart must have enjoyed especially the judgment of Edgar Lee Masters, who declared, "I have such confidence in him that I would turn him loose in Boston the rest of his life without any fear that Boston would ruin him."

Though Stuart was stung by some of the criticism, he also listened and was determined that his next volume of verse would be his masterpiece. As a matter of fact, he would take ten years before publishing his next volume, *Album of Destiny* (1944), as against the eleven months he spent on *Man with a Bull-Tongue Plow*. A.E. (George Russell) had pronounced *Man with a Bull-Tongue Plow* the greatest book of American verse since *Leaves of Grass*, and Stuart wanted to live up to this billing.

The idea for *Album of Destiny* came to him while he was leafing through an old family album and was greatly moved by the way time had changed the people whose pictures he saw there. He was struck by the mutability of life. And so with a secure structure for what he would say, for ten years he slowly developed the portraits of fifty people of W-Hollow, portraying them in the four stages of their lives from the springtime of youth through summer and autumn, and finally the winter of old age, four portraits for each person. He worked hard at it, keeping the advice of the critics in mind, but alas he apparently worked too hard, revised too much, and chipped and fit too often. In the process, he lost much of the spontaneity that was his virtue. Though he cut the number of portraits from the one hundred he started with, he failed to cut enough to avoid the charge that the volume was too great and the portraits monotonous. The volume was little noticed, appearing as it did during World War II while Stuart was in the navy. Stuart was sorely disappointed, for apparently he thought of himself as a poet first and only secondarily as a writer of prose. Meanwhile his place in the literary world was undergoing alteration with both the critics and the reading public. In 1936 he had published *Head o' W-Hollow*, perhaps his best collection of short stories; in 1938, his fine autobiographical account, *Beyond Dark Hills*, that gave some insight into his thinking; in 1940, *Trees of Heaven*, his first novel; in 1941, *Men of the Mountains*, another collection of short stories; and in 1943, *Taps for Private Tussie*, another novel, a Book of the Month Club choice and winner of the Thomas Jefferson Award for the best Southern book of the year. Whether he liked it or not, the public had come to think of Jesse Stuart primarily as a writer of fiction.

Thereafter Stuart did not abandon poetry, but he did throw more of his energies into prose. His next volume of verse, *Kentucky Is My Land* (1952), was first written as prose and subsequently revised and cut into lines and free-verse paragraphs. Though not first-rate poetry, it expresses sentiments that were always close to Stuart's heart. The first part, the title piece for the volume, expresses his love for Kentucky and celebrates the many facets of its appeal to him. The seventh (and last) part, "The Builder and the Dream," tells of the dreams of a boy, Ben Tuttle, whose vision is to reforest the neglected lands of the valley where he grew up. As a man Ben does just this, buying his land piece by piece and planting trees, until at last he has reforested a thousand acres. This was precisely what Jesse Stuart did. Twenty-seven years later, December 1979, Stuart's one thousand acres were formally dedicated to the people of Kentucky as the Jesse Stuart Nature Preserve. Under an agreement between the Stuarts and the Commonwealth half of the land was donated by Stuart and his wife, the other half purchased from the Stuarts with state and federal funds.

It was ten years before Stuart's next volume of verse, *Hold April* (1962), appeared, written after his near-fatal heart attack. In it are some excellent poems and lines, but the poems are more subdued than those that first brought him into fame. His love of the land and of people is still there, but the vibrancy of spring is gone and darker autumnal tones have made their appearance as the poet clings to beauty lest it fade. The spirit of the volume, as the title suggests, is that of middle age, the quieter pleasures, and remembered youth. It seems safe to say that in neither *Hold April* nor his total output of poetry did Stuart achieve the goals that he set out to reach. Just a year before he published *Hold April*, however, he was awarded the prestigious Academy of American Poets Award for 1961.

It is generally agreed that Jesse Stuart was more comfortable and more successful with the short story than with any of the other literary genres. What better way, given Stuart's talent and temperament, was there to portray the life of W-Hollow than with the sharp, quick focus that the short story provides? It was not, however, the traditional, carefully plotted, well-made story that interested Stuart, but a straightforward narrative following a single action in a time sequence. Nor did he create developing characters any more than he created a carefully patterned plot. Often, in fact, the narrative might seem like a tall tale, a yarn, or even just an episode. Stuart simply was not greatly interested in technique. Almost any structure or framework that could support an action and reveal character was sufficient.

A principal source of Stuart's success was the zeal, the zest with which he launched a story and carried it forward in a rushing flow of words and flood of detail to the very end. Much of the time the story is told by a narrator who, regardless of his name, is very close to being the author himself, for Stuart was always emotionally involved in the stories he told. The joy Stuart derived from telling a story is evident in the *in medias res* beginning of "Another Hanging":

> I'll remember the Bellstrase Hangin' to my dyin' day. We've had our hangin's! We've had the Sizemore Hangin', the Dimmer Hangin', Dillmore Hangin', Perkins Hangin', and the Reeder Hangin'. We never had

> a hangin' that would come up to the Bellstrase Hangin' in 1903. . . . It was one of the best hangin's this country has ever seen.

Mood, too, is another important ingredient in a Stuart short story. "I just love," Stuart says, "to write a short story. I can get ideas for short stories and put them right down on paper. Then I wonder why I don't go on and work them into novels. But the novel is too much longer. I can't sustain the mood. I can sustain a single mood in a short story."

For the most part, the characters and incidents Stuart writes about come from daily life and everyday experience in W-Hollow. Much of the time this is true, but such a statement hardly accounts for the odd and outlandish characters he sometimes writes about and their unlikely and bizarre behavior. Akin to this is his introduction of a startling or shocking incident or episode, even what has been called black-bile humor, into the midst of a scene of tenderness or lyrical beauty. To some readers the effect is that of a sharp instrument being drawn raspingly across a beautifully burnished table top. Against such an objection it is commonly pointed out that the incident can be documented in real life, but the obvious rejoinder to such a defense is that there is a higher and greater truth than the truth of fact and history that is attested to by life itself. Perhaps a better defense of Stuart's technique is that there is—or once was—something in the rigors and hardness of Appalachian life that yields best to this sort of release from life's tensions. Perhaps a reconciliation in these opposites provides a resolution that is both psychologically and artistically sound. Such episodes can be found in other Appalachian writers, among them Harriette Arnow and James Still and younger writers such as Gurney Norman. In several Stuart stories opposites are juxtaposed: kindness and cruelty, tenderness and violence, hard times and good times, beauty and ugliness, the primitive and the civilized, death and birth.

Since Stuart wrote more than 450 short stories, this discussion can only allude to some of the typical and better ones and sample some that illustrate his methods. There are, for example, stories of folk customs such as "The Bellin' of the Bride," a story of serenading a couple just married with the ringing of cow-bells, shooting of guns, beating of washtubs, and the drinking, eating, and square-dancing that follows. There are stories of lyrical beauty and pathos and magic, as in "Walk in the Moon Shadows," where a mountain mother takes her children for a walk in the moonlight in order to look for the ghosts of happier years. Here as elsewhere throughout Stuart's stories are passages of fine poetic prose: "There were a few dim stars in the sky but over the meadows, down where there were long moon shadows from the tall trees, thousands of lightning bugs lighted their ways, going here, there, and nowhere." There are stories of boyhood, such as "Thanksgiving Hunter," the story of a small boy on his first dove hunt. Though with misgivings about shooting one of the beautiful birds, he finally gives a dove call that brings a dove to a point near him, whereupon he sees that the bird is blind and knows that he cannot kill it. Then comes the voice of the bird's mate from a nearby tree and the blind bird flies toward the sound, and "I heard its wings batting the wind-shaken boughs as it ascended, struggling, toward the beckoning voice." And there are stories of old age, such as "Another April." Here an old man of ninety-one after a long winter is allowed out of doors for the first time, sees "my old friend" the terrapin, gently examines the blossoms on a dogwood tree, and goes back in the house because it is "a-gettin' a little chilly."

Stuart's subjects are almost numberless, but "Another Hangin'" may serve as an example of his vintage stuff: a flood of fast-flowing words and details, exuberant comic humor, the shockingly bizarre, and pathos, all served up with joyous gusto from the opening sentence to the last. Willard Bellstrase has committed a murder and is about to be executed in a public hanging. To witness the proceedings have come vast numbers of men, women, and children from everywhere, for the occasion is a major entertainment that can relieve the dreary, hard tedium of the mountain people's daily lives. To the reader the events and the mob behavior described in unsparing detail by the youthful narrator, Eif, are scenes of revolting horror. To Eif, with his new shoes and hat and suit, it is a holiday scene; and his happiness is complete when he meets Beadie, "the prettiest girl at the hangin," and gets to hold her and love her "all the way back to White Rock." "Bring in the man," the crowd screams, and later, "Let the Goddam door fall!" "This is a real hangin'," Beadie says to Eif; "I'm glad I come and met you." As the trap door opens and Willard's body drops through, twisting, the excitement of the crowd reaches a frenzied peak. "Cut the rope and hang him again," one man shouts; "Grab somebody else and hang 'em," shouts another. As the exhausted day finally winds to its end, the crowd breaks up into its many parts, some to load their drunken companions onto the train, some to go home to do their milking and other chores, some to rehash and relive the exciting events of the day.

Of the many short stories that Stuart published in magazines, more than 150 appeared in collections, the first of which was *Head of*

W-Hollow (1936). The volume was perhaps equal in quality to any of the collections that followed, and the themes and the subject matter of the later stories would change little through the years. *Men of the Mountains* (1941) did seem to reflect life during the 1930s and the droughts and Great Depression as they affected the people of W-Hollow, and *Tales from the Plum Grove Hills* (1946) gave more attention to the Stuart family when Jesse was a boy; but in general each volume was selected from the stories published during the intervals between collections. *Clearing in the Sky* came in 1950, *Plowshare in Heaven* in 1958, *My Land Has a Voice* in 1966, *Come Gentle Spring* in 1969, and *Dawn of Remembered Spring* in 1972.

During a span of five or six years in the middle and late 1930s Stuart had a period of remarkable achievement, culminating in 1940 with *Trees of Heaven*, which many regard as his best novel. The plot (and theme) of *Trees of Heaven* is simple enough. Anse Bushman is an austere man, a hard-working, land-greedy farmer, seventy-one years old, whose goal in life has been to own more and more land. In achieving his goal, he has worked his wife almost to death and has alienated ten of his eleven children. Boliver Tussie is a hillbilly squatter who lives off the land and is the opposite of everything that Anse symbolizes. He is carefree, likes to drink, go to dances, and follow the hounds. The plot begins to develop when Anse buys the Sexton land on which Boliver has been a squatter all his life; it builds when Anse rents the land to Boliver on a sharecrop basis and draws up articles of agreement that go beyond matters of business by forbidding the Tussie family to make moonshine, have dances, attend revivals more than twice a week, and have babies. The Tussies prove to be hard workers who grow good crops but fall short of the "moral" restrictions placed upon them by running into debt, making moonshine, and having babies, one of them the child of Anse's son Tarvin.

The resolution of the plot is less satisfactory than one would wish, but the fine portrayal of character and the vigorous flow of language are typical of Stuart at his best. One example is the passage in which Anse describes his enjoyment of food and the physical act of eating: "I'd rather watch hogs eat . . . as to eat myself. . . . Watch them white hogs try to lay down in the trough, won't you? I like to see 'em greedy like that. I like to see a person eat like a hog. I'm jealous of a man that can eat more than I can." Another occasion is when the spring equinox comes and Anse plunges into the night and walks up and down his fields in the midst of thunder and lightning and rain, exulting as he walks, "A sight like this will only come once. . . . This is the resurrection of spring. . . . Tomorrow we will have a new earth. . . . This is the best night of the year." Stuart also lavished care on Boliver Tussie, of whom he said in later years, "I loved him." Thus Stuart has Boliver say, "If I didn't have me a little snort from the jug every Saturday, life wouldn't be worth living. Just a little snort from the jug on Saturday and fox huntin' two nights out of the week and something to eat three times a day, good homemade twist to chew, and old Boliver can git along in this world."

There is, of course, much more in *Trees of Heaven*; for example, Stuart's fascination with explaining how to do farm jobs. There is celebration of the land, sometimes in poetic prose that grows out of its beauty and the cycles of the seasons, but there is no glossing over the fact that even to a man like Anse Bushman life on the land can be hard: "Town ain't no place for Boliver," Anse says to his son Tarvin; "Boliver hast his faults but he belongs to the dirt same as I belong to the dirt. He belongs to these rough slopes—these rocks and these deep hollers. Be shore, Tarvin, that you bring 'im back."

Trees of Heaven was a foretaste of other Stuart novels, and the praise it received, like the faults that were found, in general typified later criticism. Readers and critics alike have delighted in Stuart's vigor and enthusiasm, his enormous flow of words and the headlong pace of his style, his freshness, the abundance of human warmth, and his portrayal of hill people and their ways. But his faults have sometimes had a kinship with his merits. The enthusiasm for his forceful flow of language, for example, has been tempered by the regret that he is not more economical in his use of words and the wish that he were a more disciplined writer, and one who revised with greater care before going into print.

Another complaint commonly raised is that his plots are less than adequate and in general not well executed. Indeed, a talent for well-made plots expertly executed has never been a part of Jesse Stuart's equipment, in either his short stories or his novels. His greatest talent lay in creating superb episodes—a fact which explains why he is at his best when he is writing a short story and why some critics of his novels assert that they are not really plotted but are merely a series of episodes. Another complaint sometimes raised against Stuart is that his character portrayals, though often excellent, are static rather than dynamic, flat rather than developed. Such a complaint, of course, is more likely to be valid in a novel than in a short story. Skill with episodes, descriptive narrative, and "flat" characters is compatible with the short story, but not with carefully patterned plots, and dynamic, developed characters, and the novel. Stuart was simply not an experimenter with the technique of story-telling.

Taps for Private Tussie (1943), Stuart's second and most popular novel, sold more than a million copies. The plot centers upon the poor-white, hillbilly Tussies, who have suddenly come into possession of ten thousand dollars. A member of the family, Kim, was "kilt over yander" during World War II, and his life insurance money has enabled the Tussie family of five to move into the finest house in town, the Rayburn house. Here, of course, is ample opportunity for great fun as the improvident Tussies get used to fourteen rooms, use the indoor plumbing, and flip the light switches on and off, but the tempo of the wild humor and outrageous scenes rises even more when Tussie relatives swell the number of residents in the Rayburn house to forty-six. Drinking their moonshine, lolling in the yard, filling three tables at every meal, and square dancing every night, the Tussies live lives of great hilarity that gradually wreck the house, lead to their eviction, scatter the sponging relatives, and cause Grandpa and his family to move into a shack where, he says, he "feels more at home" anyway.

But another kind of humor also runs through the story. This humor centers upon the able-bodied "relief" Tussies and their use and abuse of government relief and assistance programs. Press Tussie ("Grandpa"), the leader of the clan, is skilled, among other things, at getting extra food at the Relief Office because he controls so many Tussie votes. "I'm a-livin' just the way I wany to live," Grandpa says; "I don't haf to work 'long as the government feeds me. Why should I work?" The only fault he has to find is that he must go seven miles to get his relief food. "It's a far piece to walk after your grub," he says; "If a man votes for it, b-gad, they ought to deliver it to his door." "Relief," says Sid, the boy narrator of the story, "It's one industry that keeps a-growin' right through good times."

Satiric humor underlies many of Stuart's portrayals, and sociological implications are clearly abundant; but Stuart, as always, is not a polemicist and he refuses to become involved in proletarian concerns. He is simply not a reformer. It is clear, too, that the Tussies are not just the Jeeter Lesters of *Tobacco Road*. The Tussie squatter philosophy includes a proper lack of ambition and no desire for possessions; yet Stuart does include love of the soil, among both the "sharecropper" Boliver Tussies and the "relief" Press Tussies. On his deathbed Grandpa lets some rich loam from the fifty-acre farm Vittie has bought for him trickle through his fingers: "It's wonderful to know that this land is mine," he says; "It's the first time in my life

I've ever had a deed for land. I'm a proud man to own land." Nor are the Tussies merely parasites; they are simply the particular kind of human beings they happen to be; and though Stuart has used them fully for boisterous laughter, he has employed a concomitant to humor that once caused him to characterize the novel as a "sad thing"—a sort of pathos that lies just below the surface and keeps human sensibility alive. Thus in addition to Grandpa's deathbed statement about the land, there is the narrator Sid's recollection of the family togetherness he experienced when forty-six Tussies lived together in the big Rayburn house. "I've never seen anything like the dances we had, as many as four sets a-dancin' at a time. . . . Many nights we danced all night." Sensitivity to something lost or never quite realized remains strictly subordinate to the hillbilly fun and belly-laughter, but at the same time it keeps the Tussies from being merely ciphers or merely case histories of inherited indolence in a time of rapid social change. It reflects, too, the respectful broad tolerance with which Jesse Stuart viewed his world.

Foretaste of Glory (1946) is a novel whose central structural device reminds one of a number of well-known literary works, *Spoon River Anthology* among them. On the night of September 18, 1941, the residents of Blakesburg are galvanized into action when a great display of lights appears in the sky, for they think it is the beginning of the end of the world. In a series of sketches held together by the phenomenon itself, Stuart reports on the behavior of the people of Blakesburg. Some frantically make confessions of secret wrongdoings, most seek to make peace with their Maker, others do unexpected or eccentric things. From Liam Winston, who exits from the boarding house shouting to Judge Whittlecomb, "The goddamned world's a-coming to an end," to the prisoners in the county jail who complain as they are released, "Hit's a hell of a poor time to free us now," to Charley Albright throwing away the crutches that enabled him to collect disability insurance dishonestly, the people of the town are put on display.

Such a central structure and "plot" provide, of course, an excellent vehicle for Stuart's talent. But despite the opportunity it provided him for character portrayals and although it was favorably received by the press, *Foretaste of Glory* was Stuart's least popular novel. It contains some of his best humor, but some of it may have seemed too close to reality and so close to peeking that some of Stuart's readers, including those in his home county, were offended. Doubtless, too, more judicious readers may have felt that the character portrayals did not go below the surface but existed primarily for the laughter that comes from exposing the foibles and frailties of men and women in their unguarded moments.

The Good Spirit of Laurel Ridge (1953) is another novel that fails to measure up to Stuart's best, especially in its plot and the portrayal of minor characters. Central to its merits is the main character, Theopolis Akers, known as Old Op, one of Stuart's most notable creations. Generally Stuart's characters are wedded to the soil, but Old Op goes further and is a Rousseauistic child of nature. His food comes from the land and he has an herb for every ailment. He tells time by the sun and by the animals and the insects; he hunts and traps, gathers plants from the land, and fishes with a bow and arrow. His demesne he owns not by purchase or deed but because he is coeval with the primitive rural Eden on wooded, enchanted Laurel Ridge. "There are," says Old Op, "still pockets of earth left as God made 'em"; and there are "sperets" that inhabit the land. In contrast with this spirit is the modern world of things that sometimes impinge upon it: Alf Pruitt, some people from Dayton, the foxhunters, a soldier who is AWOL, and some army officials in a jeep.

When in the 1950s after a long lapse Stuart began again to write children's stories, his return to the genre was not surprising. His career as a teacher and role in educational administration, as well as his understanding of youth as expressed in his writings, bespeak his interest in young people. Indeed, such a novel as *Hie to the Hunters* (1950) can almost be called a novel for young adults. It was not until *The Beatinest Boy* (1953) was published, however, followed during the next seventeen years by six other novels for children, that he became known as a writer of children's literature: *A Penny's Worth of Character* (1954), *Red Mule* (1955), *The Rightful Owner* (1960), *Andy Finds a Way* (1961), *A Ride with Huey the Engineer* (1966), and *Old Ben* (1970).

The Beatinest Boy is the best of these. It is the story of an orphan boy brought up by an impoverished grandmother who teaches him many practical and useful things, such as caring for a puppy, getting honey from a bee tree, learning to make decisions for himself, and being resourceful. Running through the story is the boy's effort to find or make an appropriate Christmas gift for his grandmother. The giving of the tablecloth and napkins he has learned to make from feed sacks ends the story. The novel, which was warmly received, has the qualities that make up a successful children's story: a simple and strong story line, the inculcation of moral and ethical principles, and a style and language that enhance the story and the action. Its fault, commonly found in Stuart's children's stories, is that the conversations are stiff and even stilted rather than relaxed and natural.

A Penny's Worth of Character and *The Rightful Owner* likewise have the essential features that appeal to children in the middle grades. The first centers upon a mountain boy who is tempted to cheat by including a bag with a hole in it in order to have enough bags to trade for candy and pop at the store. In the latter a boy finds a lost dog, makes it an important part of his life, and then lives in dread of the fact that some day the rightful owner may appear and claim him. Again Stuart's love of Eastern Kentucky is everywhere evident, his style is appropriate to his reading audience, and the ethical and moral problems are satisfactorily handled. *Red Mule* and *A Ride with Huey the Engineer* are interesting in that they reflect Stuart's nostalgia for a passing way of life and his apparent desire to give young people a feeling for the past. The first reflects his regret that machines are increasingly doing the work that people and animals once did, revealed through an outcast whose mission is to keep mules in the work force. *A Ride with Huey the Engineer* capitalizes upon the important part a short-line railroad used to play in the life of a rural community. These books all have boys as main characters and animals playing important roles: dogs, mules, a snake (*Old Ben*), and a calf (*Andy Finds a Way*). The characters and plots are well rooted in the earth and have a sense of community with their world.

Anyone looking for a discussion of Jesse Stuart's non-belletristic writings must look elsewhere. An examination of his lesser fiction, his autobiographical writings (including *Beyond Dark Hills* and *The Thread That Runs So True*), as well as full studies of all his works, can be found in Ruel Foster's Twayne Series volume, *Jesse Stuart* (1968), J.R. Le Master's *Jesse Stuart: Kentucky's Chronicler-Poet* (1980), J.R. Le Master and Mary W. Clarke's (eds.) *Jesse Stuart: Essays on His Works* (1977), and Harold Richardson's biography *Jesse* (1984).

It is an idle sort of guessing game to try to outwit time and assign a large or small place in either our state or national literary pantheon to a writer whose merits have been as controversial as Jesse Stuart's. During his lifetime he was accustomed to three critical reactions: an uncritical, almost mindless adulation that would make him one of America's great authors; an indifference close to scorn that either ignored him or dismissed him summarily as an undisciplined writer with few ideas and small literary merit; and a more temperate view which had lamented shortcomings while readily citing strengths and offering encouragement and critical advice. The first two of these reactions have unquestionably missed something. Even when one agrees that Stuart wrote too much, exercised too little care, and blazed no new trails, it seems fair to say that the literary establishment has been at fault in failing to discover the merit that Stuart unquestionably has: effectiveness in handling an episode, skill in descriptive narrative, power of language, and excellence in the portrayal of a static character. At the same time, no thoughtful student of literature can successfully brush away Stuart's lack of skill in technique or ignore the defects that grew out of the headlong pace at which he wrote and his seeming resistance to careful revision.

Stuart never ceased to be a bit sorry that he failed to win favor with a substantial segment of the literary establishment and with some of his fellow writers whose approval he would have relished. At the same time, it is to his credit that he never tried to be other than as he was. Stuart knew pretty well what he couldn't do as well as what he could do, and he chose to maintain his personal and artistic integrity. It seems safe to predict that his best verse and stories will have a secure place in Kentucky literature and that he will be remembered among the regional writers of our national literature of the middle third of the century.

Harlan H. Hatcher

Patterns of Wolfpen, by Harlan H. Hatcher (1898–), is different from the usual novel about the Kentucky mountains in that its subject is timber rather than coal and that the central characters are members of the upper middle class. The author's concerns are familiar, however, for Hatcher's aim was to portray the conflict between the native mountain culture and the rising tide of industrialism that would destroy it. Hatcher was born in Ironton, Ohio, but he moved to Kentucky when his father took a teaching position in the state, and as he grew up he made excursions into the Big Sandy River country and learned the history of the region and its people, his interest whetted by the fact that his own ancestors had been early settlers in the region. Not, however, till he was professor of English at Ohio State University did he begin writing about the passing of the old order as it gave way before the new.

The time of Hatcher's story is the 1880s when Sparrel Pattern sells off to a timber company most of the six thousand acres of land that Saul Pattern had come into possession of in 1790 and had passed on to generations of Patterns that nourished it well. The setting is the ancestral home of the Patterns at Wolfpen Bottoms, in Pike County, as Cynthia, Sparrel's daughter, witnesses the woodlands being stripped bare and a well-mannered way of life destroyed as the big lumber companies fell great trees in the name of progress. Hatcher's central concern is with the comfortable, well-ordered agricultural life that is now being brought to an end. Lumbering operations were better suited to the typical mountaineer's work habits and did not as seriously alter either his living habits or cultural life as did coal-mining operations with their coal camps. *Patterns of Wolfpen*, then, is an example of a not-often-found interpretation of mountain people of the upper class.

Hatcher wrote two other novels about Kentucky. *Tunnel Hill* (1931) has as its scene a brick-yard town on the Ohio River and *Central Standard Time* (1937) is a story of people in an industrialized town caught up in the aftermath of the Great Depression. Hatcher also wrote and edited several scholarly books while at Ohio State University, 1923–51; in 1951 he became president of the University of Michigan and continued in that position until his retirement in 1967.

Henry H. Hornsby

Henry H. Hornsby (1910–   ) was one of the post–World War II novelists whose purpose was to write of Kentucky mountain life as it actually was and with greater realism and candor than many of their predecessors had done. There had been novels well weighted with romantic primitivism, some that were folksy, many that were sociological, some that were full of the violence of feuding, others that were given over to strife in the coal fields. Hornsby's aim was to write of mountain people and their ordinary daily lives, not as feudists, not as unemployed coal miners, not as a misunderstood or maltreated people, but as real people without the coloration that special events give them. This he did in *Lonesome Valley* (1949).

Hornsby, a native of Clay County who came into a very successful journalistic career with the *Lexington Leader* by way of Berea College and the University of Kentucky, began his first and only novel while he was a Nieman Fellow at Harvard University in 1946. There is nothing new or unusual in the plot, which takes a bright, sensitive orphan, Johnny Baker, from the isolated community where he grew up in the home of relatives who mistreated him, sees him through college in the Bluegrass, where he does not fit comfortably, and finally takes him back to the mountains again where he marries and hopes to become a useful citizen. What makes the novel such a fine piece of writing is Hornsby's remarkable portrayal of the details of mountain life and character. In the words of the reviewer in the *New York Herald Tribune* (April 17, 1949): "Johnny's sensuous perceptions are so clear, his creator's account of them so delicately precise, that one finds oneself exclaiming again and again, 'That's it—exactly!' " Other reviewers say much the same thing in their different ways. One is pleased because Hornsby's characters are real people instead of stereotypes, another because he writes of the people and their culture as they are without either exploiting them or patronizing them. Honesty, sensitivity, perceptiveness, skill at portraying sights, sounds, and odors in the country, and the ability to relate it all to the values of a people—these are the strengths of the author.

Dean Cadle

Dean Cadle (1920–) has published little in book-length form, but the quality of his work warrants a place for him here. As a critic he has written an often-cited and often-quoted article on James Still, "Man on Troublesome," in the *Yale Review* (Winter 1968). Cadle has also published a biographical sketch of Still in *Southern Writers: A Biographical Dictionary* (1979) and written the preface for the University Press of Kentucky edition of Still's *River of Earth*.

Cadle, born near Middlesboro in a coal-mining camp, spent most of his life as a librarian in Kentucky and North Carolina colleges and at intervals was a teacher of English. His short stories have appeared in the *Carolina Quarterly*, *Southwest Review*, and other magazines, and in the *Stanford Short Stories* (1949) and *Deep Summer*, Morehead State University Press (1963). These stories, which are traditional in plot and characterization, concern coal-mining camps and miners in Eastern Kentucky, where Cadle grew up in Bell County, and in the Philippines, where he was stationed with the army air force. He has written of people who must struggle against the forces that would hold them down as they seek security and a mastery of their lives in an atmosphere that is hostile toward such strivings. As Lynne Baber (*Critical Survey of Short Fiction*, 2535) points out, Cadle reveals "a pervading tenderness . . . toward his people [and] the evil in the stories is not an inherent or developed trait of the people but an outside force imposed upon them."

Harry M. Caudill

Harry M. Caudill (1922–), a nationally known authority on the problems of Appalachia and the conservation of its natural resources, is best known for his polemical writings. His *Night Comes to the Cumberlands: A Biography of a Depressed Area* became a national textbook on the problems of Appalachia from the time it was published in 1963. In it Caudill traces the history of the highlands from the time of the first settlers to the lumber barons and the coal barons who ravaged the hillsides and the politicians who conspired with expediency. At the same time, he traces the effects upon people: how they profited when the lumber and coal business flourished, how they were hungry when business was bad, and how welfare agencies moved in to feed them, producing "a social and economic system based on public welfare that keeps on perpetuating both the welfare and those who need it." His *My Land Is Dying*, dealing mainly with strip-mining, came in 1972 and *A Darkness at Dawn: Appalachian Kentucky and the Future* in 1976. He also wrote a novel that gives him a place of considerable respectability as a writer of fiction—*Dark Hills to Westward: The Saga of Jennie Wiley* (1969).

The novel is based on historical events, but Caudill uses fictional techniques in telling the story of the white woman who was abducted from her home by Indians, probably in 1789, was kept in captivity for almost a year, and finally escaped and made her way to safety. Around such a set of events legends naturally build up, but Caudill's research has pretty well separated fact from fiction. The known facts of the abduction, however, are quite enough, for the tomahawking and scalping of three of Jennie's children before her eyes, the later murder of her two infants, and the ordeal of her captivity and flight of escape through the wilderness require no fictional embellishment. Caudill has, however, handled his scenes with the skill of a novelist as he creates a brooding atmosphere by contrasting the beauty of the place with the hardships of each day in the lives of the settlers and the brutal life confronting the captive. He has skill likewise in conveying a sense of the torment of physical exhaustion as Jennie flees from her captors and of the emotional drain of the fear that grips her. He has a good sense of timing and an ability to heighten effect as the story works toward its climax.

Caudill does more, however, than depict particular events in the life of a particular pioneer woman. He achieves a picture of a time and place in history when toughness, courage, and resourcefulness were essential human qualities if one were to survive. The Indians are portrayed as savages to whom the words "gentle" and "noble" are not applicable. In 1789, Caudill makes the reader believe, the conflict between the Indians and the white settlers was shaped by the conviction that only extermination of one race or the other was an acceptable solution.

Caudill wrote another novel, *The Senator from Slaughter County* (1973), a fictional account using the same materials he had used in his polemical writings. A hundred years ago, as the story unwinds, Slaughter County had wooded hills and independent people; now its mountains are gashed by strip-mining, its valleys defaced by great heaps of slag, its streams contaminated by run-off, and its people demoralized and on welfare. The chief contributor to this condition is Dr. Tom Bonham, once a coal-company doctor but now the chief figure in a political machine that has run Slaughter County for more than thirty years. Even up to the time when he was appointed to fill an unexpired term in the U.S. Senate Dr. Bonham qualified as a local all-American hero, for raised up as he was to render public service, he brought jobs, schools, roads, and money to his county from the state and federal governments. But while he was doing this—enjoying the power he had and his financial rewards—he failed to foresee the ills that the "progress" he aided and abetted would bring to the land through strip-mining and to the people by making them dependent on government aid. The story, told in Caudill's usual effective, hard-hitting, colorful way, provides insights into the problems of the region through probings into politics, manipulations, capitalists, and reformers.

Gurney Norman

Gurney Norman (1937–) first came to national attention when his *Divine Right's Trip* appeared in *The Last Whole Earth Catalog* in 1971. In this form his novel reached 800,000 purchasers before it was partly rewritten, expanded for separate publication and given the subtitle *A Folk Tale*. Though the latter half of the novel has much in common with the traditional novel about the Kentucky mountains, the novel begins in the flower children counter-culture movement and language of the 1960s, when Divine Right (for David Ray, but D.R. for short) Davenport, an eastern Kentucky youth, goes to California in a psychedelic paint-splattered bus. The first half reflects the passions, the communes, the rock concerts, the use of hallucinogens, and the explicit, sometimes shocking, language that gained wide use during the decade. After experimenting with the California counter-culture lifestyle, however, D.R. makes the return journey to Kentucky and there finds meaning in the place from which he started.

The novel is heavily overlaid with myth and archetypal patterns.

Thus it has been a "trip" in at least three senses: a trip to and from California in the physical sense, a trip in the sense of drug-induced hallucinations, and a trip in the sense of the emotional and intellectual maturation that leads to D.R.'s settling down, marrying, and finding meaning in reclaiming the blasted coal land on his uncle's farm. In its way, then, *Divine Right's Trip* is like Candide's discovery, after testing many optimistic philosophies, of the satisfactions to be found in tending one's own garden; it is man's journey in his search for the purpose and meaning of life. Yet it is something more than this and something less, or at least it has special applications of its own. It evokes the first pioneers who crossed the continent, but they were in search of land, whereas D.R. is in search of himself; they crossed the continent to find a new and whole land, D.R. re-crossed the continent to restore a ruined land. D.R.'s need for healing has in part grown out of the plight of a land and a people that need healing, but after a vain search away from this place he finds that his own healing comes from healing the land itself. Analogy may be drawn also between the hill folk of Trace Fork and the dome folk of the communes of the counter-culture, for the one has preserved important values and patterns that others have lost, just as the other has discovered values and patterns that it never had. Is, then, the marriage of D.R. and Estelle and of the hillbilly folk and the hippie folk at the end of the book suggestive of a new Adam and a new Eve—as in Capek's *R.U.R.*—to enter upon the scene and build a new and better world?

The plot of *Divine Right's Trip* is easy to synopsize, but it is difficult to give a sense of the nature of the writing. Perhaps some notion of it can be provided by quoting from a review in the *Courier-Journal* (September 30, 1972) by Jim Wayne Miller: "You won't believe this book—until you read it." Miller continues, describing the section after D.R. has arrived back home in Eastern Kentucky: "He comforts a dying uncle, fights a dragon in a dope vision down in a coal mine, becomes a fishworm and rabbit farmer. . . . and gets married in an all-day wedding that brings together a yard full of counter-culture freaks and local Kentucky folk. . . . The prologue is spoken by a VW bus . . . the author makes telephone calls for some of the characters. He has fun mixing up the names of friends and mentors, listed in the dedication, and assigning them to minor characters." But, concludes Miller, "The amazing thing is how this unlikely mix of California freaks and East Kentucky mountain people inhabit the same book without destroying its credibility. But Norman has brought it off. It works."

In *Kinfolks* (1977) Norman again writes of the mountains and mountain people. In this volume he brings together ten stories, known as the "Wilgus" stories, that he had published in magazines over a period of years. Arranged chronologically as they relate to the life of Wilgus Collier, the stories explore the relationships of an Eastern Kentucky family among themselves and with outsiders following World War II. Wilgus is nine years old in the first story and is in his twenties by the end of the volume, with the result that *Kinfolks*, arranged chronologically, is as much a short novel as a collection of stories. Each story deals with the relationship between Wilgus and a member of the Collier family. Starting with a story that dramatizes family loyalty, segments tell of such events and episodes as Wilgus's coming home from college on weekends, the death of his grandfather, family squabbles, family cohesion, Wilgus's initiation into manhood, and so on. Through the stories one comes to have a good sense of the mood and feeling of the mountains, and to see the members of the Collier family as cantankerous, sometimes ridiculous, but withal dignified in their particular way, and on occasion tragic. In no wise is *Kinfolks* a continuation of *Divine Right's Trip*.

One familiar with Norman's personal history will see many reflections and parallels between the events of his life and those of the characters in his stories: his upbringing in the mountains, his attendance at the University of Kentucky, where he got his A.B., his life in California, where he held a Wallace Stegner Fellowship in creative writing at Stanford University; his experience with the drug culture; and his ultimate return to Kentucky, where he has edited a newspaper in his hometown of Hazard and more recently has been teaching creative writing at the University of Kentucky. He continues to publish his "Wilgus cycle" stories and is working on two novels, one dealing with the life and mind of Daniel Boone, and a second, to be called *Crazy Quilt*, which continues the story of the Collier family of *Kinfolks*.

Jane Stuart

Jane Stuart (1942–), daughter of Jesse Stuart, spent her early years in W-Hollow, Greenup County, the area made famous by her father. Her college work was done at Case-Western Reserve University, where she received her A.B. with a major in Greek and Latin, and at Indiana University, where she did her M.A. work in classics and her Ph.D. in Italian. She has since done some teaching, but most important for her writing, perhaps, was the year when she was nineteen and taught on an emergency certificate in an elementary school in northeastern Kentucky. She and her husband live in Gainesville, Florida.

Stuart, who writes principally about Kentucky, began her writing career by publishing verse in magazines. Her first collection was *A Year's Harvest* (1957), followed ten years later by *Eyes of the Mole* (1967), and by *White Barn* (1973); each was privately printed. Her subject matter is mainly the world she grew up in as a child. As she says in *White Barn*, "I still see the dark winter hills where white barns are etched in snow; I hear the song of blackbirds, and watch the sparrow begin her flight into spring."

The year 1973 saw the publication of Miss Stuart's first novel as well as her last volume of verse. In each of four successive years she produced a novel, with McGraw-Hill as the publisher, and came more to the attention of reviewers than she had with her verse. *Yellowhawk* (1973), her first volume of prose fiction, is really less a novel than a collection of character vignettes, for the sketches are self-contained and are not linked together other than that each character has a relationship with the Yellowhawk Elementary School located in the mountains of northeastern Kentucky. Rhoda Miller, a teacher in the school, is the central figure. She looks back over her teaching experience at Yellowhawk a few years after the event—recalling students, dropouts, teachers, parents, and townspeople and speaking of what has happened to them in the interval. The volume is in no sense nostalgic or idyllic. Instead it is stark and unsparing: a youngster who is the prey of a religious fanatic; a retarded child, Tullie, strange and beautiful, and her father, who drowns her dog; a cook at the school who goes home to find her husband dead of a heart attack and puts one of the pork chops back into the refrigerator as she says, "We won't need both of them, seeing that there's only going to be one for dinner tonight."

Passerman's Hollow (1974) might be called a southern hill-country Gothic novel. Passerman's Hollow is a remote, lonely valley where suddenly one day the monotony of people's lives is ruptured by the disappearance of a girl from a Friday-night church service. Tension mounts as the search narrows to the family of the missing girl's best friend, one of whom is a retarded brother, Reuben. Finally the law makes Reuben a temporary deputy and enlists his aid in the search, thereby adding a new and strange dimension to the story. *Land of the Fox* (1975) is another excursion into a psychologically menacing world. Kay Forrester has been driven to the edge of madness by the jangling noises, the cluttered confusion, and the frantic, ceaseless demands that life and the city make on her. The novel is almost clinical as it progresses through a thicket of literary allusions and clashing fantasies into a vortex of madness—a psycho-Gothic horror tale of a person trying to cope with the demands of life in our time.

Gideon's Children (1976) is a collection of twenty-one short pieces, chiefly character sketches in which little happens. The characters in these pieces are people who would like to have lived in a happier, earlier time, or are exhausted by the constant turmoil of their lives, defeated by the marketplace, or rudderless, such as two women who sip their lives away in the afternoon or a judge who retires a second time by committing suicide. The method is not totally unlike that in *Yellowhawk*, though the characters are more sophisticated—or at least less countrified.

CHAPTER 18

Historical Fiction

In Kentucky and in the nation as a whole interest in the frontier and the Civil War as subjects of historical fiction ceased almost abruptly after it had flourished around the turn of the century. In the 1930s interest developed again, though it was not till the 1940s and 1950s that it flourished. Thus in fiction dealing with the frontier we have Elizabeth Madox Roberts's *The Great Meadow* in 1930 and Caroline Gordon's "The Captive" in 1932, after which little was written on the subject until 1940. In 1931, however, Frances Ogilvie in *Green Bondage* wrote a novel on another historical subject: the "Tobacco Wars" that took place during the first decade of the century. The subject also attracted the attention of Robert Penn Warren, Elizabeth Pickett Chevalier, and Charley Robertson. In 1940 novels of the frontier began to appear at a rapid rate: Clark McMeekin's *Show Me a Land* in 1940 and *Reckon with the River* in 1941, Caroline Gordon's *Green Centuries* in 1941, and Juliet Alves's *Huldah* in 1942. Historical fiction growing out of the frontier had begun to flower and continued to do so on through the 1950s.

The 1930s also saw the dawning of a new day nationally in Civil War fiction. Among the better-known novels were MacKinlay Kantor's *Long Remember* (1934), Stark Young's *So Red the Rose* (1934), Margaret Mitchell's *Gone with the Wind* (1936), Clifford Dowdey's *Bugles Blow No More* (1937), Hervey Allen's *Action at Aquila* (1938), Philip Van Doren Stern's *The Drums of Morning* (1942), Howard Fast's *Freedom Road* (1944), and Ben Ames Williams's *House Divided* (1947). Nor should this coming of age be surprising, especially in the Deep South. For one thing, this interest in the Civil War coincided with the Southern Literary Renascence and particularly with the Agrarian and regionalist movements and was a logical extension of the local color movement. Then too enough time had passed to provide a perspective that was not possible as long as memories harbored the war itself and Reconstruction. By the 1930s, though, a generation of authors, born after Reconstruction and mainly after 1900, were heirs to stories, traditions, and legends that blended together to form the "matter" of the Civil War. Events, motives, and outcomes would be interpreted anew.

Civil War fiction by Kentuckians came a bit later than it did in the Deep South. Most of it was intended as romances of adventure whose purpose was to engage the interest of the reader and be a part of the literature of entertainment. The same is true of those who wrote of the frontier. Most of these writers of historical fiction wrote little else and are discussed below; but others were by no means limited to fiction dealing with the past and are discussed elsewhere. First chronologically was Elizabeth Madox Roberts, whose *The Great Meadow* (1930) remains perhaps the finest piece of fiction ever written about the Kentucky frontier. Caroline Gordon's *Green Centuries* (1941) is another frontier novel which probes beneath the surface meaning of events, and to a lesser extent the same is true of Harriette Arnow's *The Kentucky Trace* (1975). Another novel of the frontier not discussed below is Harry Caudill's *Dark Hills to Westward* (1969). The Civil War inspired even more historical novels than the frontier did. These search for insights into the divisive conflict. Caroline Gordon's Agrarian novels *Penhally* (1931) and *None Shall Look Back* (1937) are heavily weighted with Civil War matters. The same can be said of Allen Tate's *The Fathers* (1938), though the novel does not have a Kentucky background. Indeed, any novel that is sympathetic with the southern cause is likely to be sympathetic with Agrarianism and more concerned with the conflict as representing the loss of a way of life than with the Civil War per se. Other novels that deal with the Civil War and are discussed elsewhere include Robert Penn Warren's *Band of Angels* (1955) and *Wilderness* (1961), Frances Barton Fox's *Ridgeways* (1934), and William McElroy Kelly's *Days Are as Grass* (1941). Owing its origins to the assassination of President Lincoln is John Patrick's play *The Story of Mary Surratt* (1947).

Clark McMeekin

Perhaps no recent Kentucky author has written more fiction about Kentucky's past with greater success than have Isabel McMeekin

(1895–1975) and Dorothy Park Clark (1899–1983), writing under the pseudonym of Clark McMeekin. For twenty years, beginning in 1940, they carried on a popular and successful collaboration that produced eleven novels and one volume of nonfiction. During this period they were writing also under their own names: McMeekin some eight volumes of juvenile fiction, verse, and nonfiction; Clark three murder mystery novels, some puppet plays, and two operettas. Their subjects were pioneer times and the Civil War era; racing, which always appears in a historical context; and the Ohio River in Kentucky's early days, including such legendary figures as Mike Fink and Johnny Appleseed.

Show Me a Land (1940), a novel about racing, was the first result of their collaboration. An interest in and knowledge of horses and the racetrack came naturally to both McMeekin and Clark. The former was born in Louisville and in 1921 married Sam H. McMeekin, sports editor of the *Courier-Journal* and later a steward at Churchill Downs. The latter was born in Iowa but at the age of four moved to Lexington (later to Frankfort) and was a frequent visitor at Bluegrass farms and racing establishments near Lexington and Versailles before moving to Louisville.

Show Me a Land begins at the Aintree Fair in England. Dana Terraine, at sixteen, is attending the fair with her father, who has gone there from his Greatways plantation, in Virginia, in order to buy thoroughbreds, and especially a stallion so that he can improve the bloodlines of his racing stable. What follows, in the words of Stephen Vincent Benét, (*Saturday Review of Literature* [Feb. 24, 1940]), "is a ramping, unashamedly romantic romance, full of beautiful girls, handsome gentlemen, fine horses, moving accidents by flood and field, and quite a lot of vivid and unpretentious historical detail. . . . it is a breathless tale and a dexterous one. It may be—and it is—melodramatic, but it makes good reading. . . . It unashamedly introduces Audubon, Lafayette, and Lincoln when and as convenient, but it doesn't make the mistake of letting prominent historical figures get in the way of the plot. . . . You are going to like this one. And what a movie it will make!" More specifically, the story tells of Dana and her father's return to their Virginia estate, the ultimate departure of the family to Kentucky and the Bluegrass, the affluent development of the new land during antebellum days, the development of the culture of the horse, the Civil War, Reconstruction, and finally the running of the first Kentucky Derby on May 17, 1875. As for the love interest, Dana has married Eben Coates, a young Scottish minister, but she has never forgotten the dashing young Irishman Rike Galphine, whom she met at the Aintree Fair. Eventually Rike shows up in Kentucky, though he too has married. By the time of the last scene at the Kentucky Derby Dana and Rike are seventy, but as one commentator puts it, "They're still as brisk and handsome as you can ask for."

During the unfolding of the story there are glimpses and vignettes that give the flavor of the times: the cholera epidemic in Lexington, tobacco auctions, slaves in the fields, duels, balls, Lexington as the Athens of the West, Henry Clay, John Hunt Morgan, the famous racehorse Lexington of Dr. Elisha Warfield, and, of course, Price McGrath's little red horse Aristides, who wins the first Kentucky Derby. Looking on at the Derby are not only Dana and Rike but also, perched in a tree, Matt J. Winn, then a boy but later the man who built Churchill Downs and the Derby into America's greatest sporting event. The thread that runs through the whole novel and holds it together is, of course, the breeding and racing of fine thoroughbreds. Its theme is summed up by Ergo, the little Irish trainer: "Show me a land where men wants none o' horses an' I'll show ye a land where there ain't no men, by God!"

Clark McMeekin did not again write a racing story that made the best-seller lists as *Show Me a Land* had done, but both *Red Raskall* (1943) and *The Fairbrothers* (1961) are successful racing novels. *Red Raskall* is an adventure story set in Tidewater, Virginia, in 1816. In it Lark Shannon, an English girl, sails for America and is shipwrecked on an island off the shore of Virginia. Another survivor of the shipwreck is the thoroughbred stallion nicknamed Red Raskall that becomes a charge of Lark and unexpectedly leads to her finding contentment and happiness in rural Virginia.

The Fairbrothers portrays the breeding and racing of horses as part of the life of a Kentucky family. The scene is the family farm and home near Louisville just three years after the Civil War. Times are hard and everyone is trying to cope with the financial problems of the new era. Major Frank, a gentleman farmer with money problems, his capable wife, "Miss Kizzie"; Tolly, who fought for the South and now gives up farming to learn more about racing; Jenny, the pretty, empty-headed widow of the elder son who was killed in the Union army; Zion, who tries unsuccessfully to pass herself off as a French teacher but becomes a loved member of the family; and Fleecy, the cook—these are the members of the Fairbrothers family who seek to regain financial security. There are the abortive effort to run a school for girls, the tobacco crop, the health spa, and the attempt to build up thoroughbred racing both in the Fairbrothers family and in the Commonwealth. The day of the first Kentucky Derby is the novel's grand finale and opens up new horizons for all the Fairbrothers.

The Ohio River during frontier days was also a popular subject with Clark and McMeekin. *Reckon with the River* (1941), their best novel on this subject, deals with the journey down the Ohio River and the area associated with it. The time is the first decade of the nineteenth century, beginning with the year 1805, when the principal character, Ma'am Cambrin, eighty years old and presumably on her deathbed, is composing the inscription for her gravestone.

Just as her farm overseer is pegging her coffin together, however, Ma'am Cambrin is galvanized into action when she discovers in her Bible a piece of birch bark bearing a map and a message. This was a deed to the fabulous Swift silver mine, together with a map showing how to find it, all given to Ma'am Cambrin by the Indian chief known to history as Joseph Brant when Ma'am Cambrin was a captive among the Mohawks. From this point on *Reckon with the River* is Ma'am Cambrin's story. She converts her coffin into a trunk, persuades her great-nephew and his family to accompany her, and goes to Redstone, where flatboats and keelboats are constructed that take settlers down the Monongahela and the Ohio to what was then called the West. Ma'am Cambrin is a dauntless, fascinating creation who dominates the rousing action of the novel from beginning to end. Nothing and no one stumps her: not those two schemers Aaron Burr and James Wilkinson, not even Mike Fink himself. But the novel is more than an exciting adventure; it gives insight into the rigors of pioneer life, from the felling of trees with which to build the flatboat, to steering the clumsy craft, to the rigors encountered in the promised land of Kentucky. It is, as one reviewer says, "a grand story."

Two legendary characters appear in the story: Mike Fink and Johnny Appleseed. Mike, that boisterous, peerless fighter, king of the keelboatmen, and master of colorful speech, is in and out of the story but makes his climactic appearance in Louisville when he agrees to come to court for trial for shooting the tails off some pigs. "Worthy to rank with the tales of Paul Bunyan and his might deeds," says the *Herald-Tribune* reviewer. Johnny Appleseed, is also in and out of the story, his appearance in Kentucky apparently resting on the legend that in the spring of 1806 he lashed two canoes together, each filled with apple seeds, and drifted down the Ohio planting seeds along both the Kentucky and the Ohio-Indiana shores as far west as Louisville. Johnny's last appearance is at Madam Cambrin's at Christmas time in

Louisville when he brings her some apple trees and hurries on down the river, "his voice floating back to them on the night wind . . . an eerie, saddening thing."

Two other novels by Clark McMeekin have the Ohio River as their setting, one of them aboard a showboat, the other aboard a showboat and a packet. In both novels the reader becomes acquainted with life aboard riverboats during the early part of the nineteenth century and with the only kind of theatrical entertainment most Kentuckians in those days ever experienced. *Black Moon* (1945) deals with a circus troupe coming down the Ohio River from Pittsburgh to Louisville in a broadhorn and playing the river towns along the way. The central figure is an exhibition balloonist, Jade Hunter, who has accidentally killed a spectator with his balloon, has been indicted for murder, and has now joined the showboat circus troupe as a fortune-teller and mesmerist in order to escape arrest. Excitement is added to the plot when the beautiful tightrope walker, wife of the circus strong man, begins to pay court to him. There are some breathless moments, but everything is in good fun. The circus atmosphere and personalities and the showboat itself seem authentic.

Gaudy's Ladies (1948) is the story of Gaudy Robertson and the women in his life as he fights his way up from an orphanage to a position of wealth and power. The time is early and mid-nineteenth century and the principal scene is Louisville, which was then a bustling town active in river traffic. As Gaudy carves out his career, however, one learns much of the Ohio River and the intense life and activity on it. The story begins with the attempted murder of Robertson and then goes back thirty years and tells of the rise of his fortunes and the women who loved him. In the first stage of his career a traveling theatrical group takes him as a small boy and trains him to be an actor. Gaudy's first love is Neal Perry, daughter of the town's leading boatbuilder, but she jilts him for a stage career and Gaudy's ambition turns to more lucrative enterprises. These include selling patent medicines, being a riverboat gambler, and ultimately being a riverboat captain, shipowner, and shipbuilder. The story portrays a great deal of river life and of the theatrical troupes of the day, both on the river and as they make their way inland to establish theaters.

The Civil War in Kentucky is another historical subject that Clark McMeekin wrote about often. *City of the Flags* (1950) and *Tyrone of Kentucky* (1954) are devoted entirely to the war, and two other novels—*Show Me a Land* (1940) and *The Fairbrothers* (1962)—make use of it. *City of the Flags* is set in Louisville during the first year of the Civil War. The story grows out of the fact that Kentucky, officially neutral though it was, was full of hotbeds of emotion as citizens held their proslavery and antislavery meetings and ladies gathered together in sewing groups to make flags—some the stars and stripes for the Union, others the stars and bars for the Confederacy. Louisville was flourishing economically as a war-time boom town, but despite the prosperity feelings often ran high as families and friends were torn apart by their divided loyalties. Into this scene comes Murray Andrews, an attractive, wealthy young widow, to visit her stepfather, Dr. Eben Tompson, a man with strong Union sympathies. As Murray seeks to renew old friendships in the social set, she finds herself ostracized by social leaders, including Ben and Malvina Purchase, whose sons, Chard and Blue, interestingly enough, ardently pursue Murray. Quite a bit is made of the glittering social life of the day, the center of which was the old Galt House.

Tyrone of Kentucky deals with the post-war period of Reconstruction with its lagging economic conditions and difficulties in healing the emotional wounds of the war. The central figure is David Tyrone, of Woodford County, who has fought for the Confederate cause and somewhat precipitously married Glen Ellen Saxton before returning home. Facing him as he returns are the girl he left behind, Cottie Thomas; a gossipy somewhat hostile atmosphere that grows out of the marriage; and David's penniless condition as he tries to farm the land and repair the buildings that have been neglected during his absence. To make matters worse, David has to cope with the marauding "Regulators" and "Avengers" who followed in the wake of the war and added to the unrest of Reconstruction with methods and attitudes not unlike those of the Ku Klux Klan.

Of these four novels, only *Show Me a Land* rates among the authors' best, but all of them are eminently readable, and all are generously supplied with incidents that keep the plot moving and maintain the reader's interest. All abound, too, in the details of the life of the day and thus both inform the reader and give insight into the times: the problems of farming the land; details of clothing, entertainment, and travel; the preparation and serving of food; the portrayal of morals and manners. The inclusion of such particulars lends credence and gives depth to the story.

The October Fox (1956) deals with love of the land. The time is the last decade of the nineteenth century, and the scene is Judge Thornberry's Bluegrass land, which is doomed as a vanishing way of life. The novel has its share of horses and hunting and pleasure, but it also has a dominating father whose determination is to keep his children about him and whose actions bring tensions into a story filled with a great deal of wit and charm and warmth. The Tod—the October fox—is a symbol of the right of people to find within themselves what they most need and want. In no sense is the novel profound or penetrating, but it is well told and is one of the most interesting the authors wrote.

Isabel McMeekin also wrote children's stories of considerable merit, the first two of which deal with the Kentucky frontier: *Journey Cake* in 1942 and *Juba's New Moon* in 1944. From the first McMeekin met with critical success, and *Journey Cake* won for her the prestigious Julia Ellsworthy Ford Award. The novel tells of the long trek of early settlers from the Yadkin Valley in North Carolina to Kentucky in 1794. The journey is different from most of its kind, however, in that it is made by six motherless children under the care of a freed black woman. The head of the family had gone ahead, expecting his wife to follow with the children, but she had died and the black woman—Juba—is bound to the Shadrow family by ties of personal devotion that cause her to undertake the role of guide and protector of the children.

The novel, which gets its name from the journey cake that Juba baked for the trip, has its share of excitement and trials. It portrays the death of an ox from a poisoned arrow and the screams of panthers, for example, but also a pioneer wedding, quilt making, and the making of soap; and there are such characters as Johnny Appleseed, whom the family meets along the way. The second volume—*Juba's New Moon*—is a sequel that tells what happens to the Shadrow family in Kentucky. Together the two volumes give good insight into the early settlement of Kentucky, but it is the heroic figure of Juba that dominates the story. With her "freedom papers" she holds the family together in spite of the tribulations that beset them, both on their journey and after they arrive on the frontier.

McMeekin's next juvenile volume was her most successful. This time the subject was racing. *Kentucky Derby Winner* was a Junior Literary Guild selection for 1949. It is the story of Aristides, the little red horse no one expected to win, and his victory at the first running of the Kentucky Derby in 1875. On that historic day owner Price McGrath had hoped to win with Chesapeake, for on May 10 Aristides had lost to Ten Broeck in the Phoenix Hotel Stakes, which for forty years had been the initial test of the season for three-year-olds. Ten Broeck was entered in the Derby too, but when Chesapeake got off to a bad start, his stablemate, the little red Aristides, was given the role not only of competing with Ten Broeck (who finished fifth) but of overtaking the leader, Volcano, which he did, and won by a length, setting a new American record of 2:37 ¾ for 1½ miles. From this beginning Aristides went on to become the champion three-year-old for the year, winning not only the Derby but the Breckinridge, the Withers, and the Jerome Stakes. He came in second in the Belmont Stakes when McGrath chose to win with Calvin. So formidable was Aristides's record by the time he was a four-year-old that only Ten Broeck was entered against him in a sweepstakes meet that McGrath arranged for Aristides's four-year-old debut on May 10, 1876.

In *Kentucky Derby Winner* the build-up and excitement surrounding the Derby are, of course, essential features, but the novel also creates fascinating pictures of the day-to-day life of a racing establishment—from the day "Risty" was born and learned to stand on his wobbly legs until he overtook and defeated Volcano, May 17, 1875. Interesting also is the depiction of the temper and atmosphere of the Bluegrass country following the Civil War. More important to the story and the plot, however, are the two human characters upon whom so much of the success of the story depends, little Jack Sprat and his grandfather. Other authentic and interesting characters also make their contribution to the story, as also do real-life persons and places. Among the latter are H. Price McGrath, owner of McGrathiana, and the boy Matt Winn.

Three years after she had published *Kentucky Derby Winner*, Isabel McMeekin published *Ban-Joe and Grey Eagle* (1952), a novel that gets its title from a banjo-playing orphan and the horse he came to have the care of when he went to Louisville and found a job in a livery stable. Grey Eagle was foaled in Lexington in 1836 and won acclaim as the greatest horse in Kentucky when at the age of three he won a two-mile race in the fastest time ever recorded in America and then a week later won another spectacular victory. Thereupon Grey Eagle was entered in a sweepstakes for all ages at the Ashland Course at Magnolia and Seventh Streets in Louisville. Among the horses entered in the race was Wagner, a five-year-old that had a long string of victories throughout the South as a four-mile racer. Grey Eagle had never run a four-mile race and not surprisingly lost to the seasoned five-year-old, though by a small margin. Supporters of Grey Eagle demanded a rematch and this time Grey Eagle won the first heat, Wagner the second by a neck; but in the final heat Grey Eagle broke down and never raced again. So widely had the match attracted attention that notables came many miles to see it, among them Henry Clay and the editor of the prestigious New York sporting magazine *Spirit of the Times*. The novel was well received by readers and critics alike, but it never manages to be quite as exciting as *Kentucky Derby Winner*, though the characters are authentic and the portrayal of life at a racetrack in Kentucky in 1839 is both interesting and convincing.

Barbara Tunnell Anderson

Barbara Tunnell Anderson (1894–1974) did not write about the Civil War as such, but about some of the problems with which the war was concerned, including one novel that deals with racial relations and another that tells the story of a quadroon who was growing up before she learned of her illegitimacy. Anderson was born in Massachusetts, the daughter of a minister, but when she was three her family moved to a small town in Tennessee and subsequently to other towns in Georgia, Alabama, and Mississippi. By 1926 she was in Louisville after graduating from Smith College, where she married Dwight Anderson, dean of the school of music at the University of Louisville. Mrs. Anderson's residence in different towns in the Deep South and Louisville not only helped prepare her for writing novels but provided her with a knowledge of the historic houses and gardens she was to write about in magazines such as *House Beautiful, Arts and Decorations*, and *Country Life*. Some of her poetry originated in this period and was published in such magazines as *Scribner's, Century*, and *Vanity Fair*.

If Anderson's two novels are reduced to a theme, it is racial tolerance in a small town. The first of the two, *The Days Grow Cold* (1941), had a very favorable reception as a Literary Guild selection. Its heroine is Lucinda, an intelligent, sensitive child who lives with her parents in a great mansion that reflects the Old South tradition. The account is largely made up of Lucinda's trying to understand her parents'—as well as the community's—attitudes toward and relationships with the blacks who serve them. Everything is seen through the child's eyes and mind as events and developments within the town touch upon her home and her home upon the town. Her reactions to the adult world are recorded with skill and restraint. *Southbound* (1949) is the story of an illegitimate, light-skinned, blue-eyed, intelligent black girl, Amanda Crane, who after being abandoned by her mother, was taken to live with a white family in Ohio and fails to learn of her Negro blood until she is eleven. Later she realizes her grandmother's ambition for her by going to study music in France because of the relative absence of racial prejudice there. After her studies in Paris are completed, Amanda returns to America and the South in order to teach black children, an experience from which she derives great satisfaction. As in *The Days Grow Cold*, Anderson makes a case for racial toleration. It would be a mistake, however, to think of her novels as having any resemblance to sociological treatises; they were written to be read for pleasure. Her narrative talent is good and her style effective.

Anderson's one play, *The Tall Kentuckian*, a drama with music by Norman Dello Joio, was published and first produced in 1953 in Louisville's Iroquois Amphitheatre as a part of the city's 175th anniversary celebration. The play is made up of episodes from the whole of Lincoln's life, including scenes that deal with the Civil War. Part of the locale of the play is historic Farmington, for it was here that Lincoln visited with his friend Joshua Speed for three weeks in 1841. Two lesser-known actual events related to Louisville appear in the play. One is Joshua Speed's help, at Lincoln's request, in smuggling arms to Union sympathizers in Kentucky. The other is the occasion when Mrs. J. Stoddard Johnston obtained a pass from Lincoln to insure her safe passage through Union lines in order to visit her husband, a Confederate soldier. Typical of the music composed by Joio is the ballad sung in the opening scene when Nancy Hanks Lincoln goes to the Knob Creek school to take young Lincoln to Indiana.

Juliet Alves

Novelists of the frontier, particularly in the nineteenth century, have commonly been conventionally moral in their portrayals. As a result the leading characters have generally been depicted as high-principled agents of progress as they pushed civilization farther and farther westward. If they did lapse into acts of barbarity or succumb to avarice or hatred, their lapses were generally softened and were represented as being for the common good and a part of Manifest Destiny, a justification often cited to explain away the conquering and killing of the red "savages" who stood in their way.

Huldah, published in 1942 by Juliet Alves (1887–1947) when the author was fifty-five, is in a different mold as it portrays the rampaging frontier of the 1790s at the river town of Red Banks, known today as Henderson. Located at the mouth of the Green River, Red Banks was less than fifteen miles above Diamond Island, the onetime headquarters of the Mason gang of outlaws and apparently the place to which Little Harpe fled when Big Harpe was beheaded during the bloody career of murder that took twenty lives. The Kentucky side of the river between Red Banks and the mouth of the Tennessee River was also the place where "Colonel Plug," representing himself as a traveler in distress would hail a passing boatman and once aboard would collapse upon the planking and covertly begin to pick away at the calking at a rate calculated to cause the raft or boat to sink at a point where "Nine Eyes," his confederate, would join him in salvaging the goods. Goings-on of this sort are reflected in *Huldah* as the red-headed heroine and tavernkeeper holds her own with the rowdies and pirates who are her customers.

As Alves tells her story of how the settlement of Red Banks began and then grew into a town, Huldah emerges, as one reviewer puts it, as a pioneer mother far less conventional than "memorial statues have accustomed us to." She is a fascinating, amoral, red-haired shrew; she knows how to cope with tavern toughs, river pirates, and the slick-talking agents of the land companies; and her language and theirs is sprinkled with profanity and coarse allusion. Courage and tenderness and motherhood have their place in the character of Huldah, but so do cunning, brutality, and passionate sensuality. Hers is a rough, untamed world, filled with danger, and she does not shrink from it.

Juliet Alves was born in Henderson in 1887 and began her writing there as a journalist. She left Henderson for New York City in 1937 with her son William Overton Johnson and in 1944 married William T. Hoyt. She died in 1947 after a long illness. Besides *Huldah,* Alves was the author of an undistinguished volume of verse entitled *Seven Oaks* and at the time of her death was working on another novel tentatively called *Ann of Kentucky.*

Cleo Dawson

Though Cleo Dawson (Mrs. George Edwin Smith), born in 1909, is the author of a frontier novel that has been through nineteen printings, was reprinted in 1973, and was made into a movie in 1981, she is best known as a platform lecturer and play reviewer. Gifted with a remarkable memory, a talent for character portrayal, and endless vitality, she has during much of her life made up to two hundred speeches or dramatic readings per year and with some frequency has appeared on such national television shows as those of Merv Griffin, Jack Parr, Steve Allen, and Johnny Carson.

Her novel, *She Came to the Valley,* was published in 1943. Although Dawson has lived in Lexington for well over half a century, she was born in Texas in 1909, received her A.B. at Southern Methodist University, and remains loyal to the state of her early upbringing. The death of her mother set her to writing the historical novel that deals with the settling of the Rio Grande country. The time represented is 1905–18, and the principal character is Willy Westall, who with her husband went to the Texas frontier to live on the land. The long journey occupies the first quarter of the book and contains some of its best writing. The mass of commonplace detail, as one reviewer puts it, "seems to cry for the blue pencil," but in the end the reader realizes that "the very jogging along of bare facts, recounted without artifice, gives the interminable journey its true weight of monotony and horror" (*Weekly Book Review*, Oct. 10, 1943). Says one reviewer, "If you like serious books that carry you along, wild-eyed with excitement, page after page, this is your book. Willy Westall is an unforgettable heroine" (*Book Week*, Oct. 17, 1943).

A.B. Guthrie, Jr.

Alfred Bertram ("Bud") Guthrie (1901–) came into fame because of *The Big Sky* (1947), *The Way West* (1949), and *These Thousand Hills* (1956), a trilogy that constitutes to date the finest expression of the fictional study of American expansion westward. Guthrie was not born in Kentucky, but as he once wrote to the present writer (Sept. 12, 1983), "In a sense I grew up there or, rather, matured, and the old town [Lexington] and its people remain a part of me." Guthrie was referring to the twenty-seven years he spent in Lexington between 1926 and 1953, twenty-one of them on the staff of the *Lexington Leader* in roles stretching from cub reporter to executive editor, and after 1947 as a novelist and teacher of creative writing at the University of Kentucky. At the age of six months he had moved from Indiana, where he was born, to Choteau, Montana, where his father became the principal of the high school. Growing up in Montana, including taking a degree at the state university, was the greatest shaping force in Guthrie's life, and his return there from Lexington in 1953 is further evidence of his love for the land of the big sky.

But Kentucky, as Guthrie's biographer, Thomas W. Ford, is careful to point out, added new dimensions to Guthrie's experience. When in 1926 he first came to Lexington from Choteau, a small ranch town, much of what he encountered sharply contrasted with where he had grown up. Lexington was still a small city and Kentucky far from populous, but both were unlike what he had known during most of his twenty-five years. Different, too, were the rolling land, the trees, and the cultivated fields, but even more different, perhaps, was the contrast between the frontier equality of Choteau and the tradition and social caste system he found in Lexington. But Kentucky had itself once been the only "West" there was and "a stage in the great American journey, east to west, where Dan'l Boone and George Rogers Clark and frontiersmen and soldiers and seekers tramped history on the land" ("Kentucky," *Holiday* 9 [March 1951], 48). Guthrie's knowledge of Kentucky was extensive, and when he was considering the epic movement of America westward and sought a character for the first novel of his trilogy, he chose a young man from Eastern Kentucky.

When Guthrie first broke into fame with *The Big Sky* in 1947, he was already the author of a melodramatic, unpromising mystery novel, *Murders at Moon Dance* (1943). With its publication, however, he began thinking about a novel of greater scope and seriousness that would do justice to the rise and fall of the "mountain men," the hunters and fur trappers of the West, between the years 1830 and 1843. The following year he made a start on it but soon laid it away as unsatisfactory. Then came the event that was "to make all the difference"—the Nieman Fellowship award that enabled him to spend the academic year 1945–46 at Harvard in the Nieman program and resume his work on *The Big Sky* under the direction of Harvard's Theodore Morrison.

To do justice to the mountain men, or "Long Knives," as the Indians called them, during the fur-trading days in the Northwest, Guthrie knew that he must depict their almost barbaric vices as well as their resourcefulness and fortitude; they must be rough and ruthless men who could be satisfied with nothing less than full independence, complete freedom, under the big sky. In 1830 when the story of *The Big Sky* opens, Kentucky's pioneer days were still fresh in the memories of many men who in the 1770s and 1780s left their homes east of the Alleghenies, stopped off along their way West, and became the stubborn, fiercely independent hill people of Eastern Kentucky. This mountain stock provided Guthrie with his hero, Boone Caudill, a seventeen-year-old boy who is somewhat on the wild side and eager to escape the confinement of home and community and the ugly fights with his vicious, drunken father.

On his way through St. Louis to the country of the hostile Blackfeet Indians at the headwaters of the Missouri River that he has heard about from his Uncle Jeb Calloway, Boone meets up with red-headed, warm-hearted, restless Jim Deakins; hunter and guide Dick Summers, the guide of the expedition; and Teal Eye, a Blackfoot Indian girl whom Jourdonnais, the French trader in charge of the expedition, has taken along as a hostage and insurance for safe conduct through hostile Indian country. Along the way Teal Eye escapes and the boat is ambushed and all the boat's company except Caudill, Deakins, and Summers are killed. Now they all know in grim earnest what Deakins meant by a land that "didn't give a damn about a man or any animal. . . . There would be other men after him and others after them, all wondering and all wishful and after a while all dead."

Perhaps better than others Guthrie has been able to get at the essence of these early trappers and hunters, why they could tolerate no other life than living as loners on a frontier of uncharted vast expanse; surviving hunger, withstanding the cold, outstalking the Indian; trapping, catching, and skinning animals. Unlike the John Jacob Astors who made fortunes in furs, the Boone Caudills had no instinct for trade, no desire to accumulate money. The pelts they trapped for had no value save that of being exchanged for the firearms, ammunition, traps, and other equipment that maintained their life as trappers and gave them total independence of other people, except maybe one night at the end of the season at an outpost they might get roaring drunk, gamble their pelts and other possessions, and buy themselves a squaw. Guthrie paints a world that is often brutal, and Boone Caudill was proud of his ability to survive in it, to fight as ruthlessly and to be as free of humane impulses as any man he knew.

But one softening memory has lingered in Boone's mind—that of Teal Eye. Finally one day when he and Jim have gone north in search of better trapping along the Teton River, they come upon a Blackfoot village and Teal Eye. Boone marries her, becomes a member of the tribe, and lives among the Indians for five years. In 1842 Teal Eye gives birth to a baby with red hair and blue eyes. Boone suspects the red-headed Jim Deakins of being the father and in a sudden fit of rage kills the one person he ever regarded as his friend. Boone returns to Kentucky to find his father dead, his mother old, and his brother married and the father of two children, both of them blonde. Thereupon Boone learns that his grandfather, whom he never saw, had red hair. His mind goes back to the child, to his having doubted Teal Eye, and his dead friend, Jim Deakins. Again Boone wanders away and ends up in Missouri, where he finds Dick Summers, now married and a farmer. He gets drunk, confesses he killed Deakins, and leaves once more, this time heading into the darkness. It has been thirteen years since the novel began in 1830, and the best years for the trappers and hunters have come and gone. "Another five year and there'll be naught but coarse fur," says one trapper; "the beaver's gone now. Buffler's next. Won't be even a goddam poor bull fifty years ahead. You'll see plows comin' across the plains, and people settin' out to farm."

The Big Sky has one excellently developed character and three others who come clear but remain subordinate to the central one. The plot is simple and the suspense well handled. The texture is rough and strong, the style natural and the story told without heroics. The historical background and the details of life and living are complete and accurate, based on Guthrie's reading hundreds of records and accounts in Harvard's Widener Library and upon a journey which Guthrie made with Bernard De Voto along the whole course of the Missouri River and its headwaters.

The response of the reviewers was instant and enthusiastic. Among them Allan Nevins, Dorothy Canfield Fisher, and Walter Van Tilburg Clark acclaimed the novel, not perhaps as a great novel but as perhaps the very best of its kind ever written. There were few derogatory or mixed reviews, and most of these expressed at least limited admiration. In the years that have followed, much has been written about *The Big Sky*, and these interpretations have broadened the scope of the criticism. Some of these criticisms discuss the novel as a landscape novel, as an epic, as a tragedy, and as a melodrama; others are concerned with it as a novel with a theme, such as the limitations of primitivism, the encroachment of civilization, the quest for truth, the passing of an era; and some have seen in it the materials for mythic and archetypal interpretations.

Walter Van Tilburg Clark's review of *The Way West* in the *Saturday Review of Literature* (Oct. 8, 1949) first made the point that the novel was more than a follow-up of *The Big Sky* designed to capitalize on the latter's popularity. This point he carried further seven years later when he reviewed *These Thousand Hills* (*New York Times Book Review*, Nov. 18, 1956). The novels as a trilogy, he says, tell the story of the opening and development of the Northwest, but each individually centers upon and develops a separate segment of the story and can stand alone. *The Way West* Clark regards as an important test of Guthrie's talent and imaginative reach, for whereas *The Big Sky* had no important antecedents that dealt with the mountain men and hence had ample new material to draw upon, its successor dealt with the Oregon Trail, a common topic from Francis Parkman onward. Guthrie, Clark thinks, met the test.

It is not uncommon to read that *The Big Sky* is more powerful and more gripping and that *The Way West* is a better novel in conception and execution; but more important is the fact that both are first-rate and that in May 1950 Guthrie was awarded the Pulitzer Prize for *The Way West*. It seems safe to say with Thomas W. Ford (*A.B. Guthrie, Jr.*, 88–89) that each volume succeeds well in presenting the facts and the spirit of the era it portrays but that the fundamental character of each age is so entirely different that the volumes are of necessity very different in character. Thus *The Big Sky* is shaped by lone individuals who range over a vast uncharted area hunting for furs, "with no set goal in mind," in contrast to *The Way West* with its "slow, plodding, straight, determined movement of people over the trail, having as its goal a simple geographical objective." *The Way West* concerns a group of settlers headed for Oregon, intent upon establishing a permanent community, whereas Boone Caudill was opposed to everything the settlers stood for.

Dick Summers is the character who links *The Big Sky* and *The Way West* together. When *The Big Sky* ended in 1843, Summers was married and had become a farmer in Missouri. When *The Way West* opens three years later, his wife is dead, he is forty-nine years old, and he has never been content as a farmer. He readily agrees, therefore, to guide the wagon train from its point of origin at Independence, Missouri, to its destination on the Columbia River in Oregon. And so the wagon train sets out on its way—to Fort Laramie, along the Platte and North Platte rivers, across the continental divide into the upper Columbia basin, thence to Fort Hall on the Snake River, and finally down it to Fort Boise, across the Blue Mountains, and down the Columbia to its confluence with the Willamette. On this long journey from the spring of 1846 till autumn, the wagon train and its people work their way. There are all sorts with wide-ranging motivations, each person hoping life will somehow be better: shiftless Hank McBee, who with his family is running away from his debts in Ohio; the Fairmans from Kentucky, who hope to find a location more congenial to their small son's health; Brother Weatherby, the Methodist minister who wants to preach religion to the Indians; Tadlock, who organized the expedition but whose petulance contributes to protagonist Lije Evans's replacing him as leader. The wagon train reveals interplay of character, the force of events, the drudgery of the journey, the accidents of fortune, the details of daily life that fill the weeks and months of the long trek. The romantic myth and dream of the Northwest are always there, but they are constantly held in check by the realistic portrayal of the rigors of the journey and its trials and tragedies. Guthrie manages to capture both the facts and the spirit of the way west to Oregon well.

Like *The Big Sky*, and *The Way West*, *These Thousand Hills* (1956) leaves the reader feeling that Guthrie's novels portray the successive stages of the settling of the West the way it really was. So thorough were his research and understanding that no matter whether it was a skirmish with Indians or cattle rustlers, the way a wolf is skinned or horses tethered, everything has an authentic ring about it. Herein, however, lay a part of the author's problem: to tell a story that grows out of the popular literary tradition of the West and avoids the charge of merely being another "Western." After all, the coming of the cowpuncher's world inevitably must deal with trail drives, cattle rustlers, and bronco busting as well as with six-shooters, gambling, saloons, and houses of prostitution. In turn, the transition to an increasingly complex way of life called for the coming of schools, churches, government, and banks, as well as for fenced ranges. Here again the materials are less than new, though Guthrie shows the reader what goes on in people's minds instead of merely their actions. *These Thousand Hills* did not wholly escape charges of being "stereotyped" and "another Western," but Guthrie's sweep of history remains intact with Lat Evans, grandson of Lije Evans, giving continuity to both the story and the development of the West. Just as Lije Evans and his family set out along the trail that led to Oregon, Lat Evans leaves Oregon for a new life in Montana. He aims for a new kind of West and a new kind of respectability and success—a far reach from the life Boone Caudill had sought out half a century earlier.

Guthrie continued to write both fiction and nonfiction throughout the period covered by this survey. *Arfive* (1971) and *The Last Valley* (1975), carrying forward the account of the development of the West, fall short of the excellence of the first three novels and especially of *The Big Sky* and *The Way West*. Perhaps the reason is that in his trilogy Guthrie had essentially accomplished "the high fictional purpose" he had set for himself of interpreting the Western movement "to the American people" in a series of what he calls "panels." *Arfive* and *The Last Valley* carry the reader into the twentieth century, ending with the period between World War I and World War II, and dealing with such problems as education, urbanization, the environment, and human relations in the midst of change. As early as *The Big Sky*, however, the problems of the advance of civilization are noted in the paradox that the mountain men have a hand in destroying the thing they love and are to become the guides for the wagon trains and permanent settlers who will despoil the land at an ever-increasing rate. Guthrie sees change as inevitable and the coming of civilization as necessary and desirable, though its coming complicates the difference between right and wrong, and the choices that have to be made are no longer "the clean choices that our youth and innocence have led us to expect." Compromise becomes inevitable and what seem like right choices sometimes turn out to be mistakes. Guthrie is in no sense a sociological or philosophical novelist, but neither is he just a chronicler and teller of Western stories.

Kentucky played a role, though not a large one, in Guthrie's fiction. Its place in his autobiography, *The Blue Hen's Chick* (1965), is greater, for the volume is an informal account of formative experiences in Guthrie's life. Here he offers accounts of the landlady who contributed to his knowledge of and interest in Kentucky history, his experiences as a newspaperman, and his warm, anecdotal recollections of newspaper associates, members of the political and legal fraternity and of the Lexington police department, friends at the University of Kentucky, and some of the "characters" who held unique places in Lexington's history. Two of the stories in *The Big It* (1960), "The Wreck" and "The Fourth at Getup," are set in the Commonwealth. Devoted to Kentucky though Guthrie has been, however, his greatest love was always for the land of the big sky.

Janice Holt Giles

Janice Holt Giles (1909–79) was Kentucky's most prolific novelist of recent time and a very successful writer of historical fiction dealing with the Kentucky frontier. She was born in Arkansas and grew up there and in Oklahoma, both of which states provided material for her historical novels. She first came to Kentucky in 1939 as a director of religious education in a Frankfort church and later was associated with the Louisville Presbyterian Seminary. She met her husband-to-be, Henry Giles of Adair County, at Bowling Green in 1943, when, as a soldier, he boarded the bus she was riding to visit her daughter in Texas. They were married in 1945, lived in Louisville for four years, and moved to Spout Springs, near Knifley, Adair County, in 1949. It was her husband, also a writer, Giles says, "who wanted me to write stories." Thus while still in Louisville she started two novels that were published after the Gileses settled on their forty-acre farm near where Henry grew up: *The Enduring Hills* in 1950 and *Miss Willie* in 1951. *Tara's Healing* came immediately afterwards in 1951 and with the two preceding novels constitutes a "Piney Woods" trilogy dealing with life on Giles Ridge and in The Knobs region of Kentucky. Thus began a writing career that was not launched until the author was forty-one. The novels were well received and reached a fairly large audience. *The Enduring Hills,* for example, sold 100,000 copies during its first nine months.

The Enduring Hills is the story of Hod Pierce, who grows up in poverty in the hill country but wants a larger life than his ancestors had in Piney Ridge. His experience in World War II has enlarged his horizon, and after the war he and his wife go to work in Louisville to find the amenities of life not available in Piney Ridge. They achieve success in the business world and gain social acceptance, but both feel the emptiness of what they have won, give it all up, and go back to the simpler and more rewarding way of life that the hills offer, convinced that the slower pace and friendliness of the hill country are preferable to comfortable material success in the midst of the hurry and stress of the outside world.

Miss Willie, the sequel to *The Enduring Hills,* is about Miss Willie Payne, the aunt of Hod's wife Mary, who resigns her teaching position in Texas and takes a job in a one-room school near the home of her niece. Miss Willie, though an earnest, well-meaning, hard-working teacher, is unfortunately convinced that a part of her responsibility is to impose more "enlightened" ways and culture upon the children and people of Piney Ridge. At first she is thwarted by her failures, but in time she comes to realize that she has erred in trying to reform the whole community and that there is no single set of rights and wrongs in cultural patterns and values for all people in all places. *Tara's Healing* concludes the trilogy by portraying the influence of Piney Ridge upon Dr. Tara Cochrane, who has had a serious nervous breakdown and has been persuaded by Hod and Mary Pierce to recuperate in their community.

Such abbreviated summaries of Giles's novels do injustice to them by making them appear hopelessly sentimental, when in fact they are not. It is more accurate to say that they are idealistic, but Giles portrays the details of hill country with honesty and candor. The people are real people who blunder along like people everywhere else. Giles unquestionably reveals nostalgia for a way of life that is disappearing and casts a rosy glow over the honesty and decency of the world she portrays; but by no means is it merely a world of sweetness and light. *The Enduring Hills* is generally regarded as the best of the three novels.

At this point Giles began her career as a historical novelist. A claim of greatness cannot be made for Giles, but she has a knack for telling a story, portrays her characters well, excels in depicting the life of the times, and is historically accurate. Most of these novels about Kentucky deal with the early settlers; first was *The Kentuckians* (1953), covering the years 1769–77. It recounts how Daniel Boone and his companions arrived in the Bluegrass region in 1769 and lived there for two years while they hunted, studied the topography of the land, and explored the terrain southward over which Boone was to guide Richard Henderson and his Transylvania Company settlers in the spring of 1775. Farther south in Green River country the Long Hunters arrived at about the same time and also remained two years. In 1777 Fort Harrod, Boonesborough, and Logan's Station were two years old and were faring well enough, though living in increasing fear of the Indian since the Revolutionary War was in progress and the British were supplying the tribes with arms, men, and leadership. In 1769 the Indians willingly tolerated the newcomers so long as they were hunters, traders, or surveyors. In 1777, two years after the arrival of the first settlers, neutrality and even friendliness had given way to hostility, and with increasing frequency both the settlers and the Indians committed atrocities. Among "The Kentuckians" on the scene were the leaders of each of the forts (James Harrod, Daniel Boone, and Benjamin Logan) and George Rogers Clark, who sought to have Virginia designate Kentucky a county, provide it with military protection against the Indians, and authorize him to raise an army with which to oppose the British and the Indians and to break the British hold on the Old Northwest. When 1777 dawned, progress had been made, but there were signs that the year ahead would be a difficult one for everyone on the frontier.

Such historical facts suggest the broad framework for the story that Giles tells, but at the human level other problems concerned the settlers: clearing the land, building cabins, planting crops; hardship and privation; being born, getting married, and dying; success and disappointment and failure; and the precariousness of life in the three little forts, situated as they were miles apart and unable to give each other much help. Giles meshes all this well, drawing on both historical and fictional characters. The latter include David Cooper, represented as having hunted and explored with both Boone and the Long Hunters, and the red-headed Bethia. David and Bethia's paths, which first crossed in Virginia, cross again when her husband Judd Jordan (later revealed to be a spy in the service of the British) and she come to Kentucky. Their story runs through the novel. There are also real-life happenings, including the capture by Indians on separate occasions of Boone and the Calloway girls, Benjamin Logan's rescue of Burr Harrison, and the conflicting land claims of Richard Henderson's Transylvania Company and those who claimed their land under the auspices of the state of Virginia.

Hannah Fowler (1956), portraying the Kentucky frontier in 1778, is the sequel to *The Kentuckians*. The central figure is Hannah Moore, who when the story begins has with her father left Major George Rogers Clark's Ohio River train to follow the Kentucky River to Boonesborough. When her father falls desperately ill from blood poisoning brought on by an axe wound, Hannah is aided by Tice Fowler, who takes her and her dying father to Logan's Station. Hannah and Tice marry, and the story focuses on the first years of their married life and their enduring the hardships and trials of pioneer life. The hardships are sometimes balanced off by hard-won triumphs, the joys of sharing, and the pleasures that come from the loyalty and kindness of neighbors. Unlike *The Kentuckians*, *Hannah Fowler* does not mix historical and fictional characters, though the actions of the former do influence the plot. The story takes its shape primarily from the central character, a woman who can track and hunt as well as a man and can shoot to kill when necessary. Giles's objective, in short, was to portray the rigors of the life of the early settlers. In *The Kentuckians* she brought her pioneers through Cumberland Gap and up the Wilderness Trail, but in *Hannah Fowler* they follow the Ohio River to the mouth of the Kentucky and from there make their way up the river to the Bluegrass region.

In *The Land beyond the Mountains* (1958) Giles combined fictional and historical people during the years 1783–92 to portray the settlers in their struggle to achieve statehood. Discontented because of the neglect they are experiencing from both Virginia and the federal government, they are divided among themselves about what the future of the territory should be: whether to maintain the status quo, press harder for statehood, or form an independent nation. After this state of affairs is set forth the central real-life character in the novel begins to play his role in the Third Convention in Danville in 1785. This was James Wilkinson, a wealthy, colorful, influential resident of Lexington recently arrived from Maryland. The story is complex since Wilkinson was an ambitious self-seeker and a skilled intriguer, playing one side against another, pretending support for statehood while receiving pay from Spain for working to establish a new Spanish empire which was to begin with Kentucky and extend westward and of which he expected to be governor. The scheme failed, of course, and Kentucky became the fifteenth state to join the Union.

Cassius Cartwright, among the fictional characters of the novel, takes the lead in thwarting Wilkinson. Through him Giles is able to portray the temper of the times and bring together the plots that center upon the settlers and the machinations of Wilkinson. Giles portrays pioneer life well, her characterizations are good, the complex material is accurate and well handled, and the story line holds the reader's attention. Giles was not the first Kentucky author to write of Wilkinson's Spanish Conspiracy. James Lane Allen made use of it in *The Choir Invisible* (1897), and Joseph Altsheler in his juvenile novel *The Free Rangers* (1909) had his young scouts go to New Orleans to confer with the Spanish governor about the rumored forthcoming attack on Kentucky.

In *The Believers* (1957) Giles covered the period shortly after 1800, when the Shakers came to America from England on the wave of the "Great Revival" that reached its climax in Bourbon County at Cane Ridge Meeting House in August 1801. Shakertown at Pleasant Hill, in Mercer County, was established in 1805, and two years later the Shaker community at South Union, in Logan County, was organized and later provided the locale of Giles's novel. At the core of the Shaker faith was belief in celibacy, daily confession, separation from the world, equality of the sexes, consecration of labor, and community of property.

The central figure in *The Believers* is Rebecca Fowler, who is married to Richard Cooper and is the daughter of the doughty pioneer Hannah Fowler. Trouble in their married life begins when their child is born dead and Richard becomes a religious fanatic, believing as he does that the infant's death was a punishment from God. Soon thereafter he and Rebecca become converts to the Shaker faith, give up their farmland, and join the Shaker community. Richard becomes increasingly fanatical and is comfortable with even the extremes of his new faith; Rebecca has intellectual misgivings, questions much of the practice she observes, and tries to win back Richard's love. In the end she withdraws from the community, returns to the home of her parents, and ultimately marries again.

The novel lacks the excitement found in Giles's novels of the rampaging frontier, but it does reflect the religious fervor that seized the frontier in its latter days and at the same time gives an interesting and sympathetic account of everyday life in a Shaker community. Giles does question the fanaticism of some of the members and the way they practice their faith, but she never calls into question the sincerity, goodness, or devotion of the leaders. Again both the details and the overall effect of the portrayal reflect accuracy and fair-mindedness.

These four novels constitute Giles's contribution to the early history of Kentucky. She was the author of other historical fiction that carries the story of the frontier west from Kentucky to Arkansas, Oklahoma, and even New Mexico and Arizona. In these works some of the main characters in her Kentucky novels, other members of these families, or their descendants are central characters. *Johnny Osage* (1960), for example, tells the story of the first white settlement in Oklahoma Territory, Johnny Osage being the son of Hannah Fowler and the brother of Rebecca. *Savanna* (1961) tells the story of the settlement of Arkansas, its title character being the granddaughter of Tattie Cartwright (*The Land beyond the Mountains*) and Hannah Fowler (*Hannah Fowler* and *The Believers*). And *Voyage to Santa Fe* (1962) employs still other descendants of the Fowlers in the move from Fort Smith to Santa Fe.

Giles is one of the few writers who has dealt with a Civil War battle within the state. This she did in *Run Me a River* (1964). The time is September 18–22, 1861, the place the Green River. The plot centers upon the five-day run of Bohannon Cartwright's ninety-ton sternwheeler, the "Rambler," from Bowling Green to Evansville to avoid capture by General Simon Bolivar Buckner and his Confederate troops, who occupied Bowling Green on September 18. Bo Cartwright, whose "Rambler" carries peacetime merchandise, livestock, passengers, and varied cargo, wants no part in the war that has split the country, but his neutrality is endangered by General Buckner, who has heard reports that downstream federal gunboats are on their way upstream to Bowling Green to attack him. Thus Buckner and his troops march on Rochester with the intention of dynamiting Lock No. 3, expecting thereby to halt the progress of the gunboats. Meanwhile Cartwright, the "Rambler," and its crew and motley passengers make their way downstream, only to find that General Buckner has preceded them to Lock No. 3. How the little steamboat gets through the Locks; evades the gunboats; jumps a dam; picks up "Sir Henry," a Shakespearean actor, and his sixteen-year-old granddaughter; copes with foul weather; and finally reaches the Ohio River and safe harbor constitute the principal events that keep the reader anxiously turning the pages and wondering whether the battered little steamboat will ever reach its destination.

As usual with Giles's historical novels, *Run Me a River* was carefully researched. The novel has fine descriptive passages, the narrative moves along well, and the regional idiom is nicely handled. In her foreword Giles writes of the historical facts upon which the story is based.

Felix Holt

Felix Holt (1898–1954) was fifty-three when he published his first novel; he died just nine days after he published his second one three years later. Even so, *The Gabriel Horn* (1951) and *Dan'l Boone Kissed Me* (1954) entitle him to a secure, even if modest place in Kentucky literature. The making of Holt as a writer started early. Through his mother he came into an interest in language, through his father a love of literature, and in Murray and Calloway County, where he was born, an understanding of the countryside, the dialect, and the descendants of the people he would one day write about.

Holt came early to a journalistic career. During World War I he was a sports reporter for *Stars and Stripes*, the army newspaper, and after the war he held positions with newspapers in Paducah, St. Louis, Memphis, Detroit, and elsewhere. He stayed longest with the *Detroit Times*, from 1923 till 1930. Then came a radio career in Detroit at station WXYZ, where he became the most prolific of the authors for the "Lone Ranger" and "Green Hornet" serials. By 1945 Holt's reputation as a scriptwriter took him to New York, where he wrote the script for CBS's "Cimarron Tavern." A year later he was writing scripts for television's "Studio One" and "Big Town."

During the years that Holt was writing for newspapers, radio, and television, two concerns stayed with him. One was his attachment to Kentucky, to which he returned frequently and where he talked about starting a country newspaper and once got as far as buying a house in Calloway County. The other concern was his desire to break free of the confines of radio and television and to write about the things he knew best. Thus he came to write a short story about early Kentucky and the Jackson Purchase where he had grown up. The periodicals he sent it to rejected it, but his confidence in what he was doing led him to rewrite the story as a novel; but publishing houses rejected the novel too. Finally in 1951 Dutton published it under the title of *The Gabriel Horn*; and soon thereafter it was being cited by critics as one of the important books of the year. The Dollar Book Club made it a selection, and after the hardback edition came the Dell paperback and ultimately a juvenile edition. In all, the novel sold more than a million copies and in 1954 was made into a very successful movie, *The Kentuckians*. A.B. Guthrie, Jr., wrote the script, and Burt Lancaster played the lead.

The Gabriel Horn is a picaresque novel about Big Eli Wakefield, who carries the hunter's horn; Little Eli, his son; and the romance of Big Eli with the indentured girl Hannah. The time is early nineteenth century, when hunters and settlers were trekking westward, and the scene is frontier Kentucky in the Jackson Purchase area. The strength of the novel lies in the author's narrative skill, his warmth and humor, his effective use of western Kentucky dialect, customs, and traditions, and his success in recapturing the spirit of the frontier.

Dan'l Boone Kissed Me (1954) is set in the Jackson Purchase also, but the time—1845—is later than in *The Gabriel Horn*. It is a story of young love, ambition, politics, and family problems, in which Pappy Duke Caldwell, a tobacco farmer and politician, is the head of the family and the principal character. Like its predecessor, the novel is full of action and moves at a rapid pace while giving, especially through the language, something of the flavor of a past way of life. The opinion of the reviewer in the *New York Herald Tribune* (May 23, 1954) is typical:

> Felix Holt's first novel, *The Gabriel Horn*, had a freshness and an appeal which one would hardly have expected the author to recapture in a second novel. It is especially satisfying to find that *Dan'l Boone Kissed Me* is in every respect an even more enjoyable book. Here is the same warmth and humor, but the flavor is fuller and more mellow, the characters are more sharply defined, and the author's narrative skill is more sure.

The place of Felix Holt in Kentucky literature is a respectable one.

Margaret Cooper Gay

Hatchet in the Sky (1954) is the only novel by Margaret Cooper Gay (1900–57), who was born in Mt. Sterling and later moved to Connecticut. The scene of her novel is the frontier town of Detroit at about the time of the French and Indian War and the Conspiracy of Pontiac. The author had a rich and full store of historical knowledge of what happened in and near Detroit during the early 1760s, and she tells her story with verve and dash. The weaknesses are the occasional overabundance of history and intrigue, some not too convincing characters, and a bit of sentimentality. The Indians are presented in a favorable light, the British unfavorably.

Alfred Leland Crabb

Perhaps no Kentucky-born novelist wrote more often about the Civil War than Alfred Leland Crabb (1883–1980). Crabb was born in Plum Springs in Warren County and after attending college and teaching public school in Kentucky, he got his Ph.D. degree at Peabody College, Nashville, in 1916. After this he taught at what is now Western Kentucky State University until 1927. The remainder of his teaching career, 1927–50, was spent at Peabody, where he published several books and many articles on pedagogical subjects.

Crabb published the first of his eleven historical novels in 1942 and continued to write at a rapid clip until the last was published in 1957. Seven of these deal with the Civil War in Tennessee, one with the war in Kentucky, two with single individuals (Andrew Jackson and Henry Clay), and one with pioneer days (the founding of Nashville). The novels cover a period from the years just preceding the war through the Reconstruction era. Nashville was the subject of five of them (*Dinner at Belmont*, 1942; *Supper at Maxwell House*, 1943; *Breakfast at the Hermitage*, 1945; *Lodgings at the St. Cloud*, 1946; *Home to Tennessee*, 1952); Chattanooga the scene of two (*A Mockingbird Sang at Chickamauga*, 1949; *Reunion at Chattanooga*, 1951); and Kentucky one (*Peace at Bowling Green*, 1955).

According to Crabb himself, the last of these novels "has been the most successful, though I can't say why." *Peace at Bowling Green* differs from his other novels about the Civil War in that it covers a much longer period of time. The others treat short periods, none of them reaching beyond the years of Reconstruction; the Kentucky novel, however, goes back to the founding of Bowling Green in 1803. Due at least in part to the sometimes grim pioneering period of Jacob Skiles, his followers, and their descendants, the novel is less a romance of the Old South than were those set in Tennessee at midcentury. The novel follows the growth and development of the pioneer community until the outbreak of war splits it apart. Delegates from sixty-eight counties met in Russellville, November 1861, formed a government to rival the one in Frankfort, and selected Bowling Green as the capital. All this, of course, receives attention in the novel, as does the tragic division among the people and the ultimate reconcilement and healing of wounds that come after the war is over.

Crabb knew he could tell a story about the southern cause with picturesque detail that would appeal to the general reader, and he wrote a great deal. Such a judgment of him seems to be encouraged by a typically whimsical, self-deprecating letter he wrote to the present author almost twenty-five years ago. "My first call to write," he begins, "was sounded by me, and I heard it from the first note. I have answered it with more words than are carried by the Oxford Dictionary. . . . My motto is that ink was made to shed." Some readers or critics might say that his novels add little to what is already familiar, that he failed to probe the depths of his characters, or that he wrote out of no guiding philosophy of history. But A.L. Crabb probably felt himself on track when a reviewer of his first volume, *Dinner at Belmont*, wrote, "This is one of those Southern novels that are fun to read, and read as if they have been fun to write" (*Books*, March 29, 1942). He was no doubt pleased also that his novels were regarded as historically accurate and could be read, as one reviewer put it, as "excellent entertainment for the relaxation of days off" (*Chicago Tribune*, Jan. 15, 1949). He was probably delighted too if he read the *Springfield Republican* reviewer's verdict that in *Breakfast at the Hermitage* the author "gives the best description of the Rebel yell this writer has ever heard" (May 27, 1947), for he liked picturesque detail. But perhaps even more he may have enjoyed the *New York Times* reviewer's statement (July 11, 1943) that in *Supper at Maxwell House* the author "makes you wish you could have attended that first magnificent evening, on September 23, 1869, when the dining room doors of the Maxwell House swung open and Uncle Jeff announced with mellow dignity, 'Suppah is served.' " A.L. Crabb was at his best when he was being that sort of historical novelist.

Gene Markey

Gene Markey (1895–1980), a reconstructed Yankee by his own admission, was born in Michigan but came to Kentucky as a permanent resident after he married Lucille Parker Wright, owner of the Calumet Farm racing establishment, in 1952. When Markey arrived in Kentucky, he had had experience in both scriptwriting for motion pictures and in movie production and had published both short stories and novels. His best novels are *Kentucky Pride* (1956) and *That Far Paradise* (1960).

More than most novels dealing with Reconstruction in Kentucky, *Kentucky Pride* enables one to understand why Kentucky became more Confederate after the Civil War than it had been during the progress of it; for it was a period when profiteers—Kentuckians as well as Yankees—took advantage of the hectic confusion that accompanied Reconstruction. Actually, of course, one could have expected Kentucky's experience to have been less trying than it actually was. On one hand, the state had remained neutral and saw twice as many of its sons fight for the Union as for the Confederacy; on another, having never seceded, it did not have to apply for admission to the Union or come under the provisions of the Reconstruction Acts as the seceded states did. Nevertheless, greedy profiteers engaged in shameless acts such as securing spurious confiscation orders and taking advantage of the confused situation and especially of those who had fought for the South and were coming home at war's end.

Markey's novel makes these post-war conditions come alive through young Major Aidan Kensal, who for four years was a member of General John Hunt Morgan's famed Raiders and returns to the Blue Grass and his ancestral home, Oakenden, near Lexington in order to resume his breeding and running of thoroughbreds. Instead of being able to make a quick transition back to his accustomed life, however, he falls victim to the chaos around him when he discovers that as a Confederate soldier he has been stripped of his civil rights and his property confiscated. Major Veach Doucain, an agent of the Reconstruction and an enemy of Kensal, impounds Kensal's farm, his home, and his horses, and even seeks to win Lacey Archer, Kensal's sweetheart.

The story that follows is filled with fast-moving action, but it also has a tight dramatic structure that reflects Markey's Hollywood know-how. Thoroughbreds, horse races, fights, duels, cross-country chases, outlaws, and murder make the action almost continuously exciting and suspenseful and keep the reader turning the pages. Though he does not probe for its underlying causes, Markey does shed light on Reconstruction and in such a way that, according to one reviewer, "Only the captious will complain that much of the script reads as though it was set up for camera angles."

In *That Far Paradise* Markey's subject was the trek of post–Revolutionary War settlers from Virginia to Kentucky, but his account deals with the gentry rather than the usual pioneer. The year is 1794, when the future of the young nation seems insecure and England, France, and Spain still have notions of further colonization in North America and even of declaring war. Against this background, and with some apprehension about the future of Virginia, General Jared Kensal decides to leave his lands in Virginia and move to Kentucky, where already he has taken up new land and built a house.

Leaving behind only the land and the buildings, the General draws upon the efficiency he had learned in military campaigns and organizes a caravan to move an entire plantation family with its retinue of slaves, furniture and other equipage, livestock, food for the journey, and implements and seed for farming the new land. Complicating the problems of logistics, General Kensal rejects the advice that he follow the Wilderness Road and elects to take the northern route, which often requires hacking out a wagon road. Finally the caravan reaches what is now Parkersburg, West Virginia, on the Ohio River, whence it floats down the river in flatboats to Maysville and from there travels overland to Lexington. With his usual crisp style and fast-moving plot, Markey tells an exciting story of how one hundred people with nine Conestoga wagons ford rivers, break trails, and cross mountains. The book has no historical thesis and is intended primarily for pleasure and escape, but it reads well and maintains the reader's interest.

Ann Hebson

Ann Hebson's *A Fine and Private Place* (1958) was in a sense a forerunner of *The Lattimer Legend*, her best work and a Civil War novel that won the Macmillan Fiction Award for 1961. The subject matter of the two volumes is quite different, but both explore the effects of sins of parents on children. In the former, the "fine and private place" is the world of childhood, symbolized by the tree-house which fourteen-year-old Travis shares with Peter, the boy next door. At the end of the long day of the novel, the world of Travis is forever shattered by the knowledge she gains of the long-ago affair between her father and Peter's mother and of its significance for the future.

The time span of *The Lattimer Legend* extends from the post-Korean War period back to the Civil War. Three characters dominate the action: Tom Lattimer, whose marriage is on the verge of dissolution; Kate Lattimer, whose diary Tom has discovered and from which he learns the story of Kate's girlhood affairs, her wretched marriage, and her eloping with one of Morgan's Raiders while her husband is missing after Gettysburg; and 110-year-old Joel Lattimer, who is the link between the plots that center upon Tom and Kate. Handling the time shifts that span seven generations and managing to keep Kate and the Civil War milieu the dominant forces in the story through which Tom discovers new meanings in his life is a difficult feat. But Hebson succeeds well enough, and the book was well received: "At its best, it is a very good story indeed" (*New York Times Book Review*); ". . . an interesting book full of laughter and earthy wisdom" (*Saturday Review*); ". . . a first-rate Civil War story" (*San Francisco Chronicle*). The opening scene of the story is in Kentucky, but it moves to West Virginia, where most of the action takes place.

Hebson (1925–) was born in Montgomery, Alabama, but grew up in Louisville, where she attended Atherton High School and the University of Louisville and studied at the Louisville Art Center. In 1947 she graduated from Grinnell College, where she met and married William J. Hebson, from whom she was divorced in 1968. Hebson early worked for the *Courier-Journal* and the *Parkersburg News*. Subsequently she worked in public relations at the University of Miami (Florida), in radio production at Mary Baldwin College, and as a writer and production assistant for Kentucky Educational Television in Lexington. Besides her two novels, Hebson is also the author of art education programs for National Instructional Television and for state agencies. At latest report she was working on a new novel, *Forests of the Night*.

Robert Emmett McDowell

Robert Emmett McDowell (1914–75), who lived most of his life in or near Louisville, was primarily the author of some undistinguished detective and mystery stories, but he published one historical novel worthy of note: *Tidewater Sprig* (1961), which centers upon a neglected aspect of the Kentucky frontier: Bullitt's Lick salt works down Salt River from Shepherdsville. McDowell's novel tells the story of Todd Medford, a member of the Tidewater, Virginia, aristocracy and an arrogant dandy, who gets into so much trouble that he leaves the Tidewater, makes his way down the Ohio River on a flatboat, and ends up at the Bullitt's Lick salt works. Todd becomes a menial laborer, destitute and without family or friends, and finally wins respect and friendship on the rough-hewn frontier. McDowell is also the author of *Home Is the Hunter*, an outdoor drama dealing with Daniel Boone that opened in the summer of 1963 in the Fort Harrod State Park Theatre in Harrodsburg and ran for several summers.

John Clagett

John Clagett (1916–), a native of Bowling Green, has written historical fiction that ranges from pioneer days in Kentucky to World War II. The best of these novels, *Buckskin Cavalier* (1954) and *Gunpowder for Boonesborough* (1965), are stories of the frontier. The first is a not very convincing account that deals with the frontier just before the Revolutionary War and tells the story of Lyon Cameron, who while on Lord Dunsmore's expedition in Pennsylvania is branded a coward for actions not wholly his fault when he fails to rescue Dawn Woodbridge from the Indians. The remainder of the action, which takes place along the Wilderness Road, at Fort Boonesborough, and in Ohio, where Lyon becomes a "son" of the Wyandotte tribe, is devoted to the rescue of the girl.

Clagett's *Gunpowder for Boonesborough*, a novel for juveniles, is a better novel than *Buckskin Cavalier*. The principal character is sixteen-year-old David Adams, who is a part of a keelboat mission from Pittsburgh to New Orleans to obtain gunpowder with which to defend the frontier against the British-led Indians. One exciting experience follows another until finally David and the Indian fighters arrivc at Boonesborough just in time to distribute the powder and repulse the final Indian charge. Such split-second timing in the hands of a lesser writer would probably repel the reader, but as the reviewer in the *New York Times Book Review* says, Clagett's success "proves that [a] good writer can transmute gimmickry into gold" (Nov. 7, 1965). Clagett's knowledge of keelboats and the Ohio and Mississippi rivers is excellent and contributes much to the success of the story.

James Robert Sherburne

No Kentucky writer of fiction in recent years has been more prolific in dealing with Kentucky's past than has James Robert Sherburne (1925–). Though he was born in Michigan, Sherburne moved to Lexington with his family in 1941 and subsequently attended Berea College and the University of Kentucky, where he received his A.B. in 1947. After working for twenty years in Chicago advertising agencies, Sherburne returned to Kentucky in 1968 and since then has lived in Midway, Woodford County, while devoting himself full time to a career as a novelist. His first two novels—*Hacey Miller* (1971) and *The Way to Fort Pillow* (1972)—are set principally in Kentucky and deal with events that lead up to and include the Civil War.

Sherburne's fictional Hacey Miller was born in 1832, the son of a Madison County planter and slave owner. He began life, therefore, with at least a tacit acceptance of slavery; but as he matured he became increasingly antislavery. The evolution of his views unifies *Hacey Miller* and ties together local and national events and episodes with Hacey's experiences in a slave society and the events and developments, especially in his schooling, that bring about his maturation. The story depicts plantation life, slave labor, the auction block, the Underground Railroad, and divided family loyalties; Hacey's attendance at Transylvania College, his reading of law, and his studies at Harvard University, where he came to know the famous abolitionist Thomas Wentworth Higginson; the Dred Scott Decision, the Kansas-

Nebraska Act, and the Fugitive Slave Law; and Hacey's dislike for John Hunt Morgan and his hatred of acts of violence toward slaves. Most important of all, Cassius M. Clay, that colorful, controversial Kentucky abolitionist, more than anyone else, led Hacey to commit himself openly to views on slavery different from those of his family and neighbors. Sherburne's discovery of Clay in 1965 while he was still in Chicago caused Sherburne to determine that some day he would write a book about Clay, Berea College, and Kentucky.

In *The Way to Fort Pillow*, Hacey, now a teacher in the school that Presbyterian minister and abolitionist John G. Fee founded at Berea with Clay's help, witnesses the pillaging and burning of the school by irate proslavery sympathizers in 1859. When the war starts, Hacey joins the colorful historic First Kentucky (Union) Cavalry under Colonel Frank Wolford and thus takes up arms aginst members of his own family. With this famous regiment Hacey fights against General John Hunt Morgan's Raiders at Lebanon, Tennessee, and saves his brother from being captured when the Raiders are defeated. Subsequently Hacey is assigned to Thomas Wentworth Higginson's black regiment in South Carolina and is well on his way to Fort Pillow. Here he is the officer in charge of a black artillery unit in the historic, bloody, controversially reported battle for the control of Fort Pillow that took place in April 1864. In the midst of the carnage where three hundred soldiers lie dead and wounded is Hacey, who has lost an arm and can only watch as his wounded comrades—most of them black—are tortured, maimed, and mutilated. In 1866 Hacey is fully recuperated. Berea College opens again, with blacks still members of the student body and Hacey one of the teachers.

Though sometimes Sherburne's novels are heavily laden with history, they are eminently readable, the narrative flows, and the action is often rousing and gripping. Furthermore, Sherburne's sense of the nineteenth century effectively evokes the life of the day and brings together his historical characters with those whom he has imagined. The volumes are not merely action novels, however. Social and moral problems and dilemmas receive attention as characters confront choices and take sides in important matters. "An historical novel of the first order," says the *Library Journal* (April 15, 1972) of *The Way to Fort Pillow*.

Sherburne's third historical novel is *Stand Like Men* (1973). Here his interest in history and research takes him into the Kentucky coal miners' struggle for survival during the early days of the Great Depression, using the Harlan County Coal War of 1931 as his subject. *Stand Like Men* is an action-packed, fast-paced tale that shows how hard times came to the mines in the late 1920s and how tensions among the contesting groups involved—mine owners, miners, and labor organizers—worsened and finally climaxed in violence that earned for the events and the place the epithet "bloody Harlan."

Sherburne has studied his subject well and weaves into his story everything from the evils of the broad-form deed to the demand for coal, mine safety, job security, yellow-dog contracts, the degradation of poverty, the abuse of power, and Communist organizers exploiting chaos. Perhaps Sherburne sees too much good among the strikers and agitators and too little among the company officials and county officials, but overall his account seems authentic. His narrative talent, coupled with an abundance of "content," and his ability to project the drama of the situation, make *Stand Like Men* a novel that reads well and is worth reading.

Sherburne is best known for his historical novels dealing with Kentucky during the Civil War, but he is also the author of a historical murder-mystery novel, *Death's Pale Horse: A Novel of Murder in Saratoga in the 1880s* (1980). Isaac Burns Murphy, in real life perhaps the greatest jockey who ever lived, is one of the principal characters. Murphy, a black, was born in Lexington in 1861 and was buried in 1896 in a Lexington "negro" cemetery that was later abandoned. Here his body lay in an overgrown grave until 1967, when Frank and Betty Borries located it and had the remains reburied at the Man o' War Park, close by Man o' War. Ten years later the remains of both Man o' War and Murphy were reinterred at the new Kentucky Horse Park on the Ironworks Pike.

Murphy's list of racing accomplishments is remarkable. He rode in every great stakes race in the country except the Futurity. He won three Kentucky Derbies (1884, 1890, 1891), a record that stood until Earl Sande equalled it on Gallant Fox in 1930 and Eddie Arcaro surpassed it in 1948 on Citation. His lifetime record was 628 wins in 1412 races, a remarkable 44 percent that to this day is far from being challenged.

Sherburne's *Death's Pale Horse* draws upon the low estate racing was falling into during the 1880s and 1890s in order to create a good yarn. It also initiates a series of murder-mystery novels that involve Paddy Moretti, Sherburne's detective. In *Death's Pale Horse*, Paddy, the lovable, bumbling but resourceful, Manhattan sports journalist, travels to the Saratoga track to witness an important race between two great thoroughbreds, Tenstrike and The Mogul, the latter ridden by Paddy's buddy, jockey Isaac Murphy. Murphy himself, Sherburne says, "was a real straight-arrow guy. He didn't throw races. He didn't booze. He didn't do bad stuff. He didn't have women. He just won races." The derring-do, therefore, has to come from other quarters: card cheats, race fixers, fraudulent mediums, as well as other rascals and swindlers. Paddy discovers three murder victims —a suspicious racetrack tout, a con-man, and an unpleasant journalist. Murphy enters the story in his role of jockey, of course, and he helps Paddy untangle the complicated skein of scams, price-fixing, and murder.

Since *Death's Pale Horse*, Sherburne has written two more murder mysteries in a historical context with Paddy Moretti as his sleuth: *Death's Gray Angel* in 1981 and *Death's Clenched Fist* in 1982. The former has an 1888 setting and deals with a fictional Confederate guerrilla raider based on William Clarke Quantrill. The latter is an 1890s story and has a New York setting of Tammany Hall, corrupt politics, anarchists, and organized crime.

CHAPTER 19

Literature of Protest

When the stock market crash came in 1929 Theodore Dreiser, Upton Sinclair, and Socialists generally had already been writing of the evils of capitalism and the exploitation of the masses, but it took the tightening grip of the Great Depression to rivet the country's attention on its economic and social woes. Furthermore, time and events played into the hands of the American Communist Party, which had been formed in 1919 by the fusion of the leftist elements that seceded from the ranks of the Socialists when the United States entered World War I. Then in 1929 the Communist Party formed a central organization for writers called the Workers' Cultural Federation, a development that coincided sufficiently with the turmoil growing out of the stock market collapse to capitalize on the long-existing Socialist impulse toward "radical" literature. Thus was born the American "proletarian novel" with its aim of using literature as a weapon in what was projected to be an American struggle between workers and their capitalist bosses.

Not all "proletarian" novelists, however, were card-carrying Communists. Some were merely "revolutionaries" who urged non-traditional solutions to specific worker/management problems, and some were "fellow travelers" whose views resembled the objectives of the Communists even though they had no connection with the Communist Party. Their novels shared some of the views advocated by the American Marxist writers, but in general they failed to conform to the requirement that the proletarian novel be tragic in tone and vision and be imbued with a deep sense of class struggle. John Dos Passos was such a writer, as was John Steinbeck.

By 1935 or 1936 American proletarian fiction pretty well ceased, for by this time the rise of Fascism in Europe obliged the Communists and the Workers' Cultural Federation to deemphasize proletarian literature as divisive and to support a united front with America against Hitler and Mussolini. The coming of World War II completely ended the writing of proletarian novels. They had never had a large audience and were generally too long on didactic purpose and too short on literary merit. They had never been a very successful instrument of class war and today are little read except by literary historians who study the relationship between literature and its times.

During the mid- and later 1920s and the 1930s Kentucky authors had ample opportunity to be among those who took the side of the workers during the Eastern Kentucky coalfields troubles. Prominent leftist literary figures came to the Harlan area to observe or participate in the spectacular events that took place there as management and labor squared off in a confrontation that saw the spilling of blood. Theodore Dreiser was the first, and then came Edmund Wilson, John Dos Passos, Malcolm Cowley, Waldo Frank, and others, but no Kentucky "proletarians" or other "radicals" were among them. Some Kentucky writers knew well what was going on and observed what followed, but their eyes were on something of larger scope than a violent confrontation between labor and management. Jesse Stuart was soon to draw upon the use and abuse of the nation's welfare system as a source for his fiction, but more for the sake of rollicking humor than for purposes of reform. Harriette Arnow and James Still wrote of the mountains, the mines, and the miners, but theirs was the long view of what they saw, and what they wrote was some of the finest fiction and verse ever produced by Kentuckians. It was to be a generation and a half later that a prominent Kentucky writer entered the lists as a writer of revolt in behalf of the people and the land of Appalachia. This was Harry M. Caudill, whose volumes of polemical prose and one novel were effective and sometimes trenchant attacks on abuse. Still later came James Robert Sherburne's *Stand Like Men* (1973), which dealt retrospectively with the Harlan County coal war of 1931. Caudill's and Sherburne's writings are discussed in the chapter on the literature of Eastern Kentucky.

Only two Kentuckians, both of them women, were ever to be known as proletarian writers. One was Olive Dargan, who moved to North Carolina and under the name of Fielding Burke wrote about labor conditions in the textile mills of that state. The other was Leane Zugsmith, who left Kentucky for New York and won a name for herself by writing about social conditions and problems with the eye of a reformer. The other two "protest" writers discussed in this chapter were of a different breed. Willie Snow Ethridge wrote about the textile mills, but her approach was more a journalistic description than a ringing call for reform. Edith Summers Kelley wrote under the influence of Upton Sinclair and the Socialists. Her tone was more moderate than that of Dargan and Zugsmith, and her artistry saved her from the pitfalls of the hard-bitten reformer. Mrs. George Madden Martin, though her writings are discussed elsewhere, should also be noted here. She took part in no labor/management disputes, but she did enter the arena in behalf of blacks and of the "new woman," as the women's suffrage movement opened up new vistas during the late 1920s and early 1930s. Her interest in education and the liberation of women also led her into challenging contemporary methods of educating adolescents, especially in biological and sexual understandings, as they entered the adult world.

Olive Tilford Dargan

Olive Tilford Dargan (1869–1968), born in Grayson County near Leitchfield, achieved considerable renown in the 1930s when she was living near Asheville, North Carolina, and writing proletarian novels under the pseudonym of Fielding Burke. She began her writing career with a series of closet dramas between 1904 and 1912 (noted in Part Two of this study), after which she turned to poetry with *Path Flowers and Other Poems* (1914) and *Cycle's Rim* (1916), the latter a sonnet sequence on the death of her husband at sea that won for her the prize for poetry given by the Southern Society of New York.

It was the death of her husband that led indirectly to the reputation Dargan was to win later as Fielding Burke, for almost at once she returned to the highland farm in the mountains of North Carolina that she and her husband had bought when they left New York in 1906. Her volume of verse, *Lute and Furrow* (1922), and her first volume of prose, *Highland Annals* (1925), a collection of short stories and sketches, signaled the change that was coming about as her portrayal of rural Arcadian scenes gave way to an increased interest in the soil and revealed her compassion and concern for those who till it. Reclaiming the water-washed ridges and slopes of the Southern Highland was different from the lowlands farming she had known as a child in western Kentucky, but the problems she faced brought a challenge similar to that which had confronted her ancestors in the Kentucky wilderness. Writing was not a primary concern with her at this time, but she did write occasional poems and stories about the mountain people around her. These she published in *Highland Annals* (1925) and *From My Highest Hill* (1942). She depicted men and women not as the typical local colorist might but realistically, as she had observed them.

Dargan's humanitarian sympathies and her sociological concerns developed rapidly in the 1920s and somewhat unexpectedly emerged in two purposeful novels that gave her an important place among the proletarian novelists of the 1930s. The first of these was *Call Home the Heart* (1932), the second *A Stone Came Rolling* (1935). The central character in both novels is Ishma Waycaster, a girl born and reared in the North Carolina mountains who, as a child, carries much of the burden in a large, improvident family. She marries Britt Hensley, but life with Britt comes to little more than bearing children and doing endless work. But Dargan does not merely portray the destitute condition of the North Carolina farmers and mountain people during the depression, she takes them into the cities and towns as they hunt for jobs, including Ishma, who goes away with a lover to a mill town called Winbury (Gastonia) and becomes involved in a strike of mill-workers. In the end, the mountains Ishma left behind constitute such a call to her heart that she goes back home to her husband and their hillside farm. In *A Stone Came Rolling* Ishma and Britt, driven by their ideals, set out to make the world a better place to live in and are led to participate in a "revolution" in Dunmow, another mill town, Ishma as a recruiter and organizer. In both novels the focus is on working conditions in the mills, the exploitation of workers, and the low salaries and credit buying that cause workers to fall increasingly into the hands of the mill-owners. The issues presented lead to the conclusion that there is no solution for the problems of the workers except for the workers to take over the mill system. By the end of the second novel the mountaineers have been transformed into workers and the case made that only a group effort—a movement—can improve the lot of those who work.

The critical response to Dargan's novels was generally very favorable, both for their content and their artistry, whereas the 1930s proletarian novels in general were lacking in literary merit. A reviewer in the *New Republic* (Jan. 29, 1936) said that in *A Stone Came Rolling* "Fielding Burke carried over into her fiction the merits of Olive Dargan's poetry, and so made a contribution to the proletarian novel" and the *Saturday Review of Literature* (Feb. 20, 1932) said that *Call Home the Heart* "is never just a preachment" and is "perhaps the best novel yet written of industrial conflict." By no means were Olive Dargan's novels in the same class as John Steinbeck's *The Grapes of Wrath* in their universal appeal, but they do rise above the narrowly topical workers' problems and the proletarian formulas. Her portrayal of the mountaineer reaches toward the timeless, for she was a person of sympathetic understanding and fair-mindness and had a literary talent well above most of her contemporaries.

Leane Zugsmith

Leane Zugsmith (1903–69) also made a significant contribution to the proletarian novel during the Great Depression. She was born in Louisville, attended high school there and in Atlantic City, spent a year each at Goucher College, the University of Pennsylvania, and Columbia University, and by 1924 was permanently located in New York City. Here she served in editorial capacities with such pulp magazines as *Western Story Magazine* and later did copy-editing for both Putnam and the Liveright publishing firms. In 1929 she published *All Victories Are Alike*, a story about a newspaper columnist's loss of his ideals, and in 1931 *Goodbye and Tomorrow*, which deals with a romantic spinster who finds her happiness in patronizing artists. Like *Never Enough* (1932) these novels attracted little attention. Zugsmith was, however, developing her techniques as a writer of fiction and working toward a subject matter of consequence; in her own words, "Great works do not come from writers who regard themselves only as entertainers."

With *The Reckoning* (1934) Zugsmith undertook the kind of writing that was to bring her a substantial reputation and give her a secure place among the better proletarian novelists. "*The Reckoning*," says the reviewer in *Books* (April 8, 1934), "is one of those experiences unusual in a reviewer's year, a really good book"; and in the view of the *New Republic* (May 23, 1934) it was ". . . very nearly a first-rate novel." This story of a New York boy from the slums who gets into trouble and lands first on Welfare Island and then in a reformatory carries out Zugsmith's professional intention of writing novels with social significance.

In *A Time to Remember* (1936) Zugsmith wrote with more maturity and more effectiveness. "I dislike using the name 'proletarian novels' for the books I have in mind," she says; "I don't know what such literature should be called, but it should be composed of works that add to our knowledge of human beings and the society they live in." But, she continues, "I do not believe that such books should be disguised economic treatises or polemics." The subject matter of *A Time to Remember*, however, did nothing to remove the tag of "proletarian" from Zugsmith's writings, for it is a story of a strike of white-collar workers against management in a great New York department store. The novel did, however, help increase Zugsmith's reputation as a writer, for her writing was becoming more incisive, her handling of the vernacular of real men and women more sure, and the force and flow of her narrative more telling. At the same time, she was becoming more even-handed in her portrayal of labor and management. No one has called *A Time to Remember* a great novel, but in the judgment of *The Nation* (Aug. 12, 1936), it was "not only the best novel that Miss Zugsmith has written, but one of the best social-minded novels anybody has written."

The Sunshine Soldier (1938), the last of Zugsmith's novels of social concern, takes five political liberals—a minister, a social worker, a playgirl, a playwright, and a university professor—to a southern milltown to observe and report on alleged violations of civil liberties, including free speech, the right of assembly, and the rights of blacks. The "committee of five" is met by hostile opposition, beaten up, and bodily thrown out of the state. Two of the five meet the challenge by electing to go back and carry out their mission, but three decide they have had enough and return home. Hence the appropriateness of the title from the ringing statement of Thomas Paine about patriots and sunshine soldiers. The characterizations, making use of stream-of-consciousness techniques, are generally excellent; the subject matter of importance.

Leane Zugsmith published other volumes, but they were of less importance to her reputation. One can only agree with her when she writes, "I think that writing should, first of all, be about human beings," but her downfall is suggested in the continuation of her statement: "However, it seems to me to be increasingly difficult to write illuminatingly about human beings without regarding their social circumstances." In short, as in proletarian writing generally, the political, economic, sociological content was too great and too specific and became dated even as the reform objectives it called for were being achieved.

Edith Summers Kelley

Edith Summers Kelley (1884–1956) was born in Ontario, Canada, and after graduating from the University of Toronto went to New York, where she found work on the Funk and Wagnalls *Standard Dic-*

tionary. In 1906 she became the secretary of Upton Sinclair and a part of the staff at Helicon Hall, Sinclair's Socialist commune in Englewood, New Jersey, and thus came under the Socialist influence being felt in American writing generally. While at Helicon Hall she became engaged to Sinclair Lewis, but instead of marrying Lewis she married Allan Undergraff, another resident of Helicon Hall. The couple had two children, but afterwards they separated. Thereupon Edith Summers moved to Greenwich Village, taught in the Hell's Kitchen district of Manhattan, did some writing, met Frederick Kelley, an artist and son of an Oklahoma farmer, became his common-law wife, and adopted his name. Soon thereafter the wanderings of the Kelleys in search of financial security began. First—in 1912–14—came a three-year stay in Scott County, Kentucky, where they grew tobacco as tenant-farmers. From this experience *Weeds* emerged. After Kentucky came Imperial Valley, California, first on an alfafa farm and then on a chicken farm. In 1923 *Weeds* was published and received generally favorable reviews, some of them enthusiastic. Nevertheless the volume was a commercial failure, and in 1926 Kelley wrote to Upton Sinclair, "I still owe the publisher a hundred and thirty dollars of the five hundred that they advanced me before publication." In 1925 she started another novel, but it had not been published when Kelley died in 1956, still virtually unknown. Finally it was published in 1974 as *The Devil's Hand*, six years after Matthew J. Bruccoli "discovered" *Weeds* in a bookshop, greatly admired it, and edited it for the Southern Illinois University Press in 1972.

Weeds was not the first novel about growing tobacco, but it was the first to dwell upon the drudgery and the destructiveness to the human spirit involved in being the share-cropper who grew it. It is primarily the story of Judith Pippinger, an above-average girl who was born to the life of a tenant-farmer. Preferring work in the fields to domestic duties, Judy rebels against the usual place of a woman in the kitchen and her role as a wife and mother. Nevertheless she marries Jerry Blackford, begins to have children, and is gradually beaten down and trapped by the monotony and unimaginativeness of the life she lives as well as by the never-ending drudgery work and child-bearing. The overall effect of the story is one of sadness and tragedy—not in the sense that something tragic happens and that life does not go beyond that point but rather because it does go on. It is in her more than in anyone else that the dreary life of the tenant-farmer is reflected, for we see her first as an adolescent girl and daughter of a tenant-farmer, then as a young and hopeful wife of a young share-cropper, and finally as a mature, and even aging, mother for whom nothing remains but relentless drudgery and resignation. In the words of the author,

> She would go on for her allotted time bearing and nursing babies and rearing them as best she could. And when her time of childbearing was over, she would go back to the field, like other women, and set tobacco and worm and top tobacco, shuck corn, and plant potatoes.

The novel is not, however, a naturalistic tale of uneducated, deprived people who have ceased to struggle. The author so handles Judith and her story that her disappointment in life is the disappointment of all women and her fate not merely pathetic but tragic. Thus though the novel is a novel of protest, it is not a reform novel that singles out the dreariness of share-cropping and offers specific cures for specific ills. Kelley was too good an artist to date or limit her writings in such a way.

Perhaps there is no better summary judgment of *Weeds* than that in the *Lexington Herald*, May 18, 1924: "It is not a pleasant book, no Pollyanna thing, but made up of the stuff of life as lived by the tobacco tenant in the Blue Grass of Kentucky. The setting is Scott County, twenty miles from Georgetown, the county seat, and the people of its pages are tenants that we have known all our lives, with this exception: Many of us, doubtless, have looked on the outside of these people; *Weeds* is the story of their insides. Their sorrows, their joys, their deaths, their births, their honesty, their dishonesty, their acceptance of life as they find it, their rebellion against life as they find it, their heartaches, their slips into profanity (there's real cussing in this book), their domestic infidelities, with not a thing explained and with nothing apologized for, with minor and major characters sinning with reckless abandon and seeking forgiveness with all their hearts. Yes, *Weeds* is the real thing. It is life."

Willie Snow Ethridge

To readers familiar with the effervescent, witty "informal-essay-autobiographical" narratives of Willie Snow Ethridge, it may come as a surprise that her second volume, *Mingled Yarn* (1938), was a novel dealing with working and living conditions in a Georgia textile town. Ethridge (1900–82) was born in Savannah, Georgia, moved to Macon when she was a child, met her husband-to-be, Mark Ethridge, when she was in high school, gained journalistic experience with the *Macon Telegraph* while she was in college, and married Ethridge in

1920. Ethridge, later to become an eminent newspaperman, came to Louisville with his wife and three children in 1936 by way of the *Richmond Dispatch* and the *Washington Post* in order to become the publisher of the *Courier-Journal.* The following year Mrs. Ethridge published her first volume, *As I Live and Breathe*, which tells of her life as the wife of a newspaperman. The next year came *Mingled Yarn*, in which the author traces the history of a southern industrial town during the 1920s.

Ethridge is no proletarian novelist crusading for the deliverance of oppressed textile laborers, but in writing the story of a wealthy mill-owner's daughter who marries a young liberal newspaperman, she does take the reader through a series of conflicts over labor questions. The ferment surrounding the organizing of workers receives attention, as does the turbulence of Ku Klux Klan activities; and almost as noteworthy in these early days of the labor movement in the South is the break with complacency when the editor of the leading newspaper and the Methodist minister in the fictional town of Hilton speak out —openly—on the side of labor. The novel makes no pretence of being a probing search into the nature of the underlying problems that face management and workers or the relationship between capitalism and labor, but it is about real people, and the materials are dealt with in honest fashion.

CHAPTER 20

Drama and Theater

Kentucky's contribution to theater and drama before 1930 was fairly considerable in quantity and if not high in quality at least respectable and representative of its time. Between 1930 and 1980 the contributions were fewer but their quality excellent: two playwrights who each won the Pulitzer Prize in drama, a drama critic of national eminence, and a theater that has taken its place alongside the best.

American drama began to rid itself of its shackles around 1915 and by the latter 1920s was in the early stages of the strongest period it had ever known. The revolution took place in a variety of interlocking ways. First of all, the power of the Theatrical Syndicate was broken, and the stranglehold of commercial profitability relaxed as a prerequisite to the production of a play of merit. The forces that led to the breaking of this hold also paved the way for the drama that flourished during the 1930s. First among these in time—and seminal in importance—was George Pierce Baker's 47 Workshop at Harvard. When Baker in 1904 began offering a course in playwriting (English 47), he was breaking new ground, for heretofore courses in drama had pretty well been limited to its history. No doubt the most important thing about the course, however, was Baker himself and the quality of the dozen or so students he accepted each year. The most distinguished alumnus of English 47 was Eugene O'Neill, but there were also Thomas Wolfe, S.N. Behrman, Sidney Howard, George Abbott, Philip Barry, John Dos Passos, and others, including Kentuckian Cleves Kinkead, whose *Common Clay* was written in the workshop. Designers such as Robert Edmond Jones and Lee Simonson, directors such as Winthrop Ames and Elia Kazan, and critics such as John Mason Brown also were graduates.

Of great importance also in the development and growth of theater and drama nationally was the "little theater" movement. In 1915 two of the most significant little theaters were founded: the Provincetown Players and the Washington Square Players. Provincetown fostered the talent of Eugene O'Neill; Washington Square achieved lasting influence through its development into the Theatre Guild in 1918. The Guild was to be the most influential theatrical organization the country has ever known. In 1919 it built its own theater; by 1925 it was strong enough to support a permanent company of actors; and by the end of the 1920s it had road companies and supported two hundred actors. By the mid-1920s theater audiences had developed a taste for the "new" theater and had accepted an honest realism that had so long been resisted. Within a ten-year span American theater had changed its character and in spite of the Great Depression during the 1930s was to achieve excellence for a decade and more. By the 1940s the Guild had begun to change too, and by the mid-1950s had become commercial and, in order to meet the mounting costs of production, sought plays that seemed likely to be "hits." Nevertheless, the Guild had already served its real mission; had done so by 1930, in fact, for by that time all respectable producers had adopted the standards that the Guild had set up. By the end of World War II the great era was pretty much at an end. The dramatists and the actors who had made opening nights times of great excitement during the 1930s—O'Neill, Maxwell Anderson, Robert E. Sherwood, Sidney Howard, Philip Barry—the Lunts, Helen Westley, Katharine Cornell, Helen Hayes—were now gone or mainly past their prime. New names were coming to the fore, among them Tennessee Williams, William Inge, and Arthur Miller, and a dynamic natively American form of entertainment—the American musical—emerged and quickly grew to maturity. Around a not very distant corner was a new phenomenon that would breathe new life into theaters and offer new opportunities for playwrights. This was the emergence and rapid growth of regional theaters. Today, perhaps no one of them is more dynamic than Actors Theatre of Louisville (ATL).

The Humana Festival of New American Plays, sponsored annually by the Actors Theatre, has been called by *Newsweek* "the most important event in the American theatre each year" and by the London *Times* "a place to give the lie to the ugly American myth" of philistinism and lack of culture. Here each year between late February and April 1 eight plays are chosen for production from among three to four thousand scripts that are submitted in competition. To this festival come playwrights, actors, directors, producers, critics, agents, and playgoers from all over America and from dozens of countries throughout the world. Many of the winning plays go on to notable production schedules in New York and elsewhere and to win distinguished prizes and honors, among them the Pulitzer Prize in drama: D.L. Coburn's *The Gin Game* (1978), Beth Henley's *Crimes of the Heart* (1981), and Marsha Norman's *Night Mother* (1983).

The Actors Theatre began in 1964 when two struggling professional companies merged. The new organization slowly gained support, but by 1969 the board of directors decided that new management was needed and accordingly employed Jon Jory, cofounder of the Long Wharf Theatre in New Haven, Connecticut. Under Jory's leadership ATL moved to new quarters composed of two structures: the old Bank of Louisville, designed and built in 1837 by Gideon Shryock, the father of Greek Revival architecture in Kentucky, and adjacent to it an 1860s red brick warehouse building to house administrative offices and production areas. Within six months ATL had raised $1.2 million locally and secured $360,000 through a Ford Foundation challenge grant. When renovation of the two structures was completed, ATL had the 637-seat Pamela Brown Auditorium, the 161-seat, three-quarter arena Victor Jory Theatre, and, in the rotunda of the bank building, one of the most impressive lobbies in the nation.

While this was happening, attendance was increasing, a children's theatre series was added, and a plan for conducting tours was adopted. By 1980 ATL had an operating budget of $1.7 million, of which 70 percent was earned income, and the subscription list for the seven-play season in the Pamela Brown Auditorium was 18,700. By this time, Jory had a dozen actors in residence working under his supervision and directorship, plus others brought in from time to time for particular roles.

The ATL New Play Program was initiated in 1975–76 and included four distinct segments: a playwriting contest which came to elicit up to four thousand scripts, a festival at which winning plays were produced, workshops for playwrights, and a commissioning program for new plays. By 1980 the winning play received a prize of five thousand dollars. During the first festival in 1977 only four plays were premiered, but by 1980 the number had increased to eight, of which ninety-four performances were given before an audience of almost thirty thousand. There have also been variations in the programs offered at the festival. In 1979–80, for example, one pattern was a program of short plays all related to a single theme. Another device, conceived for the benefit of people who could not attend the whole festival, was to reserve one weekend for seven premiered productions to be staged over a three-day period.

Among the plays featured at the Festival of Plays between 1977 and 1980 have been Frederick Bailey's *The Bridgehead*, Marsha Norman's *Getting Out*, Beth Henley's *Crimes of the Heart*, Olwen Wymark's *Find Me*, John Pielmeier's *Agnes of God*, and Adele Edling Shank's *Sunset! Sunrise!* The ATL won the Margo Jones Award in 1978 for its production of new plays and its encouragement of new playwrights; the James N. Vaughan Memorial Award in 1979 for exceptional achievement and contributions to the American theater; and the Tony Award in 1980 for regional theaters. In 1984 ATL completed its twentieth year, in which it won a three-year grant from the National Endowment for the Arts, the only theater to do so. Since the grant is to be matched by three nonfederal dollars for every federal dollar, this means that ATL can expect to see the grant reach a total of $1.35 million over the three years. According to producing director Jon Jory the grant "will allow Actors theatre to grow as both a regional company and a nationally prominent organization. It will give us the opportunity to take on projects that will assist our long-range artistic stability and provide us with a firm base to support future growth."

Jory himself has won honors, none more satisfying perhaps than the Distinguished Service to the Theatre citation he received in 1983 from the American Theatre Association in convention at Minneapolis. Earlier recipients of this citation include Helen Hayes, Eva Le Gallienné, John Housman, Walter Kerr, Brooks Atkinson, Thornton Wilder, and Tyrone Guthrie.

John Mason Brown

John Mason Brown (1900–69), as his biographer George Stevens puts it in *Speak for Yourself, John* (1974), "was called to the theatre" at the age of eight in his native Louisville when he saw Robert Mantell in *King Lear* at the Macauley Theatre. By way of Harvard, George Pierce Baker's 47 Workshop, and the Hasty Pudding Club, he never wavered in his determination to spend his life in the theater. Drawn more to criticism than to acting or directing, he took his first job as a dramatic critic with the *Theatre Arts Monthly Magazine* (1926–28).

In 1929 he became the drama critic for the *New York Evening Post* and remained there until he took a similar position with the *New York World-Telegram*, 1941–42. Then followed a stint in the navy during World War II, after which he became drama critic and associate editor of the *Saturday Review of Literature*, a position in which he remained until 1955, when he took a leave of absence in order to devote himself more exclusively to the study of Robert E. Sherwood. Brown's theater and drama criticism, therefore, grew out of the journalistic career he practiced in his daily play reviews, the weekly columns he wrote, and the volumes he composed as separate entities.

If one must select from among Brown's twelve volumes on theater and drama, perhaps the place to start is with *Dramatis Personae: A Retrospective Show* (1963), published a decade after he gave up his reviewing and writing of a weekly column in order to work on his study of Sherwood. *Dramatis Personnae* is a 563-page volume in which Brown reprinted his *Modern Theatre in Revolt* (1930) and selected essays, reviews, and criticisms from his writings for the *Theatre Arts Monthly*, the *Evening Post*, the *World-Telegram*, and the *Saturday Review*. "This is one of the great theater books of this century," says the *Library Journal* (June 1, 1963). *Modern Theatre in Revolt* pulls together the history of the theater during the preceding hundred years and shows how each new generation has torn down the work of its predecessor and built anew on top of the old, and how it in turn was replaced by still another generation. It ends with a discussion of the new theater of revolt in Russia. The shorter selections in the volume are sixty in number and were chosen from ten earlier volumes, plus some previously uncollected articles. These selections, representative of his best work, display Brown's qualities as a critic and reveal why those who reviewed his writings spoke of him with enthusiasm and generally concurred in saying that he was the best of his kind.

Brown came to maturity on the American theatrical scene at a high point in its history. During the years of the Great Depression occurred the Theater of Revolt, of which Elmer Rice's *We the People* and Clifford Odets's *Awake and Sing* and *Golden Boy* are examples; but more important were Eugene O'Neill's *Mourning Becomes Electra* and *Ah, Wilderness*, T.S. Eliot's *Murder in the Cathedral*, Thornton Wilder's *Our Town*, Philip Barry's *Philadelphia Story*, Robert Sherwood's *Reunion in Vienna* and *Abe Lincoln in Illinois*. As for revivals, Maurice Evans appeared in *Richard II*, Katharine Cornell in *Romeo and Juliet*, John Gielgud in *Hamlet*, the Lunts in *The Taming of the*

Shrew, Blanche Yurka in *Electra*, Eva Le Gallienne in *Hedda Gabler*, and Nazimova in *The Cherry Orchard*. And among those who wrote about the golden years of Broadway there were Brooks Atkinson, George Jean Nathan, Alexander Wollcott—and John Mason Brown.

No one ever claimed for Brown the quality of being a great seminal theoretical critic. His role was to make judgments of playwrights, plays, productions, and actors, daily and weekly, while faced with the usual deadlines of New York newspaper drama critics. In writing such reviews there is no time for lengthy contemplation and the maturing of judgments. Not only is there the necessity to be quick, there is the need to be right and to be readable, free of the charge of dullness. On all scores Brown came off well. Time after time at the end of the theater season *Variety* found that Brown surpassed his fellow critics in identifying the plays that would succeed and those that would fail. As for readability, as one critic put it, Brown knew how "to split the difference between erudition and entertainment" and to do so without sacrificing standards in the process; how with a reading audience that ranged from highbrow to lowbrow to appeal to "brows of every type of conformation." With his flair for phrases, Brown's judgments sometimes are framed in such a way as to lay him open to the charge of smartness; even so, such phrases and the images they produce make their point in memorable fashion. Thus he says that Sherwood in *Abe Lincoln in Illinois* does not prepare the audience for Lincoln's greatness; instead, greatness "overtakes" Lincoln during intermission. Of T.S. Eliot and his awesome reputation he wrote of *Murder in the Cathedral*: "Slow in beginning as it was, it rose to moments of high beauty, became dramatic almost in spite of itself, and brought poetry back to a prosaic stage." As for Ethel Merman, "It is hard to understand how anyone who had not heard [her sing] could have invented the calliope." But if such statements are judged to be a bit "flip", innumerable others make soberer points with equally telling language. Thus he said of Arthur Miller's *Death of a Salesman*, "Mr. Miller's play is a tragedy modern and personal, not classic and heroic. Its central figure is a little man sentenced to discover his smallness rather than a big man undone by his greatness." In comparable fashion he catches the essence of Thornton Wilder's *Our Town*: "It is not so much of the streets of a New England town he writes as of the clean white spire that rises above them." And he crystallizes the significance of a lesser play of John Patrick when he declares, "*The Hasty Heart* is not only a play about a dying soldier, but it is a study . . . of the inadequacy of words in wartime farewells, or in any other of the serious crises of that quieter warfare we call peace."

Brown was a humanist in the broadest sense. His reviews of plays encompass much more than just a stage production—they attach themselves to life and to the world and bring to criticism a cultural breadth and human warmth that is too generally missing in the work of others. In addition, he had a single-minded dedication to the theater that never wavered from the time he was eight years old. His omnivorous reading habits gave him wide knowledge not only of the theater but of literature in the large. At the same time, he was a man of taste who instinctively had the right feelings about what he read or saw as well as the verbal talent to explain why he liked what he did.

Among Brown's collections are *Upstage* (1930), *The Art of Playwriting* (1936), *Two on the Aisle* (1938), *Broadway in Review* (1940), and *Seeing Things* (1946). But it is perhaps *Letters from Greenroom Ghosts* (1934) that should take precedence over any one of these if one wishes to read more of Brown's criticism than *Dramatis Personnae*. This work contains five letters from some great actor or playwright or theater person of the past to some person of the theater now living: Mrs. Siddons to Katharine Cornell on the acting of tragedy, Peg Woffington to Ina Claire on comedy, Inigo Jones to Robert Edmond Jones on stage design, Richard Brinsley Sheridan to Noel Coward on the dangers of facility in writing, and Christopher Marlowe to Eugene O'Neill about play-writing. Such an approach, of course, calls into play both the breadth and the depth of Brown's knowledge of the history of drama and of the stage. The volume, said John Corbin in the *Saturday Review of Literature* (Dec. 15, 1934), "is not without ineptitudes, but at its best it stands on the summit of dramatic criticism."

It has been well said that John Mason Brown was an ambassador of good will for the theater. He preferred to appreciate a play than to depreciate it and to speak well of a production than ill of it. At the same time he was honest and could be devastating when he thought this was called for; but always he was even-tempered and fair-minded, and he had the human touch. Perhaps there is no better way to end this discussion of Brown than to quote from Alistair Cooke's tribute to him in the *Manchester Guardian*. Cooke, who had watched Parkinson's disease sap away Brown's stamina and strength, concludes by saying, "It was, for too many years, a continual sadness to think of the slow decay of the blythe and irrepressible gentleman from Kentucky, who managed for so many years, and by some subtle chemistry of character, to applaud the brave, to slap down fools without malice, to combine gaiety with goodness, to blast pretension, and leave no enemies."

John Patrick

John Patrick, born John Patrick Goggan in Louisville in 1906, is known internationally as the author of *The Hasty Heart* and the Pulitzer Prize–winning *Teahouse of the August Moon*, but his success in writing screen adaptations has been almost as great. Among these adaptations have been *The President's Lady* (1953), *Three Coins in a Fountain* (1954), *Love Is a Many-Splendored Thing* (1955), *High Society* (1956), *The Philadelphia Story* (1956), *Les Girls* (1957), *Some Came Running* (1959), and *The World of Susie Wong* (1960). By 1980 Patrick had written more than thirty plays, was coauthor of nineteen film scripts, and had adapted many works for motion pictures. The quality of his writings as literature does not match the reputation he has gained as an entertainer, but in his better plays his craftsmanship and his flair for drama with a strong dash of theatricality have won him a wide audience.

Abandoned early by his parents, Patrick grew up in foster homes and boarding schools, became a hobo in his teens, and at nineteen was a radio announcer in San Francisco. Here he legally dropped his last name, began writing scripts for NBC radio by the early 1930s, and by 1940 was doing adaptations for NBC that were performed by Helen Hayes. During World War II he served first as an ambulance driver for the American Field Service and later with Montgomery's Eighth Army in Egypt, with the British Ninth Army in Syria, and under Lord Mountbatten with the South-East Asia Command.

After the war Patrick quickly won a name for himself with *The Hasty Heart* (1945), but as early as 1935 he had written the unsuccessful *Hell Freezes Over* and in 1942 *Willow and I*, a play with Gregory Peck in one role that received some favorable critical attention, although its success was short-lived. *The Hasty Heart* pleased critics and attracted large audiences, running 205 performances in the Hudson Theatre in New York. Based in part on patients Patrick had known when he was being treated for malaria in a Burma hospital, the play has seven principal characters: five soldiers who are recovering from injuries, a nurse, and a Scottish soldier who has not been told that his one remaining kidney will fail in a matter of weeks and that he will die. Everyone knows this but him. The other soldiers take it upon themselves to add cheer to "Lachie's" days by offering friendship, but the Scot is an intensely private, distrustful, uncommunicative loner who has always been fearful of a heart too hastily given. His resistance to all overtures frustrates and angers those who would be friends and thus leads to their giving him the rough and silent treatment. These tactics achieve their purpose, and he comes to understand that it is simply friendship that they offer and that nothing is expected in return except friendship. Then he learns of his impending death and is angered and resentful as he concludes that they offer only pity. The play could end at this point—tragically—but Patrick likes to affirm the goodness of human nature and thus has Lachlen reverse himself again and accept the proffered friendship—and so is won out of himself.

Despite the toughness and sincerity of the play, Patrick came dangerously close to sentimentality. No reviewer, however, found him maudlin. John Mason Brown best explains why. In a review entitled "When Words Fail" (*Saturday Review of Literature*, March 3, 1945), Brown sets forth his view that despite its shortcomings as literature, Patrick's irresistible play is more than just an exercise in sentimentality. The answer he finds in Patrick's concern with "those emotions which especially among men in wartime, resist statement." It is, he says, precisely at the moment when a separation is at hand which threatens to be final, "when the deepest emotions demand utterance . . . that men and women are apt to be most mute" and likeliest to fall back upon threadbare words and phrases or "prattle on about everything except what they wish most to say." Thus, he says, *The Hasty Heart*, though it is "merciless in its tugs at our sympathies," deals "with emotions as human as they are poignantly male" and comes to grips with truth.

Patrick's next play was *The Story of Mary Surratt* (1947), a somber play based on the trial and hanging by a military court of a woman who was alleged to have played a hand in Lincoln's assassination. The immediate response to it was favorable, but it was a box office failure. It did, however, win recognition by being included in the Burns Mantle *Best Plays of 1946–1947*. Patrick now turned to comedy with *The Curious Savage* (1950). The play met with quite a bit of negative criticism largely because of its subject matter, but since its initial short run it has become a favorite with community theatres. At one time, in fact, it was surpassed only by *Life with Father* and *Arsenic and Old Lace* in the frequency of its revival. It is the story of an extremely wealthy lady whose children get her committed to an insane asylum in their effort to gain control of her money. The grim humor arises from the contrast between the insane greed of the children and the gentle humanity of the inmates of the asylum.

The Teahouse of the August Moon (1953), adapted from Vern Sneider's novel, brought international fame to Patrick and won him the Pulitzer Prize in drama for 1953, as well as numerous other awards, including the New York Drama Critics Prize. Produced in at least twelve countries in Europe and in Israel, South Africa, Japan, Mexico, and South America, the play has literally been seen around the world. The plot is simple. An American occupation force is sent to the remote village of Tobiki, in Okinawa, to teach democracy, industry, and agriculture to the conquered natives. Amiable, bumbling Captain Fisby, who is under the command of blustering, pompous Colonel Purdy, is charged with bringing efficiency to the little community and carrying out the orders handed down from Washington. Everyone, however, has overlooked the cultural habits and philosophy of the islanders and their ability to outwit their conquerors. Thus Fisby comes to use the lumber intended for a schoolhouse shaped like a pentagon to build instead a teahouse for the Grade A geisha girl who has been sent to him, and the natives are diverted from making cricket cages, strawhats, and lacquer bowls to distilling a high-powered brandy from sweet potatoes to sell to army and navy officers' clubs. From beginning to end the play is delightful, hilarious entertainment, but it is also more, for it exudes a warm human philosophy, is touching at times as well as uproarious, and pokes fun at the Pentagon, Manuals of Occupation, and political and military ineptitude generally. In showing to audiences around the world that Americans could poke fun at themselves, the play, as John Mason Brown put it, was the best goodwill ambassador the United States could have devised.

Despite the spectacular success of *Teahouse*, however, Patrick has not again scored so well with either the critics or the public. After two new near-failures, he wrote the first of a series of five plays about Opal Kronkie, who is a crotchety but likeable junk collector. The first of these, *Everybody Loves Opal* (1961), met with limited success in New York, but both it and its sequels had considerable success in summer theaters and have attracted such talented actresses as Jean Stapleton, Martha Raye, and Imogene Coca. Patrick turned again to Broadway in the late 1960s, but *Love Is a Time of Day* (1969) closed after eight performances, and *Lovely Ladies, Kind Gentlemen* (1970), a musical version of *The Teahouse of the August Moon*, ran for only sixteen. It is likely that the war in Vietnam had something to do with the lack of success of the latter, but apparently, too, Patrick was no longer in step with entertainment tastes on Broadway. Since that time he has continued with reasonable success to write plays for community theaters.

Marsha Norman

An author who gives promise of becoming Kentucky's foremost playwright is Marsha Norman (1947–), whose first play, *Getting Out* (1977), was chosen by the American Theatre Critics Association to be the best play produced in a regional theater during 1977–78, and whose *'night Mother* won the Pulitzer Prize in drama for 1983. Born in Louisville in 1947, Norman attended the public schools there, got her A.B. from Agnes Scott College in 1969 and her M.A.T. from the University of Louisville in 1971. Since that time, she has written for the *Louisville Times*, taught gifted children, and worked with disturbed children at the Kentucky Central State Hospital. She now lives in New York City.

Few critics have denied the strength and effectiveness of Norman's plays, but her bleak subject matter and sometimes daring techniques have antagonized some viewers even as they have admired what she has written. Such reservations—or even controversy—do not disturb Norman, however, for she has strong feelings about what for her is worth writing about. "I always write about the same thing," she told *Contemporary Authors*: "people who have the nerve to go on. The people I care about are those folks you wouldn't even notice in life—two women in a laundromat late at night as you drive by, a thin woman in an ugly scarf standing over the luncheon meat at the grocery, a tiny gray lady buying a big sack of chocolate-covered raisins and a carton of Kools." To Linda Stahl (*Courier-Journal Magazine*, May 20, 1984) she explained, "My plays are always conversations I would like to hear, conversations people have or would like to have, but don't, for fear of what would happen if they did." As Stahl observes, "Marsha Norman writes plays that jolt and jab, that unearth buried feelings, that leave people discussing the previously undiscussed."

Getting Out, Norman's first play, reached the Theatre De Lys on Broadway in May 1979 by way of Actors Theatre in Louisville, the Mark Taper Forum in Los Angeles, and the Phoenix Theatre, off-Broadway. In the play a woman who has spent eight years in prison for robbery and homicide makes her way back into the workaday world. The scene is her shabby Louisville apartment to which she has just come after being released from prison; the staging technique is having her present self—Arlene—and her former self—Arlie—on stage at the same time. Thus two actresses more or less simultaneously reveal past and present in parallel fashion: the Arlene who is trying to rehabilitate herself and the Arlie who went from bad to worse and ended up in prison. This is achieved through direct communication between the two, through conversation with a third person, and through flashbacks and fade-outs and other skillfully handled devices. Secondary characters include the lecherous prison guard who resigned his job and brought Arlene to her apartment, hoping to move into it with her; the junkie who was once her lover and pimp, ready to take up where he had left off; her mother, a sloppy, vicious cab-driver who informs her daughter that she will not be socially acceptable in her home; and a neighbor upstairs who has also served time in prison. It is a bleak and forbidding world into which Arlene is let loose and in which she must fight her way to respectability or sink again. Whether she makes it remains conjecture, for the play is almost documentary in the objective way the action is presented.

The play was almost universally praised. Douglass Watt (*Daily News*, May 16, 1979) objects to the dual-character staging device and Walter Kerr (*New York Times*, June 9, 1979) thinks "the barrage of ills" that assail Arlene as she "takes her first step toward freedom" is too overwhelming to be convincing. More general, however, is the praise that singles the play out for its honesty, its emotional impact, the way it turns the searchlight on a prison experience, its "untearful" compassion and humanity, and the promise it offers as a first play.

Third and Oak: The Laundromat and *The Pool Hall*, two one-act plays, came in 1978 and were produced at the Actors Theatre of Louisville, the former being taped for National Public Radio. *Circus Valentine* was next in 1979 and *The Holdup* in 1980, both being produced at the Actors Theatre, and *In Trouble at Fifteen* was televised on the program "Skag," also in 1980. In the meantime in 1978–79 Norman held a National Endowment for the Arts playwright-in-residence grant at the Actors Theatre of Louisville and in 1979–80 a similar grant from the Rockefeller Foundation at the Mark Taper Forum in Los Angeles. Other work followed, and then came *'night Mother*.

First produced at Harvard's American Repertory Theatre in Cambridge in December 1982, *'night Mother* opened at the John Golden Theatre on Broadway the following March, was runner-up for the Susan Smith Blackburn prize as the best play by a British or American woman, and before the end of the year won the Pulitzer Prize in Drama. From the first, however, critics have differed sharply on its merits. To Frank Rich in the *New York Times*, *'night Mother* "is a profound achievement," and to Robert Brustein in the *New Republic* Marsha Norman "is the genuine article—an American writer with the courage to look into the black holes from which we normally turn our faces." On the other hand, Stanley Kauffmann, writing in the *Saturday Review*, sees the play as "a device, a stunt, and not an authentic drama"; and to Richard Gilman in *The Nation*, "Yes, the play's *honest*, yes it's sincere; but have we reached the point where we find such minimal virtues something to rave about?"

'Night Mother is a ninety-minute play without an intermission where two women who live together—Jessie, a woman in her thirties and divorced, and Thelma, her mother and a widow—are going about their routine Saturday evening activities. As the daughter is about to give her mother a manicure, she casually and calmly declares, "I'm going to kill myself, Mama." Jessie, we soon learn, is in earnest and is forewarning her mother so as to reduce the shock to her and so that they can tidy up the house and draw up lists of things that will have to be done and people who will have to be called after the suicide. But as the evening progresses there is much else that we learn about what appears to be the "meaning" of the play. First of all, it is neither for nor against suicide, but is, as Frank Rich expresses it, "about contemporary life and what gives it—or fails to give it—values." As the women talk, the audience (or reader) realizes that despite the life-long relationship the two women have had they have only a superficial knowledge of each other—or any other member of their family or of their friends; that they have never expressed their real feelings to each other or revealed the truth about themselves; that they have never asked questions that might have given insights into and understandings of themselves or others. In negation of Thelma's protest that "people don't really kill themselves unless they're retarded or deranged," the audience learns that Jessie's decision grows out of a sense of emptiness and the meaninglessness of her life. She is not morose about life or about specific things in her life that went wrong; she is at peace with her decision, for she is convinced that nothing will change. The real problem is "nobody out there, but my own self." That self—her interior life—is something that "got lost." She has spent years waiting for herself to arrive, but "I never got here," and now there's no use waiting any longer; years hence she will only be in "the same place."

Norman has written a taut, dramatic, uncompromising play that focuses narrowly on a troubling subject and has done so without flinching or obtruding the author's views as the grim dialogue carries the action to its logical end. As noted earlier, Norman likes to write plays that are "conversations I would like to hear" if the people in them felt free to speak the truth. In doing so, she has set the teeth of some critics on edge, but invariably she has stimulated sharp response and has impressed all alike with her unflinching honesty and the excellence of her economical, lucid, incisive use of language. Her most recent play (*Traveler in the Dark*) took a drubbing at the hands of the reviewers, but in view of Norman's conviction that "there is no way to do significant work without [sometimes] falling," it seems reasonable to predict that she will continue full steam ahead.

CHAPTER 21

Literary Criticism

It is almost a cliché to say that in general the greatest contribution Kentucky has made to our national literature has been in the novel. Less well known is the fact that its contribution to literary criticism between 1930 and 1980 has been likewise significant. Of principal consequence has been the work of the New Critics—Allen Tate, Robert Penn Warren, and Cleanth Brooks at the first level of importance and Caroline Gordon at the second level. By any measurement these are major critics on the national scene. Lesser critics, but still national in visibility, have been Burton Rascoe, David Morton, and Elizabeth Hardwick. With the exception of Rascoe, it should be noted, these writers are also discussed under other headings.

The New Criticism

Perhaps no other development in literary studies has achieved in its own day the fame and influence that the critical movement known as the New Criticism did during the late 1930s, 1940s, and 1950s. Dedicated to textual analysis rather than the historical scholarship that had dominated the study of literature since Hippolyte Taine's *History of English Literature* (1863), the origins of the movement trace back to the early 1920s. The central figures were John Crowe Ransom, Allen Tate, Robert Penn Warren, and Cleanth Brooks, all but Ransom being Kentuckians and all but Brooks tracing their relationship back to the Nashville Fugitive group and to the Agrarian movement that grew out of it. In England in the early and mid-1920s T.S. Eliot and I.A. Richards began applying many of the principles from which the New Criticism was to draw, and as the 1930s dawned other distinguished critics became a part of the movement, including R.P. Blackmur, Yvor

Winters, William Empson, Kenneth Burke, and William K. Wimsatt. Tennesseean John Crowe Ransom, professor of English at Vanderbilt University and teacher of Tate, Warren, and Brooks, was the dominant figure in the movement. His writings state and clarify many of the views held by the New Critics, though it would be a mistake to suppose they ever were in complete agreement on details.

In *God Without Thunder* (1930) Ransom expresses his dislike for science; sees "progress" as an outgrowth of the technological advances that have led to industrialism, urbanization, and the destruction of a way of life that has served the South well; and reveals his fondness for myth as a mode of expression. *The World's Body* (1938) continues the attack on the sciences and sees poetry as the ultimate source of the knowledge and order that can solve the world ills which political, social, and economic theory seem incapable of curing. Poetry, he says, comprehends the "world's body," science only the skeleton, and can communicate truths that are communicable in no other way. By the time Ransom's *The New Criticism* (1941) appeared, the movement was already pretty well established in the universities, but the book gave a name to the movement and strongly supported the use of myth, icons, and archetypal patterns as methods of conveying meaning.

Allen Tate, the most philosophical and theoretical of the original New Critics, has left a body of work that sets forth his views of what poetry is and how it is to be read and interpreted: *Reactionary Essays in Poetry and Ideas* (1936), *Reason in Madness, Critical Essays* (1941), and *On the Limits of Poetry* (1948). The principles enunciated in these works are far too complex to be analyzed with care here and too arcane for substantial inclusion in this volume. Suffice it to say that in the beginning it was Tate who first came under the influence of Eliot and made the other Fugitives aware of his ideas. More than Ransom, Tate advocated "pure" poetry—poetry that has only aesthetic effect and no moral, political, religious, or sociological values. A poem, therefore, is a complete entity, a self-contained construct, which must be examined without reference to its relationship to an author or the age that produced it.

Such a view, of course, clashed immediately with the literary historian's belief that a piece of literature bears the imprint of its author and its age much as a fossil bears the imprint of a once-living plant or animal. Thus the literary historian seeks to recreate the tangible world of events and the less tangible world of taste, attitude, and spirit that prevailed when an author lived and a particular work took its shape. In this way, the scholar argues, a reader is enabled to discover meanings that would otherwise remain hidden. When, therefore, the teachings of the New Critics penetrated college classrooms, the scholars—with Douglas Bush of Harvard the chief guardian and spokesman for traditional literary studies—struck back. The controversy between the scholars and the New Critics found its way into the annual meetings of the Modern Language Association of America and the scholarly journals. The New Critics did in time modify their emphases, but never did they fail to insist upon their focus on the text. Today, half a century later, with the New Criticism a historical phenomenon still settling into place in literary history, few would deny that the methods of the New Critics have improved the study of literature.

It is not difficult to understand why the New Critics took the positions they did. The post–World War I world seemed headed in directions which many thoughtful people considered disastrous. Here we must turn to Ransom and Tate's contention that poetry, not politics, economics, or religion, can lead the world out of the abyss into which it is sinking. On the one hand, there is the age-old view of the poet as the sage who sees truth whole and does so without the bias that characterizes men and women of science, religion, and practical affairs. From the time of the vatic power ascribed to the poet among the ancients through the "Defences" of Sidney and Shelley to *The World's Body* of Ransom, the "sciences," it has been contended, can only analyze and strip the world down to its constituent parts, whereas poetry synthesizes, sees interrelationships, and creates and celebrates the world's full body. The poet, Tate held, was capable of transcendent knowledge. No advocate—or defender—of poetry ever claimed poetry to be "useful" in the ordinary sense of usefulness. Indeed, Tate in "Three Types of Poetry" declared that poetry "finds its true usefulness in its perfect inutility." The aim of the poet is at one with Matthew Arnold's dictum that poetry operates out of a perfect "disinterestedness" that seeks to promulgate the best that has been known and thought in the world and to help it to prevail.

At a more practical level of the workaday world it must be remembered that at the time the principles of the New Criticism were being enunciated the Great Depression was in progress, that social and political thinkers were troubled by the direction in which they perceived the world to be going, and that some of them sought to influence that direction by the proletarian and leftist-leaning, admittedly propagandistic, literature they wrote. Allen Tate, a conservative political and social thinker, was opposed to the ideology of these writings. Thus in the preface to *Reactionary Essays on Poetry and Ideas* (1936) he declared his opposition to any literature dominated by a practical purpose, against "trying to make an art respectable by showing that after all it is only a branch of politics." He insisted that above all else the literary quality be kept high. Such a view, of course, pointed the way toward the importance of the text and away from the sociopolitical and economic backgrounds with which both Marxist and literary historical scholarship deals. "The completed poem," he wrote, "is neither exact nor inexact, but what it is, and does not refer to any other order than its own." Some of the New Critics could not go this far, saying that a poem has many relations with the world. More given to theoretical criticism than Brooks and Warren, Tate, unlike them, did comparatively little analyzing of poetry as a free-standing form. His best analysis is "Narcissus on Narcissus," a commentary on his own celebrated "Ode to the Confederate Dead."

In this context we must note Robert Penn Warren as the author of "Pure and Impure Poetry," published in the *Kenyon Review* in 1943, one of the more consequential statements in modern criticism. Tate's views on "pure" poetry as an aesthetic experience are at odds with Warren's. "Poetry," Warren begins, "wants to be pure but poems do not." If the poet could create in the laboratory under controlled conditions, he says, he could produce a distillate of "pure" poetry, but the fact is that he creates in the world, where "impurities" crowd in upon him: "cacaphonous, jagged rhythms, ugly words and ugly thoughts, colloquialisms, cliché. . . ." Love, for example, is a subject upon which the "pure" poet often writes, and since it is what Warren calls a "soft" subject, the poet (and he cites Shelley and Tennyson) is likely to portray love as beautiful and pure and ethereal; when in fact love is often sensual and bawdy, and unless the poet makes it clear that he is aware of this paradoxical nature of love, he is laying himself open to ridicule and parody. Warren's own practice as a poet exemplifies such a view, for his poetry is full of folk speech and dialect, slang and syntactical oddities—a startling combination of elegance and earthiness, and a notable mixture of metrical forms and patterns. Thus in his view he can best be faithful to the "pure" idea embedded in what he writes by being faithful also to the "impurity" that is certain to be present.

Warren has written excellent critical essays on individual authors, such as those on Coleridge ("A Poem of Pure Imagination: An Experiment in Reading") and Ransom ("John Crowe Ransom: A Study in Irony"), but in general his excursions into theoretical literary principles have been infrequent and less consequential than his "Pure and Impure Poetry." His greatest contribution to the New Criticism was his collaboration with Cleanth Brooks in writing textbooks that reached an enormously large audience. Brooks (1906–), a year younger than Warren, was born in Murray and grew up, therefore, not far from Warren, who was born in Guthrie. Both attended Vanderbilt University and became acquainted during the academic year 1924–25; both had John Crowe Ransom's advanced writing courses with their stress on theories of prosody; both studied in detail selected poems from English literature and engaged in the close textual analysis they would broaden and systematize in their textbooks on poetry. In 1928 Warren went to Oxford as a Rhodes Scholar and while there was joined by Brooks in 1929; there the two of them no doubt had discussions that paved the way for their later collaboration. In 1932 Brooks became a member of the English department at Louisiana State University and two years later was joined by Warren; the next year they were invited to found and edit a literary and critical quarterly, with Charles W. Pipkin serving as editor-in-chief. This journal—the *Southern Review*—ran for seven years and became what Ray B. West has called "the most highly respected literary journal in America during the 1930s." During these seven years, in addition to editing the *Southern Review* and teaching three courses each semester, Warren published *Thirty-Six Poems* (1935), *Night Rider* (1939), *Eleven Poems on the Same Theme* (1942); Brooks published *Modern Poetry and the Tradition* (1939); and the two published in collaboration *An Approach to Literature* (1936, 1939, 1952, 1964, 1975) and *Understanding Poetry* (1938, 1950, 1960), the former with John T. Purser.

It would not be fruitful to analyze the textbooks just cited or the two that followed: *Understanding Fiction* (1943), by Brooks and Warren, and *Understanding Drama* (1945), by Brooks and Robert B. Heilman. A few words about *Understanding Poetry*, however, may be instructive, for this was the most significant and most influential of the volumes. In order to get rid of the traditional organization of textbooks on literature, the poems selected for study were not arranged chronologically, by country of origin, or by literary type, but rather in order of complexity; the groupings were under such headings as metrics, tone and attitude, imagery, and theme. An analytical approach was thus almost insured. To further guarantee formal analysis, the editors included model analyses and questions to assist the student, at the same time in the prefatory material enjoining the teacher not to use biographical and historical materials, to avoid didactic and inspirational interpretations, and not to be satisfied with mere narrative or logical paraphrase. Instead emphasis on the structure of the poem and the organic relationships of the parts was encouraged. Rather than dealing with the relation of a poem to its age, an author, or a tradition, then, the student was guided to concentrate on semantics, syntax, meter, texture, imagery, metaphor, and symbol.

Distinguished though his contribution to the Brooks-Warren collaboration was, Brooks during the decade ahead distinguished himself even more in his own volumes: *Modern Poetry and the Tradition* (1939) and *The Well-Wrought Urn: Studies in the Structure of Poetry* (1947). In neither of these volumes was he—nor did he pretend to be—a literary theorist; he was indebted ideologically to others. But Brooks did have a theory of how to read poetry and perhaps said more sensible things about more poems than anyone else in his time.

Modern Poetry and the Tradition is a sort of synthesis of T.S. Eliot, I.A. Richards, John Crowe Ransom, and Allen Tate and extends the discussion of the metaphysical tradition in poetry down to the moderns. Many nineteenth-century poets in the romantic tradition, he feels, had strayed from the tradition when they began to reject the wit and the concrete, complex metaphors of the seventeenth-century metaphysicals such as Donne and Marvell. He believes the mingling of emotion and intellect in paradoxical literary conceits provides the best way for poetry to achieve insight into reality. Thus he looks for and favors the qualities of wit, irony, paradox, symbolism, and intentional ambiguity. Among the moderns he embraces Yeats and Eliot in particular as representatives of the tradition.

The Well-Wrought Urn develops his theory further through a series of essays on poetry in which structure, resting upon the principle of "paradox," is the central point. He then examines Shakespeare, Yeats, Milton, Wordsworth, Keats, and Tennyson in light of this principle. Of the essays in the volume "Keats' Sylvan Historian," an analysis of the "Ode on a Grecian Urn," is representative and certainly the best known. The central point is, of course, that the "truth" of the poem is not found in any assertion made in the poem or in any paraphrase but in the metaphor of the poem as a whole. "The Heresy of Paraphrase," in which Brooks discusses meaning in "structure" and poetry as myth, ends the volume.

Brooks remained at LSU when Warren took a position at the University of Minnesota in 1942. In 1947 he joined the English department at Yale and in 1950 was joined by Warren, whose place at Minnesota was filled by Tate. At Yale the two long-time friends continued with their writing. Together they revised *Understanding Poetry* in 1950 and 1960 and *An Approach to Literature* in 1952, 1964, and 1975; in 1949 they published together *Modern Rhetoric*; and in 1957 Brooks and William K. Wimsatt, Jr., published *Literary Criticism: A Short History*. Beginning in 1963 Brooks again began to publish his essays as collections, first *The Hidden God: Studies in Hemingway, Faulkner, Yeats, Eliot, and Warren*, and then *A Shaping Joy: Studies in the Writer's Craft* in 1971. During this period he also began a sustained study of the works of William Faulkner, of which *William Faulkner: The Yoknapatawpha Country* (1964) is but the first principal outcome. Here Brooks is the patient researcher and literary historian as well as the critic and skillful close reader. Never was he merely an *explication de texte* critic, but as time passed he came increasingly to combine his sensitive and subtle reading of texts with his ability to carry on the investigations that are traditionally the contributions of the literary scholar.

Attention must be given here to Caroline Gordon, who was married for thirty-five years to Allen Tate. The Tates first became acquainted in the summer of 1924 when Tate, then living in New York, visited at some length with Warren in Guthrie. At the same time Caroline Gordon was visiting her parents on Merry Mount Farm, where she was born, near Trenton and not far from Guthrie. Tate and Gordon already knew of each other, for Tate was one of the Fugitives, a group Miss Gordon enthusiastically admired and about which on February 10, 1923, in her role as a reporter for the *Chattanooga News* she wrote an article entitled "U.S. Best Poets Here in Tennessee." In November 1924 Tate and Gordon were married and lived together until their divorce in 1959. Gordon was never a member of the Fugitive group and was not an Agrarian in the literal sense of having written one of the essays in *I'll Take My Stand*, but she was closely associated with members of the group and wrote several Agrarian novels; and though she may not readily come to mind when one thinks of the New Critics, she was associated with them and wrote both essays and analyses of fiction somewhat in the manner of Brooks and Warren.

The House of Fiction: An Anthology of the Short Story with Commentary, of which she was the principal author and to which Tate was a contributor, was published in 1950, a second edition in 1960. *How to Read a Novel* appeared seven years later in 1957. In the Preface to the former "C.G." and "A.T." declare that they believe there are "certain 'constants' or secrets of technique which . . . have been handed down from master to master throughout the ages" and that the identification of them is "the most profitable exercise a student of the craft can engage in." In the appendix of *The House of Fiction* and in *How to Read a Novel* these "constants" are set forth and applied to fiction.

With these "constants" Gordon has not developed any new theories of fiction, but she has synthesized several diverse ideas, drawn mainly from the *Poetics* of Aristotle, the use of symbolism in Dante, the practice of Flaubert, and the theory and practice of Henry James. She is not a philosophical theorist; she is practical in her critical views as they apply to both readers and writers. Gordon takes the position that a slice-of-life cannot be a short story or a novel. To her Aristotle's definition of a play as "the imitation of an action . . . of a certain magnitude" is equally applicable to a piece of fiction. Following Aristotle again, she holds that this action must include the complication and the resolution, the two interlocked by having the complication subtly foreshadow the resolution. Thus a piece of fiction must resolve the complication.

From Dante she derives her theories of symbolism and levels of meaning. Thus she intends that there must be a literal meaning, an allegorical meaning, and in works of true excellence a moral meaning. The fullest meaning is achieved, she says, by symbolic naturalism, a technique derived from the practice of Flaubert, with symbols found in the natural world used to dramatize emotional states. Examples of symbolic naturalism are to be found in such stories of Gordon as "The Brilliant Leaves," "Old Red," "The Forest of the South," and "The Presence." Thus images and symbols reinforce the overt action by providing mood and tonal qualities that give depth and meaning beyond mere exposition and paraphrase.

Finally, she draws upon Henry James's "central intelligence," an improvement as she sees it over Flaubert's "concealed narrator," as a technique for achieving immediacy in drama while maintaining the flexibility of the author's omniscient point of view generally present in fiction. Thus characters are revealed as in drama, not only by what they say but also by what their family, friends, and others say about them. Thus as Gordon sees it, the best fiction through the years has been moving from the expository method to the methods of drama.

Not everyone, of course, agrees with such theories of fiction; some object to the rejection of slice-of-life fiction, to the failure to take into account the novel of ideas or the hero who thinks but does not act. Despite these or other objections, however, most readers would agree with a reviewer who said that the criticism and analyses in Gordon's two volumes "are occasionally irritating, frequently controversial, and always stimulating."

Burton Rascoe

Burton Rascoe (1892–1957), author, editor, and critic, was born in Fulton, moved to Oklahoma with his family when he was a boy, and while he was a student at the University of Chicago began his whirlwind professional career as a book reviewer for the *Chicago Tribune*. During the next seven years he served the *Tribune* as a star reporter, literary and dramatic critic, feature writer, and chief book reviewer. In 1917 he began his battles in behalf of H.L. Mencken, James Branch Cabell, and other young men who were just appearing on the scene. In 1920 he was fired by the *Tribune* and during the next four years was associate editor of *McCall's* and literary editor for the *New York Herald-Tribune*, only to be fired by the latter in 1924. Rascoe's stormy career, however, is less important than what he wrote.

By 1923 Rascoe had written critical introductions for the Alfred Knopf French authors series and for Modern Library. In 1925 he published his first book, *Theodore Dreiser*; in 1931 *Titans of Literature*; and a year later *Prometheans*. In addition he wrote book reviews that were carried by more than sixty newspapers and a syndicated column called "The Daybook of a New Yorker" that appeared in almost four hundred. In 1931 he was literary critic and book reviewer for the *New York Sun* and in subsequent years for *Newsweek*, the *American Mercury*, the *Chicago Sun*, and the *New York Herald-Tribune*. And in 1936 there was *Before I Forget*, an autobiographical account, and in 1947 a continuation of it, which he called *We Were Interrupted*.

Unfortunately Rascoe's views as a critic did not grow with the years, and his temperament failed increasingly to fit the age he lived in. During the 1920s and the early 1930s he had prominence and influence as an avant-garde critic and editor, but during the decade of the Great Depression literary fashions and critical assumptions changed. By the 1940s and the 1950s—the causes he had fought for already won—Rascoe no longer seemed to matter. His contribution had been considerable and in 1929 the *New York Herald-Tribune* had called him "the most gifted Journalist of his generation," but during the last two decades of his life he was all but ignored. Today, literary handbooks give short accounts of his career, but histories of criticism take no note of him. One full-length study of him (*Burton Rascoe*, by Donald M.

Hensley, in the Twayne series) has been written. Here may be found the details of Rascoe's career and accomplishments.

David Morton

David Morton, both a poet and a critic, first undertook the discussion and criticism of poetry in *The Sonnet Today—and Yesterday* (1928). Beginning with the conviction that the sonnet is a noble form, he seeks to say something about its form that will not be "at the expense of poetry." To do this, he briefly surveys sonnet literature, analyzes the qualities of the sonnet, and discusses the main forms, showing the differences between the twentieth-century sonnet and that of earlier periods. "The fundamental principle of the sonnet," Morton says, is "the statement of a single idea, followed by another derivitive or related statement." With this guiding principle, he presses beyond the Petrarchan sonnet for the origins of the form, finding it in the Greek epigram, the Egyptian Book of the Dead, the sacred books of the East, the Book of Psalms, and the Japanese tanka and hokku. All of these, he points out, "possess this same quality of two-fold development within unity." Quoting a poem written three thousand years ago in one of the Vedas, he says, "A sonnetteer today wishing to put the passage into the formal sonnet," would have to supply the meter and rhyme, "but as to structure, the skeleton stands ready, every part in place." The point, Morton concludes, "is the evidence it offers of the high authority for the sonnet's mode. . . . Where a mode of thinking and feeling is so old, so universal and so persistent, the presumption arises that that mode is instinctive and inherent in man's mental and emotional processes." It is remarkable, Morton says, that the sonnet has survived in this century against "the late passion for 'free and full expression.'" There is, however, he continues, "no longer such a thing as the 'proper' subject for a sonnet, nor such a thing as an 'appropriate' manner and language." The sonnet, he concludes, is still the instrument of majestic utterance, but the range is wide—"from sublimity at one end, to clever flippancy at the other."

In preparation for his second volume about poetry Morton went to Ireland to immerse himself in Irish atmosphere and history and to gain the acquaintance of writers involved in the Irish Literary Renaissance. The result was *The Renaissance of Irish Poetry, 1880–1930* (1930), a systematic discussion of the subject matter and the methods of the movement.

Morton's other critical writings have not been collected. Some of his most perceptive remarks on poetry are to be found in his column, "Poems for Our Time," which appeared in several newspapers, including the Sunday *Courier-Journal*. Here on a weekly basis he selected a short poem and commented on it. An example is his remarks on Gerard Manley Hopkins's "Pied Beauty," which concludes, "His alliterative, hyphenated, propulsive syllables come catapulting into the mind with force of shock that compels attention. A reader may like or dislike them; he cannot ignore them."

Morton was perhaps at his best in his telling, brief remarks on the relationship of poetry to life. "The history of poetry," he writes, "shows that she has been most herself and most acceptable when she has concerned herself with the joys and the travails of man, without enlisting in the political or social nostrums." "I doubt," he concludes, "if we will have advanced very far beyond the old epigram which says: " 'Poetry was not meant to save the souls of men; it was meant to make them worth saving.' " Morton was, if anything, a moral critic.

Elizabeth Hardwick

Elizabeth Hardwick (1916–) first won attention with her novel *The Ghostly Lover* in 1945, but in 1946 a telephone call gave new direction to her life and started her on her career as a critic. The call was from Philip Rahv, editor of the *Partisan Review*, asking her to become a contributor to the magazine. "Thus," says Hardwick, "was a lowly reviewer born."

For seventeen years she wrote reviews, essays, and short stories for the politically liberal *Partisan*. Then in the spring of 1963 the New York printers' strike shut down the book reviews of the *New York Times* and the *Herald-Tribune* and led Hardwick and some of her friends to start a new review journal. Few thought that such a venture could survive for long in competition with the established *New York Times*, *Herald-Tribune*, and *Saturday Review of Literature*, but the *New York Review of Books*, as their journal was called, not only survived, it flourished. Dedicated to reviewing only the best books and being critically honest in witty, polished fashion, the new magazine soon became the darling of the intellectual elite. Its editorial credo, run in the first issue, stated that only "reviews of some of the more important books will be published" and that "neither time nor space will be spent on books which are trivial in their intentions or venal in their effects, except occasionally to reduce a temporarily inflated reputation or call attention to a fraud." "What style," wrote Philip Nobile in *Intellectual Skywriting*, "What class. What brass." By the spring of 1971 the *Public Opinion Quarterly* reported that 50 percent of a selected sample of writers, professors, and editors regularly read the *New York Review*. Though always controversial, the *Review* had become a prime literary and cultural influence.

Hardwick was born in Lexington, where she grew up, attended the public schools, and received A.B. and M.A. degrees at the University of Kentucky in 1938 and 1939. Even before she had finished her M.A. her mind was made up that New York was the place where she wanted to try her wings. The city's sophistication and intellectual challenge appealed to her and seemed to promise an opportunity to exercise the natural skepticism that had early characterized her intellectual equipment. She enrolled in Columbia University's doctoral program in English, but after two years she withdrew in order to devote her full time to "serious writing." *The Ghostly Lover* was the first highly visible product of her decision to undertake a writing career. Though never a popular novel, it was readily accepted as a first novel "with promise" and won her what has been called a "quiet" reputation with a generally select and sophisticated audience. During the next thirty-four years Hardwick wrote only two more novels and numerous short stories, eight of which gained some eminence by being reprinted in prestigious annual "best" story collections. She also wrote essays and reviews not only for *Partisan Review* and *New York Review of Books* but also for *Harper's Magazine*, *New Republic*, the *New Yorker*, the *Yale Review*, the *New York Times Book Review*, and other journals; and she published three volumes of essays and criticism. In recognition of her merit she was awarded a Guggenheim Fellowship and won the prestigious George Jean Nathan Award for her "distinguished service of reviewing plays and discussions of the situation in the American theatre." Later significant honors include being asked to serve on the Advisory Board of the National Book Awards and being a member of the Pulitzer Prize Jury for drama.

During the 1940s and 1950s, Hardwick published some essays and criticism that shed light on her views. In November 1959, for example, in *Harper's Magazine*, her "Decline of Book Reviewing" deplores the banality of American reviewing: "Sweet, bland commendations fall everywhere upon the scene," she declares, "a universal if somewhat lobotomized, accommodation reigns. A book is born into a puddle of treacle; the brine of criticism is only a memory." Hardwick has a talent for the "brine of criticism" when she chooses to exercise it. A good example is her review of the revival of Lillian Hellman's *The Little Foxes* at the Lincoln Center in 1967. "It is nearly always said," she writes, "that Lillian Hellman's plays are triumphs of craftsmanship. Actually the question of motivation, the construction of plot, are quite awkwardly managed in most of them. . . . Behind Lillian Hellman's plays is a torn spirit: the bright stuffs of extensive production and the hair-shirt of didacticism. Between these two her genuine talent for characterization is diminished" (*New York Review of Books*, Sept. 21, 1967).

A View of My Own: Essays in Literature and Society (1962) was the first published collection of Hardwick's essays; its appearance enhanced her reputation in New York literary and cultural circles. Among the subjects of the essays are Edna St. Vincent Millay, Hart Crane, William James, Mary McCarthy, Graham Greene, Dylan Thomas, and Eugene O'Neill. As usual with her writing, there are many memorable passages. F. Scott Fitzgerald, she says, "had in the midst of chaos the rather cross-eyed power of gazing upon his deterioration as if he were not living but somehow observing his soul and body as one would watch a drop of water dry up slowly in the sun." Of a Mary McCarthy story containing a good deal of realistic sex she says, it "is about contraception in the way Frank Norris's *The Octopus* is about wheat. There is an air of imparting information—like whaling in Melville." And of the indulgence of Dylan Thomas when he was in the United States on one of his visits she observes, "There was a certain amount of poison in our good will."

Seduction and Betrayal: Women and Literature (1974), an advance over Hardwick's first volume of critical essays, contains ten studies based on lectures given at Vassar College and the Christian Gauss Seminar on Criticism at Princeton University, and on essays that appeared in the *New York Review of Books*. Their genesis traces back to Hardwick's interest in women writers, an interest that appeared in *A View of My Own* and shaped *Seduction and Betrayal*. The women Hardwick studies are both fictional and real. Among the former are Hawthorne's Hester Prynne; Hardy's Tess; Ibsen's Hedda, Nora, and Rebecca; Dreiser's Roberta; Richardson's Clarissa; and George Eliot's Betty. Among the latter are Dorothy Wordsworth, Jane Welsh Carlyle, and Zelda Fitzgerald, all closely associated with geniuses; and the Brontë sisters, Virginia Woolf, and Sylvia Plath, all writers. As the *New York Times* reviewer (May 5, 1974) says, "Hardwick addresses herself to female vulnerability, to women's relations to men, to their own work, their options and lack of options, the real and the fictional alike." In a sense the volume encompasses the role and changing status of the "undone" woman in literature through two hundred years.

The final chapter, "Seduction and Betrayal," surveys the theme of seduction and its evolution from Richardson's *Clarissa* through Tolstoy, Hardy, and others to the naturalists and Zola's *Nana*. Sex as an exalted and tragic theme, she concludes, ends with the nineteenth-century novel; in the twentieth century it becomes a casual encounter. In Hardwick's own words, "You cannot seduce anyone when innocence is not a value."

Elizabeth Hardwick's last collection of essays—*Bartleby in Manhattan*—in 1983 seems to hold no surprises. At no time has she pretended to be an original thinker or a critical theorist who, as she told John Ed Pearce (*Courier-Journal*, May 26, 1974), "discovers the nature of tragedy. I'm not trying as much to set up principles as to provide insights. . . . to look at old books in new ways." Yet her indifference to recent fashions has not really allowed the world to pass her by, for basically her criticism is an age-old approach. In *Bartleby in Manhattan* she carries further her view that the touchstones of our civilization are being eroded by subverting ephemera, "something pitiless and pathological [that] has seeped into youth's love of itself, its body, its politics." Many regard moral criticism as an anachronism today, but Hardwick seems willing to trust the future of such criticism and to rest her case on what she regards as a fundamental principle: that literature—and life—must be rooted in something "that matters."

CHAPTER 22

Poetry

Through the years it has been a commonplace to observe about Kentucky literature that whereas the Commonwealth has produced even more than its reasonable share of writers of fiction its contribution to the nation's poetry has been negligible. The last half-century has thrown such a judgment into doubt, as a quick glance backward over the careers of Kentucky's recent major writers readily makes clear: Elizabeth Madox Roberts first, followed by Allen Tate, Robert Penn Warren, Jesse Stuart, James Still, Thomas Merton, and Wendell Berry. The verse of these writers has already been examined.

There are a few other writers, however, whose claim to a place in literary history is primarily due to the verse they have written. Most of these writers have small or no recognition at the national level, but two of them—Thomas Merton and John Jacob Niles—in distinctively different ways are internationally known.

David Morton

The poetic career of David Morton (1886–1957) extended over two literary periods. As early as 1914 he began publishing verse in the better magazines, and his last verse (except for a volume that came out after his death) was published in 1955. His content and manner, however, belong more to an earlier generation. To appreciate the extent of his active career we must remember that Morton began publishing in magazines in the year Robert Frost published *North of Boston* and Vachel Lindsay *The Congo*, and that the year before he died Allen Ginsberg published *Howl*.

Morton was born in Elkton, graduated from Vanderbilt, and started a career in journalism in Louisville immediately thereafter. He was first a reporter for the *Louisville Evening Post*, was subsequently employed by the Associated Press, and still later became an editorial writer for the *Courier-Journal*. From 1915 to 1918 he taught English at Louisville Boys' High School and English and history at Morristown, New Jersey, 1918–24. During this latter period he also contributed editorials to the *New York Sun* and the *New York Evening Post*. In 1924 he became a member of the English department at Amherst College, a position he held until 1945, at which time he became poet-in-residence at the Deerfield (Massachusetts) Academy. In the 1950s he became professor of English at the American International College in the Azores, where he remained until his retirement in 1957 because of ill health.

Morton, a lyric poet and sonnet writer, began his publishing career in 1914 when his verse began to appear in such magazines as *Harper's*, *Poetry*, *Smart Set*, and *North American Review*. During the next forty-odd years he published eleven volumes of poetry and two volumes of prose, one dealing with the sonnet, the other with the poetry of the Irish Renaissance. He first attracted attention in 1919 when the Poetry Society of America gave an award to his poem *Wooden Ships*. In the same year the Lyric Society of New York conducted a nationwide search for manuscripts and gave first prize to Morton's *Ships in Harbor*. When the manuscript was published two years later, it received the Poetry Society of America award for the year. Morton was, then, rather well known when his first volume appeared in 1921.

Reviews of *Ships in Harbor*, though mixed, were generally favorable. Thus Clement Wood declares in the *Bookman* (Sept. 1921), "Mr. Morton is surely one of the leading sonnetteers writing today. . . . [his] rank as a lyricist is high indeed"; but Wood finds a troubling "limitation in poetic attitude" and is concerned about lines which though exquisite in phrasing are prone to be "unemotional, dehumanized; life seen at dusk through a rose window." *Harvest: A Book of Sonnets* (1924), Morton's second volume, causes an *Outlook* reviewer (May 28, 1924) to speak of Morton's "almost flawless taste and true ear for the melodies of word and phrase" but also to warn that "his prevailing mood of tender melancholy is likely to pall upon the minds of our restless moderns." *Nocturnes and Autumnals* (1928) meets with much the same reception as one reviewer speaks of hearing for ten years "the same note of nostalgic melancholy" and listening to "the same scales on the same perfect flute. . . . a stiff shot of vitality would put him up with the very greatest of modern sonnet makers" (*Book-*

man, Sept. 1928). And the same view is expressed by the *Saturday Review of Literature* (Nov. 5, 1932) in a review of *Earth's Processional* (1932): "He can build a strong sonnet, as in 'The Mountain,' but most of his sonnets seem merely graceful. . . . there is nothing in his book that leaps like fire from the page, as, in my view, poetry should."

Spell against Time was next in 1936, followed by *All in One Breath* in 1939, *Angle of Earth and Sky* in 1941, and *Poems, 1920–1945* (1945), which was Morton's last volume for ten years. Of this volume the *Saturday Review of Literature* (Nov. 17, 1945) writes, "David Morton, probably the foremost American nature lyricist in the years 1920–1945, has taken from all his poems nearly three hundred and made this long, undivided sequence. . . . The book in its entirety leaves much the same impression which a single poem would—of gentle sadness, almost a passing bell. . . . what remains most strongly with the reader is the poet himself, as poet, conscious of the beauty of the world, gently, inexorably slipping from him while he tries to capture it complete."

Such a statement could be taken as a summing up, but Morton would publish one more volume, *Like a Man in Love* (1955), and a posthumous volume, *Journey Into Time* (1958). He would, too, be honored again as he entered his last decade. In 1949 he was elected vice-president of the Poetry Society of America; in 1952 and 1953 respectively he was granted honorary degrees by the University of Kentucky and the University of Massachusetts; and in 1955 he received the Borestone Prize for Poetry for his *Like a Man in Love*.

Morton, then, achieved some recognition, though in no sense was he a great poet. Society and the contemporary world were no part of his concern; he wrote of the seasons and his imagery, generally conventional, was drawn from field, wood, and stream. Strong passion was not part of his equipment, and though he had technique and his style was charming and graceful, the impact of what he said was small. His was the poetry of a sensitive spirit responding to loveliness, and he did it well. Especially was he haunted by the passing of time, the brevity of life, the mutability of lovely things, and our inability to build a defense against "the clamorous ticking of the clock."

Hortense Flexner

Hortense Flexner (1885–1973), who spent most of her life in Louisville, had a versatile career as an author. After receiving her A.B. and her M.A. from the University of Michigan, she was employed by the *Louisville Herald* and did editorial work for the Curtis

Publishing Company in Philadelphia. In imaginative writing she first turned to drama and between 1914 and 1920 wrote several plays, one of which was produced by Stuart Walker's Portmanteau Theatre as *Voices* (1916); others were produced in little theaters in Indiana, California, and Louisville: *The Broken God* (1915), *The Faun* (1915), and *The New Queen* (1920). In 1919 the Poetry Society of America awarded her first honors for her poem "Mask of Soldiers." In the same year she married Wyncie King, a cartoonist, who in later years illustrated her children's books. In 1920 appeared the first of the three volumes of verse she was to publish.

Of this first volume of poetry, *Clouds and Cobblestones*, one reviewer said, "there is nothing in these pages that will long endure," but like other reviewers he admired her technical proficiency and commended the way "the verses touch human values with sincerity." More merit was found in *The Stubborn Root, and Other Poems*, published ten years later. Here the *Bookman* finds "occasional flashes" of excellence; the *Outlook* speaks of the "high quality" of the verse; and the *New York Times* declares that the poems are "something a little out of the ordinary. Not often does one happen on a book of verses the quality of which is kept so constantly at a high level of achievement" (Sept. 28, 1930).

The first of these two volumes was broad in its subject matter, being concerned with everything in life between clouds and cobblestones; the second, with "the sense of life reaching forth, but never quite achieving the ultimate aim of beauty." Her third volume, *North Window, and Other Poems* (1943), contains short, crisp poems like notes on present-day life. It won warm recognition from such review journals as the *Saturday Review of Literature*, *Poetry*, the *New York Herald-Tribune*, and the *New Yorker*. The reviewer in *Poetry* finds faults but speaks in praise of "fifteen or twenty" of the seventy-four poems in the volume; the *Saturday Review of Literature* is pleased with Flexner's "adult and very individual talent," adding, "If perhaps her poetry is too much preoccupied with bitter inquiry and unresolved speculation, it is always interesting, always provocative" (July 24, 1943).

After Flexner's death at eighty-eight, admirers, unwilling to let memory of her die, published selections from her poetry. The first, edited by Laurie Lee, was published by Hutchinson in London in 1963; the second, edited with an introduction by Harvey Curtis Webster and Joy Bale under the imprint of the University of Louisville, in 1975. Miss Flexner also published much verse in magazines that was never collected, including enough light verse, she said, to make a volume, most of it in the *New Yorker*.

Flexner was fifty-six in 1941 when she published her first children's book, *Chipper*, about the friendship between a chipmunk and a human "giant." The book was not widely noticed, but it did receive a warm reception in *Books* and *The Horn Book*, as well as in the Louisville press. Her next book for children, published in 1942, received wide attention, for both its quality and its subject matter. *Wishing Window* (1942) is a story of two little French children whose family has been driven from their home and village during the Nazi invasion of France. The volume was warmly praised, for one reason, because, as Dorothy Canfield Fisher puts it in the foreword, it introduces children to the reality of war, with the door "at least ajar, but so tenderly told that it ought not to frighten most six- to ten-year-old readers." The *New York Times* praised it for telling its story "with a lovely simplicity and a complete absence of melodrama"; and similar commendation was given by the *Saturday Review of Literature*: "Without any brutality or excesses it tells its little story—frequently gay, and always honest." The volume ends as it began, with children peering through the window of Madame Bon Bon's shop at the wonderful tarts, buns, and cakes while the fragrance of the warm oven fills the air.

Puzzle Pond (1948) is a story that tells how Wedge, a beaver, lives on Puzzle Island off the coast of Maine and how Davy, a small boy, saves him from being caught in a steel trap. Eventually Davy catches Wedge in a box and takes him back to Juniper to live with his beaver family. Though the story is very simple, each reviewer—and especially the one in the *New York Herald-Tribune*—is struck by the way it held the interest of seven-to-ten-year-old boys.

Leah Bodine Drake

A Kentucky poet who has not received the attention she deserves from those who have written about Kentucky literature is Leah Bodine Drake (1904–64). Born in Kansas, Drake was to live in Lexington and attend both Hamilton College and Sayre College. Subsequently she was married and divorced and at some time moved to Evansville, Indiana, where from 1945 to 1955 she wrote movie, music, drama, and book reviews for the *Evansville Courier*. In 1955 she began writing feature articles, including book and music reviews, for the Henderson, Kentucky, *Gleaner and Journal* and in 1957 moved to Parkersburg, West Virginia, where she became society editor of the *Parkersburg News*. Her poems appeared in the *Atlantic Monthly*, *Commonweal*, *Contemporary Poetry*, *Cornhill Magazine* (London), *New Yorker*, *Poetry*, *Saturday Evening Post*, *Saturday Review*, the *Southern Literary Messenger*, and in many other magazines, such as *Weird* and *Magazine of Fantasy and Science Fiction*.

Drake's first volume of verse was *A Hornbook for Witches: Poems of Fantasy* (1950). As the title suggests, the subject matter is specialized, dealing with the dark of the moon, witches and potions, ghoulies and ghosties. Drake's "The Ballad of the Jabberwock," which first appeared in *Dark of the Moon* and later in *A Hornbook for Witches*, won the Stephen Vincent Benét Ballad Contest in 1946:

My grandmother tells me,
  When the lights are low,
How the Jabberwock appeared
  In Squankom long ago.

First a frightened farmer,
  Tearing into town
Told how his wife had seen
  Something big and brown.

Horned like a billy-goat
  And scaled like a dragon,
Perched cross-legged on
  Their brand-new wagon.

The twenty-three stanzas of this poem do not constitute great poetry, but as in other poems in the volume the lines move easily, skillfully create a mood, and in general provide entertainment for those who enjoy accounts of the macabre and are interested in the unknown.

The volume that brought Drake most favorable attention was *This Tilting Dust*. Drake received the $1250 Borestone Mountain Poetry award for the manuscript on January 28, 1954, at the Poetry Society of America annual awards dinner in New York City. Other awards (Drake's was the largest) were given at the dinner, among the recipients being Conrad Aiken, Witter Bynner, Marchette Chute, and Dylan Thomas. Drake was living in Henderson at this time.

"Cobra," originally published in the *New Yorker*, is representative of *This Tilting Dust*. It is not a mood poem, as many of her poems are, but a nine-stanza comment on a seeming contradiction in nature, in that one of the most venomous snakes in the world is fond of milk and music. At the time of her death Drake had partially assembled more poems for an additional volume of verse.

Thomas Merton

To many it would come as a surprise to read a review of *The Seven Storey Mountain* in 1948 stating that the volume is "an autobiography of a young American poet" who, after his conversion to Catholicism, entered a Trappist monastery in Kentucky. The fact is, however, that in that year Thomas Merton's published work consisted of three volumes of verse with which he was winning himself a substantial reputation as a religious poet: *Thirty Poems* (1944), *A Man in the Divided Sea* (1946), and *Figures for an Apocalypse* (1948). It was, however, *The Seven Storey Mountain* (1948) that brought Thomas Merton (1915–68) into fame with a national audience. Later he was to say of the volume, "It is a youthful book, too simple in many ways." But with the million copies it sold, which were followed by more distinguished writings such as *The Waters of Siloe* (1949) and *The Sign of Jonas* (1953), he was to become America's most widely known theologian and religious poet.

Merton was born in Prades, in the French Pyrenees, the son of a New Zealander and post-impressionist painter of some note who met his American (Ohio) wife-to-be while both were students in Paris. Because of World War I the Mertons came to America (Long Island) in 1916. In 1921 Merton's mother died, and his father, partly to find subjects to paint, went respectively to Bermuda, France, and England, taking his son with him. In 1931 Merton's father died, and young Merton in 1933 won a scholarship to Clare College, Cambridge University. He won reappointment for a second year, but despite his successes in languages and literature, his passion for hard drinking and frivolity led to his being sent to Long Island to live with his grandparents. Merton then entered Columbia University, where he was an enthusiastic fraternity man; but he also found a circle of literary-minded undergraduates, became a contributor to Columbia student publications, including the literary quarterly, and thus started a prolific career of writing that he never abandoned. Perhaps best of all, he found Mark Van Doren teaching there, which led him to major in English and to write his master's essay on William Blake under Van Doren's guidance. He received his A.B. in 1938 and his M.A. in 1939. During these years he also wrote reviews for the *New York Times* and the *Herald-Tribune* and no fewer than four and a half novels, all but one of which he totally destroyed. This one, *My Argument with the Gestapo* (1969), was published after his death. Merton had found Columbia very stimulating. "There was," he says, "a kind of genuine intellectual vitality in the air."

After his graduation, Merton considered entering the Franciscan Order, taught at St. Bonaventure University, worked in a Harlem slums Friendship House, and continued to write. But the pull of the contemplative life led him to enter the Trappist monastery at Gethsemani near Bardstown on December 10, 1941, to become a member of the Cistercian Order, the most austere offshoot of the Benedictines. Before his death twenty-seven years later he wrote fifty volumes. It was a paradox that a career of silence should speak to so many people, Catholic and Protestant, Christian and non-Christian, the world over.

The discipline at Gethsemani was severe, demanding almost complete silence, laying great stress on work and obedience, and requiring adherence to detailed rules. Merton was fearful of the conflict that might arise between his life of contemplation as a monk and his desire to be a writer, but he received only encouragement from the Abbot, who saw that Merton's life as a contemplative and as a writer were likely to support and feed upon each other. And indeed Merton's writing was prolific and broad: poetry, autobiography, philosophy, theology, religious history, comparative religion, even world affairs. Here we are interested only in the poetry.

Merton's first volume was *Thirty Poems* (1944). Written over a substantial period of time, including the years leading up to World War II, the range of subject matter is fairly broad. There are poems like "Dirge for the City of Miami" about war and cities and the manifestations of disorder and violence in the world:

> And there the gentle murderer stands,
> And sadly, sadly wipes his hands.
> There the forger and the thief
> And the bank robber bow in grief.

But there are poems also in the lyric mode, some of them dealing with travel and places, among them "Song for Our Lady of Cobre," which he wrote in Cuba:

> The white girls lift their heads like trees,
> The black girls go
> Reflected like flamingoes in the street.
>
> The white girls sing as shrill as water
> The black girls talk as quiet as clay.
>
> The white girls open their arms like clouds,
> The black girls close their eyes like wings:
> Angels bow down like bells,

Angels look up like toys,
Because the heavenly stars
Stand in a ring:
And all the pieces of the mosaic, earth,
Get up and fly away like birds.

And there are poems such as "The Trappist Abbey: Matins" and "Dirge for the Proud World" about leaving the world for a monastic retreat. *A Man in the Divided Sea* (1946) was written at about the same time as *Thirty Poems* and is a continuation somewhat in the same manner of the earlier volume: poems about travel and places ("Tropics," "The Ohio River—Louisville") and his retreat from the world ("The Trappist Cemetery—Gethsemani," "Dirge for a Town in France"). But new themes, including the sacramental view of nature, take their place alongside liturgical themes. Among them are "Trappists, Working" and "Advent," a poem about winter nights. *Figures for an Apocalypse* (1948) was Merton's third volume of verse and his first effort at a long poem. Made up of eight sections it somewhat parallels the biblical book of the Apocalypse, though greatly modernized. The remainder of the volume is not unlike Merton's first two volumes. Here, as in the earlier volumes, one can trace the influence of such English seventeenth-century Metaphysical poets as Andrew Marvell, John Donne, Richard Crashaw, and George Herbert, and of Gerard Manley Hopkins and T.S. Eliot; but in the last of the three volumes the influence of William Blake and his mysticism may be detected—an influence that was to grow with the years. *The Tears of the Blind Lions* (1949) was to be Merton's last volume of verse for eight years. Devoted largely to saints, monastic life, and other religious subjects, the poems differ from Merton's earlier work by being little concerned with places, travel, and retreat from the world. In general, they were less successful than the earlier poetry, though again nature poems such as "On a Day in August" and "In the Rain and Sun" may equal them. In all these volumes Merton was generally well received and was acclaimed by some as the best Catholic poet since Francis Thompson.

By the time *The Strange Islands* appeared in 1956 Merton's ideas were changing, and he was abandoning his view that a monk is someone who retreats from the world. His opinions on civil rights and disarmament were taking shape, and his poetic style was in transition. The short lyrical poem was giving way to longer, satirical, complex poems. He was engaged in experiments intended to match his poetic manner with his widening range of subject matter of race and war and violence. Merton's changing views were encouraged by the election of Pope John XXIII, who set an unprecedented example for tolerance, provided an atmosphere for change, and proclaimed the need for liberty of belief and the practice of faith. Before John's death in 1963 the Second Vatican Council (Vatican II) had made history.

The stern discipline in Gethsemani began to relax, and Merton, once a temporary Communist in the 1930s, now rediscovered his compassion for the disinherited and regained his social militancy. He experimented with new forms and what he called the "anti-poetry" of indignation, and he broadened his reading; he began to translate the poetry of the Third World. *Conjectures of a Guilty Bystander* (1966) is his principal prose work of this time that parallels his poetic development. He became more earthy in his writing, more direct, more compact, less elevated. He broadened his relationships with other faiths. He became reconciled to Protestantism and found a growing attraction toward unbelievers; he saw monasteries as too rigid and stifling. He was impelled more and more to speak out on issues and to seek to express his vision of a just society. He saw hope in the new radicalism of the counterculture of the 1960s and in the early New Left with its concern with immediate ends in civil rights and disarmament. He admired Gandhi and Martin Luther King and was convinced that the black problem was really rooted in the larger white society.

Merton dealt with his awakened social concerns in both his essays and his poetry during the 1960s. *Original Child Bomb* (1962) is his first volume in this vein. Here in satiric fashion he deals with the explosion of the first atomic bomb, putting together adapted snippets from news reports in ironic, stark, telling fashion. *Emblems of a Season of Fury* (1963) is made up of lyrics, translations, and prose poems dealing with the problems of a troubled world. In the volume he abandons meter, poetic diction, imagery, and symbols as a way of speaking and turns to poetry as statement, even as a news story is a statement —and does so in human terms. In "A Picture of Lee Ling," for example, a Chinese girl is trying to flee to Hong Kong but is turned back at the border. His method is sometimes that of the existentialist and even of the absurdist.

As early as 1949 in *The Sign of Jonas,* when Merton was immersed in monastic life, there is evidence of his interest in Asian religions and Asian contemplative ways. No one was more aware of the theological differences between Christianity and the religions of the East, but Merton believed that for the spiritual disorders of the world to be healed there must be rapprochement between the East and the West and that the Western Church must be willing to learn from Eastern religions just as earlier it had learned from the teachings of Plato and Aristotle and the Islamic theologians. As a contemplative he desired to explore the similarities between the Asiatic and European mystical traditions, for there were many points at which he saw resemblances between Christian and Zen or Taoist insights. By December 10, 1968, the day he was electrocuted by touching an exposed wire of an electric fan in Bangkok, Thailand, he was on this mission and was attending a conference of Benedictine and Cistercian superiors of Asia. He had spent forty days with the Buddhists, including three long meetings with the Dalai Lama. His end thus came before his journey eastward was completed, twenty-seven years to the day after he entered the monastery at Gethsemani.

Two more volumes of Merton's verse remain to be noted. *Cables to the Ace* (1968) appeared the year of his death, *The Geography of Lograire* (1969), which was incomplete, the year after. The old Merton is not present in either volume. The joyful psalms are no more, his religious and nature imagery is absent, metrical form is gone, the old rhythms are not there. The poet, he says, has "changed his address and his poetics are on vacation." The cruelty of the world provides much of the content, the tone is often one of irony and the mood one of sadness; and there is wit, along with parody and mock pathos:

> Weep, weep, little day
> For the father of the lame
> Experts are looking
> For his name

Most of *The Geography of Lograire* is "found" poetry in the sense that it is extracts from Merton's reading of the time, some of it copied almost without change, some of it converted into free verse. The fragments are arranged to produce counterpointing of mood between our urban civilization and other cultures. In literary form the volume is an experiment to discover new forms of expression, just as his spiritual search led him into world religions and even among primitive peoples to explore grounds of resemblance.

The change in Merton's poetry has been great, but in retrospect it could have been anticipated as early as *The Tears of the Blind Lions* (1949). There are poems in that volume that reveal mystical experience and do so with new techniques. *Emblems of a Season of Fury* (1963) represents quite an advance in what has been called "a Zen mystical dimension." Progressively his themes have become more existentialist, his structures more surrealistic. He gives more attention to conditions that hinder human freedom; increasingly he directs his critical thrusts at a technological system that "fails to communicate to man as total man." *Cables to the Ace* reveals such views as well as Merton's inner urge to open himself to the contemplative East. *The Geography of Lograire* goes even further into his probing of existentialism and his effort to fathom the unknowable and develop a methodology to enable him to commit his insights to words. In his "Message for Poets" (1964) he writes, "Let us be proud of the words which are given to us for nothing, not to teach anyone, not to prove anyone absurd, but to point beyond all objects into the silence where nothing can be said." Thus Merton came to write what unsympathetic critics call "puzzle" poetry. Where he was leading and with what success can never be known because he died too soon. Only recently have his works been published in collected form, his *Collected Poems* in 1977 and his *Literary Essays* in 1981. With the body of his works brought together, both the published and the previously unpublished, the way has been paved for more definitive study than has been possible heretofore. Between 1970 and 1980 at least twenty books and many, many articles have been written in order to clarify and appraise Merton's place in both theology and literature. More will have to be done, for he was a complex man and his poetry the result of increasingly complex creativity. In the meantime, those who try to understand Merton's poetry must—as we have done here—be guided by studies such as George Woodstock's *Thomas Merton: Monk and Poet* (1978), which stresses the monastic backgrounds, and Thérèse Lentfoehr's *Words and Silence: On the Poetry of Thomas Merton* (1979), which is more concerned with the poetry itself. Definitive studies have yet to be written.

Albert Stewart

In his mild-mannered, soft-spoken way Albert Stewart (1914–) bridges the gap between the old and the new in the role of poetry in Appalachian Kentucky. Around 1960 an expanded interest began to develop in Appalachian literary studies, and Stewart was one of those who fostered it. He was born at Yellow Mountain, in Knott County, and attended the Hindman Settlement School, where he knew Lucy Furman and was a student of Ann Cobb, Eastern Kentucky's first published poet. Later he received his A.B. in English at Berea College and his M.A. at the University of Kentucky, where he did further graduate work before taking a teaching position at what was then called the University's Community College of Northern Kentucky. Later he took a position at Morehead State College, which took him back closer to the region where he grew up and to which he was quietly dedicated. At Morehead he was given the opportunity to do two things that were important to him: to assemble well-known Kentucky writers as teachers in a series of summer writing workshops which he directed, and to institute a Morehead Press, from which came several volumes, including an annual anthology of poems and short stories—*Kentucky Writing*—by students in the workshops and by Kentuckians at large. Finally he accepted a position at Alice Lloyd College at Pippa Passes and thus made his way deeper into the mountains near where he grew up and where he could carry on his career as a teacher and encourager of young people who might have a talent for self-expression. At Alice Lloyd College, Stewart continued to direct writing workshops, but he enlarged his "Appalachian" role by founding and for twelve years editing *Appalachian Heritage: A Magazine of Southern Appalachian Life and Culture*. After Stewart's retirement, the magazine was moved to Berea College.

While Stewart was encouraging others to write and was abetting the study of Appalachian culture, he never ceased to be a writer himself. His *The Untoward Hills* (1962) is a selection from the many poems he had written and published in magazines through the years. Bearing the characteristic trademarks of Stewart's careful and sensitive handling of language and imagery, the volume was warmly reviewed in *Masterplots: 1963 Reviews of 100 Outstanding Books Published . . . during 1962*. It is, as the reviewer says, "the poetic history of a clear-seeing spirit moving lyrically against the background of its native hills . . . into that larger world . . . among the terrible colors of war." The sections are titled: "The Hills of a Child," "Yellow Mountain Country: The Outlying Hills," "Yellow Mountain Country: The Inmost Valleys," "West of Easter Island," "Interludes," "The Hesitant Mirror." The poems encompass two parallel movements: the actual physical journey outward from home in the mountains and the return home, the framework for the symbolic inner journey—the human odyssey. As the reviewer observes, the volume is made up of "a series of thematically connected instants in time, a gradual drift of mountain leaves, a growth of geometric frost, a movement of fiddlers' hands, a tableau of Civil War horsemen, a swell of U.S. naval warships in 1945, and finally a movement of return."

There are many attention-catching lines in the volume, such as: "Counting the way the memory counts time . . ." and "No words will sing you backward into life." But even more plentiful are lines with delicate traceries such as these from "Winter Landscape":

The crystal world was drawn with crystal hands
So deft the eye may never see
Aught but intricate tracery that stands
As lonely signature of cry or ghost . . .

Jim Wayne Miller

Jim Wayne Miller (1936–), like Albert Stewart, is dedicated to matters Appalachian. Unlike Stewart, however, Miller looks back retrospectively upon the Appalachia about which Jesse Stuart, Harriette Arnow, and James Still wrote. His perspective is that of a new generation. By the 1960s when he arrived on the scene, the "Great Society" programs of President Johnson's administration were being put in place in Eastern Kentucky and the exploitation of the land and the arrival of industrialization were accomplished facts. Old values were in a shambles, and a new culture that could replace them and give direction to life had not been born. The sociologists had long been involved in a study of Appalachia, but more than analysis and managerial devices were needed; there was a need for synthesis and for a new myth—or set of myths—to live by. Literary scholars and writers turned their attentions to this effort.

Kentucky-born Cratis William's monumental three-volume dissertation, *The Southern Mountaineer in Fact and Fiction* in 1961 (published in abridged form in *Appalachian Journal*, vol. 3) charted a way through a maze of writing that revealed the richness of the literature not only of Kentucky but of the whole of Appalachia. Other scholars such as Ruel Foster (also Kentucky born) broadened and deepened the course of literary investigation; and now, it appears, Jim Wayne Miller—both a scholar and a poet—has taken on the role of leadership in fostering literary studies, as witness, for example, his article in *Appalachian Journal* 5 (Autumn 1977), 82–91, in which he surveys the scholarly work that has been done and needs to be done and in general cites the challenges and opportunities that lie ahead for both the scholar and the creative writer.

Miller is perhaps the leading poet among a new generation writing about Eastern Kentucky. Born in Appalachian North Carolina, Miller majored in English at Berea College, received his Ph.D. in German from Vanderbilt University in 1965, and has taught German, folklore studies, and writing at Western Kentucky State University since 1963. Miller's first volume of verse was *Copperhead Cane* (1964), his second a set of ballads called *The More Things Change the More They Stay the Same* (1971); but *Dialogue With a Dead Man* (1974), published by the University of Georgia Press, brought him a wider audience and some national critical attention. The poems, grouped in three sections ("Copperhead Cane," "Dialogue With a Dead Man," and "Family Reunion"), constitute a dialogue between the poet and his father (or a father figure) and collectively make up a narrative. The first section (seventeen poems from the author's first volume) reveals in a series of still pictures the poet's and the deceased "father's" lives as they did things together and the poet's sense of grief and loss, especially now that he does alone the things he once had done with the deceased. In the second part a dialogue takes place as the two go their separate ways, a process of self-healing begins, and a rejuvenation of spirit emerges. In the last part the poet finds security in family ties, in a sense of place, and in the memories left which death cannot take away. As in an elegy, then, the poet has moved from death and grief through a reflective mood to one of resolution and acceptance. The sixty-four poems in the volume are rich in Appalachian lore: folk customs and superstition, farming and logging, and the events that make up the life and rituals of the poet's world.

Miller's next volume—*The Mountains Have Come Closer* (1980)—is a set of poems whose dominant mood is alienation. In this volume the author has invented a persona, a mountain folk character who serves him well—"the Brier." The Brier is a person of intelligence and sensibility who is aware of the fact that people of the mountains are trying to live in two worlds—or between them. He abhors what "progress" has brought to Appalachia—things such as huge smelly diesel trucks and tapedecks and the lifestyle of the technological world—and laments that it has left in its wake a fragmentation of life and a dislocation of values. Finally, "One Friday night the Brier felt called on to preach," and he preaches a synthesis of the ideas set forth in *Dialogue With a Dead Man* and *The Mountains Have Come Closer*. The poem is thus a sort of jeremiad in which the mountain people are told that they must again find a sense of place, must lose their state of rootlessness, and be "born again," not into the world of nostalgic romanticism for things long past, but into rejection of the superficial, technological glitter of the present; they must develop a new awareness of present problems and discover a firm footing on "native ground" where it is possible to build a new self.

Miller is also a writer of short stories where motivation is comparable to that found in his poetry and his scholarly writing. Taking his readers into the very houses of his characters, he writes of men and women of Eastern Kentucky whose families have been broken up and scattered by the inducements of business and industry. The plots and the action arise from the tension that grows out of the conflicts that reflect present-day life in the hill country and the juxtaposition of ways and values that characterize the life of the traditional mountaineer with those of the young people who have been alienated from "the old ways."

John Jacob Niles

Anyone familiar with the name of John Jacob Niles (1892–1980) probably thinks of him first as a folksinger, a performer, and second as a collector of folksongs and folkmusic, of which the principal outcome has been *The Ballad Book of John Jacob Niles* (1960). But Niles was a composer of music as well as a collector of it, and he was a poet as well as a collector of ballads. Here we are concerned with *Brickdust and Buttermilk: Poems by John Jacob Niles* (1977).

Niles was born in Louisville, began collecting folk songs of the Ohio Valley when he was fifteen, and from his high school graduation in 1909 until 1917 collected songs and tunes in Eastern Kentucky. His first composition of note was "Go 'Way from My Window," based on a song he heard from a workman on his father's farm. After service as a pilot in Europe during World War I he studied music in France and later at the Cincinnati Conservatory of Music. His collection of ballads, words and music, throughout the Appalachia area, was done in the late 1920s and early 1930s. He married Rena Lipetz in 1937 and from 1939 until his death lived at Boot Hill Farm in Clark County. Many regard him as America's foremost balladeer and folksinger.

Brick Dust and Buttermilk, Part 1, begins

> I have not studied the philosophy of human love
> Nor set a slide-rule on the yearnings of my heart
> But I have loved you well and very long
> And taught my heart the way you'd have it go.

Fifty-odd pages later Part 4 and the volume end:

> The locusts have eaten nearly all of my years
> And left the husks and hulls of endless days.
> And now I must discover how to live with the bitter
> Husks and the tattered fragile hulls
> Of days I shall never see again.
> So if you see me trying to piece the shards

Of broken days and tiny fragmented moments together
To brighten the dark night of my loneliness,
Be kind, be gentle, be affectionate to an old man
Who has given his years to the locusts: be kind.

Between these two poems are more than fifty others selected from the many that Niles had written through the years and that he thought good enough, when he was eighty-five, to be remembered by. Near the midpoint is a masterwork, the four stanzas of "I Wonder as I Wander." To what degree the piece is original and to what extent it is an adaptation has been debated, but it seems safe to predict that the carol itself—words and music—will be sung down through the centuries as long as the Christmas story is told.

I wonder as I wander out under the sky,
How Jesus our Saviour did come for to die,
For poor orn'ry people like you and like I,
I wonder as I wander out under the sky.*

Other Poets

A few more recent and contemporary poets and some selected titles from their works must be cited. These writers have not been as well known outside Kentucky as the authors just noted, but each has a regional following. More about most of them can be found by turning to volume 3 of the John Wilson and Dorothy Edwards Townsend volumes on Kentucky literature, *Kentucky in American Letters*. Three of these authors are as much associated with their contribution to the cause of poetry in Kentucky as with their own poetry.

Joy Bale Boone (1912–) first came to the attention of Kentucky literary circles as a reviewer for the *Courier-Journal*, beginning in 1945 as Joy Bale. She has edited two collections of *Contemporary Kentucky Poets* (1964, 1967) and in 1964 founded *Approaches*, a literary magazine which ran for ten years and provided an outlet for Kentucky poets. In the tenth issue Bale's principal poem, *The Storm's Eye: A Narrative in Verse Celebrating Cassius Marcellus Clay, Man of Freedom, 1810–1903*, was published. She is also the author of *never less than love* (1972).

Wade Hall (1934–), professor of English at Bellarmine College, has also been of service to poetry in Kentucky. For more than ten

* "I Wonder as I Wander," copyright © by G. Schirmer, Inc., reprinted by permission.

years, with the assistance of Joy Bale (Boone) and others, he has been the main force behind the *Kentucky Poetry Review* (1976–), which has published poetry by Kentucky poets and sponsored special issues honoring individual Kentucky poets. In addition to *The High Limb: Poems by Wade Hall* (1973), he has also written *The Truth Is Funny: A Study of Jesse Stuart's Humor* (1970).

Jonathan Greene (1943–) has had a hand in encouraging the writing of poetry as well as in writing it himself. While production manager and designer for the University Press of Kentucky, he founded the Gnomon Press in Lexington, and later moved to Frankfort, where he now lives and is its editor and publisher. Here Greene has published verse by several Kentucky writers; and in 1976 he edited, with a preface, *Kentucky Renaissance: An Anthology of Contemporary Writers,* in which he reprinted verse and some prose of selected contemporary Kentucky writers. Between 1966 and 1980 he published ten volumes of his own verse in various small presses. Readers generally are not acquainted with these volumes, however, for small presses usually set their type by hand on handmade paper with the result that the number of copies printed is very limited and generally not available in bookstores. Greene's work, according to his own statement, "often delves into psychological/philosophical ruminations as well as being concerned with living in a rural setting." He often deals with archetypal materials. Among the volumes he has published with small presses are *The Reckoning* (1966), *The Lapidary* (1969), *Scaling the Walls* (1974), and *Quiet Goods* (1979).

Nor is **John D. Engle, Jr.** (1922–) lacking in support of the cause of poetry. Born at Yocum, he earned his A.B. and M.A. in English at the University of Kentucky, has taught English in both Kentucky and Ohio high schools and has been active in statewide writing programs and conferences. He has published many poems in the *Saturday Evening Post*, the *Christian Science Monitor*, the *Ladies' Home Journal*, and other magazines as well as publishing two volumes of verse, *Modern Odyssey* (1971) and *Laugh Lightly* (1974). Engle has reasonable range in his style and subject matter, but nothing seems to appeal to him more than light verse. The dust jacket of *Laugh Lightly* describes his verse aptly enough in this way: "short, pointed, paradoxical in thought . . . humanly relevant, timely, and cleverly structured," often hinging upon paronomasia, or a slight changing of a key word. The following poem on morality in the good old days is an example:

It's not that we
were paragons
with virtue
unassailable,
it's just that then
so much sin
was simply
unavailable

A poet who received some attention during the 1970s is **Richard Taylor** (1941–), who has now published two volumes of verse: *Bluegrass* (1975) and *Earth Bones* (1979). Taylor's poetry is in the agrarian tradition and reveals the author's sense of close relationship to the land. Often it is at its best when in simple fashion he writes of simple things: mending a fence, sawing wood, planning a garden, a wild cherry tree, a pot-bellied stove, trees versus new subdivisions, the death of a relative.

Girty (1977), a narrative in prose and verse, deals with the Kentucky frontier white renegade Simon Girty, who at eighteen was adopted into the Seneca tribe and was a scout, trader, interpreter, and "white Indian" warrior who fought for the British during the Revolutionary War. Through a mélange of excerpts from actual diaries, quoted history, verse, fiction, and excerpts from an old historical romance, Taylor has devised effective passages and in the process has left a sense of the savagery of both the Indians and the whites on the frontier.

Taylor, who lives in Frankfort, has operated a bookstore, taught at Kentucky State University, been a poet-in-the-schools under the auspices of the Kentucky Arts Commission, 1973–1975, and in 1976 edited *Cloud Bumping: A Collection of Poems by Students in Kentucky Schools*. In the preface Taylor points out that adults take things for granted and lose their sense of wonder while "children, whose image of reality is not fixed, re-shuffle the deck for us. They revive our dulled senses. They restore wonder." Taylor held a National Endowment for the Arts fellowship in 1976–77.

Five other poets—all with roots in Appalachia—remain to be noted here.

Sylvia Trent Auxier (1900–69) was a vigorous, strong-spirited woman who rode horseback through Pike, Knott, Perry, and Leslie counties as a public health nurse and later taught school at Johns Creek High School. Her first volume, *Meadow-Rue*, was published in 1948 and was followed by *Love-Vine* (1953), *No Stranger of Earth* (1957), *The Grace of the Bough* (1958), *The Green of a Hundred Springs* (1966), and *With Thorn and Stone* (1969), posthumously. Perhaps the most familiar lines in Mrs. Auxier's verse are those in "Someday in a Wood," beginning, "Death never was a match for me . . . As Death and I rushed on headlong. . . ."

Lois Hiers (1910–) is the author of one volume of verse, *My House and My Country* (1958), published poems often in the *New York Times*, the *New York Herald-Tribune*, the *Christian Science Monitor*, the *Washington Evening Star*, *Lyric*, *Kaleidoscope*, and elsewhere. Her verse won a number of awards, including the Reynolds Lyric Award of the Poetry Society of America in 1954.

Lee Pennington (1939–) has written oftener on Appalachia than he has on any other subject. More prolific than disciplined, Pennington by 1975 reportedly had written seven hundred poems, ten thousand newspaper articles, fifty or more short stories, and half a dozen plays. A maverick as a teacher, writer, folksinger, and tale-teller, Pennington attracted some not wholly favorable attention while he was teaching at the Southeast Community College of the University of Kentucky in Harlan County. His teaching methods inspired a student publication called *Tomorrow's People*. The hard-hitting lines on coal mining, poverty, ignorance, stripmining, and pollution generated enough hostility in the community to cause him to move to Jefferson County, where he now teaches at the Community College. *Scenes from a Southern Road* (1969) was Pennington's first volume of verse. Its attention to people, places, and things is reminiscent of his early teacher, Jesse Stuart. Pennington's best volume—more even and more controlled than his earlier verse—is *I Knew a Woman* (1977).

Woodridge Spears (1913–), grew up in Greenup County, graduated from Morehead State College, received his M.A. and Ph.D. at the University of Kentucky, and took a teaching position in Georgetown College in 1953, where he remained until his retirement in 1978. *The Feudalist* (1946) was his first volume of verse. Here, as in his later poetry, Spears draws upon a sense of place as the source of much that he writes and of a region that he knows and understands. Often it is time in a framework of time long past. After *The Feudalist* came *River Island* (1963) and *Concord* (1975).

Charles Semones (1937–), born in Mercer County, graduated from Eastern Kentucky State University, and has taught in the public schools. At the time when *Witch Cry* (1973), his one volume of collected verse, appeared the author lived in the community where he was born. "It is the landscape there, both inviting and forbidding," as the preface observes, "which informs his imagination and affords the solitude in which his poetry is written."

As John Crowe Ransom has noted (see preface), "Semones' poems often reveal a despairing cast of mind," but also a poet in search of meaning, the ring of honesty, and firmness and clarity of language and imagery. The following lines from "The Sabbath Country" are representative:

> To grow old in that country was to hurt with idleness.
> We felt the creek turn cold. Our Sunday afternoons
> droned sad. Clouds loomed tall to northward and the dusk
> came early. We lighted lamps and counted secret guilts
> like old coins. We did not venture into darkened rooms
> or attics. For each of us, in time, a bed was made.
> The tender wives of our young manhood haunted us.
> We recalled the cries that terrified us when our sons were born.

CHAPTER 23

Children's Literature

In 1919 the Macmillan Company became the first publishing firm to establish a children's book department with its own editor, and in the same year Children's Book Week was inaugurated in order to encourage more reading by American children. In 1922 the American Library Association established the John Newbery Medal as an annual award for "the Most Distinguished Contribution to American Literature for Children." In 1924 the *Horn Book Magazine*, a very influential journal in the world of children's literature, began publication. During the 1920s there also came into being regular reviewers for children's books and reading lists for the guidance of librarians, teachers, and parents. In 1919, 433 new works for children appeared on the market; in 1928, 931. In the 1920s and 1930s technical innovations made possible experimentation in picture design and the format of books, and in 1938 the American Library Association established the Caldecott Medal for the best picture book of the year.

Such developments could but affect the number and quality of children's books. Just as Frank L. Baum's *The Wonderful Wizard of Oz* in 1900 became the first of his fourteen "modern" fantasies for children and paved the way for a new kind of American child's book, so other landmark volumes came during the 1920s and 1930s. In 1937 the Dr. Seuss books gave a new impetus to fantasy, followed by E.B. White's *Charlotte's Web* in 1952, and Maurice Sendak's stories such as *Where the Wild Things Are* in the 1960s. We cannot here name all of the important or significant books written for children in this period, but we must not fail to mention *The Little Engine That Could* (1930) and *Little Toot* (1939), two very human little machines that shore up the will and character of young readers. And there have been realistic stories, among them the Laura Ingalls Wilder's "Little House" stories (1932–43), Marjorie Rawlings's *The Yearling* (1938), and the Lois Lenski novels such as *Strawberry Girl* (1945).

During the last half-century Kentucky has not been in the forefront of the states producing the "best" or the "most popular" children's books; but many Kentucky productions have been better than "good," and some writers have carved out special niches for themselves. Furthermore, a few Kentucky authors not discussed here have written novels which appear on reading lists for high school students and young adults. These novels were not written with young people in mind, but their nature is such that, like John Fox, Jr.'s *Little Shepherd of Kingdom Come* in an earlier day, they are appropriate for young adults as well as older ones. Among these are Harriette Arnow's *The Kentucky Trace* (1974), a frontier–Revolutionary War story; Harry Caudill's *Dark Hills to Westward* (1969), a fictionalized account of the capture of Jennie Wiley by Indians and her ultimate escape; and any one of several of Janice Holt Giles's stories, such as *The Land beyond the Mountains* (1950), *The Kentuckians* (1953), and *Hannah Fowler* (1972)—all stories of the Kentucky frontier; *The Believers* (1957), a story of the Shaker community; and *Run Me a River* (1972), a story of the Civil War.

Biography is not included here as children's literature, though many excellent biographies for young people have been written. Katharine E. Wilkie (1904–80), of Lexington, has been a prolific writer of biographies of Kentucky figures such as Zachary Taylor, Mary Todd Lincoln, George Rogers Clark, Simon Kenton, Henry Clay, and Mary Breckinridge. More distinguished, however, is the one "children's book" that John Mason Brown (1900–69) wrote about Daniel Boone. When the critics reviewed this book about Boone and the opening of the wilderness, the adjectives they used were "fresh," "distinguished," and "superb." (Other authors of children's books are cited in the index under "Children's Literature.")

Rebecca Caudill

Rebecca Caudill (1899–1985), Mrs. James Ayars in private life, began her career as a writer relatively late in life. She was born in 1899 "on a rocky farm squeezed between the Black Mountains and the Poor Fork River in Harlan County," where both of her parents were teachers. At the age of four she moved with her family to Tennessee "in search of level land and better schools," but till her death more than eighty years later she proudly called herself an Appalachian and a Kentuckian even though after 1937 she lived in Urbana, Illinois, with her husband. From her first book, *Barrie & Daughter*, written in 1943, to her last ones in the 1970s—twenty-one in all—almost all have had their roots in Appalachia.

Her books focus on characters who are ordinary people doing ordinary things, but the stories are not told in commonplace fashion. Four of them achieve an excellence that sets them apart; two or three more are runners-up; and the rest reflect some of the skills that make Rebecca Caudill one of Kentucky's best writers of children's stories. *Barrie & Daughter*, an unusually good first novel, draws upon her early childhood memories of her father and the place where she grew up. It attracted favorable critical notice and was followed by other stories that dealt with life in Appalachia at the beginning of the century: *Happy Little Family* and *Schoolhouse in the Woods* in 1948 and 1949, and then *Up and Down the River* in 1951 and *Saturday Cousins* in 1953. In the last, for example, three Tuttle cousins visit three other Tuttle cousins every Saturday in a time when there was neither radio nor TV to provide entertainment. Instead, the children watched the train go by, listened to a talking machine, played the player piano, and slid down the banister on a quilt. *Schoolhouse in the Parlor* (1959) was a "Bonnie" story and was followed by *Time for Lissa* (1960), an orphan story with a difference, and *Higgins and the Great Big Scare* (1961), which "should delight any dog-lover."

All of these stories met with friendly receptions, but *House of the Fifers* (1954) and *Susan Cornish* (1955) won a place of distinction for Caudill. The first became an "Honor Book" on the *New York Herald Tribune*'s annual list and the latter won the Nancy Bloch Memorial Award in 1956 as the best juvenile book dealing with international relations. *Tree of Freedom* had been honored by being made No. 2 on the Newbery Medal vote for 1949. The story takes place in 1780 when the Venable family makes the long journey over the mountains from the Carolinas to Kentucky. Thirteen-year-old Stephanie Venable has brought with her an apple seed, just as her grandmother had carried an apple seed from France to Charleston. The tree she planned to grow was to be the symbol of the new life in the new land of promise in which in 1780 there were still Indians to contend with, land to be cleared, and houses and outbuildings to be built. Furthermore the Revolutionary War had not been left behind in the East, and the legality of land claims was in question. Caudill's excellence in treating such problems caused the *Saturday Review of Literature* (May 21, 1949) to declare, "This is a story that should have a long and prosperous career." In the mid-1960s Caudill's high degree of skill was again manifested when she published in successive years three of what are perhaps her four best volumes.

It is never easy to identify or describe the alchemy by which a better writer achieves the results a lesser writer fails to achieve. The subjects Rebecca Caudill chooses have been written about over and over with commonplace results by a host of writers, and often enough Caudill herself has achieved little more than others who have written on basically the same subjects. But sometimes she does, and herein lies the difference. Three stories in which she has done so are *A Pocket Full of Cricket* (1964), *A Certain Small Shepherd* (1965), and *Did You Carry the Flag Today, Charley?* (1966). Certainly there is nothing remarkable about a small boy who becomes emotionally attached to a cricket, a handicapped boy who is a shepherd in a Christmas pageant, or a school boy who wants to experience the honor of being selected to carry the flag. Yet in each case Caudill achieves the extraordinary, maintaining successfully the precarious balance between sentiment and sentimentality, between the believable and the far-fetched.

In *A Certain Small Shepherd*, little Jamie, a mute since birth, is able to speak for the first time in his life when he plays the role of a shepherd at the birth of a child and lays an orange beside the baby's hand. The event could be characterized as sentimental, but as a reviewer in the *New Yorker* noted (Dec. 4, 1965), "instead it is moving; it has a kind of charm and dignity because none of its points are stressed." The reviewer of *A Pocketful of Cricket* in the *New York Times Book Review* (Nov. 29, 1964) notes Caudill's success in making an unbelievable action believable: "A sweet apple, a yellow butterfly, a hickory nut . . . from such things Rebecca Caudill evokes an entire world." Thus a small, lonely farm boy makes a pet of the cricket which in the fall he takes to school in his pocket. When the cricket begins "to fiddle," the teacher copes with the disturbance by inviting the boy to "share" his pet with the class. "With magical simplicity," says the reviewer, "Miss Caudill tells the story of the farm child. . . . [It is] a modest tale, but such a compassionate one that it will strike a blow of nostalgia to the hearts of many grown-ups. To children, it will simply seem to be true."

In *Did You Carry the Flag Today, Charley?* the honor of being the one to carry the flag to the school bus at the end of the day eludes Charley Cornett because his curiosity about how rocks feel, why books in a library have their backs turned outside instead of their faces, and how a spigot works, somehow keeps him from being the best-behaved child in school that day. When Charley's chance does come, it is a double honor, for finally he has done everything right and got to carry the flag. The importance of the occasion to Charley, says the *Book Week* reviewer (Oct. 9, 1966) is successfully portrayed because Caudill brings her story to its end "without ever departing from Charley's own eager unsentimental view of the world."

Still to come was Caudill's nostalgic, nonfiction reminiscence, *My Appalachia* (1966); her tall-tale sort of book, *Contrary Jenkins* (1969); *Come Along* (1969), a volume of Haiku describing the four seasons; and *Wind, Sand, and Sky* (1976), a girl's statement of feeling for the land. Of Caudill's twenty-one volumes, seven have been Junior Literary Guild selections; and a *Pocket Full of Cricket* was a runner-up for the Caldecott Medal and was chosen in 1966 by the Hans Christian Andersen Award Committee as the American book to be recommended for translation into other languages. Caudill's books do not combine great artistry with great inventiveness as do *Alice in Wonderland, Charlotte's Web,* and *The Wind in the Willows,* but at her best she does enable her readers to view the ordinary world, may we say, without the encumbrance of the world-colored glasses of adults.

Rachel M. Varble

Rachel M. Varble (1893–1976) grew up in Shelby County, graduated from the Science Hill Academy in Shelbyville, and attended Eastern Kentucky State University and the University of Kentucky. Her writing career began while she lived in Shelby County and served as a *Courier-Journal* reporter for the area. She married Pinckney Varble III of Louisville in 1917 and subsequently moved to Ft. Mitchell. Here her career as a writer of children's stories flourished. She was buried in Cave Hill Cemetery in Louisville.

Mrs. Varble's forbears came to Kentucky from Virginia not long after the American Revolution, a fact which contributed to her interest in both American and English history. This interest, plus a talent for research, led her to write children's stories with their setting in a bygone time. The first, *The Red Cape* (1928), tells of the adventures of a twelve-year-old princess who fled from her country during a revolution, found a safe hiding place, and remained there until it was safe to return to her own country in triumph. In her next volume —*Marie of the Gypsies* (1931)—Varble tells the story of fourteen-year-old Marie, who has been adopted by the chief of a gypsy tribe. When Marie learns that she is not really a gypsy but the daughter of a French artist who traveled with the gypsies until his death, she runs away and is ultimately taken in by a kindly lady who has a collection of paintings by her father. The story is enriched by Varble's knowledge of gypsy ways and manners; but her next novel undertakes to expand the knowledge and horizons of her young readers even more. This was *Beatrice the Brave* (1934), which tells the story of the daughter of a weaver of tapestries in the reign of Charles V. Like Varble's first two stories, this one was well received.

With her fourth story, *Julia Ann* (1939), Varble moved into American and Kentucky history, gave the novel a strong biographical core, and told a true story about Kentucky that, though fictionalized, records the founding of Science Hill Academy in Shelbyville. The account is based on the memoirs of a real person and is the story of Julia Ann's childhood in Kentucky during the early 1800s through her marriage and the founding of the school. The portrayal of the historical period is solid, and the volume is characterized by the *New York Times* (Nov. 12, 1939) as "a fine book to put among the choice volumes of American biography."

Romance for Rosa (1946) reaches further back in history and again tells a story based on events that lead to Kentucky. This is a seventeenth-century story of an indentured servant, Rosa Wickliffe, who at the age of twelve sails from London to Virginia. Here she makes a place for herself, marries, and has indentured servants of her own. The author's remarks about descendants during the course of the story prompted Jean Howerton (*Courier-Journal*, Nov. 20, 1946) to pursue the subject and to report that even the most improbable parts of the story are based on fact—that two great-granddaughters of Rosa (who had married Tom Waters) married Wickliffes, from whom the Kentucky Wickliffes are descended.

In two novels Varble turns again to seventeenth-century England. *Pepys' Boy* (1956) and *Three against London* (1962) have as their background the London of Restoration England. The former grows out of references made by Samuel Pepys in his famous diary to a boy who worked for him. It is an exciting story that extends from the household of Pepys himself to the London waterfront, to a highway robbery, and to young William Penn. Well praised by the *Chicago Sunday Tribune*, the *Christian Science Monitor*, the *New York Times*, and the *Library Journal*, the novel, in the words of the last of these, "is an outstanding story of life in seventeenth-century England. . . . Its many improbable though not necessarily impossible situations, its hair-raising escapades and humorous incidents, will remain in the mind of the reader long after he has closed the book" (Feb. 15, 1956).

Three against London is also indebted to Pepys in that his serving maid, Susan Stokes, is one of the "three" referred to in the title. Like its predecessor, the story is full of excitement, and its setting ranges from the elegance of the Pepys household to the rough-and-tumble life of London.

Scarcely less warmly received was *Seth and Beth* (1961), a novel that returns to American and Kentucky history again. The action begins in 1836 and continues for a few years thereafter; the scene is first Maryland, then Pennsylvania and Ohio, and finally Kentucky, as Beth Counts and Seth McAdam travel west in a Conestoga wagon with Seth's uncle, Andrew McAdam, an ancestor of Varble and a distant kinsman of the man from whom macadamized roads got their name. As the three make their way in a covered wagon, Beth and Seth are constantly at odds, but despite some mishaps good fortune finally comes their way, leading Seth to propose marriage to Beth and be accepted and Mr. McAdam to become a construction commissioner on the National Road that was then being built through Kentucky.

Varble was also the author of two volumes for adults. The first was a novel, *A Time Will Come* (1941), dealing with the rights of women in the early 1900s; the other was a biographical account, *Jane Clemens: The Story of Mark Twain's Mother* (1964). Twain's mother, born Jane Lampton, grew up in Columbia, Adair County.

Billy Curtis Clark

A discussion of Billy Clark (1928–) may aptly begin with *A Long Row to Hoe* (1960), a narrative of reminiscences and perhaps Clark's best and most warmly received volume. His seventh published book and the story of his life through high school, it makes clear that the wellspring of his career was his background growing up in a semiliterate, impoverished home on the Big Sandy River near Catlettsburg. The volume tells of a ragged family living at the junction of the Big Sandy and the Ohio: an intelligent father, a shoemaker and a fiddle player, whose literacy was limited to signing his name and who told his son about poor people "having a hard row to hoe"; the mother, a laundress who played the piano and was so generous of heart, according to her husband, "She'd give away a chair with someone sitting in it"; and eight children. One of Clark's greatest regrets has always been that his parents were unable to read his books.

"In nineteen years of growing up in the valley, hunger was my most vivid memory and an education my greatest desire," Clark declares as he tells of how as a boy he trapped for muskrats, set trotlines, salvaged flotsam, and scrounged for whatever small sums of money he could get. It is not psychological scars, however, that Clark writes about but the learning and the lore that came from the rivers, the community, and the people who were a part of his growing up. In fact the the *Time* review of *A Long Row to Hoe* (July 25, 1960) concluded that Clark, "far from trying to forget his boyhood miseries . . . has dignified them through grit and awareness of the natural beauty around him." And the *San Francisco Chronicle* reviewer (Oct. 2, 1960) observed that Clark's reader "comes to the end of his book envious of his opportunity to have had such a wonderful childhood."

After graduating from high school—the point at which *A Long Row to Hoe* ends—Clark spent four years in military service during the Korean War and then entered the University of Kentucky in 1953. He tried to pay his way with the help of the GI Bill, carry on his studies, and do the writing that had been a compulsion even during high school days. Clark says that when he was enrolled in a writing class, "Hollis [Summers] recommended that I drop his class" on the grounds that, "You are the first natural-born writer I've ever met, and your writing is changing in class." But Clark insisted on completing the course, and as his works make evident, he managed to preserve his own way of looking at things and the distinctive characteristics of style and manner that in another writer might be called defects.

During his years as a college student Clark managed to publish *A Heap of Hills* (1956), a collection of stories, and to get ready for a burst of publication—five volumes during the next five years. One was *Song of the River* (1957), a novel he had written when he was a freshman in high school. It is the story of an aging man who lives in a shantyboat on the Big Sandy and whose aim in life is to catch a legendary great catfish known as Scrapiron Jack. The main thread of the story is reminiscent of Hemingway's *The Old Man and the Sea*, but what makes the novel distinctly Clark's own is his detailed portrayal of life on the river.

In The Trail of the Hunter's Horn (1957) a boy, Jeb, has worked long and hard to earn a pup of his uncle's wonderful hound, Lucy, and is bitterly disappointed when the pup turns out to be stub-tailed and blind in one eye. As the novel progresses, however, and in its sequel, *Mooneyed Hound* (1959), love between the boy and the dog replaces all other considerations, the animal shows prowess as a coon dog, and Jeb enters him in the annual trials for the best coon dog in Kentucky. Reviewers noted two qualities in these novels that make them something more than just juvenile stories about a boy and a pet. One is the author's sensitivity in developing the relationship between the boy and his dog; the other is his responsiveness to the rugged beauty of the land. "This book," says the *Saturday Review* of the first volume (Oct. 19, 1957), "has a quality of universality which makes it one of those stories which haunts the reader, no matter what his age. It is evident that Mr. Clark loves the hills and rivers and people about which he writes."

Riverboy was published in 1958 and was followed by *A Long Row to Hoe* and then by three more volumes that are characteristic of Clark at his best: *Goodbye, Kate* (1964), a story of a vagrant mule that becomes a community nuisance; *The Champion of Sourwood* (1966), which tells of an agreement whereby thirteen-year-old Aram Tate agrees to teach a wily woodsman, moonshiner, and cockfighter to read and write if the latter will get Aram a hound dog and teach him about "the varmints and the mountains"; and *Sourwood Tales* (1968), a collection of eighteen stories that picture life in the Big Sandy region during the Great Depression. In all these works Clark's sometimes extravagant yarns hold his stories together, but nothing perhaps equals the author's portrayal of local life and lore and his responsiveness to the surrounding natural beauty. The sounds of rustic music, the roughhewn and unsophisticated mountain and river characters, and the humor and pathos in human and life situations—these make Clark the chronicler of the Big Sandy region.

Martha Bennett Stiles

Martha Bennett Stiles (1933–), a Virginian with a University of Michigan degree in chemistry, became a Kentuckian in 1977 when with her family she moved to Bourbon County, where she still lives on a thoroughbred horse farm. She has published articles in such magazines as the *Thoroughbred Record* and the *Maryland Horse*; but it is her writings for children that we are concerned with here. *One among the Indians* (1962) was her first; *The Strange House at Newburyport* (1963) came a year later. Neither was widely noticed, but then came *Darkness over the Land* (1966), for which she received *The Horn Book Magazine* award for the notable children's book of the year.

As Hortense Flexner had portrayed with great success the impact on a French family and village of the Nazi invasion of France during World War II, so Stiles dealt with the impact of that war on a

German boy and family in Germany. Mark Elend is nine years old when the war begins. Thus at a very impressionable age he grows up constantly buffeted by the bewildering contradictions that exist between what his Nazi teachers tell him in school and what his parents say guardedly at home, what he hears from official government broadcasts and what he hears clandestinely on BBC programs, what he hears at youth meetings and what he gathers from remarks whispered by adults. Strong commendation for *Darkness over the Land* was general. "Believable and moving from the very first page," said *Book Week*; "it is monumental in its scope and terrible in its honesty . . . with a maturity that is lacking in most juveniles. . . . an enormously worthwhile book" (March 19, 1967). The *New York Times Book Review* was less enthusiastic, but the reviewer concluded that in spite of any shortcomings "this chronicle will give young Americans an idea of how it felt to grow up in the terror and twilight of Hitler's Germany" (Jan. 15, 1967).

During the next thirteen years Stiles wrote four more children's books: *Dougal Looks for Birds* (1972), *James the Vine Puller* (1975), *Tana and the Useless Monkey* (1979), and *The Star in the Forest* (1979). The first three are light and undemanding. *Dougal Looks for Birds*, for example, is a pleasant and useful book with bright-colored pictures of birds and a story that details some of the rudiments of bird-watching. It is calculated to delight small children because it is the boy, Dougal, who spots the great blue heron that his father is so anxious to see. And *Tana and the Useless Monkey* is often amusing because of the monkey Pepito's antics, while Tana, somewhere in a Spanish-speaking jungle, is finally successful in getting her monkey blessed as a "useful" animal.

The fourth of these volumes, *The Star in the Forest: A Mystery of the Dark Ages*, constitutes a marked change of pace as Stiles turns to a demanding subject. It is a historical novel with its scene in Gaul during the latter part of the sixth century after the Frankish barbarians have wrested control of the region from Rome. Designed for high school students, the novel is a rousing, headlong romance of love, intrigue, and murder, and the plot is filled with forebodings, omens, and dark spells that reflect pagan beliefs of the day. Such an abundance of exotic and spectacular subjects could constitute pitfalls for an unwary writer. Stiles has not escaped scot-free, but she has proved that she can cope with difficult materials of this sort and maintain her credibility.

Lillie D. Chaffin

Though Lillie D. Chaffin (1925–), who was born in Pike County and has spent most of her life there, is the author of at least five books for adults, her reputation rests principally on her children's books. No matter whether she is writing for adults or children, however, Appalachia is always at or near the center of her concerns.

Chaffin's first children's books to gain attention were nonfiction: *A Garden Is Good* (1963) and *I Have a Tree* (1969). For each of these she was awarded first prize by the National League of American Pen Women. She received more critical attention, however, for *Bear Weather* (1969), a volume of juvenile verse about a mother bear and her cub during their winter of hibernation:

> Sleeping through dark, sleeping through light
> They never knew the day from the night. . . .

The poem is a sort of mood poem rather than a narrative or story and is illustrated with round friendly bears and country landscapes. One reviewer characterizes the verse as "affectionate" and the illustrations as "cuddly." The *New York Times* selected *Bear Weather* as one of the fifteen best juvenile books of 1969.

John Henry McCoy (1971), a novel for the upper elementary school grades, also received favorable notices and won the 1971 Award of the Child Study Association for being "the best book for children or young people that deals realistically with some problem in their contemporary world." The story grows out of the lives of coal-mining families, where work is scarce and they drift from place to place, even to mid-western industrial cities, looking for a temporary job. This is what John Henry's mother and father have done, though John Henry has remained in Eastern Kentucky with his grandmother and, like her, wants to put down roots. There is not much action in the novel and no real resolution, but the plight of the poor in Appalachia is depicted effectively. The novel was nominated for the Newbery Award.

Chaffin is the author of more than fifteen children's books, all of them dealing with Appalachia in verse, fiction, or nonfiction. Of those not yet discussed, perhaps the best is *Freeman* (1972). Like *John Henry McCoy*, it deals with the problems of a boy and a family in coal-mining Appalachia. Freeman Sloan puzzles out the history of an old feud and the prolonged absence of his parents while he lives with his grandparents.

Chaffin's best-known works for adults are *A Stone for Sisyphus*

(1967) and *Lines and Point* (1968). Her anger rises quickly on such subjects as strip-mining and pollution. She resents, too, the mountain stereotypes that the public has come to accept and the commercialism that came in the wake of the "Great Society" days of the Johnson Administration during the 1960s and the subsequent cornshuck dolls on sale on Fifth Avenue. Tourists, she says, come to the mountains "in search of front porch washing machines, feuds, moonshine stills . . . unfriendly natives, pot-bellied children . . . barn-dance frolics, ecstatic preachers battling unadulterated sin." And, she adds, "They find what they're looking for, and much more. We lay it on." "Tourism in Appalachia" and "Old Timer to Grandchild" are representative of her hard-hitting methods.

George Ella Lyon

George Ella Lyon (1949–), a native of Harlan, has written a play (*Braids*, produced at Transylvania University), poetry (in *Prairie Schooner*, *Kentucky Poetry Review*, and elsewhere), and an article entitled "Contemporary Appalachian Poetry" (in *The Kentucky Review* 2, no. 2 [1981], 3–22). She has, however, attracted more attention as a writer of children's stories. Lyon graduated from Centre College and received her Ph.D. from Indiana University. She, her musician husband, and son live in Lexington, where she teaches at the Community College of the University of Kentucky.

Lyon's first children's book was *Father Time and the Day Boxes* (1985). Father Time, who wears a white linen suit and a blue tie but has a traditional white beard, sits in his time vault somewhere in the heavens and each day tosses earthward a time box, which as it falls billows out, covering the earth. There is something each day for everyone in the world and Father Time admonishes, "Help yourself to this day, but you can't come back for seconds." Not much happens in the beautifully illustrated volume, but there are interesting philosophical observations about time that give children something to think and talk about. Robert Andrew Parker is the illustrator.

The following year she published *A Regular Rolling Noah*, which is the story of a Kentucky mountain boy who has been hired to take care of the animals of a family moving from their mountain farm to Canada. *Father Time* was well received, but *A Regular Rolling Noah* evoked more enthusiasm from reviewers. Again the illustrations (by Stephen Gammell) are credited with adding charm and warmth to the story and "extending" the author's narrative: a stoic hen, a contented cow, a shiny red engine, a boxcar barnyard with a line for laundry, and the cheerful young hero attending to the livestock. The *School Library Journal* reviewer concludes his remarks by saying, "Author and artist combine their considerable skills in this tale of one boy's trip West that echoes the spirit of those involved in the Westward expansion" (Nov. 1986).

CHAPTER 24

Other Writers

The myriad details that coalesce to become literary history remain indifferent to the problems of the literary historian and not only resist being grouped under convenient and instructive headings but lead to such catchall headings as "Other Writers." Actually, of course, it is really too much to expect all authors to fit hand-in-glove under headings that are familiar to the student of literary history. In addition, some headings that are appropriate at the national level may not work at the state level, where the number of authors may be too small to warrant grouping. Of the writers who follow, Pati Hill and Jane Mayhall can be said to be in the *Catcher-in-the-Rye* tradition, but all the others seem to have little in common and hence are arranged in chronological order under the date of their first volume. For reasons not fully understood yet, it appears that after the 1950s it has become increasingly difficult to classify authors under the traditional (or other) headings of literary history.

Eleanor Mercein Kelly

Though Eleanor Mercein Kelly (1880–1968) began her writing career with stories and novels about Kentucky, she was born in Wisconsin and received her education in Washington, D.C. She came to Kentucky—Louisville—in 1901 when she married Robert Morrow Kelly, Jr., and there spent the rest of her life. Her first story, *Toya the Unlike* (1913), was a "charming trifle" about a Japanese girl in America. Three years later when she published the first of her novels about Kentucky, she showed improvement, but it was not until she wrote a trilogy about the Basque country in Spain that she did her best writing.

John Mason Brown. Photo courtesy of the *Courier-Journal*.

Kelly's first novel about Kentucky, *Kildares of Storm* (1916), is set in and around the grim old house of Storm in the foothills between the Bluegrass and the uplands. Before the story begins, the beautiful Kate Leigh has been carried away at seventeen by the dashing Basil Kildare. Basil turns out to be nothing more than a hard-drinking, hard-riding squire, but Kate bears him two daughters, falls in love with Dr. Benoit, a gentle, sensitive man, sees her husband come to

A. B. Guthrie, Jr. Photo courtesy of the *Courier-Journal.*

a violent death, and witnesses Benoit's unjust conviction and life imprisonment as Kildare's murderer. The story which follows tells how Kate Kildare, a strong, dynamic woman with two daughters almost arrived at womanhood, brings the daughters to maturity and succeeds in finding fitting husbands both for them and herself. Though lacking in depth and significance, the story has vitality, and the action moves swiftly and with dramatic effect. The author also reveals a talent for characterization and the creation of atmosphere.

The scene of Kelly's second novel about Kentucky, *Why Joan?* (1918) is Louisville, and the time is just before and during World War I. The central character is Joan Darcy, and the action involves her choosing among three suitors. Again Kelly has written a readable novel designed particularly for female readers. The pictures of Louisville society among the "good families" are well done, and there

Elizabeth Hardwick. Photo courtesy of the *Courier-Journal*.

is deftness in the author's creation of atmosphere and her portrayal of character. But again significance is lacking and the motivation is weak. *The Mansion House*, the last novel in the Kentucky trilogy, tells the story of Judith, an orphan, and her rearing in the ancestral "Treaty Oak," the Mansion House. The novel excels in the atmo-

Thomas Merton. Photo by Ralph Eugene Meatyard. Courtesy Thomas Merton Studies Center.

sphere it evokes, has excellent individual scenes, and reads well. Like the earlier novels, too, it received favorable attention and won a substantial reading audience.

These three novels provided a sort of apprenticeship through which Kelly came to her best novels, another trilogy, the scene this time being the Basque country. No doubt Kelly's interest in the subject was whetted by the fact that on her father's side her forbears came from the region of the Pyrenees along the French-Spanish border and were of Basque origin. As preparation Kelly went to the Basque country and studied the region and the people, their customs and way of life. In the *Saturday Evening Post* in 1926 she published her first stories on the subject and in 1927 *Basquerie*, the first and best of her Basque novels. A favorable critical response and a large reading audience were immediate. Not every review was as unrestrained as the one in the *New York Times*, but all expressed pleasure and delight. Said the *New York Times Book Review* (Nov. 27, 1927): "It is almost impossible to praise it too extravagantly. It is a book to read and to reread, to close with regret and to reopen with enthusiasm, to tell one's friends about, to cherish always." The novel so caught the public interest that not only did babies, dogs, and country-houses get their names from it but even millinery-shops, dress fabrics, and tea-rooms. The novel was made into a movie in 1931.

Basquerie's hero is a dashing, romantic character named Esteban Urruty. The love interest is provided by the frivolous but winning Emily Weldon, an American girl seeking a wealthy husband who finds her true love in Esteban. Several characters are romantic stereotypes: the wealthy hero disguised as a poor man, the strong-willed heroine tamed by the dominating man, and the frivolous wife ennobled by the rearing of children. No character in the novel, perhaps, is more interesting than Mme. Urruty, Esteban's grandmother, the formidable matriarch who rules her tribe with an iron hand. Fully as interesting as the characters, however, is the Basque country background and the depiction of quaint ways and old-time customs.

Kelly continued to publish magazine stories about the Basque people for the next fifteen years; she also produced two more Basque novels in fairly quick succession: *The Book of Bette* (1929) and *Nacio: His Affairs* (1931). The former is the story of Esteban's younger sister Bette and includes, along with some false starts, her betrothal and marriage to a proper husband in the Basque tradition. The latter is about Esteban's younger brother, Nacio, and the harmless and amusing affairs he has, no one of which leads to marriage. Neither novel is up to the level of *Basquerie*, but both were popular with readers. Kelly wrote to entertain and to amuse. Her flair is for the romantic and her predilection is for happy endings. Her Basque novels are not intended to probe deep into the Basque character and soul. On the other hand, she gives insight into Basque customs and ways and the picturesque world in which they live. Furthermore, she does this in charming fashion with a light touch that is appropriate to her optimistic outlook.

Kelly took many trips abroad, and, as she put it, "I didn't go to foreign parts looking for stories, but stories came out of my trips." *Spanish Holiday* (1930) grows out of her travels in Spain, *Arabesque* (1933) out of Moorish Africa and Syria; *Sounding Harbors* (1936) has the Dalmatian Coast of Jugoslavia and the Island of Corfu as its scene; and *Mixed Company* (1936) divides its time primarily among Poland, Hungary, and Italy. Though by no means the equal of the Basque novels, these are very readable, for the author is a good storyteller with a knack for describing a country and its people.

It was fourteen years before Kelly wrote another novel, *Richard Walden's Wife* (1950). Drawing upon the experiences of her own grandparents, it tells a story of pioneer days in Wisconsin just before and during the Civil War. Her last novel, *Proud Castle* (1951), grew out of a trip she made to Hungary the year before World War II began, but it is different from earlier stories about exotic places, for the Europe she knew and had written about before the war no longer existed. *Proud Castle*, therefore, is about the departed splendors and the customs and culture of "the Magyars, one of the saddest places behind the Iron Curtain."

Ben Lucien Burman

Ben Lucien Burman (1895–1984) was Kentucky's premier writer of fiction about rivers and boats and the people who work on them. Covington was his birthplace and boyhood home and the place where he became fascinated by the riverboats he saw on the Ohio and by the rivermen he saw on the waterfront and on the streets. His love affair with the people he was to spend his life writing about, however, was reinforced by a later event, so that one can say that Burman's life career really began in 1929 when he was thirty-four. This was after he had been a journalist, had been seriously wounded in World War I, and had come back to Lookout Heights, a suburb of Covington, for recuperation and to find a place where he could think about what he was going to do with his life. It was after he had tried his hand at short stories and detective fiction; had written some Kentucky mountain ballads and an article on Kentucky for the *Nation*; had married Alice Caddy (1927), who was to be his illustrator and almost constant companion for the fifty years she was to live. The big event of 1929 came when he and his wife signed on with the "Tennessee Belle" at Natchez as roustabout and cook. The rest of Burman's life was spent in writing about the river and the people he increasingly came to love.

An interesting array of unusual river characters appears in his picaresque-like novels. Some readers and critics complain that Burman's books are too gentle and too sweet and that, in spite of a certain kind of realism in both his selection of characters and his portrayal of them, they ignore the seamy and criminal aspects of the world he writes about, that there is no penetrating analysis and no earnest search for meaning. Indeed, it must be said that seldom does he allow anything very bad to happen; nor does he delve into the darker side of the social structures he chose to represent. He prefers to portray a gentle world and to write from a kindly frame of reference. His characters have their faults, but they are childlike faults, and Burman has chosen to view them understandingly and in the context of the needs they grow out of. He is not unaware of evil, but that is not what he is writing about.

Mississippi (1929) was the first of Burman's "river books." During the next fifty years he wrote seventeen more that dealt in part or as a whole with river life and river people. Some are concerned exclusively with the Mississippi, and almost all of them make some use of it, but some are also set on the Kentucky and the Ohio. *Mississippi* is the story of a feud between Captain Lilly, a steamboat owner and pilot, and the shantyboat people who live on the river where his boat operates. *Steamboat Round the Bend* (1933), Burman's most famous novel, is the story of a gentle couple: Miss Robbie, who paints china and dresses in the fashion of a bygone time, and Doctor Jim, who lives on a shantyboat and sells herb remedies so that he can buy a steamboat. *Blow for a Landing* (1938) is the story of Willow Joe, a riverman who can make music on a plate or a cigarbox and aspires to play the calliope on a showboat. Burman's popularity was growing, so that even before *Big River to Cross* (1940) he had won the reading audience that publishers had insisted did not exist. *Big River to Cross* is a sort of anecdotal account of various types of riverboats: packets, showboats, shantyboats, barges, steamboats. Then came the interruption of World War II and the publication of some non-river volumes, though the river books never ceased. *Children of Noah,* in 1951, is a series of narrative essays on Burman's adventures among fishermen, steamboaters, shantyboat dwellers, and showboat thespians. And last came *Look Down That Winding River* (1978), a sort of account of life on the Mississippi during the 1920s, 1930s, 1940s.

Such are Ben Lucien Burman's works about boats and boat people. Though not profound books, they are not devoid of meaning. As a matter of fact, Burman repeatedly insists, "The theme of every book I have written is the child-likeness of all humanity. We are all children, groping our way through life, we know not how, seeking the Holy Grail." The Grail for Doctor Jim in *Steamboat Round the Bend*, he says, "happened to be a steamboat," and in order to get one he became a seller of Indian herb medicine. In *Blow for a Landing* another good river man, Willow Joe, achieves his life's goal by becoming the calliope player on a showboat. Not a high ambition, perhaps, but all things are relative, and for Willow Joe it was the one thing that gave point to his life. For Little Doc in *The Rooster Crows for Day* (1945) the goal is again a simple one: after much travel and many experiences in Africa's Congo, the red-headed Mississippi River pilot finally wends his way homeward, where at last he realizes his dream of being a member of the Cotton Valley Booster's Club. In *Everywhere I Roam* (1949) Captain Asa, a Kentucky mountaineer, is every man who ever tried to realize his dream of a better life, even if the dream came late and the search for a place "where people's still nice, and living the way they used to do" is a futile one. The world that this little man of the back country has lost has been destroyed by industrialization, by "progress" in the form of coal mines, steel mills, juke boxes, pool rooms, and cosmetics. In his search Captain Asa crosses rivers and hills and rolling farmlands; he travels swamp roads, goes into roadside cabins, visits great cities, sees the unsightliness of an oil boom town, experiences the weather in all seasons, and sees beauty as well as ugliness. He never finds the place where "people's living the way they used to do," but he has nevertheless learned from experience and has gained wisdom. In *The Four Lives of Mundy Tolliver* the principal character is again a native of the Kentucky Cumberlands. "I keep trying to figure things out," Mundy says, "about being lonesome, and what makes people happy, and why some people's got money and some ain't." Again the searcher is an adult who, in childlike manner, is groping his way toward his place in life. His four lives—on a towboat, as a partner in a store on wheels, as a timber-cutter and moonshiner, and as a shrimp fisherman—constitute the four episodes upon which the search and the structure of the novel depend. His native Cumberland hills, timber-cutting, moonshining, mountain jails, construction jobs, flood camps on the levee, Cajun country, and swamps constitute the parts of his learning experience. In the end he seems to find contentment with Essie, whom he had loved but thought he had lost. The "four lives" of Mundy Tolliver and Little Doc's experience "on the water, in the jungle, and on the desert" may seem to suggest symbolic or mythic levels in the characters' search and some sort of progressive refining process, but the author keeps the search at the level of the characters' perception. He pretends to no philosophical profundity, but simply follows Doctor Jim, Captain Asa, Little Doc, and Mundy in their search for happiness and dignity of spirit.

Two more of Burman's works give some attention to showboats: *Big River to Cross* (1940) and *Children of Noah* (1951). The former focuses on the kinds of boats that go up and down the big rivers of central United States and the roles they play. Like *Children of Noah*, it devotes one chapter to showboats. The structure and appearance of showboats are discussed, as are programs, the actors, bill-posters, calliopes, and a wide range of topics related to showboating. "There are," says Burman, "five large showboats on the inland rivers today," and he names them and writes of their masters and their areas of operation. By the time of *Children of Noah* only one showboat was left on the rivers: the "Goldenrod," tied up as a dinner theater at St. Louis, and nightly offering typical showboat fare. Giving his attention to the master of the "Goldenrod," Captain Bill Menke, "who for fifty years made theatrical history," Burman touches on almost every aspect of a showboatman's experience.

Other volumes of a very different character grew out of Burman's experiences as a war correspondent in Africa during World War II. He was the first writer to reach the Free French capital in Brazzaville after the French collapse and the first to send his historic cables exposing Petain and the Vichy government. For this and subsequent services while attached to the French and the British Eighth Army he was decorated with the French Legion of Honor. The first book to come out of this experience was *Miracle on the Congo* (1942), which is principally concerned with politics, Petain's life in Brazzaville, and Burman's (and his wife's) journey across Africa to find General Le Clerc and his camel troops in the Lake Tchad country, and later to Cairo, Syria, and Suez. A novel, *The Rooster Crows for Day* (1945), portrays the beauty and menace of Africa, but this time Burman is back to paddlewheels, as Little Doc, a Mississippi River pilot, seeks adventure on the Congo. *The Street of the Laughing Camel* (1959) is a quixotic trip along the coast and through the heart of Africa, with Yance Cullum merrily skirting the edge of disaster after disaster.

Burman's novels have won a warm spot in the hearts of many readers. They have also won honors aplenty. *Steamboat Round the*

Bend was made into a very successful movie starring Will Rogers; *Blow for a Landing* was awarded the Southern Authors Prize for most distinguished work; *The Rooster Crows for Day* won the Thomas Jefferson Memorial Award; *The Street of the Laughing Camel* was produced by the Theatre Guild; and *It's a Big Country* (1956) and *It's a Big Continent* (1962) were both book club selections.

The fourth and last stage of Burman's career as an author was his children's books. As a young man he was a journalist, did some writing in American folklore and Kentucky ballads, and tried his hand pseudonymously (Burton L. Benham) at detective fiction. Then came the stage that brought him fame in the 1930s and 1940s. The 1950s witnessed another and even greater turn in the direction of Burman's writing, for it was in 1952 that he published the first of his Catfish Bend stories for young people. The seventh and last was published thirty-two years later, three months before Burman's death at the age of eighty-eight.

Burman's Catfish Bend stories blend an interest in rivers that traces back to his birthplace in Covington and a tradition of animal stories and beast epics that reaches back to Greece and Aesop around 600 B.C. and comes down through European beast fables to the present. Doubtless the best-known example in the United States has been the Uncle Remus stories of Joel Chandler Harris. All such stories have animals as characters and can generally be read at two levels: at the adventure level for children and at the level of satire—usually gentle—for adults.

Burman's Catfish Bend is a mythical village in a swampy bend of the lower Mississippi River not far from Baton Rouge. In fact, the fame of the fictional place and the endless inquiries by tourists at filling stations along the Mississippi River led the Baton Rouge Chamber of Commerce to seek Burman's help in selecting the precise place along the river bank to be designated officially on a marker as Catfish Bend. As a result a river light near Baton Rouge has been named in Burman's honor by the Lighthouse Service of the U.S. Coast Guard and an official historical marker erected bearing the essential information.

Doc Raccoon is the mayor of Catfish Bend, the leader of the community, and the link between the other members of the community and the human reporter of events, the author. Judge Black is the gentle, vegetarian black water-snake who is trying to live down the bad reputation that snakes have. These two are the central characters, but there are also J.C., the sporty fox, who is a sort of smart-aleck; the silly, giggling rabbit, who is given to unfinished rhymes; and the pessimistic frog, who conducts the Indian Bayou Glee Club. These were the original animals, but as story was added to story new animals were added—good guys and bad guys—eagles and crows, a one-eyed rapscallion fox and a gang of wharf rats, moles, minks, fire-ants, a Sherlock Holmes sort of bloodhound, and an army of tough tomcats. In the first volume (*High Water at Catfish Bend*, 1952) the reader learns of beginnings, of the need for levees, of the pact of the animals, and of how the mayor of New Orleans was too busy with Mardi Gras and everybody else too unconcerned with flood control to build the levees. As a result, Doc Raccoon says, it was the animals, not the farmers, who went to New Orleans and by trickery got the levees built. The next six volumes deal with the problems and crises that confront Catfish Bend as time passes. Just as the first deals with the problem of flood control, so the second (*Seven Stars for Catfish Bend*, 1956) deals with the crisis created when the state turns the Catfish Bend area over to a hunt club, which almost destroys the animal sanctuary before the devastation is stopped. The third story (*The Owl Hoots Twice at Catfish Bend*, 1961) perhaps received more attention than any of the other six. It tells how the gray fox, with the assistance of the storm-trooper wharf rats, virtually becomes the dictator over the whole community.

In these three stories, as in all the others, there is the narrative, or adventure, appeal to children; at the same time there is the satiric humor that is apparent to the more sophisticated reader. As each story adds animals to the fictional world, that world becomes more complex in its social and political structure. In the first volume the satiric thrusts are largely at government, but by the time of *The Owl Hoots Twice*, propaganda, demagoguery, social change, tenement housing, and (by inference) racial bias have become targets. By the time the other four volumes have been published (*Blow a Wild Bugle for Catfish Bend*, 1967; *High Treason . . .* , 1977; *The Strange Invasion . . .* , 1980; and *Thunderbolt . . .* , 1984), the killer-coyote with his slogan of "Coyotes are the Super-Race" has hypnotized the animal world for a while, the young animals have become disenchanted with their bucolic life and go off to California for a period, some young upstarts rebel against the oldsters, and some of the oldsters travel the world as hitchhikers and stowaways looking for a friendly and better place to live.

In short, the more the animals develop their world into greater complexity, the more like the human world their world becomes and the more like human beings they themselves become. As anyone who knows Burman's other writings would expect—and as in general is true in beast fables—the satire and the humor at the expense of the human race is gentle. Burman sees the foibles and the stupidities of the world around him, but he is too understanding of human beings to carry a reformer's banner or consign the world to perdition.

Burman's animal stories—like his stories of real people on the rivers—are not for everybody, but they have reached an astonishingly large audience the world over. It has been estimated that sixteen million copies of the Catfish Bend stories have been sold in English and the ten languages into which they have been translated: German, French, Italian, Spanish, Urdu, Vietnamese, Thai, Burmese, Polish, and Czechoslovakian. As another measure of their success, *High Water at Catfish Bend* won the New York Public Library's prize as its favorite children's story of the year and the international first prize at the German People's Book Festival. *Seven Stars for Catfish Bend* was the choice of four book clubs, and leading Puppeteer Luo Bunin has made *The Owl Hoots Twice at Catfish Bend* into a movie. The Walt Disney Studios have plans for a feature-length picture of the Catfish Bend characters, and the makers of the game "Scrabble" have produced the "Catfish Bend Storybook Game." The remarkable success that these stories have had has no doubt been due in part to the excellent drawings of Burman's wife, Alice Caddy.

Sarah Litsey

Sarah Litsey Nye (1903–) writes under her maiden name. She was born in Springfield but moved to Louisville with her family in 1912. After graduating from Radcliffe College, she taught for one year at Mary Baldwin College and then for almost a decade at Atherton High School in Louisville. In 1933 she married Frank W. Nye and moved with him to Redding, Connecticut, where she still lives. Like her father, Edwin Carlile Litsey, she writes both verse and fiction.

From her early years Litsey published poetry in magazines. In the mid-1930s, before turning to fiction, she published two volumes of verse, a narrative poem, *Legend*, privately published in 1936, and *For the Lonely*, in 1937. It was, however, a novel, *There Was a Lady*, published in 1945 that caught the attention of a wider audience and of the reviewers. The novel tells the story of a small Kentucky town to which, just before World War II, two strangers come, one—a tobacco agent—an older man; the other—a beautiful young lady—who lives with him as his housekeeper. The town never comes to know much about them, but the lady, Miss Cammy, through her intelligence, her helping hand, her civic enterprises, and her music, wins a place for herself. In time, however, unfounded rumor brings the ostracism of the town down upon her, but she weathers this as she has weathered other gossip and criticism. Litsey is at her best when with a light stroke she portrays the foibles of the town, characterizes the local "Bach Circle," and depicts the attitudes and decorum of small town life. Unfortunately the novel, despite its merits, loses some of its effectiveness because of melodrama and sentimentalism.

Intimate Illusions (1955), Litsey's second novel, also has a small Kentucky town setting. The principal characters are Joseph Revington, a successful merchant, and his daughter Josephine. When Josephine was born and her mother died in childbirth, Joseph was prepared to hate his daughter, for he had been determined that the child should be a boy. But as Josephine grows up in the image of her father, a close bond develops between the two, leading the father to neglect his other two children and threatening Josephine's self-fulfillment as she pushes aside from childhood to middle age the normal life she should have lived. On her father's death, Josephine is left the family home and store but is unfulfilled and rudderless. When Frederick Marbrey, the only man Josephine was ever attracted to, moves next door with his alcoholic wife, it brings disaster for her. The novel has considerable merit but is weakened by a conclusion that does not live up to the first three-fourths of the story.

Litsey's third novel, *A Path to the Water* (1962), attracted less attention than had her first two. In it she chooses as the setting a wealthy, sophisticated suburban community in Connecticut. Here she is concerned with the erosion of meaning and values in the lives of young people as a result of the amoral lives of their elders.

Sarah Litsey published another volume of verse, *The Oldest April*, in 1957. Here as elsewhere in her writing she deals often with nature and with her native Kentucky, for which she had never ceased to maintain a warm affection. Frequent too in her musings are lines on her father and her childhood reminiscences. Representative are these lines from the title poem, "The Oldest April":

> I remember the oldest April;
> Thinking of a peeled sapling switch with the grace of a girl
> And the feel of a pebble I once closed into my hand
> And a plum tree that I knew that bloomed one night
> And trembled standing between me and the moon.
> For each of these there is a song I made

Long ago on the green hill of childhood.
Only for the plum tree I made no song
Because it was too beautiful.
Even in a child's heart it is like that.

Toward Mystery (1975) is Litsey's last volume of verse. As the title suggests, she has become more concerned with abstract subjects than she was in her earlier verse—with the mystery of being, of death, and the unknown. The first section, called "Words for Kentucky," deals with her recollections of childhood. The poems that follow are concerned with the broader experiences of adulthood and the mystery of life and the future life.

Willie Snow Ethridge

"Informal-essay-autobiographical" books qualify only marginally as a literary genre to be included in this study, but such is the merit of those by Willie Snow Ethridge and so much were they read and delighted in during the 1940s in and out of Kentucky that their omission could only be an offense against the literary history of the state. Ethridge (1900–82) was the author of fifteen books, among them two novels and a biography, but the ones for which she will be remembered longest reflect the life she lived day by day. Like her distinguished husband, Mark Ethridge, she was born in Georgia and lived in Louisville for twenty-eight years while Mr. Ethridge was publisher of the *Courier-Journal* and the *Louisville Times*. She finished out her life in North Carolina via New York, where Ethridge edited *Newsday* for two years, and Chapel Hill, where he taught in the School of Journalism at the University of North Carolina until he retired the third time at the age of seventy, and he and Mrs. Ethridge built a house near Moncure.

Ethridge published her first volume the year after the Ethridges arrived in Louisville in 1936. This was *As I Live and Breathe*, which grew out of her experiences while she and her husband lived in Georgia and she was occupied with being the wife of a newspaperman, raising a family, and generally living the full days of a homemaker. In the words of one reviewer, "Here is a rare book. And, one may say, so simple. Just an everyday record . . . No plot. No problem. No tragedy. No argument. . . . But by and large this book ought to bring joy to almost any family" (*New York Times*, March 7, 1937). *Mingled Yarn* (1938), a novel of protest about the textile mills in Georgia, was next; then came *I'll Sing One Song* (1941), a successor in kind to her first volume. By now the Ethridges had four children, and it is about them, her "room mate," her house and garden, and her and her family's social and personal activities, that Ethridge wrote. "Anyone," says the *Christian Science Monitor* (June 21, 1941), "who has ever been a hostess, or tried to be; who has ever tried to skate on ice, taken up a movie camera, made a wild flower garden, had a baby, hired a plumber, tried to keep peace in the family, owned a dog, or ridden a horse will have a fellow-feeling with the author." In *This Little Pig Stayed Home* (1944) come the war years in the life of a housewife coping with the problems of the home front: wartime scarcities, gas rationing coupons, war bond drives, food rationing cards, victory gardens, and the rest. "It was time," one reviewer says, "that somebody came right out and said being a civilian isn't all beer and skittles."

After the war Ethridge adapted her talent for writing to a new set of conditions. Beginning in 1947 her husband went on three missions to troubled areas in the world to represent the state department: to Bulgaria, Rumania, and Russia, to Greece, and to Israeli and Arab trouble spots; and later to the Middle East as a representative of the Ford Foundation. Mrs. Ethridge went along and recorded her impressions in books whose characteristic titles suggest the contents and tone: *It's Greek to Me* (1948), *Going to Jerusalem* (1950), *Let's Talk Turkey* (1955), *Russian Duet* (1959), and *There's Yeast in the Middle East* (1963). Of the first, the *Christian Science Monitor* (Feb. 4, 1948) declares, "It is the fourth book heralding the intimate misadventures of Willie Snow Ethridge [whose] three previous books have already identified her as a vital new name in American humor . . . also as one of journalism's able women reporters." Of the second another reviewer says that it is "a painless introduction to a painful problem"—to, that is, the Arab-Israeli problem.

These volumes were generally well received both for what they had to say and for their way of saying it. Some critics—like some readers—did think Ethridge was sometimes "cloyingly cute" and sometimes guilty of oversimplifying a complex problem. Despite such complaints, however, and the annoyance her style and manner were to some readers, Ethridge had a loyal and substantial following. Some found her writing both "informative and diverting"; others felt that in spite of the "gay and flippant style" the reader was not put off but read right through to the last chapter; her casualness, says another, is deceptive—she is a "more perceptive observer than she would have you believe."

After these volumes Ethridge returned to the kind of writing with which she made her debut: *I Just Happen to Have Some Pictures* (1964) and *You Can't Hardly Get There from Here* (1965); but the temper of the times had changed and the response was not as warm as it had been in the 1940s. In 1971 she wrote *Strange Fires: The True Story of John Wesley's Love Affair in Georgia* and in 1972 *Summer Thunder*, a historical novel dealing in the main with James Oglethorpe; but neither volume was really successful. In 1973 she returned again to the old manner in *Side by Each*, her last book, which tells of her and her husband's retirement in 1963 and the road to Moncure, North Carolina, where they built a house. *Side by Each* includes the building of the house, the taming of fifty acres of sandhills seven miles from Moncure, and other experiences of the Ethridges' later years. At last, Mrs. Ethridge says, Mark "is really retired and I find it perfectly delightful to have a man around the house. Mark knows how to spell and I don't. He knows a lot and what he doesn't know he makes up."

Ann Steward

Ann Steward (1898–), born in Cincinnati, published her first novel when she was forty-two. Between the time when she graduated from the University of Michigan and began writing fiction, she worked on a newspaper, acted in and wrote plays for the Theatre Workshop in Cincinnati, wrote stories, poems, and plays for children, and did social work. During this period Steward kept longing to own a farm "across the river" in Northern Kentucky. Eventually she and her husband bought a farm, which they named "Skyfields," near Hebron, in Boone County, and began living there in 1935 except for the severest months of the winter. This farm gives point and meaning to Steward's two novels, *Let the Earth Speak* (1940) and *Take Nothing for Your Journey* (1943), which are deeply concerned with the relationship of humankind to the land. Both are kin to the legend of Anteaus and to the notion that strength and healing can be drawn from renewed contact with the earth.

Let the Earth Speak tells how the Jarrell family, sophisticated city people whose lives are weary and somewhat shattered, have been sent by the owner to his farm called Hayes El in search of healing. Arriving in March, "the real beginning of the year in the country," the Jarrells spend the next twelve months on the land. Such a back-to-the-soil plot is, of course, commonplace, but *Let the Earth Speak* tells more than a commonplace story. The Jarrells observe the cycle of the seasons and see how each in turn brings life and death in the universe of things. Through a neighbor, Zayda, they learn of "Old Hayes" and how he had created the land on the estate from a barren nucleus of a few acres, how he had lived to be almost a hundred years of age, and how even in death, almost as if he were an earth-god, he still dominated the land that has passed to his nephew. Other neighbors and the land and its living things contribute to the Jarrells' heightened experience, leaving them strangely changed by the time March comes again.

Only a reading of the novel can enable one to understand how Steward, through her poetic and sometimes difficult style and through her handling of her materials, creates an atmosphere that broods over the land and heightens the reality of Old Hayes and his mystic kinship with the earth. *Take Nothing for Your Journey* uses the same scene and characters as *Let the Earth Speak*. The core of the book is still the fate of the Hayes land. Like its predecessor, the volume is difficult reading, the style elaborate and sometimes extravagant, and the characters, the mood, and the story tantalizing and elusive. The reviewer in the *New York Times* says it best: "Ann Steward will not be a popular author . . . but she undoubtedly will attract and hold a small critical audience. Those caught by the rhythm and mysticism of her expression will return to rereading her pages as to a volume of poetry. The meaning is there, clothed in language that betrays it only to the ear attuned to its truth and the heart willing to accept it. Perhaps this is asking too much of readers who turn to a novel only for story. This book is not for them but for those who do not run while they read, for those who can enter a world of enchantment unmarked by time" (Oct. 13, 1940).

Gwen Davenport

Gwen Leys Davenport (1910–60) was born in the Canal Zone, where her father, Vice-Admiral James F. Leys, was stationed with the U.S. Navy. As she grew up, she lived at various naval ports and in England. She received her A.B. from Vassar College in 1931 and took a job as an advertising and publicity copywriter in New York City. In 1937 she moved to Louisville on her marriage to John Andrews Davenport, a business executive.

Davenport's first published volume was *A Stranger and Afraid* (1943), a wartime spy novel written in collaboration with Gustave Bruerer. Her second, no doubt reflecting the theatrical interest she had shown in college, was *Return Engagement* (1946), about a world-famous actress who in her old age comes back to the Maine coast where she was born and scandalizes the neighborhood with the unconventional way she lives. But it was *Belvedere* (1947), Davenport's third novel, that brought her fame.

The reviews of Belvedere were mostly neutral, with the principal exception of the *Saturday Review of Literature* (June 21, 1947), which found it "witty, warm, and loving." A full appreciation of *Belvedere* requires that the reader understand that the action takes place during World War II when almost every qualified male was in military service, and that others—including many females—were employed in essential wartime jobs. As a result, domestic help was almost impossible to find. Under such circumstances Harry and Tacey King, parents of three small children, in desperation advertise in a literary magazine for a resident babysitter in their Hummingbird Hill home in Louisville. When the "mother's helper," who is to launder diapers, prepare formulas, fix lunches, wash dishes, set tables, shop for war-rationed foods and supplies, arrives, however, it is Lynn Belvedere, a man whose objective in life is to write the great American novel. Furthermore, he hates children and has a low opinion of marriage and the home. Best-seller lists, Hollywood, and Broadway claim his attention, and though he likes nothing about his duties, he is willing to tolerate them in return for being well housed and well fed. *Belvedere* was made into a movie the next year under the title of *Sitting Pretty*, with Clifton Webb as Belvedere and Robert Young and Maureen O'Hara as Harry and Tacey King. So successful was the motion picture that the novel won renewed attention and came out in a paperback edition. Davenport would not again achieve such a degree of celebrity, but her name would no longer be unknown.

In *Family Fortunes* (1949) Simon and Hattie Brackenwood are living in the ancestral Bluegrass mansion built in Revolutionary times. Unable to bear the expense of so great a structure, they live mostly in the kitchen during cold weather because they cannot afford to heat the other innumerable rooms. Just as they are about to sell enough furnishings and land to move into a comfortable little cottage, Martha, Simon's sister and the guardian of family tradition, at the urging of outraged antiquarians, begins serving meals to tourists and opens the doors of the mansion so people from all over the country can see its wonders. The peeping and the prying as these tourists view the place where Henry Clay and Zachary Taylor slept, see the fine furniture and staircases, look at the Jouett portraits and rare books, and learn of the ballad that tells of a family tragedy, are the materials upon which Davenport draws for the humor and gay-hearted satiric thrusts that characterize the novel.

In *Candy for Breakfast* (1950) the more lunatic aspects of Progressive Education are Davenport's targets, each represented by a character of her invention. *The Bachelor's Baby* (1958) depends less on satire and more on humorous situations. In it Oliver Custer loses his efficient, indispensable secretary because she is going to have a baby. In quick succession four replacements for her fail to work out. At last Oliver persuades his original secretary to come back to work, but she will do so only under the condition that the baby come too, thus giving rise to the farcical situations that follow. In a return to gentle satire, *The Wax Foundation* (1961) strikes out in a new direction for its fun-poking: a foundation set up by the will of Evalina W. Wax to house and support an organization whose purpose is "The Improvement of Society." The winners of the fellowships and their projects, of course, prove to be a strange assortment and therefore the subject for satiric treatment.

The common denominator in all of Gwen Davenport's work is a situation where funny things inevitably happen. In some cases—*Candy for Breakfast* and *The Wax Foundation* in particular—the humor is achieved largely through satire, but Davenport never tries to be severe or malicious. On the other hand, her wit sometimes puts sting into words and she obviously enjoys gentle fun-poking and chuckle-provoking satire. This is most obvious in *Family Fortunes* where antiquarianism, ancestor adulation, and tourist gawking are on parade. Although not one of Davenport's novels is totally free of laughter at the expense of human foibles, her human warmth does not permit her to devise situations merely for the purpose of taking a few scalps.

Jane Morton

Though she wrote only one novel, Jane Morton Norton, who wrote under her maiden name of Jane Morton (1908–), has won a place of esteem in Kentucky literature not usually accorded a one-novel writer. Morton is a fifth-generation resident of Louisville, her family ties tracing back as far as General George Rogers Clark and Joshua Speed, and including her brothers, Senator Thruston Ballard Morton and Congressman Rogers C.B. Morton, Jr. After the death of her husband, George W. Norton, Jr., and of her son in separate automobile accidents, Morton became a business executive, succeeding her son as president of Station WAVE, which her husband had founded in 1933. Her business career did not, however, eclipse her lifelong interest in art and music. In her early years she studied art in the Art Students League in New York and later in Paris, and throughout her life she has remained active in art and music circles, being both a painter and sculptor as well as a collector of art.

Morton's *Blackbirds on the Lawn* was published in 1944 and met only with commendation. No one called it a great novel, but all spoke of it warmly and with respect. It is, says the *New York Herald-Tribune* (May 7, 1944), "the work of an artist whose warmth and insight stem from deep sources of creative understanding," and to the *New York Times* reviewer (April 30, 1944) "the author achieves no small triumph." To Henry Hornsby in the Lexington *Sunday Leader* (May 14, 1944), "the book has a gentleness and strength and beauty which would challenge any seasoned writer."

Blackbirds on the Lawn is a Kentucky story that has its origin in what can be called a land-feud. The families concerned are the Tarnols and the Merrils, Bluegrass landowners whose farms adjoin each other and who for years had been friends and good neighbors but whose friendship had turned to anger and bitterness because of some land that had changed hands as the result of a bet. There were no killings, but enmity and hatred kept the quarrel alive for generations, until in time the feud was more a formality than anything else, save for Linda Tarnol, who remains vindictive.

The scene is a present-day small town, Sommertown, and the nearby countryside. The principals, besides Linda Tarnol, are her brother Henry, former editor of a Sommertown newspaper, Dagma Merril, and her son, a doctor. When a malpractice suit is brought against Dr. Merril, Henry, who has tutored a backward son of Dagma and is in love with her as she with him, intervenes in behalf of the "enemy clan" of Merrils and in so doing uncovers a tragedy that centers upon his sister Linda and reaches out to threaten the whole community. The author, as her spokesman Henry Tarnol makes quite clear, portrays what happens in Sommertown as a microcosm: "I like to think of [it] as the world. . . . the true victory for humanity depends on Sommertown and all the Sommertowns. What they fail to win the nations cannot win—or winning—cannot count as victory."

Elizabeth Hardwick

Elizabeth Hardwick (1916–), a native of Lexington who earned her A.B. and M.A. in English at the University of Kentucky, had her mind set on going to New York City to test herself against the challenges she thought she would find there. Entering Columbia University in 1939, she spent two years in a doctoral program in English before deciding to devote herself full time to serious writing. Her first novel, *The Ghostly Lover* (1945), was panned by critics for its weak plot and poor character development but won praise for the author's style and her talent for descriptions of people and places. Then came an important turn in her writing career, an invitation to become a reviewer and contributor to the *Partisan Review*. In her new career she began to blossom and quickly won a reputation as a reviewer and an essayist on literary, social, and political matters. Her second novel, *The Simple Truth* (1955), met with much the same critical reaction as *The Ghostly Lover*. It was to be twenty-four years before Hardwick published another novel—*Sleepless Nights* (1979)—but this time with great critical success. The chief fruits of her critical writing she has published in *A View of My Own* (1962), *Seduction and Betrayal* (1974), and *Bartleby in Manhattan* (1983). These volumes and her critical views are discussed at some length elsewhere in this volume.

The Ghostly Lover's central character is Marian Coleman and its anchor points are a small Kentucky town and New York City. Marian's mother and father have spent their years in a sort of nomadic existence as they go from place to place working at jobs that always turn out poorly. As the story opens, Marian, with her brother Albert, is living with her indolent grandmother, and her parents are returning home after a two-year absence. Marian, a sixteen-year-old adolescent, is ready for college. Her parents have no money to support her in school, have little understanding of her, and soon wander off again. Next door is Bruce, about thirty years of age, who becomes Marian's lover and gives her the money for a year in college. Thus Marian goes to college in New York City, where she comes to know a young man who wants to marry her. Her grandmother dies and Marian takes the five hundred dollars she inherits from her and goes West to see her parents, hoping to find a meaningful relationship that will relieve her loneliness and give her a sense of family. Her parents, however, only want to borrow her money, and Marian, disappointed, goes to New York to find a job. The young man who wants to marry her is waiting for her at the station, but on sudden impulse, as she sees him waiting at the wrong exit, Marian leaves without speaking to him and faces the city alone.

The novel can dubiously be said to have a plot, and such theme as it has is obscure. Nor is there really an action in the complication-resolution sense, though there is a sort of turning point when Marian goes West to see her parents. Her failure on this occasion seems to mature her and send her off to New York a second time to make a life of her own. If this was the freeing action, then her avoiding the young man at the terminal gate is an act of independence and the first act of the new life she hopes to build. The novel constitutes an early expression of a theme not uncommon in Hardwick's writings: the effort of the human soul to break through the barrier of intolerable loneliness and find another searching soul. However imperfectly Hardwick may have achieved her objectives her talent did not go unnoticed, for scarcely a reviewer failed to note the author's sensitivity and her skill in writing.

Hardwick's short stories began to appear with regularity through the latter 1940s and the 1950s and less frequently thereafter. "People on the Roller Coaster" (1945) and "What We Have Missed" (1946) were reprinted in the *O. Henry Memorial Prize Stories*; "The Mysteries of Eleusis" (1946), "The Golden Stallion" (1947), "Evenings at Home" (1949), "The Purchase" (1950) were selected for inclusion in *The Best American Short Stories*; and "The Classless Society" (1957) was one of the selections in *Stories from the New Yorker: 1950–1960*. "The Golden Stallion," originally published in the *Sewanee Review*, was also published in *The Best World Short Stories in 1947* and Thomas Blair's *Fifty Modern Stories* (1960). These stories have never appeared in a collected edition. The "content" varies from an exposé of social and intellectual snobbery ("The Classless Society") to a witty tale of the gallantries of an aging doctor ("The Faithful") to a delinquent girl embarking upon marriage with a soldier she barely knows ("The Mysteries of Eleusis"). The early short stories and *The Ghostly Lover* earned Hardwick a Guggenheim Fellowship for fiction in 1947. In 1949 she married the poet Robert Lowell, a marriage that lasted till 1972. For three years they lived in Europe, after which they lived in Boston for six, and then moved to New York and the house where Hardwick still lives.

In 1955 Hardwick published her second novel, *The Simple Truth*. Set in an Iowa country town, the story deals with the murder trial of a young college student, Rudy Peck, a poor but upstanding young man accused of murdering his sweetheart, a beautiful and rich sorority girl. About the only known facts are that the girl was in Rudy's room at the time of her death and that his hands had been at her throat. To the defense, the girl's death was a tragic accident brought on by the couple's frolicking play; to the prosecution, it was murder. The focus of the story, however, is not on what happened or on the defendant or the legal contest, but on two people who attend the trial daily and through whose eyes the reader sees the trial. One is Joseph Parks, a student, and the other a faculty member's wife, Anita Mitchell. Both are convinced the young man should be freed, the faculty wife because she considers herself gifted with psychological insights that make Rudy blameless because he became temporarily irresponsible; the student on the social ground that Rudy is a poor boy who will not stand a chance against the girl's wealthy family. The jury, they feel confident, lacking their sensitivities, will find Rudy guilty of murder. Then comes the irony of the whole book: the jury finds him not guilty —and Parks and Anita are stunned. Reduced to its simplest terms, the novel is about snobbery—snobbery of insight. It is too much for Parks and Anita that twelve ignorant, ordinary Iowa townspeople and farmers could have come to the same verdict that they had. They can only conclude that the jury members did the right thing for the wrong reasons.

Again the critical reaction was mixed. Some found fault with the novel's one-dimensional characters, the absence of action, and the dullness of too much talk and too much attention to ideas. "Miss Hardwick's world ends," says one reviewer, "not with a whimper but with a yawn." Counterbalancing such views were those that praised Hardwick's style, originality, and skill in the handling of ideas.

For Hardwick's next novel, *Sleepless Nights* (1979), praise came from just about every quarter. "I have almost nothing negative to say about this novel," says Laurie Stone in the *Village Voice* (May 7, 1979), a sentiment fairly typical among the reviewers. There was some uneasiness because the book, by following along the borderline between autobiography and fiction, was marginally a novel and because the reminiscences so generally dealt with "losers"; but those who registered complaint did so gently.

Sleepless Nights is a series of reminiscences told by a narrator named Elizabeth as on sleepless nights she remembers people and places and events from her past. The scenes are from everywhere—Kentucky, New York, Boston, Amsterdam, Maine; but the people are not important people and there are no intellectual gatherings and no brilliant literary conversations. Instead, they are insignificant people made significant only because they are remembered. They are the people next-door, friends of friends, people observed on a train, a stranger met in the course of a journey, a cleaning woman, a bag woman, a laundress in Maine, an old woman in a nursing home, a doctor in Amsterdam–people who for one reason or another stick in the memory; and recollections of them come in the way that memory moves, by free association, from place to place, and back and forth in time.

The most poignant memories seem to focus upon lonely people, rootless people, people—many of them women—who have been let down by life. Indeed, Hardwick says of herself that she has "a prying sympathy for the tendency of lives to obey the laws of gravity and to sink downward, falling as gently and slowly as a kite, or violently breaking, smashing." The reminiscences are not, however, merely stories of losers. Most of the characters have a reasonable share of will and determination, and their stories are about the way people are overpowered by the events of their lives and endure their fates with courage and without complaining. From Kentucky come recollections —and vignettes— of Elizabeth's childhood, a dancehall near Lexington called Joyland Park, and a mother who bore nine children: childbearing is "what she was always doing, and in the end what she had done." There was Josette, a Boston cleaning lady, who was the victim of "unfair diseases," and Alex A. of New York, an intellectual and a failed academic who did not marry the woman who might have made his life different. And, unforgettably, there was Billie Holiday with "the creamy lips, the oily eyelids, the violent perfume," who went nightly from club to club and who, self-destructive her life through, died in agony, with the police at her bedside.

But despite the preponderance of tales about people who were betrayed by life, the book is far from being just that. To one reviewer *Sleepless Nights* is "a useful book . . . one that even our daughters' granddaughters will want to consult—if not for comfort, then for truth"; to another it reveals "unexpected adherences, lifelong conjunctions of [caring] people who might not be expected to stick together"; and to still another, "This is a bitter trembling book of memories to keep us all awake. But if the dose is bitter, it is also life." And all of it, says another reviewer, written in "sentences so burnished you can skate across them."

Each of Hardwick's novels has troubled her critics because each imperfectly fits the critics' perception of what a novel should be. As a person she has also often been a puzzle. To Philip Nobile (*Intellectual Skywriting*, 105), "the Hardwick persona, hard-bitten in print, brims over nicely with a comforting Southern accent in person. Blithe-spirited Elizabeth Hardwick can come on like a blend of Martha Mitchell and Blanche Dubois." Others who have known her as a founder of the *New York Review of Books* and a leading member of a New York group of literary sophisticates have asked, as it were, how she could be what she has been and come from where she did. And Hardwick baffles them when she says, "This was, is, truly home to me, not just a birthplace. . . . I have always, since my first breath, been from Kentucky."

Hollis Summers

Hollis S. Summers (1916–87) was born in Eminence, Kentucky, and grew up in parsonages in Campbellsville, Louisville, and Madisonville, where his father served as a Baptist minister. He received his A.B. at Georgetown College (1937), his M.A. at Middlebury College (1943), and his Ph.D. at the University of Iowa (1949). He began his teaching career as a teacher of English at Holmes High School, in Covington, and later taught at Georgetown College, the University of Kentucky (1949–59), and Ohio University (1959–86). He has been the recipient of many awards and honors: a grant from the Fund for the Advancement of Education (1951–52), the *Saturday Review* poetry award (1957), a Danforth Lectureship (1963–64), a grant from the National Foundation for the Arts (1975), a Fulbright Lectureship (1978), and lectureships at a number of writers' conferences, including the Bread Loaf School of English and Antioch College. He has written as a novelist, a short story writer, a poet, and an editor.

Summers's publishing career began with his novel *City Limit* in 1948. During the early 1950s he published a good deal of verse in literary journals and "little magazines," but his next three volumes were novels: *Brighten the Corner*, 1952; *Teach You a Lesson* (as Jim Hollis, pseud. for Summers and James F. Rourke), 1956; *The Weather of February*, 1957. Then came an eleven-year period during which he published no fiction but did publish four volumes of verse. From this point onward till 1980 his volumes of verse and fiction almost alternated, with his collection of short stories, *How They Chose the Dead* (1973), adding variety.

Summers's early fiction, though not autobiographical, had its roots in his experience and the places he had lived. *City Limit* grew out of his teaching in the public schools in Covington, *Brighten the Corner* out of his birthplace and other towns where his father held churches, and *The Weather of February* out of his residence in Lexington while teaching at the University of Kentucky and his sabbatical leave, which he spent in Mexico.

City Limit is the story of two high school students who fall in love, spend an idyllic day together as they play hooky, and then face condemnation and punishment from the school and their parents. Critics found fault with the portrayals of the main characters, but were friendly and saw promise in the author's honesty and the carefulness of his writing.

Brighten the Corner is about the society revolving around a Baptist church: the retired minister who tries to continue to dominate the church, the zealous, well-meaning matronly church member who also loves to run things; the black sheep of the congregation who is always falling from grace and then begging forgiveness. There are members who are rigidly righteous and overbearing, those who are devout and sincere and gentle, and the hypocrites. There are board meetings and committee meetings, Sunday School classes, and prayer-meetings. And there is the parson, a man of expediency who tries to remain on good terms with everybody, and his two sons, Albert and Joe. More notable is six-year-old Joe, who is perceptive, possesses an inquiring mind, and has an uninhibited and sometimes embarrassing way of asking questions and making remarks about things he has overheard and not quite understood. Materials such as these are ready-made for satire, but Summers's way is to be gentle and tolerant and amused as he portrays these people and their frailties. His pen is skillful, his touch and his humor light and glancing.

The Weather of February caught the attention of the critics more widely than Summers's first two novels and brought some national attention to his fiction. The main character is a woman of forty whose home is in Lexington, but the story is set largely in Mexico City, where she is recuperating from a serious automobile accident sustained when she accompanied her lover, a Texas businessman, to Mexico. Now, during the month of February, at the challenge of this lover (now gone home to his wife) she is weaving the events of her life into a sort of diary or journal as a means of speeding her days. Organizing her revelations as "some variations on the theme of love," she reconstructs her life pretty much around the men who have been a part of it. The novel won the commendation of most reviewers. "This many-dimensioned study of what makes a twentieth-century woman tick," says the *Saturday Review*, "is uncanny, perceptive, and convincing" (Oct. 5, 1957). "A fascinating, convincing, and unusual heroine for a novel of quality," is the opinion of the *New York Herald Tribune* (Sept. 22, 1957). Summers does not, however allow himself to become involved in the lives of the characters. He is understanding of the middle-aged woman, sensitive and subtle in his responses, but he writes as a detached observer. The style, as usual with Summers, is deft and seemingly effortless.

The Walks Near Athens was Summers's next volume and the first of four volumes of verse he would publish before returning to the novel again. In the main, reviewers were favorably inclined toward it, though there were diverging opinions: some admired his "fine eye" for homely things, his rhythms and line movement because they are the rhythms of colloquial speech, and his whimsical interest in the mundane and the O. Henry–like twist he sometimes uses at the end of his poems. Others were annoyed with a certain tentativeness in the manner and the content. One reviewer was irritated by the style, which others found more interesting than the content. According to another (*Poetry*, Feb. 1960), "Mr. Summers is so much his craft's master that his facility sometimes leads him into a pyrotechnical display that defeats itself. . . . Most of [his] poems are what used to be called *vers de société*—fashionable writing whose chief characteristic is lack of commitment."

Irony is a common feature in Summers's verse, as exemplified by the title poem. The title may suggest classic Athens, but the scene is Ohio, not Greece, and the "walks" are not "pleasant strolls" but the actual pavement on which people walk. Summers deals with everyday subjects of many sorts: a lawnmower, a butterfly, blackbirds, swifts, a flicker, a robin, a hamster, the author's children, academic life, committee meetings, classrooms. The variety is great, and the subjects are viewed in relaxed fashion. His approach to the subject matter is personal, and he commonly views things from an unusual angle, often adding a twist at the end.

Seven Occasions (1965) won the attention of the critics more than did *The Walks Near Athens* or Summers's second volume of verse, *Someone Else: Sixteen Poems about Other Children* (1962). "Another testament to wit," says one reviewer; and another calls the poems "nervy," full of wit and a somber sort of playfulness. The author seems more confident of himself as the conversational quality of the poems makes friends with the reader, or, as one critic puts it, takes hold of the "listener's lapels." Summers's whimsy works well when he writes of Sears Roebuck in "The Catalogue Tells You What You Are Interested In," and he is delighted with the printed sign on the preserved wreck of a ship at Cape Hatteras:

> Do not disturb.
> Please leave the wreck for others to enjoy.

Four more volumes of Summers's verse were to appear during the decade ahead: *The Peddler* (1967), *Sit Opposite Each Other* (1970),

Start from Home (1972), and *Occupant, Please Forward* (1974). Summers continues to write about the world he lives in and in verse that is well crafted. Economy of language—even to the point of spareness—continues to characterize his style. The practice of building toward the concluding stanza remains a favorite device, and he often gives the thought an unexpected twist, sometimes providing a flash of insight, but sometimes also doing injury to matters of mature importance when the temptation to toy with words becomes too great.

Summers returned again to fiction with *The Day After Sunday* in 1968 and *The Garden* in 1972. The former is the story of the Watts family, "the best society" in Lexington. There is Maribeth, the thirty-eight-year-old wife and mother, who is frigid and unloving and finds her outlets in being a compulsive spender; David, the husband and father, sexually starved, who has lost contact with his wife and son and taken refuge in reading, memories, and alcohol; Joe Bill, the seventeen-year-old son, newly awakened to sex and drinking too much; and Beulah, a lonely thirty-year-old spinster church secretary who one night admits Joe Bill into her bed for her first and only indiscretion. The novel does a good job stripping away the facade that hides these "best" people, but the probing is not deep and little is changed in their lives. *The Garden* is about people who are living lives of quiet desperation: two Americans who go to Malta for a month's vacation to find a new life for themselves, but despite their experience in "The Garden" they are not freed of their ordinariness or the commonplaceness of their lives.

Summers has always been interested in the short story. In 1954 he edited *Kentucky Story: A Collection of Short Stories*, in 1963 he edited *Discussions of the Short Story*, and in 1973 he published a collection of his own short stories, *How They Chose the Dead*. The last contains twelve stories whose subjects vary from an account of an English professor who observes events in light of their usefulness to him as anecdotes to discussions of the "twilight zones" of human psychology and of the connections between reality, illusion, and madness in "The Man from Cord's" and "The Terrible Death of Mister Vimont." Summers's latest volume—another collection of short stories—is *Standing Room* (1984). Containing nine stories, this new volume represents a maturing in his style and content. There is less playfulnes with words, and the stories are more tightly focused and move with more directness to their denouement than did his earlier stories.

David Alexander

Half-a-dozen or so mystery writers in Kentucky wrote a respectable whodunit or two, but only one was a true professional. David Alexander (1907–73), though lacking a major reputation, did have visibility on the national scene. No other Kentuckian except Foxhall Daingerfield has made the writing of literature about crime a serious objective. Evelyn Snead Barnett wrote *Dragnet* (1909), the first murder mystery by a Kentucky writer worth noting. That prolific novelist Charles Neville Buck has left a mystery novel—*Mountain Justice* (1935)—that compares favorably with his novels about feuding, but Buck was not a mystery writer any more than was Hollis Summers, who under the pseudonym of Jim Hollis, in collaboration with James Rourke, wrote a well-received murder mystery called *Teach You a Lesson* (1955); the same is true of Leane Zugsmith, who with Carl Randau wrote *The Visitor* (1944). Dorothy Park Clark wrote three change-of-pace mystery stories, two of which—*Roll, Jordan, Roll* (1947) and *Poison Speaks Softly* (1948)—are cited elsewhere, though neither adds anything to her reputation. Robert Emmett McDowell has written a number of "bread-and-butter" pieces of fiction, but his serious interest in history contributed to his making *Hound's Tooth* (1966), a mystery with a Civil War background, worth mentioning. Ann Armstrong Thompson (1939–) has written *The Swiss Legacy* (1974), *Message from Absalom* (1975), *The Romanov Ransom* (1978), and *The Man Caine* (1979)—all involving international intrigue—and has gained some regional following. James Robert Sherburne has been developing a fascination for murder stories, the best of which is *Death's Pale Horse*.

David Alexander was born in Shelbyville, moved to Louisville when he was a boy, attended the University of Kentucky, 1926–28, and began his writing career with the *Lexington Herald*. He was early attracted to horse racing and breeding and soon (1930) was in New York working for the *Morning Telegraph*, one of the country's leading turf publications. At the age of twenty-six he was managing editor and columnist for the *Telegraph* and there remained for more than ten years. He then returned to Lexington, where he contributed to the *Blood Horse* and the *Thoroughbred Record* and continued to do so even after returning to New York. Back in New York he became racing editor for the *New York Herald-Tribune* and remained in this position until the newspaper ceased publication.

Alexander published his first murder mystery in his mid-forties.

To prepare himself for his new profession, he took a program of study at the New York Institute of Criminology, from which he graduated with high honors. He was offered a number of positions in detective work, but his mind was set on a writing career. His first murder mystery was published in 1951 and his last in 1962—fifteen of them in all. In 1962 he returned to his early love, horses and racing, with *The History and Romance of the Horse* (which won the Boys' Club of America Juvenile Book Award) and in 1966 with *A Sound of Horses: The World of Racing from Eclipse to Kelso*. Before his death in 1973 he turned twice more to mystery stories: a juvenile story, *The Red Coat Mystery* (1966), and *Tales for a Rainy Night*, which he edited.

Most Men Don't Kill and *Murder in Black and White*, his first novels, both published in 1951, were rather widely reviewed and stirred strong reactions: "Flabbergasting characters . . . tingling suspense and delirious burlesque"; "the characters are certainly different"; "tremendous clowning with murder"; ". . . some of the strangest people who ever got in a book." Alexander grew in favor with readers and critics, but remarks such as these never ceased to appear in the judgments that were made of him. In fact, in the opinion of Bill Pronzoni in *Twentieth-Century Crime and Mystery Writers* (1985), David Alexander has remained an underrated writer partly because of his idiosyncracies and his "sometimes self-consciously poetic and mannered style" that puts readers off. But, says Pronzoni, "his plots are unusual and compelling, as are his offbeat, colorful characters, and the best of his work has undeniable power."

By 1955 the adverse criticism began to soften and his merits to be recognized. Thus the *Saturday Review* (Oct. 22, 1955) called *Shoot a Sitting Duck*, "his best yet," and a year later the *New York Times* (May 6, 1956) declared, "The steady improvement in David Alexander's work makes *Die, Little Goose*, the best yet of his Broadway-focused mysteries." In 1957 the *Chicago Sunday Tribune* (Oct. 27, 1957) said of *Death of Humpty Dumpty*, "Rich in night life atmosphere and swift in turbulent sequences"; and even the normally hostile *New York Herald-Tribune Book Review* (Oct. 28, 1957) was complimentary of the volume. *Hush-a-Bye Murder* the same year won praise from the *San Francisco Chronicle* (June 30, 1957): "The Broadway scene is as fantastic and wonderful as ever, and this yarn is a good example of Alexander's specialty."

In short, Alexander had won his place as a maverick sort of detective story writer. Those who read him and judged him had adjusted somewhat to his sort of story and writing, and he in turn had adjusted in some measure to their occasional bludgeoning. By 1959 the British press began to review his books, the *Guardian* (Oct. 21, 1960) declaring of *The Death of Daddy-O*, "Mr. Alexander can usually be relied on for a startling new idea, and this time he has come up with a daisy." *The Times* [London] *Literary Supplement* (June 29, 1961) was more lukewarm in appraising *Hangman's Dozen* (1962), a collection of Alexander's short stories and the last volume of original work he was to publish, concluding, "Some are macabre, some sentimental, one is pure fantasy, and two are historical; none is exactly a detective story. They are competently told but contrive to be unusual without becoming really memorable."

Perhaps such an appraisal is also a reasonable judgment of Alexander's work as a whole. Certainly he is not one of the great American writers of detective fiction; at the same time, even when registering frustrated annoyance, critics knew they were dealing with a writer who belonged on the national scene. He was perhaps an even better short story writer than a novelist, as a reading of *Hangman's Dozen* will tend to prove. Indeed among the thirteen stories in the volume "The Man Who Went to Taltavul's" won second prize in the *Ellery Queen Mystery Magazine* contest in 1956. Alexander also won the Edgar Allan Poe Award of the Mystery Writers of America, was at one time an officer in that organization, and in 1967 edited *Tales for a Rainy Night* for the same group. His own best stories, it is generally agreed, were among the eight in the series that focus on Broadway and Times Square in the 1950s and in which Bart Hardin is his most celebrated detective.

Henry Giles

Most of the writers of fiction of the midcentury who have explored the collapse of the social structure of the Kentucky hill country have addressed social conditions and the way these conditions produced social problems and social degeneration. A few writers, however, more psychological than sociological in their approach, looked for the collapse within the people themselves. The best novel by a Kentuckian taking this approach is *Harbin's Ridge* (1951), by Henry Giles (1916–86), husband of the novelist Janice Holt Giles and at least as talented as his prolific wife. James M. Cain, of California, has written a better-known seamy novel of this sort (*The Butterfly*, 1946) dealing with coal mine troubles in Mingo County, West Virginia, but *Harbin's Ridge* is a better work. It tells the story of two men who were friends for many years but whose friendship was cursed before it began. The details of the story come out as the reading of Jeff Harbin's will reveals how years ago he had grown up in the Knobs section of Kentucky as the bosom friend of Faleecy John Squires, how Faleecy was in fact his illegitimate half-brother, and how he had shot and killed Faleecy John one day when he found him and his own mother locked in an embrace near the Harbin cabin. With its theme of illegitimate sex, revenge, and violence, therefore, the novel has something in common with Cain's novel. It is, however, much more than a sensational potboiler, for, somewhat in the tradition of Elizabeth Madox Roberts's *The Time of Man*, it is a story of farming and farm life enriched by a poetic style that makes memorable its record of the sights and sounds and odors of the ridge country of Adair County. The plot is well constructed and the suspense well maintained. The novel, published by Houghton Mifflin, was well received and was a selection of the Doubleday Book Club and a Bantam Book reprint.

Robert Hazel

Robert Hazel (1921–), novelist and poet, was born in Indiana, near Bloomington, and received his A.B. from George Washington University in 1946 and his M.A. from the Johns Hopkins University in 1951. He has taught creative writing at George Washington University, Oregon State University, the University of Kentucky, and New York University. He won a Saxon Memorial Fellowship in Fiction in 1955. In the early 1950s he lived in Louisville and drew upon this experience for his first novel; from 1955 to 1961 he lived in Lexington while he taught at the University of Kentucky.

Hazel's first novel, *Lost Year* (1953), received limited attention and was generally disparaged for its "appalling" content, principally about a boarding-house that doubled as a brothel. The author was seen, however, as having "a way with words." Hazel's next novel, *A Field Full of People* (1954), fared much better and received generally favorable reviews. The action, which takes place in rural Indiana, centers on Tom Flood, whose weakness for drink leads to his falling asleep at the wheel of a car and having an accident that kills his best friend. Critics found fault with the novel but admired the "beautifully detailed rituals" of farm life and the author's skill with language. The *Herald-Tribune Book Review* concluded its appraisal: "With clean, unswerving direction, Mr. Hazel carries his story to its tragic end. His talents both as poet and novelist are stirringly revealed in this chronicle of ill-starred revel."

It was not till 1972 that Hazel published his third novel. *Early*

Spring, in which a twice-divorced college professor in a Kentucky university, "alienated from his Indiana origins. . . . shares his bed and board with Heidi Johnson, one of the more attractive students in his writing class." The affair leads to his losing his job, but not, as one reviewer puts it, "before he has displayed his contempt for the university and most of its people." A reviewer in the *Nation* commends the novel but says it "will satisfy nobody's stereotypes of the situation." Other reviews are less favorable, some of them sharply so.

Hazel often intersperses verse in his novels and has published individual poems in such journals as *The Hopkins Review*, *The Nation*, *Minnesota Review*, *Prairie Schooner*, and *Poetry*. He has also published in collected editions: *Poems: 1951–1961* (Morehead Press, 1961), *American Elegies* (Crazy Horse Press, 1968), and *Who Touches This: Poems, 1951–1979* (Countryman Press, 1980), the last being selections from the first two. As in his fiction, Hazel is perhaps at his best when writing about the Indiana countryside he knew as a boy—scenes, backcountry graveyards, small towns with their filling stations—but there are poems also about the city and about people. Running through Hazel's poetry is the author's often oppressive sense of mutability. His imagery is sometimes startling and in general is integral to the development of his poems. Often, however, this development is not easy to follow and hence produces "difficult" poetry. In the words of one re-reviewer, "The trouble with this sort of imagery and this sort of poetic structure is that sometimes . . . it doesn't come off." As Hazel himself puts it, his verse "is not a poetry of statement." Tense and often elusive, sometimes blunt and painful, Hazel's poetry, despite its virtues, has not attracted a wide audience.

Pati Hill

Pati (Patricia) Hill (1921–) was born in Ashland, moved to Virginia, where she spent much of her childhood, attended private boarding schools, and spent two years at George Washington University. She then became a Powers model in New York and subsequently moved to Paris, where she was a fashion model, began writing for the *Paris Review*, and began her first book, *The Pit and the Century Plant* (1955), which was more a journal than a novel. The scene is a rundown stone cottage near the village of Montere, some sixty miles southeast of Paris, where Hill spent much of a two-year period cleaning up and refurbishing the place and making friends with the neighbors. The result is a charming set of vignettes on the way of life in provincial France.

Hill's first novel was *Nine Mile Circle* (1957). The title comes from a stretch of road on the outskirts of a small town in the Upper South that winds past the race track and village green, out into the country, and then back again. Along this road two thirteen-year-old girls, Linda and Jan, walk every Saturday. As they walk, these preadolescents invent imaginary adventures for the people they know in the town, often being a part of the invention themselves, little knowing that the situations they imagine cannot equal the actual ones about them. Among these, years ago Jan's father and Linda's mother had been in love, and now, this very summer, her mother's mind relives the past as she wonders if she might have done better with Jan's father. The volume contains many excellent vignettes and characterizations and memorable insights into the two girls, some of them through flashbacks. And there are many episodes and events through which Hill makes her characters real and convincing as she portrays their little foibles and idiosyncracies. Like *The Pit and the Century Plant, Nine Mile Circle* met with a warm reception at the hands of the review press.

In *Prosper* (1961) the author returns to France. This time the critical reception was even warmer. *Prosper*, says Chad Walsh in the *New York Times Book Review* (Sept. 11, 1960), "reads as though it were a previously unpublished work by Stendhal or Maupassant, translated with exquisite skill into English." The central figure is Prosper Cadot, a young peasant farm worker with a deep attachment to the land. With an immediate family consisting of an alcoholic father and an imbecilic sister, Prosper is cut off from young ladies of good families and drifts into an affair with the widow of a former employer. The liaison ends with the death of the middle-aged widow, who has become pregnant and commits suicide in order to escape disgrace. Then follows Prosper's loveless marriage to a young woman through whom he comes into possession of the land he desperately desires, after which he settles down into the contented life of a peasant farmer.

In her fourth novel, *One Thing I Know* (1963), only ninety-three pages long, Patti Hill returns to America for her setting. Her theme is not only one she has used before but one—in the wake of J.D. Salinger's *The Catcher in the Rye* (1951)—that was popular with writers as late as the early 1960s: the problems of adolescence and growing up. The heroine is sixteen-year-old Francesca Hollins, whose diary contains the source of the title: "One thing I know, I will never be in love again." The book uses language effectively and economically, and the tone is well handled as it avoids being solemn, escapes the sentimental, and manages to keep a sense of humor.

Hill's last novel, *Impossible Dreams* (1976), is about a heroine who marries well and suffers from ennui. "Tomorrow," she says, "I'll likely sleep in Marseille. Or maybe I'll stay where I am. Who knows, anything can happen." The book failed to win the critical approval that her earlier works had.

Walter Tevis

Though mostly a writer of science fiction stories, Walter Tevis first came to the attention of readers in 1959 through a realistic, sometimes seamy, novel about a pool shark. When it was published, it received a good press as "a fine, swift, tightly-plotted, offbeat novel" and the author was called the master of an athletic, packed, curiously effective style. Two years later the novel was made into a watershed motion picture with Paul Newman as Fast Eddie Felson, Jackie Gleason as Minnesota Fats, and George C. Scott in a supporting role. When the movie gained national acclaim with eight Academy Award nominations and three "Oscars," the game of pool had at last come of age with a tension-taut story worthy of the pastime; and Walter Tevis would be forever known as the author of *The Hustler*.

Tevis (1928–84), who moved to Kentucky from San Francisco when he was ten, picked up the experience that led to his writing the novel when he entered the University of Kentucky, where he earned both A.B. and M.A. degrees by 1956. He held a job at a poolroom near the campus, where he learned the game and gained experience, and he frequented the Phoenix Hotel poolroom, where he observed the hustlers and the professionals as they made their circuits. Characters and episodes that he would write about later began to take shape in his mind. Gambling he says he learned while he was stationed for seventeen months on Okinawa during his service in the navy. His first published story about playing pool, written in a writing course he had with A.B. "Bud" Guthrie, then teaching at the university, appeared in *Esquire* in 1953. The plot that fully tied the knowledge, the characters, and the events together, however, did not take on book form until 1959 while Tevis was doing editorial work for the research division of the Kentucky Department of Highways.

In pool a hustler is a skilled player who makes the rounds of smoky, ball-clacking, often sleazy, airless poolhalls peopled with gamblers, suckers, sharpies, losers, the broke and the well-heeled—all ready for a game and a swift buck. Successfully plied, the hustler's scam is to be highly skilled but to look only fairly good, to play awkwardly, look merely lucky, perhaps drink too much, and thus con the right victims into a game they think they are certain to win. He then pyramids the bets, wins, and quickly moves on. Tevis's novel begins when Fast Eddie Felson thinks he is the best and is ready for a big money game with Minnesota Fats—the best of them all—who rules at Bennington's in Chicago. "In Eddie's world," says *Time* magazine (Jan. 12, 1959), "Fats's name is spoken in reverence. Huge, lardy, and gross, Fats plays with the grace of a virtuoso." For forty hours he and Eddie matched their skills, and at one time with Eddie $18,000 ahead it appears that Fats has met his master. But Eddie cracks, looks to his bottle for help, and finally staggers out a loser. Eddie has learned that skill with a cue-stick is not enough—that in the midst of a crisis a player's inner resources may be more important than a good shot. Eddie's comeback is slow as he sets about earning a return match with the master—the subject of most of the novel.

After he sold the movie rights for *The Hustler*, Tevis went to Mexico for an extended visit, but things did not go well for him there. He kept coming back to Kentucky in search of both a spiritual renewal and a setting for his stories, even for the science fiction novel he would write next. Two kinds of subjects, he says, have always played a role in his fiction. The first is one-on-one competition, the role of the winner and the loser, the contest between two loners. "I'm obsessed with the struggle between winning and losing," he says; "pool is a dazzling game, a loner's game." He wrote of loners and winners and losers again when he turned to chess in *The Queen's Gambit*. The other kind of subject, he says, is the "speculative fantasy that goes back to falling in love with The Wizard of Oz when I was young." He had already tried his hand at science fiction short stories as early as the latter 1950s; then in 1963 came a novel, *The Man Who Fell to Earth*.

The Man Who Fell to Earth is the story of Thomas Jerome Newton, who has been sent from the dying planet of Anthea to Earth to prepare a refuge for Anthea's last few survivors. Newton is making progress toward his goal through advanced Anthean technology but is apprehended by the FBI and imprisoned. Finally he is released but abandons his project and becomes an alcoholic exile. "I worked very hard to become an imitation human being," he says, "and of course I succeeded." His failure came, he says, through what Thoreau called "quiet desperation"; not because of military might or scientific excellence but because of smothering bureaucracy.

Tevis's reputation was growing. "Far from Home," a science fiction story, appeared in Doubleday's annual collection of *The Best from Fantasy and Science Fiction* and received a citation as the best science fiction short story of 1958. *The Man Who Fell to Earth* received The Little Green Man citation as the best science fiction novel of 1963. Having completed his M.F.A. at the University of Iowa, Tevis was now ready to combine writing with teaching and took a position in 1965 at Ohio University, having earlier taught in the public schools of Science Hill, Hawesville, Irvine, and Carlisle between 1949 and 1954 and as a graduate student at the University of Kentucky. Despite his enjoyment of teaching, however, Tevis decided in 1978 to give up the security of his professorship and went to New York so that he could give himself to full-time writing.

Mocking Bird (1980), another science fiction novel, was the first of five novels that Tevis would publish before his death at fifty-six in 1984. The setting of the novel is the twenty-fifth century and its aim is to foretell, somewhat in the manner of *Brave New World* and *1984*, the sort of world America's present tendencies are leading to. In this world of the future robot-like people are not allowed to learn to read and are brought up to be responsive to catch-phrase aphorisms such as "When in doubt, forget it" and "Don't ask—relax." Anyone who teaches himself to read is regarded as an enemy of the state. *Far from Home* (1981) is a collection of thirteen short stories that Tevis began writing as early as 1958. Like his science fiction novels, these stories are well crafted and reveal the author's eye for the realistic detail that aids the reader in bringing about a willing suspension of disbelief in extraordinary events. The tales vary from one about a man haunted by the ghost of his mistress's dead lover to one about a whale that materializes in an Arizona swimming pool.

The three volumes Tevis was yet to write—*The Steps of the Sun* (1983), *The Queen's Gambit* (1983), and *The Color of Money* (1984)—must be cited at least briefly. The first, a science fiction novel, is set in the year 2063 and takes place during a massive energy shortage that threatens the world. To solve the problem, tycoon Ben Belson secures a spaceship and goes prospecting for uranium in distant worlds. On Planet Belson he not only finds the object of his quest but makes other discoveries. His return home triggers a series of events that Tevis writes about with wry humor as he looks into the twenty-first century and sees the directions in which political and social change have gone.

The Queen's Gambit is the story of an orphan girl, Beth Harmon, who is taught to play chess by the janitor in the orphanage. At fourteen she wins her first tournament, at eighteen she becomes the American champion, and at nineteen she makes her way through international competition to the pinnacle where she ultimately plays the world champion in the Moscow tournament. Tevis, who was a qualified Class C player himself, seeks to penetrate and portray the workings of the mind, the quality of memory and power of synthesis the game requires, the emotional and physical stress of competition, and the dedication, concentration, and spiritual resources that genius must have. A Book-of-the-Month alternate selection, the novel is characterized by the (London) *Times Literary Supplement* as displaying "the obsessive quality of the chess-player's allegiance to his craft. . . . The authority of *The Queen's Gambit* derives from Walter Tevis's technical and historical knowledge of chess . . . his strategy and tactics are immaculate. Familiarity with chess is not needed in order to enjoy the book" (April 22, 1983).

Tevis's last volume was a sequel to the one that first brought him to the attention of the public. Taking its title, *The Color of Money*, from the brushed green cloth beneath the shaded light of a pool table, Tevis returns to Fast Eddie Felson, now fifty and "washed out and frightened." For pressing personal reasons Fast Eddie undertakes a comeback and gets his old enemy, Minnesota Fats, now living in comfortable retirement in Florida, to team up with him in shopping mall exhibitions staged by a cable television company. But few people, Eddie learns, remember an old legend, and besides, nine ball has replaced straight pool. Eddie changes his game, however, and learns to cope with the new breed of hustler, until at last he reaches Tahoe before the cameras of "Wide World of Sports." "The writing is taut and evocative," says *Publishers Weekly*; "Tevis is unequaled when it comes to creating and sustaining the tension of a high-stakes game. Even readers who never lifted a cue will be captivated" (June 29, 1984).

Sallie Bingham

Sallie Bingham (1937–   ), a member of the Bingham family that once owned the *Courier-Journal* and other media enterprises, was born in Louisville. She majored in English at Radcliffe College, where she received her A.B. in 1958. Subsequent to her graduation she married A. Whitney Ellsworth in 1958, lived in the Boston area for a time, published her novel *After Such Bondage* in 1959, and moved to New York, where she continued to write. After a divorce she returned to Louisville in 1977, having in the meantime published two collections of short stories, *The Touching Hand* (1967) and *The Way It Is Now* (1972). Since her return she has married Timothy Peters, has done some writing, has served on national award committees, and has been book-page editor for the *Courier-Journal.* This position she resigned in the spring of 1985, having served in it for some three years. Since that time she has set up the Kentucky Foundation for Women, which is intended to achieve three objectives: to provide women writers with grants that will give them more time for writing; to publish a quarterly literary magazine, *The American Voice*; and to establish an archive for women's papers (diaries, journals, oral history, etc.). Devoting more time to her own writing is also a part of Bingham's plan for the future.

Of the pieces of fiction in *The Touching Hand, and Six Short Stories* (1967), all but one had already appeared in such magazines as the *Atlantic Monthly*, *Mademoiselle*, and *Redbook*. The opening novella, the strongest piece in the volume, is the story of a "life-starved" housemaid who is escorting a small boy and his older sister on a sea voyage to meet their parents in England and tells how an encounter with a lonely old gentleman affects their lives. As one reviewer described the volume, the stories deal with "the interdependence of people and their persistent resentment of it." There are, for example, in other stories a divorcee trying to regain not so much her ex-husband as the support that marriage has provided her, and a woman leaving a house where she had remained childless. Though lacking in real distinction, the stories are well constructed and well written. Each may be said to be a character study and as such is well done.

The Way It Is Now: Stories is a collection of fifteen short stories. As with Bingham's first collection, the stories are concerned with unhappy women of various ages who, immersed in themselves, are also caught up in situations common to women's lives. Some of the stories deal with the traditionally romantic, sugar-coated experiences in women's lives—weddings, for example, and births—and examine these occasions in clear-eyed fashion "the way it is now." Others deal with times of crisis, as when women grow up and grow away from parents, from brothers and sisters, and from children and husbands. Family tensions of all sorts are portrayed, from bored little girls in rebellion against parental authority to the trying care of the mentally ill.

The most recent work by Bingham to attract attention is *Paducah*, a play (her fourth), which was produced by the Horse Cave Theatre in the summer of 1984 and opened again the following spring in the off-Broadway American Place Theatre. Set in the city of Paducah and portraying the troubled life of retiring banker and community leader

Clay Baker, the play at the larger level of meaning is concerned with the disintegration of the privileged southern aristocracy under the impact of social change.

Jane Mayhall

Jane Mayhall (1921–) was born in Louisville and spent her early years there. She attended Black Mountain College, 1937–40, and had further training in music schools. She married George Katz, a publisher in New York City, in 1940. Subsequently she started her publishing career, first in the *Sewanee Review* and the *Partisan Review* and later in the *Antioch Review*, *The Nation*, the *Paris Review*, *Harper's Bazaar*, and other magazines and reviews. In 1947 and 1949 one of her stories was selected for inclusion in the Martha Foley *Best American Short Stories*; in 1973 another was published in *The Prize Stories: The O. Henry Awards*. She has participated in writers' workshops on a number of college campuses, including New York University, the New School for Social Research in New York City, Ohio University, and Hofstra College. Her ties with Kentucky have remained strong. Louisville has provided her with settings, and she has participated in summer workshops in writing at Alice Lloyd College and Morehead State University.

Cousin to Human (1960), Mayhall's first novel, is the work for which the author for a time received quite favorable attention. "One of the finest new novelists on the scene," said the *Saturday Review of Literature* (March 12, 1960); "a new writer of very substantial abilities," said the *New York Herald-Tribune* (Feb. 14, 1960). Mayhall was to write three more volumes—*Ready for the Ha Ha and Other Satires* (1966), *Givers and Takers: Poems* (1968) and *Givers and Takers II* (1973)—but none of them rivaled the acclaim that she won for her first volume. *Cousin to Human* is in the *Catcher in the Rye* mold. The place is Louisville, the time is the mid-1930s, and the central character is Lacy Cole, a girl not yet sixteen who is a senior in high school facing the problems of growing up and finding out much not only about herself but the people she has lived with all her life: her mother, a hill-country woman with a great deal of strength of character; her father, an improvident, non-caring person; a teacher who recognizes her potential both as a person and as a student with talent in music; and others. The story is made up of everyday events in the life of a family in a very ordinary neighborhood faced with a meager existence, and the heroine runs headlong into trying experiences while she works her way through to self-realization as an individual and as a musician. The novel comes off as unpretentious and credible because of the freshness and honesty with which the story is told.

David Madden

The writing career of Jerry David Madden (1933–) has been unorthodox and individual. Both in his personal life and in his writing he has been the sort of person who takes risks, sometimes wins and sometimes loses, and always comes out undaunted with his zest and his ego unimpaired. Born in Knoxville, Tennessee, he attended the public schools there, enrolled at the University of Tennessee but dropped out, held odd jobs in New York, Boston, and Maine, went to sea as a merchant seaman, and spent more than a year in the army by the time he was twenty-two. Subsequently he enrolled in Iowa State Teachers College, where he met the girl he was to marry, received his B.S. at the University of Tennessee (1957), his M.A. at San Francisco State College (1958), and attended the Yale Drama School (1959–60). Since completing his academic training, Madden has published seven novels, a volume of short stories, and six critical studies; edited nine volumes that range from *Tough Guy Writers of the Thirties* (1968) to *Studies in the Short Story* (1975); and published scores of uncollected short stories, plays, poems, and critical essays. At the same time he has taught at Centre College (1960–62), the University of Louisville (1962–64), Kenyon College (1964–66), Ohio University (1966–68), and Louisiana State University (since 1968), as well as holding shorter appointments at Appalachian State College and the University of Delaware and participating in summer writing workshops at Morehead State University and Alice Lloyd College in Kentucky and in the Bread Loaf Writers' Conference.

The Beautiful Greed (1961), written as his M.A. thesis at San Francisco State College, was Madden's first published novel. It was based upon his experience as a merchant seaman and though not without merit lacks, by Madden's own admission, a real story to support the idea which the novel seeks to convey. His next novel, *Hair of the Dog,* was concerned with a private detective but was never published in book form. It appeared serially in *Adam* (1967) during Madden's "men's-magazine" period and like his *Tough Guy Writers of the Thirties* (1968) reveals the author's interest in such writers as James M. Cain, about whom he was to write a volume for the Twayne Series of biographical studies (1970).

Cassandra Singing (1969), Madden's second published novel, caused him no end of trouble. For fifteen years he worked on it, producing more than a dozen versions and casting it variously in the form of a play, movie script, radio script, and novel, before settling on the form in which it was published. The scene of the story is a squalid coaltown in Eastern Kentucky. The principal character, Cassie (Cassandra) McDaniel, a fifteen-year-old bedridden victim of rheumatic fever, is cured by her "old-time-religion" uncle and becomes a gospel singer on the local radio. Other characters include her brother, "Lone," who is in jail for dynamiting a coal tipple and robbing a company store; Boyd Wheeler, a leather-jacketed, dishonorably discharged ex-Marine who rides a motorcycle and sells moonshine; a drunken father, a whorish mother, and a grandfather in the junk business. The novel was damned by some reviewers, but others found strength in it and praised the author's ability to tell a story.

Brothers in Confidence (1972), set partially in Kentucky, is a story about con men and has definite virtues, but what Madden had learned about writing from his trials with *Cassandra Singing* did not pay off till *Bijou* (1974), a Book-of-the-Month alternate that the *New Republic* saw as an "important novel" and the *Library Journal* as "a fine and entertaining novel." During this interval Madden had also learned from his critical studies of the work of others. Among these were *The Poetic Image in Six Genres* (1969), *James M. Cain* (1970), *The Shadow Knows* (short stories, 1970), *The Popular Culture Explosion* (1972), *Nathanael West* (1973), *Contemporary Literary Scene* (1974), and *Remembering James Agee* (1974).

In *Bijou* Madden traces the physical, emotional, and artistic development of an eighth-grade boy, Lucius Hutchfield, during the year 1946, at home, at school, and in his job as an usher in the Bijou Theatre, where Lucius sees movie after movie. As he watches, he escapes his home, his drunken father and strange mother, his brother Earl, who is a criminal and abuses him, and his brother Bucky, an odd tormented youth always getting into trouble. Lucius daydreams about life, outlines romantic plots, and composes love poems. At the end of the novel, having discovered the writings of Thomas Wolfe, Lucius runs away from home and finds his way to Asheville, where he will walk the streets that Wolfe walked.

The Suicide's Wife (1979), Madden says, could "almost be called *The Beginning*." It too is a story about tortured, isolated people. The title character, Anne, has grown up in a ghetto shamed by the fact that her mother was a drunkard and her brothers criminals and in prison. She marries a college professor who one day kills himself without leaving a clue to why he has done so. Anne tries to come to terms with what has happened and asks questions of herself and others in order to try to understand better the man she had married. In the process she comes to know a great deal about herself, realizes she has grown, and is ready for a new beginning.

Pleasure-Dome (1979) is a sequel to *Bijou* with Lucius Hutchfield six years older and still fascinated with the way fact interacts with reality. In the first half of the novel Lucius seeks through his storytelling to get his brother Bucky out of prison. In the second half the focus shifts to Lucius and an old woman, Zara Jane Ransom, now living in the Blue Goose Hotel, near Boone, North Carolina, who claims she was once seduced by Jesse James. Lucius sets about learning Zara Jane's story, but before he has finished, the hotel burns with Zara Jane in it.

Madden's aim has been to entertain, though he has had no objection if what he writes also has a message. He has been fascinated with the relationship between the storyteller and his audience and how, in the telling of a story, each affects the other. This interest is reflected in *On the Big Wind* (1980), with its subtitle, *Being Seven Comic Episodes in the Fitful Rise of Big Bob Travis from Disc Jockey in a Small Eastern Kentucky Town to Network News Reporter*. He has been concerned too with the tension that builds between the life of the imagination and the life of action, of which *Cassandra Singing* is an example. The last third of *Pleasure-Dome* is given over to an introspective questioning of the moral consequences of a writer's art.

Madden's views have spilled over into his technique. For some readers the connections between parts of his work may seem chaotic, the stories merely wild yarns, and the plots to defy summary. "Accidents, not logic," says Webster Schott, "run *Pleasure-Dome* . . . it's clear that [it] is a writer's notebook of plot possibilities, social observations, narrative lines, character sketches and his own sentiments about the meaning of his craft or art. . . . One hundred pages into *Pleasure-Dome* I thought it was one of the few novels I couldn't force myself to finish. Madden seems incapable of controlling his impulses to collect scenes, a writer writing with nothing to say." Then, says Schott, he turns serious "at exactly the right point—with a town and a life doomed—his novel becomes an elaborate serio-comic commentary on U.S. middle-class trash culture." *Pleasure-Dome*, he concludes, "is troublesome, demanding, and sometimes a bore. But at its height it is indeed a work of art." (*Washington Post Book World*, Jan. 6, 1980).

Wallace Edward Knight

Wallace Edward Knight (1926–) has followed writing as a career in varied ways. Born in Charleston, West Virginia, he became a reporter and business editor for the *Charleston Gazette* (1950–55) after getting his M.A. degree at Ohio University. Subsequently he moved to Ashland, Kentucky, where for sixteen years he worked for the Ashland Oil Company in public relations, a job that included being principal writer and editor for the company's quarterly magazine. Since 1982 he has been a member of the school of journalism at Marshall University, while still living in Ashland.

In addition to being a journalist, Knight has published poetry and long and short fiction. His short story "The Way We Went" was published in the *Atlantic Monthly* in 1972, reprinted in Martha Foley's *Best American Short Stories in 1972*, and published in the *Junior Great Books Series* of the Great Books Foundation in 1980. Most widely recognized among Knight's writings, however, was *Lightstruck*, published by the Atlantic Monthly Press in 1979.

Lightstruck did not win favor with all who read it, but in general it was commended by the critics. *Kirkus* (Dec. 1, 1978) did not like the ending or the style. The *Washington Post Book World*, on the other hand, found the book "beautifully written"; *Publishers Weekly* found it a "beautifully crafted, deliberately cryptic novel" (Dec. 11, 1978); and the *Library Journal* considers it an "intelligently constructed, clever parable" (Jan. 1, 1979). The story reports what happens one night when a brilliant, unexplained light falls upon a small Midwestern town. Among the inhabitants portrayed are a burglar who dies of a heart attack, a boy who is being beat up by a gang, a pair of backseat lovers, a young lady who claims she has been raped by spacemen, a hack writer who smacks his lips as he thinks of writing a best-seller, an old newspaperman who just wants to get his facts straight, and a host of others. The story is told with sardonic humor rather than with a sense of heavy purpose or of sudden death.

Hunter Thompson

Hunter Thompson (1939–), whose writings can marginally be called belletristic, was the inventor of "Gonzo, or Outlaw Journalism." True Gonzo reporting, Thompson explains in *The Great Shark Hunt*, "needs the talent of a master journalist, the eye of an artist/photographer . . . the writer *must* be a participant in the scene." Thompson has won considerable attention: his writings have been very widely reviewed, he has been parodied in a movie called *Where the Buffalo Roam,* and a character in Garry Trudeau's cartoon strip "Doonesbury" has been modeled on him—"Duke, the bald, vicious, foreshortened elf" (*Courier-Journal,* Jan. 10, 1982). Thompson, who grew up in Louisville, has had a phenomenally varied writing career, which has seen him in the role of a sports writer in Florida, a correspondent for *The National Observer* in South America, the "Washington Correspondent" for *Rolling Stone,* and the author of four long volumes.

Hell's Angels: A Strange and Terrible Saga (1967) was his first full-length book. Dealing with the notorious California motorcycle gang, its history, its day-to-day life, and the experiences of its members with speed, violence, sex, and drugs, the account attracted a good deal of attention. It was, however, *Fear and Loathing in Las Vegas: A Savage Journey to the Heart of the American Dream* (1972), first published in *Rolling Stone,* that was to become a counterculture classic. A review in the *Library Journal* (Aug. 1972) describes the contents and reveals a typical critical reaction: "This is a tale of 'fear and loathing' on both sides of the freak culture; it's the American Dream and its savagery seen from both sides of the same gap, Horatio Alger stoned. The writing is some of the cleverest, funniest, and best-paced material in a long while. Thompson's Marx Brothers' movement through these incredible days in Las Vegas creates a terrifying, fascinating tale that is meant to be read in one gulp, as it appears to have been written."

The Great Shark Hunt: Strange Tales from a Strange Time (1979), benefiting from Thompson's reputation as the High Priest of Gonzo Journalism, became a best-seller, but the critics were cool toward it, for they found the volume repetitious of Thompson's earlier work and the author "teetering on a fine edge between brilliance and burnout." *The Curse of Lomo* was published in 1983 and is typical Thompson fare, this time growing out of a journalistic assignment to Hawaii.

Coleman Dowell

Coleman Dowell (1925–85) was a writer often acclaimed in literary circles but a commercial failure. He was born in Adairville, attended high school in Franklin, and moved to Louisville, where he lived for five years before moving to New York in 1950. Though he mostly wrote fiction (short stories and five novels), he also wrote plays and music, including the score for the musical *The Tattooed Countess* (1961), based on a book of the same name by Carl Van Vechten, and for a weekly television show called "Once upon a Tune." But Dowell's success in music and the theater was limited, and he turned to fiction.

Dowell's unpleasant subject matter partially accounted for his lack of financial success as a novelist. In his obituary Bradford Morrow, Dowell's editor, speaks of his works as "an examination of sexual obsession, homosexuality, and social issues" and of his characters as creations with which most readers cannot identify. Dowell's first novel, *One of the Children Is Crying* (1968) is set in Kentucky and concerns what one reviewer calls "the twisted wreckage" of "the mixed-up children" of Murdoch McChesney as they return home to attend their father's funeral. *Too Much Flesh and Jabez* (1977) perhaps received more attention than any other of Dowell's novels. Like his first novel, *Too Much Flesh* also deals with decadence in a small town. It tells how a seventy-year-old retired schoolteacher copes with her loneliness and desolation by fantasizing about one of her former students and then writing down her long-repressed feelings for him. Other novels by Dowell include *Mrs. October Was There* (1974), *Island People* (1976), and *White on Black on White* (1983).

Dowell's novels reached a small audience and received mixed reviews and judgments: "Ahead of his time—a novelist's novelist"; "drenched in sensuality"; "novels depicting Southern decadence died with novels such as this"; "a bold examination of black pain and anger and white guilt that crackles with insights"; "the reader may be outraged or disgusted or pleased."

Jack A. Cady

Jack A. Cady (1932–), who grew up in Louisville, has had a remarkably varied career ranging from being an auctioneer to a tree climber in Massachusetts and a truck driver in southeastern U.S. His first published volume was his best and his most successful. This was *The Burning and Other Stories* (1972), which won the Iowa School of Letters Award in Short Fiction from among two hundred entries and was published by the University of Iowa Press. One of the best stories is the title piece, "The Burning," which grew out of Cady's three years of experience as a heavy-truck driver. It is the story of a driver trapped in the burning cab of his multiwheeled truck, in which the author describes the scene and sequence of events in matter-of-fact, unemotional, but chilling fashion as he leads up to a bystander with a gun who would put the victim out of his misery. The volume was reviewed rather widely and the criticism was upbeat. One reviewer pronounced Cady to be in "the front rank of contemporary short-story writers"; no one failed to find merit in Cady's stories, though some found fault with his unevenness.

Cady has written other stories and five novels. These reveal his interest in mystery and the supernatural, but like *Singleton* (1981), which returns to truck-drivers and the Jack Kerouac tradition of the road, they lack the freshness and force of *The Burning and Other Stories*.

Leon V. Driskell

Leon V. Driskell (1932–), a native of Georgia, teaches creative writing at the University of Louisville. Driskell is also a writer of fiction and has published short stories in the *Carolina Quarterly*, the *Georgia Review*, and elsewhere. Three of these have been listed among the best stories of the year in *Best American Short Stories*, and he has received the Lawrence Award from *Prairie Schooner* magazine. His *Passing Through* (1983) is a collection of nine stories which work together as a chronological narrative. The setting is Owen County, and the characters are members of the Waters clan, with Mama Pearl presiding over a household of women and children, grandchildren, and great-grandchildren of her first husband's first wife. The experiences of this motley set of eccentrics constitute the story. As one reviewer puts it, "Driskell writes with affection and humor of particular people making the best of hard lives and loss" (*Publishers Weekly*, July 15, 1983).

Driskell is also a critic and scholar. He is a frequent reviewer for the *Courier-Journal* and is coauthor (with Joan T. Brittain) of *The Eternal Crossroads: The Art of Flannery O'Connor* (1971).

Some Novels about Tobacco

Despite the chronological ordering of authors in this chapter, perhaps it is an admissible interruption to bring together five lesser authors who wrote about a common subject, though not extensively enough to warrant a separate chapter. The subject was tobacco and the authors who wrote novels about it include Frances Ogilvie, William Woodrow Chamberlain, Elizabeth Pickett Chevalier, Virgil Steed, and Charley Robertson—the last the only one among these writers to publish more than one work of fiction. Prior to this little eddy of interest in tobacco during the 1930s and 1940s, however, others had written about the subject, and their works are discussed elsewhere. These include John Fox, Jr., whose *The Heart of the Hills* has Jason Hawn becoming involved in the Tobacco Wars when he comes from the hills to the Bluegrass to get an education. In Elizabeth Madox Roberts's *The Time of Man* (1926) the principal character, Ellen Chesser, is the daughter, and later the wife, of a tobacco-growing sharecropper. Tobacco also plays a role in Jesse Stuart's novels—in *Trees of Heaven* (1940), for example, with those two memorable characters, landowner Anse Bushman and sharecropper Bolliver Tussie; and in *Hie to the Hunters* (1950), where in careful detail Stuart describes the steps involved in tobacco-growing. Tobacco figures in Caroline Gordon's fiction, especially in *The Garden of Adonis* (1937); and, more recently, in Wendell Berry's *A Place on Earth* (1969) and *The Memory of Old Jack* (1974). Edith Summers Kelly was the first Kentucky writer to devote an entire novel—*Weeds* (1923)—to tobacco tenant farming; but best known of the tobacco novels is *Night Rider* (1939), by Robert Penn Warren.

Frances Ogilvie Frances Ogilvie (1902–42), born in Princeton, Caldwell County, was the first Kentucky writer after Edith Summers Kelley to make tobacco and tobacco-growing the central focus of a novel. Ogilvie wrote several novels, but she submitted only one of them to a publisher. This was *Green Bondage* (1931), which draws on incidents the author witnessed or knew about when she was a child. One of these was the burning of three tobacco warehouses in Princeton. The story itself is a tale of two generations of tobacco farmers in Caldwell County—from the death of Sam Davis, killed while night-riding, to the time of his daughter's settling in for a life of hard work just as her parents had done before her. This realistic story portrays the toil and drudgery of tobacco farming and gives an account of the Tobacco Wars.

William Woodrow Chamberlain Another lesser novel about tobacco is William Woodrow Chamberlain's *Leaf Gold* (1941). In it Chamberlain (1914–), a native of Glasgow and a graduate of Centre College, writes with understanding of farm life in general and of tobacco-growing in particular. His novel tells the story of a tenant-farmer, Bert Perkins, his young wife, Nolie, and the Parks family, on whose farm Bert works. It portrays the demanding year-round cycle of planting, growing, and harvesting, and the hardships of tenants as they try to get ahead. But the novel is no "tobacco road" sort of story and in certain respects contrasts with Edith Summers Kelley's *Weeds*; for although it depicts hard work, disappointment, and even tragedy, none of it is portrayed as drudgery or as heavily burdensome. Instead, the portrayal is softened by the fact that among landlords there are many who are generous and charitable, that love of the soil and working with it is or can be a noble and rewarding experience, that there is always the reasonable hope of owning one's own farm, and that the hard and unrewarding life of tenant-farmers is often due to their own shiftlessness. *Leaf Gold* is a warm-hearted story, as one reviewer puts it, that is told in a leisurely fashion and with "the fidelity of a slow-motion cinema."

Chamberlain now lives in Richland, Washington.

Elizabeth Pickett Chevalier *Drivin' Woman* (1942), by Elizabeth Pickett Chevalier (1896–1984), covers a period of fifty years following the Civil War. Its heroine is America ("Merry") Collier Moncure, who is eighteen at the end of the war. Her father is dead, her brother is a fugitive, and she herself flees from her ancestral home in Virginia to Mason County, Kentucky, for having killed a lecherous Yankee who assaulted her sister. Here she successfully grows tobacco and teaches school near Maysville. Then she marries a rapscallion cousin, a Mississippi River riverboat gambler who becomes a murderer but to whom she remains loyal through thirty years of hardship and disgrace as she has trysts with him and bears him two daughters whom she explains as illegitimate, for nobody must know that the hunted murderer is still alive. Of Merry, *Time* magazine says, she "catches the womanly public coming and going: she is at once a Jezebel, a faithful wife, a W.C.T.U.-pledgee, a patrician, a pauper, a farmer, a mother of ingrate daughters sired by a worthless husband, a passionate creature, an unsatisfied creature, a high-grade businesswoman" (Aug. 3, 1942). The novel was published on the sixth anniversary of *Gone with the Wind* and rivaled it for a while, but its early success faded, for in the movie version there were no Clark Gable and Vivien Leigh to immortalize it.

Nevertheless, *Drivin' Woman* made quite a stir. When the Macmillan Company saw the manuscript in the summer of 1940, it contained more than a million words; but six months later under the guidance of editor Maxwell Aley the manuscript was cut to book size, with the movie rights sold to Metro-Goldwyn-Mayer. It became the Literary Guild selection for July 1942, sold 300,000 copies during the first six months, was translated into five languages, was serialized in the *Ladies Home Journal*, and the author was catapulted into fame.

Though Chevalier was born in Chicago, worked for the Red Cross in Washington, and assisted in the making of such motion pictures as *What Price Glory?* (1926) and *Seventh Heaven* (1927), she was also well qualified to write about growing tobacco on a Kentucky farm.

In 1928, she says, while she was working with David O. Selznick on *Thunderbolt*, the inspiration for *Drivin' Woman* came to her in a childhood memory of her grandfather's farm in Mason County: a moonlit night with Night Riders pounding down a country road and minutes later a barn ablaze against the horizon. Thereupon she set out for Tuckahoe Ridge and for eight years lived there, learning first hand all she could about farming and especially about tobacco. The knowledge she gained about raising, cutting, stripping, grading, and auctioning tobacco informs the novel. Chevalier also tells the story of the Tobacco Wars, but she does something not done in other novels about tobacco: she covers both the birth and the death of the tobacco trust. The canvas is large as she goes back in time to Virginia and "Tugger" Blake, a Tarheel trader and friend of the Moncures, who peddles Durham tobacco in little drawstring sacks, becomes a financial genius, and organizes the southern tobacco trust. The story moves to New York and the offices of the trust and even of financial institutions and the stock exchange. Years later the story continues in Mason County when Merry and other farmers, unable to manage with the prices paid by the trust, rise in rebellion and organize the Night Riders.

Reviews of the novel were mixed. The *Christian Century* characterized it as "a dramatic tale that has never been told and well deserved to be," maintaining that the author "handles her materials with real mastery," but also adding, "Apparently it was written with one eye, if not both, on Hollywood" (Aug. 12, 1942). *Time*'s judgment was that "*Drivin' Woman* reads like an inspired high-school prize composition packed with cinematic moments. It revolves around a character who may turn out to be the most satisfying heroine since Scarlett O'Hara" (Aug. 3, 1942).

Virgil Steed A less memorable novel was *Kentucky Tobacco Patch* (1947) of Virgil Steed (1901–). Born in Georgia, Steed went to New York, where he met his wife-to-be, a Lexington, Kentucky, native. In time the two of them became farmers on land now occupied by the Eastland Shopping Center in Lexington. For seventeen years Steed was a grower of tobacco, but following a divorce he moved to Louisville, leaving his former wife on the land that was her inheritance. His novel lays no claim to distinction, but it does reflect the interest in tobacco during the 1930s and 1940s, for no fewer than fourteen novels about tobacco were written during this period. Steed's novel is a semifictional story that deals with farming in general but centers primarily on tobacco-growing.

Charley Robertson Charley Robertson's *Send for Miss Cora* (1948) is a story about the Tobacco Wars in Western Kentucky. Robertson (1907–81) grew up in Smithland, Livingston County, in the between-the-rivers section of Kentucky. After graduating from Western Kentucky State University, Robertson taught in Florida, became a W.P.A. administrator in the Kentucky mountains, and finally moved to Louisville when he took a position with the E.I. du Pont De Nemours Company. Writing, however, had been in Robertson's blood from the time he was a boy, and two novels—*Send for Miss Cora* and *Shadow of a Cloud*—bear witness to his success.

"There are stories a-plenty in these old hills and rivers. Stick to the things you know," an old lady once counseled Robertson. How well he heeded her advice is revealed by some of the reviews of his first novel, *Send for Miss Cora*. A *New York Herald-Tribune* reviewer identified Robertson's achievement as a "faithful and understanding portrayal of the day-to-day life 'between the rivers' of Kentucky" (Feb. 29, 1948). And in the words of a *Chicago Tribune* reviewer, "Mr. Robertson is a master of descriptive detail. You can hear the crackle of freezing mud, feel the bouncing gallop of the big horse, sniff the nighttime warmth of the old barn, and sense the backbreaking weariness that comes with making a tobacco crop" (July 4, 1948).

The story has a secondary plot that deals with Miss Cora and Bayless Calhoun, a man of great respect and goodness in the community, who sends for Miss Cora when domestic chores need to be done. The central story is about the teen-age Lennie Bogard, who one night finds his father dead, murdered by Night Riders. For three years, obsessed with his desire for retribution, Lennie seeks to learn the identity of the masked man who rode the gray pacer at the head of the Night Riders group that killed his father. In time he learns that Bayless Calhoun—Miss Cora's friend, Lennie's own benefactor, and the father of his fiancée—is the guilty one. The way Lennie deals with the problem of retribution provides what one reviewer calls a "natural, unforced ending" that need not be told here.

Robertson's other novel was *Shadow of a Cloud* (1950), perhaps the best story about moonshining writtten by a Kentuckian. The principal character is Paul Worden, from Orchard Mills, Kentucky. Paul, who is writing a novel, works at a plant in Detroit, but his rather uneventful way of life is interrupted when his fellow worker, Max Shafer, convinces him that big money can be made running moonshine from Kentucky to Detroit. The characters in the story are believable: Eva, a dipsomaniac; Harry, who plays lonesome music on his guitar; and "Little Preacher," who knows his Kentucky whiskey. The action, reminiscent of Golden Pond, the between-the-lakes area, and the Al Capone, Dutch Schulz, Waxie Gordon booze-running days, has truckstops and rendezvous, bullet-riddled corpses, and twisted wreckage of cars loaded with illegal whiskey. The novel had a mixed reception, ranging from "Absorbingly interesting from start to finish" to "a crude and uneven thing . . . with self-conscious realism . . . entirely lacking in the significance of Anderson, Norris, or Dreiser."

CHAPTER 25

The Current Scene: 1975–1985

During this last quarter of the century there is reason to believe that the Commonwealth's literary future is still in good hands. Elizabeth Hardwick is still publishing, and Robert Penn Warren is writing the finest poetry of his long career. Wendell Berry is in mid-career, and a new generation that has attracted an unusual amount of national attention has come along during the past decade. Guy Davenport published his first volume of short stories in 1974 and has received little but praise from the avant garde since then. Gayl Jones's first novel had a warm reception when it appeared in 1975, and she followed this success with another two years later, only to fall almost silent since then. Bobbie Ann Mason became an important writer on the national level overnight with her volume of short stories in 1982 and won equal acclaim for her first novel in 1985. Joe Ashby Porter got off to a good start with a volume of short stories in 1983, and Ed McClanahan won rave reviews for his first novel in 1983 and for his collection of stories and sketches two years later. Marsha Norman, who wrote her first play in 1977, won the Pulitzer Prize in drama in 1983. Only two of these writers are more than two volumes into their careers, and all but two have used Kentucky almost exclusively as their subject.

Guy Davenport

Hilton Kramer, reviewing Guy Davenport's *Tatlin! Six Stories* (1974) in the *New York Times* (Aug. 26, 1974), begins by saying that Davenport "is one of our most gifted and versatile men of letters—

critic, poet, classicist, translator, teacher, and book illustrator—and in *Tatlin!*, his first work of fiction, he has written a most unusual book." After writing at some length on the volume, Kramer concludes by saying, "Like Pound, he is given to quoting half a dozen languages, incorporating paraphrase and translation and indulging in obscure references. *Tatlin!* will thus offend the innocent reader and be an absolute delight to the literary connoisseur." Almost two months later, Andrew C.J. Bergman, reviewing the same volume in the *New York Times Book Review* (Oct. 20, 1974), and also writing at some length, complains about Davenport's "pedantic self-display" and his "exasperating penchant for the arcane." Near the end of his review Bergman concludes, "We get much of man's works but little of man; there is much here to praise but little to remember." Other objections are raised by other reviewers and critics: that there is "too much cleverness" or that the stories are a "webwork of meanings imprecise behind a screen of fussily virtuosi prose." On the other hand, John Gardner in *On Moral Fiction* (1977) asks who among writers now living "will outlast the century?" Gardner answers that of four or five who have such a chance, one is "conceivably Guy Davenport, if sheer precision and uncompromising artistry count." And George Steiner in a long article on Davenport in the *New Yorker* (Nov. 30, 1981) declares, "The fact is that Guy Davenport is among the very few truly original autonomous voices now audible in American letters," and concludes by saying that "he is . . . not everyone's cup of tea. But to a growing number he will, I am confident, be nectar."

Davenport (1927–) was born in South Carolina, received his A.B. in Classics and English at Duke, earned his B.Litt. from Oxford, where he was a Rhodes Scholar, and received his Ph.D. in English at Harvard. Before becoming a member of the English department at the University of Kentucky in 1963, he taught at Washington University in St. Louis and at Haverford College.

Davenport's first published volume was *The Intelligence of Louis Agassiz* (1963), followed by two translations: *Carmina Archilochi* (1964) and *Sappho: Songs and Fragments* (1965). Other work followed in the latter 1960s that showed Davenport's versatility, but it was not till the 1970s that his name came prominently to the attention of critics and readers. This was for his short fiction, first *Tatlin! Six Stories* (1974) and later *Da Vinci's Bicycle: Ten Stories* (1979). Next came his translation, *Archilochos, Sappho, Aikman* (1980), for which he was nominated for the second annual American Book Award. Since 1980 he has published other collections of stories, *Eclogues: Eight Stories*

Wendell Berry. Photo courtesy of James Baker Hall.

(1981) and *Apples and Pears and Other Stories* (1984), and a critical volume, *The Geography of the Imagination: Forty Essays* (1981), the latter, like the stories, pleasing some critics very much but scowled at by others. Critical reaction to Davenport is never of the ho-hum variety.

Davenport has also reviewed many, many books, notably in the *New York Times Book Review*; has often lectured or conducted seminars on Pound, Joyce, and other recent writers at such universities as Columbia, Yale, Princeton, and the University of Toronto; has served on three Pulitzer Prize juries; and has won numerous awards and honors, including the Leviton-Blumenthal Prize for Poetry in 1971, the American Academy of Arts and Letters Prize for Fiction in 1981; he has had short stories reprinted from the *Hudson Review* in Martha

Guy Davenport. Photo courtesy of University of Kentucky Photographic Archives.

Foley's *Best Short Stories of 1973* and the *O. Henry Prize Stories*, 1974. At the University of Kentucky, he holds one of the prestigious University Alumni Professorships.

To say that *Tatlin!*, the volume that brought Davenport into the limelight, is made up of short stories is correct, but the statement is also just a bit misleading, for the stories in a certain sense are histori-

Bobbie Ann Mason. Photo courtesy of James Baker Hall.

cal fiction with an unusual amount of intellectual content. How does he use history for the purposes of fiction? How, as one critic puts it, does he "play idiosyncratic fictional games with historical personages and occasions?" In "Robot" Davenport starts from the known facts of the discovery of Cro-Magnon paintings in the Lascaux Cave in southern France during World War II and the investigation of them by an aging expert on prehistoric art, L'Abbé Breuil. To this Davenport adds

Marsha Norman. Photo courtesy of the *Courier-Journal*.

some French boys who are rabbit hunting with their dog "Robot" and are led to discover the treasure of the prehistoric paintings because of Robot's misadventures.

Davenport's contribution is far more, however, than just the invention of the elemental features of a plot. Stressing the importance of research in the fiction he writes, Davenport explains that he read everything he could about the paintings and the life of Breuil, about the cave, about everything related to the time and place. "I read some forty books about prehistory," he says, "visited the site of Lascaux, talked with Jacques Marsal, have heard first-hand accounts of refugees fleeing the Germans across that part of France." Seven years, he says, passed as he gathered the information he needed in order both to make "Robot" an adventure tale and an essay on the impulse toward art in prehistoric man and to provide a portrait of recent modern history, including a portrait of L'Abbé Breuil.

Comparable research and use of an informed imagination led to the writing of "The Aeroplanes at Brescia." The story, Davenport relates, began as a scholarly article when he learned that Franz Kafka attended the Italian air show at Brescia in 1909 in the company of his friends Max and Otto Brod. Kafka wrote about the occasion in a newspaper article and this "I combined . . . with Brod's memory of the occasion in his biography of Kafka, and with what I could discover of other people (D'Annunzio, Puccini) who were there, as well as of people who might have been there (Wittgenstein). At that time Wittgenstein was an aviator, not a philosopher. "To realize certain details I studied the contemporary photographs of Count Primoli, read histories of aviation, built a model of Blériot's *Antoinette* CV25, and collected as rich a gathering of allusions to the times as I could. I played over the story like a playful Calvinist God who knew what would happen in years to come." In all, Davenport says, "ninety-three historical personages are named in 'The Aeroplanes at Brescia' " ("Ernst Machs Max Ernst," *The Geography of the Imagination*, 174).

Sometimes the known historical facts from which Davenport works are even fewer than for the foregoing stories. For "Tatlin!," the story about the Soviet engineer, painter, and theoretician Vladimir Tatlin, Davenport says, "I literally used up every significant fact known about him in the Western world." We cannot here, however, pursue additional subjects dealt with in *Tatlin!*, *Da Vinci's Bicycle*, *Eclogues*, or *Apples and Pears*—twenty-eight stories in all—interesting though the pursuit would be. No doubt the best way to gain understanding of Davenport's critical principles, his views of the relationship of the past to the present, his indebtedness to certain recent writers, and his practice, would be to read at some length from *The Geography of the Imagination*; but some random jottings here may be enlightening.

A plot of sorts, as one reviewer puts it, encases a Davenport story "like a skimpy bikini," but it would be inaccurate to think of his stories as short stories in the conventional sense. Instead, they are the product of a process that brings together facts, events, and miscellaneous knowledge out of which is constructed a story that grows out of the past and connects the past with the present. The excitement which the stories generate is cerebral, and their purpose is to celebrate the human mind and to make the past and the present a sort of continuum. As Davenport says in "The Pound Vortex," one "can animate the dead past and make it live again . . . , one can find out the causes of wars, and can educate the people and make them noble . . . *find the best in the past and pass it on.*" Though Davenport is historically accurate in what he writes, the subjects he has chosen are so little known that in most cases they are "in the position of being, in fact, almost not there," thus leaving the author artistic freedom. "It is my sense," he says, however, "that I am always telling a story rather than projecting an illusory fictional world. . . . My Tatlin is not Tatlin, nor my Poe Poe. But my stories are about them." His aim, too, he says, has been "to let nothing of myself get into these stories." Instead, the essential requirement of fiction is "to imagine how others feel, what a Saturday afternoon in an Italian town in the second century was like. . . . In a sense my texts are translations of an obliterated original that can never be reconstructed again."

When complaint is raised against Davenport's writing, it is usually because of his method rather than because of content. One target of criticism is the way his themes and motifs appear in one story and then reappear in others in a complex pattern. Thus *Tatlin!*, as Davenport points out in "Ernst Machs Max Ernst," "begins with the invention of an archaic flying device, recognizable in other technological dialects as Pegasus, Chinese kites capable of reaching the moon, Daedalus's wings, the Wright Flyer, Eros as a *pteros* or winged phallos, da Vinci's ornithopter. *Tatlin!* ends with Commander Neil Armstrong stepping onto the dust of the dead moon. The book therefore spans the history of flight, a sustained symbolic web woven throughout with images of birds, *pteroi*, machines. . . ." And, of course, other themes run through the stories and tax—sometimes overtax—the mind of the reader.

Also confounding the uninitiated reader is Davenport's practice of juxtaposing unlike persons, places, and events without the benefit of connectives or clarification to reveal relationships. For example, in "The Richard Nixon Freischütz Rag," from *Da Vinci's Bicycle*, Nixon visits China and listens intently as a poem by Chairman Mao is read to him. "He wrote that?" Nixon says. "Made it up? . . . My! but that's interesting." Then this is followed by a piece on Leonardo da Vinci, which in turn is followed by one on Gertrude Stein. "For making these particulars cohere I tried to learn from certain highly elliptical writers how much can be omitted from a page." He cites Hugh Kenner, Osip Mandelstam, Samuel Beckett, Wyndham Lewis, Ezra Pound, and Charles Doughty; these are writers, he says, "who do not waste a word, who condense, pare down, and proceed with daring synapses."

No complaint is raised more often than the degree to which the author's erudition—his knowledge of archaeology, lexicography, mythology, cultural history, languages and literatures both ancient and modern—intrudes on the story. Such allusiveness can, of course, be wonderfully illuminating to the well-stocked mind, but other readers may be baffled and still others offended by such lavish historical and literary collages. To them such displays are ostentatious, a needless freight of arcane knowledge. And indeed the range in time, the span of subject matter, and the store of knowledge which this "specialist in the unheard of" seems to handle with ease is staggering. In *Tatlin!* alone he ranges from the sixth century B.C. to the 1960s and from Ephesus to Amsterdam. Seven different languages in six different countries with their six different cultures flow through the pages in dazzling array. A *Los Angeles Times* reviewer of *The Geography of the Imagination* exclaims, "There is no way to prepare yourself for reading Guy Davenport. You stand in awe before his knowledge of the archaic (the cave paintings of Lascaux, Heraclitus, Diogenes, Homer) and his knowledge of the modern (Joyce, Mahler, Gaudier-Brzeska, Marianne Moore). Even more, you stand in awe of the connections he can make between the archaic and the modern; he makes the remote familiar and the familiar fundamental."

James Baker Hall

James Baker Hall (1935–) began writing in earnest in the 1970s and appears to have come into full career in the 1980s. He was born in Lexington and was a student at the University of Kentucky at a time when four young writers who would succeed remarkably well during the years ahead were just beginning their careers: Wendell Berry, Ed McClanahan, Gurney Norman, and Hall himself. Each did graduate work at the University of Kentucky and each went on to Stanford University in order to work in the Stanford writing program under the direction of Wallace Stegner and to hold one of the Stegner writing fellowships. Hall received his M.A. there in 1961. Hall was also greatly interested in photography and worked with Gene Meatyard, a distinguished Lexington photographer. Subsequently he taught English and photography at the Massachusetts Institute of Technology and at the University of Connecticut. Hall's expertness in photography is reflected in his attention to detail and his eye for contrast in his writings, and especially in his poetry. Hall is a member of the creative writing program at the University of Kentucky.

Hall's first published novel was *Yates Paul, His Grand Flights, and His Tootings* (1963). The novel grew in part out of the author's interest in photography and has been described as "a comic novel about fear and loneliness, about several kinds of darkrooms, and about the courage and help it takes to come out of them." The novel was neither a critical nor a popular success. The 1980s arrived before Hall published another novel, *Music for a Broken Piano* (1983), set in the Berkshire Hills of Massachusetts during the summer of 1969, the year of Woodstock and a time of much political and social turmoil. Forty young people in their twenties and thirties, all of liberal persuasions, have given up their workaday pursuits for the summer in order to live in a communal organization and search for more meaningful lives. The novel recounts the interplay of personality within the group and how the lives of the participants are changed by the experience. Dramatic tensions and stresses of many sorts develop—ideological, racial, sexual, and other—as the unconventional members of the group assert their differences and struggle for influence within the group. In Makar, the only black in the group, Hall has created an especially interesting character, a gifted, angry, flamboyant provocateur. Two other central characters share the spotlight: Makar's opposite number, Toni McHugh, an angry, calculating feminist, and Nathan, who seeks to bridge differences and is Jewish, liberal, and egalitarian. The book is thoughtful as the author sympathetically portrays the flower-child idealism that emerged in the 1960s, while at the same time portraying and examining the way conflicts and the potential for self-destruction arise in communal living with its free-love and revolutionary idealism.

Hall also published short stories in periodicals, among them the *Saturday Evening Post*, *Cimarron Review*, *Shenandoah Review*, *Chicago Review*, and the *Paris Review*. Around 1970 he began writing poetry that likewise was published in periodicals, and within fifteen years had published perhaps 150 poems. These appeared in *Sewanee Review*, *Southern Poetry Review*, *Massachusetts Review*, *Hudson Review*, *American Scholar*, *Antioch Review*, *Denver Quarterly Review*, *New Yorker*, and *Poetry*. He has published two volumes of verse: *Get-*

ting It on Up to the Brag (1975) and *Her Name* (1981). The former, which contains only twelve poems, may be characterized variously as restrained, lyrical, humorous, and whimsical. Perhaps the following passage is a fair sample of the poems in the volume. Here the poet imagines himself writing poems on the dusty sides of trailer trucks which travel all over America displaying his poems:

Straight to Topeka, Kansas, to Wayne Willis,
and old Wayne and his girl, pulling
up beside my big poem, they'll see
how the letters are all equally clear,
and he'll say to his girl, Gee Whiz,
that poet who found the ephemeral home
in the truck stop on the Jersey Turnpike
licks his motherhunching finger
after every letter, he's eating
America's road dirt for us!

The later volume, *Her Name*, also a thin one, is different in tone from the earlier volume and its lines slower to yield up their meaning. Perhaps the following segment from "The Cloudless Sky Takes Charge" is representative:

3/ The place to see
lightning is the desert, the sky
behind it, all around it

Like a great lizard
flicking out its tongue

The egg of darkness cracked.
a brief glimpse
at the other side

We lie there
face to face
back to back

caught in the shadows
on the wall

Gayl Jones

Gayl Jones was born in Lexington in 1949, received her A.B. in English from Connecticut College in 1971, and earned her M.A. and D.A. in creative writing at Brown University in 1973 and 1975 respectively. In 1975 she accepted an assistant professorship in English and Afro-American studies at the University of Michigan. Her writing career began early with her first novel, *Corregidora*, in 1975, a second novel, *Eva's Man*, in 1976, and a volume of short stories, *White Rat*, in 1977. Her work, which may be characterized as bleak and brutal, has been praised for its power, partly because of which she has won a number of awards and honors: Frances Steloff Award for Fiction, 1970; Breadloaf Writer's Conference Award, 1973; Shubert Grant for Playwriting, 1973–74; Rhode Island Council on the Arts Grant in Writing, 1974–75; Howard Foundation Award, 1975; National Endowment for the Arts Fellowship, 1976; Michigan Society of Fellows Grant, 1977–79. Despite Jones's productivity during the 1970s, she is included here both because her work is more in tune with a new spirit in literature and because at her age the greater part of her writing career lies ahead.

Jones quickly won considerable national reputation with *Corregidora*. The principal character is Ursa Corregidora, a fourth-generation descendant of a Portuguese seaman who became a Brazilian plantation coffee-grower and took Ursa's beautiful great-grandmother out of the plantation slave-fields, turned her to his own sexual use, and then did likewise with her daughter, his own child. Thus he fathered the generations from which Ursa sprang and in each of which the mother passes the story along, underscoring the fact that "the important thing is making generations." This admonition is important to Ursa, who is concerned with the way miscegenation and female exploitation, coupled with slave brutality, have debased black male-female relations and how this debasement lingers on as a buried, hidden thing in male-female relationships. Thus to Ursa femaleness among blacks and the rooting out of an ingrained racial memory becomes central.

Ursa is a blues singer in a seedy club in Lexington in the 1940s. She marries Mutt Thomas, whom she loves, and thus faces the burning question of whether after generations of incest and prostitution and male exploitation she can escape her heritage and find a man who will love her without hurting her and destroying her. But Mutt is driven almost to madness as he watches his wife sing before boozing men; and when she refuses to give up her singing, in anger he knocks her down a flight of stairs, causing injuries that lead to her having a hysterectomy. A divorce follows and then marriage to Tadpole, the owner of the club. But this fails too and—unable to "make" a new generation—Ursa for psychological survival gives herself over to her singing and to regaining her own maimed femaleness.

The novel is full of black anger, but it is not a polemical nov nor an indictment of whites, nor even a novel of woman's liberation. With sordid detail, raw emotion, and explicit sexual language the novel works its way through frigidity and passion, pleasure and pain, love and hate. But to most critics this sexuality and the unflinching language are handled with good taste and the author is regarded as "a powerful and gifted writer" as she probes "the bleak side of love." "No black novel since Richard Wright's *Native Son*," says one reviewer, "has so skillfully traced psychic wounds to a sexual source" (*Time*, June 16, 1975).

Jones's second novel, *Eva's Man*, is an excursion into abnormal psychology and the lower depths of savage sexuality. Eva tells her story from her cell in a prison ward for the criminally insane, where for five years she has been confined for murdering a man and then mutilating him sexually. Like *Corregidora*, *Eva's Man* is about sex "as an act, as a burden," but whereas in the first work there was sometimes tenderness, in the latter there is nothing but brutality. Eva has come up through an environment devoid of purpose and value. "People," says Jones, "are made up of their memories, their pasts, and the pasts of their ancestors," and Eva accordingly has been heir to "squalor, with its beatings, shootings, sodomy, cockroaches, deformity, and child molestation." Bit by bit, disjointedly, as Eva tells her story to psychiatrists, her cellmate, and others, the reader learns of the events that have made her what she is and that ended in a five-day sexual orgy and nightmare and with the death of Davis, a man she came to know by chance.

Few critics have failed to find power in *Eva's Man*. To many it is a taut and compelling story, the dialogue precise and spare and lean, and the narrative sometimes lyrical. Few question Jones's seriousness as a writer. The starkness of the story and its terror, the brutalization of human beings in an environment devoid of plan or motive, however, alienate some readers and critics. "In many ways," says Jones herself, "*Eva's Man* is a horror story. It really is."

While writing these novels, which constitute her major work thus far, Jones was also writing poems, plays, and short stories. *White Rat* (1977), is a collection of her short fiction, the themes of which are much like those of her novels: female exploitation, adolescent courtship, lesbianism, sodomy, neuroticism, and so on. The title story is about a black man who looks white and his troubled search for identity. Jones explores this use of the white rat as the symbol of miscegenation which eats away black identity.

Jones's novels and short stories were written during the 1970s when the civil rights and feminist movements were matters of central interest to both blacks and women, but her writing avoids being polemical or explicitly political. The victimization of blacks by whites is clearly implicit in what she writes but is not her real subject. At the same time, she avoids preachiness. In *White Rat* Jones has not added significantly to what she has already said in her novels, but her writing is powerful and her handling of the vernacular of black speech excellent.

Since *White Rat* in 1977 the rate of Jones's publication has slowed down. Her next full-length publication was *Song for Anninho* (1981), an epic poem of love and freedom in colonial Brazil, but it has not received the attention that her fiction did.

Bobbie Ann Mason

Bobbie Ann Mason (1940–) has been a slow starter but a sudden achiever. She grew up in Mayfield, attended the University of Kentucky, where she got her A.B. in English in 1962, became interested in writing, and went to New York, where she worked as a writer for movie magazines. But this, she says, "wasn't the writing career I had in mind when I was an iconoclastic columnist on the University of Kentucky *Kernel*." As a result she entered graduate school in English and received her Ph.D. from the University of Connecticut. Then she "lapsed back into my childhood and started reading Nancy Drew books," from which was to grow her *The Girl Sleuth: A Feminist Guide to the Bobbsey Twins*, a descriptive, semi-critical study, published in 1975. During this period she also married (1969), began teaching at Mansfield State College in Pennsylvania (1972), and by the end of the decade embarked upon a career in fiction writing that quickly blossomed.

"Shiloh," a short story published in the *New Yorker* in October 1980, won attention at once and was selected for inclusion in Houghton Mifflin's *Best American Short Stories of 1981*. Mason continued to write stories for magazines and in 1982 published *Shiloh and Other Stories*, a volume that brought instant acclaim from the critics. "Vision and technique come exhilaratingly together," says the *New York Review of Books* (Dec. 16, 1982); "Go buy this book. Don't borrow it, don't look for it in the library," exclaims the *New Republic*, "but buy it as a way of casting your vote for real literature" (Nov. 1, 1982). During the year that followed Mason received repeated recognition because of the volume: The Ernest Hemingway Foundation Award for first fiction and the PEN/Faulkner Award, as well as a National Book Critics Award nomination and an American Book Award nomination. In addition she received a National Endowment for the Arts fellowship (1983), a Pennsylvania Arts Council grant (1983), and a Guggenheim fellowship (1984).

"Just about everything I write is about Kentucky," Mason says, but as one reviewer puts it, she "never lets us forget that her small district encompasses much of the U.S." Primarily Mason's stories grow out of the rural and working-class people she grew up with in Western Kentucky—their problems, their sorrows, and their frustrations; people, as one reviewer put it, "just trying not to get lost in the shuffle." They are, in the main, people who are experiencing a sense of loss, for they have been severed from a time they remember when people lived by inherited values. "Shiloh" is about the crumbling of a sixteen-year-old marriage between Leroy Moffitt, a disabled truck driver who is locked into the past, and Norma Jean Moffitt, who works at the Rexall store and is changing with the times as she attends the local community college. Like some other Mason characters, Leroy is floundering in a world that is passing him by; subdivisions have been spreading around him and the ways of doing things have changed without his really "noticing." In "Detroit Skyline" a child from Kentucky learns about television, tall buildings, and "Reds" when she goes to Detroit for a visit with her kinsfolk. "The Retreat" is about an electrician and part-time minister trapped in an unfulfilling marriage. Over and over Mason's people find themselves emotionally and intellectually distanced from each other by the way in which they respond to their changing world. The stories are not, however, a series of tragedies in the classic sense, but stories told lovingly and compassionately—not sentimentally or condescendingly—of farmers, blue-collar workers, housewives, K-Mart clerks, truck drivers, in a world where mutability alters their lives faster than they can comprehend and adjust to what is happening.

Mason's first novel, *In Country*, published in 1985, was enthusiastically received and widely reviewed. The scene of the novel, like that of her short stories, is a small town near Paducah where everything is becoming the same as everywhere else in the country: fast-food outlets, K-Marts, shopping malls, and cable TV; farms are dying and industrial parks are spreading. The spiritual milieu is one of ordinary people experiencing the malaise of the new homogenized way of life that has replaced the old one and to which is added the delayed effect of the war in Vietnam. The central character is Sam (Samantha) Hughes, whose father was killed in the war before she was born, and who is now increasingly afflicted by the syndrome that has afflicted so many other veterans of the Vietnam war. Mason, who has mastered the way teen-agers talk, has succeeded well in catching the laconic manner and limited emotional range of her young people while at the same time reflecting the ambivalance of their lives.

Joe Ashby Porter

Though Joe Ashby Porter (1942–   ) has spent most of his adult life outside Kentucky, he grew up in Madisonville and has often chosen Kentucky as the subject of his fiction. He took his A.B. at Harvard (1964), studied at Cambridge University on a Fulbright fellowship (1964–65), and did his M.A.(1966) and Ph.D. (1973) at the University of California at Berkeley. He is now a professor of English at Duke University, where he teaches creative writing. In addition to being the author of a novel and a volume of short stories, Porter has published a scholarly volume, *The Drama of Speech Acts: Shakespeare's Lancastrian Tetralogy* (1979).

Eelgrass (1977), a novel, was Porter's first published volume. The story originates in the flower-child and drug culture movements of the 1960s and takes place, as one writer puts it, on "a magic island peopled with fairies, supernatural folk, and foolish mortals." The volume was not a critical success, but Porter was commended for his good writing. *The Kentucky Stories* (1983), published by the Johns Hopkins University Press, received more critical attention. Porter says in the foreword, "Kentucky became what it is in these stories, a state of mind. It is a state of listening for the grave and reedy voice that comes out of nowhere and with complete assurance begins its inexplicable tale." When one says that Porter writes about Kentucky, however, one must remember that this is true in a special sense. With other authors we find Kentuckians living in a context and involved in actions we are familiar with. Porter's characters and actions are at least once removed from reality. People and events are reported in a straightforward fashion by a narrator who tells his story in an easy, relaxed, comfortable way that makes the reader a sort of intimate listening audience. The story, however, is often about violence—child abuse, incest, murder, and madness. The events are not within the narrator's personal acquaintance, but rather he is telling a story he has heard and perhaps added to. In "A Child of the Heart," for example, we are told that "we have managed to piece it out together in the course of many long evenings when the talk turns to neighbors and their people"; and, "It is likely that each one who hears the story has his private version of the occurrence." Porter's short stories, then, are told at second- or third-hand, and the account is not intended to be a realistic record of what happened as it is in, say, Mason's *Shiloh*, McClanahan's *The Natural Man*, or Berry's *A Place on Earth*.

"Bowling Green" with its startling ending draws upon the old story of a young man who goes away to college, jilting the girl to whom he had been offering his attentions; "A Child of the Heart" deals with a disaster triggered by a peddler; "Nadine, The Supermarket, The Story Ends" is a short story with three loosely related parts which end in a post–nuclear holocaust Kentucky. "The Vacation" (which has been reprinted in *Best American Short Stories*) is a wistful and sometimes whimsical story about a misunderstood husband who decides that he, his wife, and his no-account son all need a year's vacation from each other and runs into unanticipated complications.

The scenes of Porter's eight stories range from the Jackson Purchase to the Pennyrile to the Blue Grass to the mountains. Each story is told well and in generally excellent language and style. They start in a casual matter-of-fact way and readily win the reader's interest. This done, the author comfortably leads the reader quickly into the midst of the story with unhurried and carefully pruned language. Thus the first story in the volume, "Bowling Green," begins, "So, you come from there, did you? Maybe they told you about R.W. Pritchett." From that point onward, as one reader puts it, Porter has the Ancient Mariner's knack of holding readers' attention almost against their will.

Ed McClanahan

For more than twenty years between 1961 and 1983 Ed McClanahan (1932–) was writing short stories and nonfiction prose and trying to finish a novel that refused to be written. To make a living, having received his A.B. in English at Miami (Ohio) University and his M.A. at the University of Kentucky, he taught creative writing at Oregon State College, Stanford University (where he held a Stegner Writing Fellowship), the University of Montana, and the University of Kentucky. The novel he was working on was *The Natural Man*, which was published in 1983 and brought McClanahan a degree of acclaim that first novels seldom earn.

The novel is about growing up, about adolescence—and male adolescence in particular. Harry Eastep, a fifteen-year-old boy, is the central figure. He is more sophisticated and more intelligent than most of his peers, but he is still "a slouching, shambling, gangling tangle of ganglia." He is growing up in Needmore, in Burdock County, located in "south-central northeastern" Kentucky, and according to Harry it is "to all intents and purposes out of business." One day at the bus station arrives the streetwise Monroe "Monk" McHorning, a fifteen-year-old orphan from Newport weighing 238 pounds and measuring 6'5". He has been recruited and adopted by the Burdock County High School principal and basketball coach to win games for his Bulldogs and to please the local sports boosters. Monk lives up to his billing on the basketball floor and in the poolhall, and his stock of dirty jokes is unlimited and awe-inspiring. He and Harry become friends, and Monk sets about educating Harry, for according to Monk, "There was a big secret of 'carnal knowledge' going around and everyone except Harry was getting in on it." Before long Harry is plotting how to be rid of the shackles of sexual innocence and soon has his eye on "Oodles" Ockerman, whose scent of drugstore cologne hangs over her "like a slightly sordid idea."

It is not the characters and events of the novel, however, that make *The Natural Man* a remarkable success; rather it is the author's handling of his materials. In the words of a reviewer in the *New York Times Book Review*, the novel is "superbly written. . . . I predict it will eventually find its place beside great coming-of-age books like *The Adventures of Huckleberry Finn* and *Catcher in the Rye*" (April 24, 1983). Several qualities help account for such an enthusiastic appraisal. For one, the rite-of-passage action is set in a context where the passing of a way of life is portrayed in other ways. For example, newly invented television is crowding out the movies and closing down the New Artistic Theatre just as a few years earlier movies had crowded out minstrel shows, lectures, exhibits, and talent shows. And there is the war for which Monk tried to enlist when he was fourteen and in which later as a master sergeant he was killed by his own men. The novel supports two levels of awareness. It is written largely in the language of the poolroom and the high school gymnasium, while at the same time the impeccable prose of the prologue and epilogue frames and makes sense of the raucous and crude materials of the inner story.

Still another two-level feature of the novel is the way it works from rejection to reconciliation for both the characters and, one may say, the author. Perhaps the best-known fact about the writing of *The Natural Man* is that it required twenty-two years. McClanahan started it in 1961. "I write slowly, painfully slowly," he said in excuse for the delay. Actually, apparently, the thing that had to happen was for time to pass so that he could achieve the perspective, the maturity, to enable him to find his proper artistic relationship to his subject. When he began to write about adolescence and Harry Eastep's growing up in Needmore, he was too close to his own growing up at Brooksville, in Bracken County. No adjectives today are more often applied to *The Natural Man* than *funny, hilarious,* and *comic*—"the funniest novel I've read since *A Confederacy of Dunces*," say in essence the reviewers in *Newsweek* and *Kirkus*. But when McClanahan started writing it, "It wasn't the least bit amusing. It was about how I suffered as a young man; the subject was rejection." What McClanahan had to learn, of course, was that as author he had to have two simultaneous relationships to his characters and the action: he must be with them in their midst, see as they see and feel as they feel, and be at one with them in their adolescent rejection. At the same time, he must view them with detachment from a safe place, understandingly, lovingly. He must be both the creator and the created. Only then could he reconcile himself to his own experience and finish the book. In the epilogue ten years after the main events of the story when Harry is on his way to Lexington to be interviewed for a teaching position, he gets off the bus at Needmore and views again the place he knew when he was fifteen. Through this experience he makes his peace with his old home town and with growing up, and one can believe that the author does too.

With *The Natural Man* a critical success and the movie rights sold, McClanahan completed *Famous People I Have Known*, a collection of nonfiction pieces, some of which he had already written. *Famous People I Have Known* was published in 1985 and met a warm reception. The period that the volume draws upon is primarily the 1960s, the years of student rebellion, the drug culture, and the sexual revolution. The accounts are not totally lacking in bona fide "famous" people, but the real heroes are such figures as the rock 'n' roll singer Little Enis, assorted barflies, and the lady in Clovis, New Mexico, "whose earrings featured her late husband's gallstones"—the "loose ends" of life. McClanahan knows how to tell a story, even at his own expense, and the reader may be tempted not to take him seriously; but as one reviewer puts it, "this is, at heart, a serious book, though never solemn, and good-hearted and generous."

Joe Coomer

Joe Coomer (1958–), whose father's family was from Breathitt County, was born in Texas and came to Kentucky when his father took a job in Lexington. The family moved to a farm near Danville, and Coomer graduated from Boyle County High School. He then spent two years at the University of Kentucky, where he enrolled in a creative writing course and decided to give up the business career he had planned and to become a writer. Later his family moved back to Texas, where Coomer studied English at Southern Methodist University. During his senior year he began writing *Decatur Road: A Novel of the Appalachian Hill Country*.

Decatur Road (1983) opens with Mitchell Sparks walking down a two-rut road on his way to propose marriage to his sweetheart, Jenny. Jenny accepts his proposal and the novel tells the story of their fifty-year marriage, ending with old age and Jenny's death. Coomer tells a warm story about a simple people who have their share of good times and bad, and when it is over the reader feels good about the people in it and about life itself. The remarks of the reviewer in *Publishers Weekly* are typical: the author, the reviewer says, "captures time, place, and hearts exceedingly well in this close-to-the-land, warm evocation of Appalachia. A first novel from a promising new writer" (Sept. 9, 1983).

Kentucky Love (1985) has its setting primarily on a farm near Decatur (Danville) and the campus of the University of Kentucky, where Hart, the principal character, attended college. During the course of the novel Hart is spending his first year out of college on his grandfather's farm remembering his first love affair, which took place between his freshman and sophomore years. Brief though it was, it shook him so deeply that four years later he is still trying to rid himself of poignant memories of it by writing it out in a novel. Coomer's novel, as one reviewer (in *Newsday*) puts it, could have been "a gusher, a sappy, sentimental book to stop them all. But it's not." Instead, critics speak of it as an "infinitely charming" book and an intense and believable story about "the possibilities of life—and hope."

Louise Murphy

The Sea Within (1985) is another first novel that offers promise for the future. It is the story of Camille Anderson, thirty-one years old, who after years of marriage to a workaholic, "mildly philandering" husband goes back from California to Tom's Creek, Kentucky, her childhood home, with a desperate sense of failure. Pitching a tent on the one plot of ground she owns—a lot in a cemetery—she sets about getting her bearings again by re-examining her roots. This she does by exploring her traumatic past, in the process exorcising many painful memories.

Such a synopsis, however, fails to reveal the novel's full nature. One reviewer speaks of the "unexpected turns and twists in style, story and tone" and of its being "ludicrous, grotesque, absurd, off-beat, bizarre, cinematic, surreal . . . Kentucky Gothic." Then he adds, "It's hard to find the right words to describe the original work displayed in this major first novel" (Wade Hall, *Courier-Journal*, May 2, 1985). Not every reviewer considers *The Sea Within* a "major first novel," but hardly one fails to find merit in it. "Over-busy and over-gothic . . . but . . . an energetic and attractive debut," reported the *Kirkus Review* (March 1, 1985); "a lovely, brave piece of work by a first novelist of shining promise," says the *New York Times Book Review*, (April 21, 1985).

The author (1943–) was born Louise Natcher in Bowling Green and grew up in Kentucky. She took her A.B. degree at the University of Kentucky, taught in a junior-high school in Delaware, married Michael Murphy (her second husband) and with him moved to the San Francisco Bay area, and took her M.A. in creative writing at San Francisco State University. Though no longer married, she still lives in California.

Richard Cortez Day

A Kentucky writer who has come on the scene too late for more than brief notice is Richard Cortez Day (1927–), whose *When in Florence* (1985), a cycle of short stories, gives promise for the future. Day lives in California and teaches at Humboldt State College, but his connections with Kentucky are strong. He was born in Covington; his father was a native of Knott County; and Day has returned to Kentucky four times during the past four years to teach in the summer Appalachian Writer's Workshop at the Hindman Settlement School. He is working on another volume of short stories and on a novel which will deal at least in part with Kentucky.

Leon V. Driskell starts his review of *When in Florence* by saying, "Once in a great while a book so good comes along that it makes one want to take to the rooftops or rent a billboard space to spread the news" (*Courier Journal*, April 20, 1986). The volume includes fifteen short stories (some of them slice-of-life sketches) linked together in a way that lends interest and appeal to the whole. In the first, "A Chagall Story," for example, a colorful old man, a native of Florence, dies of a heart attack outside a neighborhood grocery. One witness of the event becomes the central character in the next story, and some stories link both forward and backwards. The characters are either native to Florence, are tourists there, or have temporary business there, like Day himself, who spent a sabbatical year in Italy and learned his Florence well. Not all reviewers are enthusiastic, but all do find it an appealing book. The *New York Times*, for example, concludes, "The stories have a guileless charm as though each were composed by a writer who loves deeply and well."

Selected Bibliography of Secondary Sources

More than 160 authors have been discussed in this history of Kentucky literature, and most of their more important works have been named, described, analyzed, or otherwise commented on, thereby identifying the "primary sources" with which the volume deals. Little attention, however, has been given to the secondary sources with which we have worked, nor have we cited additional readings to which an interested reader may turn. The materials upon which the present volume depends are of many kinds: the primary works themselves, reviews, books and articles about individual authors and works, and volumes more general in nature that deal with the context out of which authors and their works grew.

The books and articles that follow have been selected because the compiler feels they are good examples of the scholarly work that can enhance a reader's understandings. Some have been selected because they are "best" books for the advanced student with scholarly and critical expectations; some have been selected because they may better meet the needs of an interested but general audience. In the latter category are reference works such as the *Dictionary of American Biography*, the *Dictionary of Literary Biography*, and the Twayne Publishing Company's series of literary biographies. The accounts in the first two are usually limited to a few pages, but in general they are trustworthy and are analytical as well as biographical. The Twayne biographies are normally shorter than two hundred pages and are sometimes the only existing biography of an author. These will seldom be the best work available on a major author about whom there are a number of full-length studies. They are, however, generally good introductions, provide critical analysis, contain lists of "primary works" and of annotated readings for further study, and are widely accessible. All three of these sources—the *Dictionary of American Biography*, the *Dictionary of Literary Biography*, and the Twayne biographies—are to be found in many small libraries, both school and public, and all three are regularly listed below when the discussion of an author appears in them.

Secondary Sources: General

Arnold, Coleman. "A History of the Lexington Theater from 1887 to 1900." Ph.D. diss., University of Kentucky, 1956.

Bradbury, John M. *Renaissance in the South: A Critical History of the Literature, 1920–60*. Chapel Hill: University of North Carolina Press, 1963.

Browning, Sister Mary Carmel, O.S.O. *Kentucky Authors: A History of Kentucky Literature*. Evansville, Ind.: Keller-Crescent, 1968.

Channing, Stephen A. *Kentucky: A Bicentennial History*. Norton, 1977.

Clark, Thomas D. *A History of Kentucky*. Lexington: The John Bradford Press, 1960.

———. *Kentucky: Land of Contrast*. New York: Harper and Row, 1978.

Contemporary Authors: A Bio-Bibliographical Guide to Current Authors. Detroit: Gale Research, 1867–. (Various editors and series.)

Cowan, Louise. *The Fugitive Group: A Literary History*. Baton Rouge: Louisiana State University Press, 1959.

Dictionary of American Biography. 20 vols.; suppls. New York: Scribner, 1928–36.

Dictionary of Literary Biography. 86 vols. (to date). Detroit: Gale Research, 1978–.

Foley, Mary Donne, comp. *Kentucky in Fiction: An Annotated Bibliography*, Lexington: University of Kentucky Library, Occasional Papers, no. 2, 1980. (Supplement to Thompson and Thompson, *The Kentucky Novel*, below.)

Graham, Philip. *Showboats: The History of an American Institution*. Austin: University of Texas, 1951.

Hackett, Alice Payne, and James Henry Burke. *80 Years of Best Sellers, 1895–1975*. New York: Bowker, 1977.

Hill, West T. *The Theatre in Early Kentucky, 1790–1820*. Lexington: University Press of Kentucky, 1971.

James, Edward T., ed. *Notable American Women, 1607–1950*. 3 vols. Cambridge: Harvard University Press, Belknap Press, 1971.

Leisy, Ernest E. *The American Historical Novel*. Norman: University of Oklahoma Press, 1950.

Magill, Frank N. *Critical Survey of Drama. English Language Series*. 6 vols. Englewood Cliffs, N.J.: Salem Press, 1985.

———, ed. *Critical Survey of Poetry*. 8 vols. Englewood Cliffs, N.J.: Salem Press, 1982.

———. *Critical Survey of Short Fiction*. 7 vols. Englewood Cliffs, N.J.: Salem Press, 1981.

Mainiero, Lina, ed. *American Women Writers: A Critical Reference Guide from Colonial Times to the Present*. 4 vols. New York: Frederick Ungar, 1979.

Moore, Arthur K. *The Frontier Mind: A Cultural Analysis of the Kentucky Frontiersman*. Lexington: University of Kentucky Press, 1957.

Poupard, D., ed. *Twentieth-Century Literary Criticism*. 23 vols. (to date). Detroit: Gale Research, 1978–. (Extensive excerpts from criticism of writers who died between 1900 and 1960. See also *Contemporary Literary Criticism*.)

Ray, Bess A. ed. "Biographical and Critical Materials Pertaining to Kentucky Authors." Kentucky Work Projects Administration Library Project. Louisville: Louisville Public Library, 1941. Mimeo.

Richey, Ish. *Kentucky Literature, 1784–1963*. Tompkinsville, Ky.: Monroe County Press, 1963.

Riley, Carolyn, ed. *Contemporary Literary Criticism*. 43 vols. (to date). Detroit: Gale Research, 1973–. (Extensive excerpts from the criticism of contemporary writers. See also *Twentieth-Century Literary Criticism*.)

Roach, Abbie Meguire. "Louisville Poets of the Early Nineteen-Hundreds." *Filson Club Historical Quarterly* 33 (Jan. 1959), 26–31.

Roland, Charles P. "The South of the Agrarians." In *A Band of Prophets: The Vanderbilt Agrarians after Fifty Years*, edited by William C. Havard and Walter Sullivan. Baton Rouge: Louisiana State University Press, 1982.

Shapiro, Henry D. *Appalachia on Our Mind: The Southern Mountains and Mountaineers in the American Consciousness, 1870–1920*. Chapel Hill: University of North Carolina Press, 1978.

Sicherman, Barbara and Carol H. Green, eds. *Notable American Women. The Modern Period*. Cambridge: Harvard University Press, Belknap Press, 1980.

Stewart, John M. *The Burden of Time: The Fugitives and the Agrarians*. Princeton: Princeton University Press, 1963.

Thompson, Lawrence S. *Kentucky Tradition*. Hamden, Conn.: Shoe String Press, 1956.

———. "The War between the States in the Kentucky Novel." *Register of the Kentucky State Historical Society* 50 (Jan. 1952), 26–34.

Thompson, Lawrence, and Algernon D. Thompson. *The Kentucky Novel*. Lexington: University of Kentucky Press, 1953.

Townsend, Dorothy Edwards. *Kentucky in American Letters, 1913–1975*. Vol. 3. Georgetown, Ky: Georgetown College Press, 1976.

Townsend, John Wilson. *Kentucky in American Letters, 1784–1912*. Vols. 1 and 2. Cedar Rapids, Iowa: Torch Press, 1913; rpt. 1974.

Wagenknecht, Edward. *Cavalcade of the American Novel*. New York: Holt, 1952.

Ward, William S. "Anni Mirabilis: Kentucky Literature at the Turn of the Century." *Kentucky Review* 5, no. 3 (1985), 32–45.

Ward, William S., and Alfred L. Crabb, Jr. *Literary Landmarks in Kentucky*. Lexington: Kentucky Council of Teachers of English, 1961.

Watts, Emily Stipes. *The Poetry of American Women from 1632 to 1843*. Austin: University of Texas Press, 1977.

Williams, Cratis. *The Southern Mountaineer in Fact and Fiction. Appalachian Journal* 9, nos. 1–4 (1961). (An abridgement of Williams's three-volume Ph.D. dissertation.)

Secondary Sources—Authors

James Lane Allen

Bottorff, William K. *James Lane Allen*. New York: Twayne, 1964.

Knight, Grant C. *James Lane Allen and the Genteel Tradition*. Chapel Hill: University of North Carolina Press, 1935.

Nelson, John N. "James Lane Allen." In *Dictionary of American Biography*, vol. 1: 195–97.

Pattee, Fred Lewis. *A History of American Literature since 1870*, 365–72. New York: Century, 1915.
Petry, Alice. "Universal and Particular: The Local Color Phenomenon Reconsidered." *American Literary Realism* 12 (1979), 111–26.
Quinn, Arthur Hobson. *American Fiction: An Historical and Critical Survey*, 472–83. New York: Appleton, 1936.
Rhode, Robert D. *Studies in the American Short Story of Local Color*. The Hague: Mouton, 1975.
Shapiro, Henry D. "The Local-Color Movement and the 'Discovery of Appalachia.'" In *Appalachia on Our Mind*, 26–31. Chapel Hill: University of North Carolina Press, 1978.
Wagenknecht, Edward. "The Finely Wrought Art of James Lane Allen." In *Cavalcade of the Novel*, 186–91. New York: Holt, 1952.

Mary R. Shipman Andrews

Kondelik, Marlene. "Mary Raymond Shipman Andrews." In *American Women Writers*.

Harriette Arnow

Baer, Barbara L. "Harriette Arnow's Chronicles of Destruction." *Nation* 222 (Jan. 31, 1976), 117–20.
Eckley, Walton. *Harriette Arnow*. New York: Twayne, 1974.
Edwards, Lee R. *Psyche as Hero: Female Heroism and Fictional Form*. Middletown, Conn.: Wesleyan University Press, 1984.
Goodin, George. *The Poetics of Protest*, 40–46. Carbondale: Southern Illinois University Press, 1985.
Hobbs, Glenda. "Harriette Arnow." In *Dictionary of Literary Biography*, vol. 6: 3–8.
———. "A Portrait of the Artist as Mother: Harriette Arnow and *The Dollmaker*." *Georgia Review* 33 (Winter 1978), 851–67.
———. "Harriette Arnow's Kentucky Novels: Beyond Local Color." *Kate Chopin Newsletter* 2 (Fall 1976), 27–33.
———. "Harriette Louisa Simpson Arnow." In *American Women Writers*.
Lawson, Lewis A. "The Knife and the Saw in *The Dollmaker*." In *Another Generation: Fiction Since World War II*, 58–74. Jackson: University of Mississippi Press, 1984.
Lee, Dorothy H. "Harriette Arnow's *The Dollmaker*: A Journey to Awareness." *Critique: Studies in Modern Fiction* 20, no. 2 (1978), 192–98.
Oates, J. C. "An American Tragedy." *New York Times*, Jan. 24, 1971, pp. 12–16.

Wendell Berry

Collins, Robert. "A More Mingled Music: Wendell Berry's Ambivalent View of Language." *Modern Poetry Studies* 11 (1982), 35–56.
Ditsky, John. "Love As a Farm and a Forest." *Modern Poetry Studies* 5 (1974), 92–93.
———. "Wendell Berry: Homage to the Apple Tree." *Modern Poetry Studies* 2, no. 1 (1971), 7–15.
Driskell, Leon V. "Wendell Berry." *Dictionary of Literary Biography*, vol. 5: 62–66.
Elder, John. *Imagining the Earth: Poetry and the Vision of Nature*. Urbana: University of Illinois Press, 1985.
Hass, Robert. "Wendell Berry: Finding the Land." *Modern Poetry Studies* 2, no. 2 (1971), 16–38.
Hicks, Jack. "A Wendell Berry Checklist." *Bulletin of Bibliography* 37 (1980), 127–31.
———. "Wendell Berry's Husband to the World: A Place on Earth." *American Literature* 50 (May 1979), 238–54.

Morgan, Speer. "Wendell Berry: A Fatal Singing." *Southern Review* 10 (Oct. 1974), 865–77.
Murphy, Patrick D. "Two Different Paths in the Quest of Place: Gary Snyder and Wendell Berry." *American Poetry* 2, no. 1 (1984), 60–68.
Tolliver, Gary. "Wendell Berry." In *Dictionary of Literary Biography*, vol. 6: 9–14.
Robinson, J. K. Review of *The Country of Marriage*. *Southern Review* 11 (July 1975), 668–680.
Young, I. D. Review of *The Unsettling of America*. *Sewanee Review* 86 (Fall 1978), 595–604.

Sarah T. Bolton

DeMarr, Mary Jean. "Sarah Tittle Barrett Bolton." In *American Women Writers*.
Shumaker, A.W. "Sarah T. Bolton." In *Notable American Women, 1607–1950*, edited by E.T. James et al. Cambridge: Harvard University Press, Belknap Press, 1971.
Starr, Harris E. "Sarah T. Bolton." In *Dictionary of American Biography*, vol. 1: 424.

John Mason Brown

Stevens, George. *Speak for Yourself John: The Life of John Mason Brown*. New York: Viking, 1974.

William Wells Brown

Farrison, W. Edward. *William Wells Brown: Author and Reformer*. Chicago: University of Chicago Press, 1969.
Heermance, Noel. *William Wells Brown and Clotelle: A Portrait of the Artist in the First Negro Novel*. Hamden, Conn.: Archon, 1969.
Katopes, Peter J. "William Wells Brown." In *Dictionary of Literary Biography*, vol. 3: 27–29.

Madison J. Cawein

Covi, Madeline. "Madison Cawein: A Landscape Poet." *Kentucky Review* 3, no. 3 (1982), 3–19.
Gosse, Edmund. "Introduction." *Kentucky Poems by Madison Cawein*. London: Grant Richards, 1902.
Guthrie, William N. "A Southern Poet." *Sewanee Review* 1 (May 1893), 290–308.
Hart, Paula A. "Madison Cawein." In *Dictionary of Literary Biography*, vol. 54: 29–35.
Howells, William Dean. "The Poetry of Madison Cawein." *North American Review* 187 (Jan. 1908), 124–28.
Knight, Grant C. "Madison Julius Cawein." In *Dictionary of American Biography*, vol. 2: 578–80.
Peckham, H. Houston. "Madison Cawein." *South Atlantic Quarterly* 14 (1915), 279–84.
Perkins, David. *A History of Modern Poetry*. Cambridge: Harvard University Press, Belknap Press, 1976.

Thomas Holley Chivers

Damon, S. Foster. *Thomas Holley Chivers, Friend of Poe*. New York: Harper's, 1930.
Leonard, Charles M. *Thomas Holley Chivers*. Boston: Twayne, 1979.
Lombard, Charles M. "Thomas Holley Chivers." In *Dictionary of Literary Biography*, vol. 3: 57–61.
Watts, Charles Henry. *Thomas Holley Chivers*. Athens: University of Georgia Press, 1956.

Irvin S. Cobb

Chatterton, Wayne. *Irvin S. Cobb*. Boston: Twayne, 1986.

Dilliard, Irving. "Irvin Shrewsberry Cobb." In *Dictionary of American Biography*, supplement 3: 170–71.

Lieb, Sandra. "Irvin S. Cobb." In *Dictionary of Literary Biography*, vol. 11: 82–88.

Maurice, Arthur Bartlett. "The History of Their Books: Irvin S. Cobb." *Bookman* 69 (July 1929), 511–19.

Neuman, Fred Gus. *Irvin S. Cobb: His Life and Achievements*. New York: Beekman, 1974.

Pattee, Fred Lewis. *The New American Literature, 1890–1930*. New York: Coope Square, 1968.

Riley, Sam G. "Irvin S. Cobb." In *Dictionary of Literary Biography*, vol. 25: 48–57.

Van Gelder, Robert. *Writers and Writing*, 232–36. New York: Scribner's, 1946.

Yates, Norris W. *The American Humorist: Conscience of the Twentieth Century*, 127–33. Ames: Iowa State University Press, 1984.

Joseph Seamon Cotter, Sr.

Brooks, A. Russell. "Joseph Seamon Cotter, Sr." In *Dictionary of Literary Biography*, vol. 50: 62–70.

Hatch, James V., ed. *Black Theatre, U.S.A.: Forty-Five Plays by Black Americans*. New York: Free Press/Macmillan, 1974.

Kerlin, Robert T. "A Poet from Bardstown." *South Atlantic Quarterly* 20 (July 1921), 213–21.

Sherman, Joan R. *Invisible Poets: Afro-American Writers of the Nineteenth Century*. Urbana: University of Illinois Press, 1974.

Shockley, Ann Allen. "Joseph S. Carter, Sr.: Biographical Sketch of a Black Louisville Bard." *College Language Association Journal* 18 (March 1975), 327–40.

Townsend, John Wilson. "Kentucky's Dunbar: Joseph Seamon Cotter." In *Lore of the Meadowland*, 23–26. Lexington, Ky.: J.L. Richardson, 1911.

Joseph Seamon Cotter, Jr.

Hammond, L.W. *In the Vanguard of a Race*, 162–76. New York: Council of Women for Home Missions, 1922.

Payne, James Robert. "Joseph Seamon Cotter, Jr." In *Dictionary of Literary Biography*, vol. 50: 70–73.

Olive Tilford Dargan

Cook, Sylvia. "Olive Tilford Dargan." In *American Women Writers*.

Knickerbocker, F.W. "American Writers." *Times Literary Supplement*, March 21, 1936, p. 244.

Lathrop, V.T. "Olive Tilford Dargan." *North Carolina Libraries* 18 (April 1960), 68–76.

Polsky, T. *North Carolina Authors: A Selective Handbook*. Chapel Hill: University of North Carolina Press, 1952.

Reilly, John M. "Images of Gastonia: A Revolutionary Chapter in American Social Fiction." *Georgia Review* 28 (1974), 498–517.

Rideout, Walter B. *The Radical Novel in the United States, 1900–1954*. Cambridge: Harvard University Press, 1956.

Guy Davenport

Dawson, Fielding. "On Olson, with Reference to Guy Davenport." *Sagetrieb* 1 (1982), 125–32.

Gardner, John. *On Moral Fiction*. New York: Basic Books, 1978.
Morace, Robert A. "Invention in Guy Davenport's *Da Vinci's Bicycle*." *Critique: Studies in Modern Fiction* 22, no. 3 (1981), 71–87.
Shannon, John, ed. "A Symposium on Guy Davenport." *Margins* 13 (Aug.–Sept. 1974), 3–23.

Charles T. Dazey

Quinn, Arthur Hobson. "The Height of Melodrama." Ch. 17 of *A History of the American Drama*. New York: Harper's, 1927.

Ann Crawford Flexner

Londré, Felicia. "Ann Crawford Flexner." In *American Women Writers*.

Sallie Rochester Ford

Chew, Martha. "Sallie Rochester Ford." In *American Women Writers*.

Stephen C. Foster

Howard, John Tasker. *Stephen Foster, America's Troubadour*. New York, Crowell, 1962.

John Fox, Jr.

"John Fox Jr. and His Kentucky." *Nation* 109 (July 19, 1919), 72–73.
Marcosson, Isaac F. "The South in Fiction." *Bookman* 32 (Dec. 1910), 363–69.
Shapiro, Henry D. "The Local-Color Movement and the 'Discovery of Appalachia.'" In *Appalachia on Our Mind*, 70–78. Chapel Hill: University of North Carolina Press, 1978.
Titus, Warren Irving. *John Fox, Jr.* New York: Twayne, 1971.
Tucker, Edward L. "John Fox, Jr." *Dictionary of Literary Biography*, vol. 9: 25–27.
Wade, John D. "John Fox." *Dictionary of American Biography*, vol. 3: 570.
Wagenknecht, Edward. *Cavalcade of the American Novel*. New York: Holt, 1952.

Caroline Gordon

Baker, Howard. "The Strategems of Caroline Gordon; or, the Art of the Novel and the Novelty of the Myth." *Southern Review* 9 (1973), 523–49.
Brown, Ashley. "The Achievement of Caroline Gordon." *Southern Humanities Review* 2 (1968), 279–90.
Cheney, Brainard. "Caroline Gordon's Ontological Quest." *Renascence* 16 (Fall 1963), 3–12.
Fraistat, Rose Ann C. *Caroline Gordon as Novelist and Woman of Letters*. Baton Rouge: Louisiana State University Press, 1984.
King, Lawrence T. "The Novels of Caroline Gordon." *Catholic World* 181 (July 1955), 274–79.
Koch, Vivienne. "The Conservatism of Caroline Gordon." In *The Southern Renascence; the Literature of the Modern South*, edited by Louis D. Rubin, Jr., and Robert D. Jacobs. Baltimore: the Johns Hopkins University Press, 1953.
Landess, Thomas H., ed. *The Short Fiction of Caroline Gordon: A Critical Symposium*. Irving: University of Dallas Press, 1972.
Lytle, Andrew. "Caroline Gordon and the Historic Image." *Sewanee Review* 17 (1949), 360–86. (Reprinted in Lytle's *The Hero with the Private Parts*, 1966.)
McDowell, Frederick P.W. *Caroline Gordon*. Pamphlets on American Writers, no. 54. Minneapolis: University of Minnesota Press, 1966.

O'Connor, William Van. "Art and Miss Gordon." In *South: Modern Southern Literature in Its Cultural Setting*, edited by Louis D. Rubin, Jr., and Robert D. Jacobs, 314–22. Garden City: Doubleday, 1961. Rpt., Greenwood Press, 1974.
Rogers, Cynthia H. "Caroline Gordon." In *Dictionary of Literary Biography*, vol. 4: 178–80.
Squires, Radcliffe. "The Underground Stream: A Note on Caroline Gordon's Fiction." *Southern Review* 7 (1971), 467–79.
Stuckey, William J. "Caroline Gordon." In *Dictionary of Literary Biography*, vol. 9: 76–80.
———. *Caroline Gordon*. New York, Twayne, 1972.
Thorp, Willard. "The Way Back and the Way Up: The Novels of Caroline Gordon." *Bucknell Review* 6 (Dec. 1956), 1–15.
Warren, Robert Penn. "The Fiction of Caroline Gordon." *Southwest Review* 20 (Jan. 1935), 5–10.

A.B. Guthrie, Jr.

Astro, Richard. "The Big Sky and the Limits of Wilderness Fiction." *Western American Literature* 9 (Summer 1974), 105–14.
Attebery, Louie. "The American West and the Archetypal Orphan." *Western American Literature* 4 (Fall 1970), 205–17.
Barasch, Marc. *Writers of the Purple Sage*. Viking, 1984.
Clark, Walter Van Tilburg. "Emigrants on the Oregon Trail" [A review of *The Way West*]. *Saturday Review of Literature*, Oct. 8, 1948, pp. 21–22.
Cracroft, Richard H. "*The Big Sky*: A.B. Guthrie's Use of Historical Sources." *Western American Literature* 6 (Fall 1971), 163–76.
Folsom, James K. *The American Western Novel*, 64–76. New Haven: Yale University Press, 1966.
Ford, Thomas W. *A.B. Guthrie, Jr.* Boston: Twayne, 1981.
Kohler, Dayton. "A.B. Guthrie, Jr., and the West." *College English* 12 (Feb. 1951), 249–56.
Prescott, Orville. "The Art of Historical Fiction: Richter, Guthrie." In *In My Opinion: An Inquiry into the Contemporary Novel*, 133–45. New York: Bobbs-Merrill, 1952.
Putnam, J.K. "Down to Earth. A.B. Guthrie's Quest for Moral and Historical Truth." *North Dakota Quarterly* 39 (Summer 1971), 47–57.
Stegner, Wallace. "Foreword." *The Big Sky*. Boston: Houghton Mifflin, 1968.
Stewart, Donald C. "The Functions of Bird and Sky Imagery in Guthrie's *The Big Sky*." *Critique: Studies in Modern Fiction* 19, no. 2 (1977), 53–61.
Vorpahn, Ben Merchant. "A.B. Guthrie, Jr." *Dictionary of Literary Biography*, vol. 6: 122–27.
Walker, Don D. "The Mountain Man as Literary Hero." *Western American Literature* 1 (Spring 1966), 15–25.
Williams, John. "The 'Western': Definition of the Myth." *Nation* 193 (Nov. 18, 1961), 401–406.

Elizabeth Hardwick

Axelrod, Steven Gould. *Robert Lowell: Life and Art*. Princeton: Princeton University Press, 1978.
"Bartleby and Manhattan." *New York Review of Books*, July 16, 1983, pp. 27–31.
Branin, Joseph J. "Elizabeth Hardwick." In *Dictionary of Literary Biography*, vol. 6: 133–36.
Didion, Joan. "Meditation on a Life." *New York Times Book Review*, April 29, 1979, pp. 1, 60.

Gray, Francine Du Plessix. "Elizabeth Hardwick: A Fresh Way of Looking at Literature—and at Life." *Vogue* 169 (June 1979), 202–203, 250.

Nobile, Philip. *Intellectual Skywriting: Literary Politics and the "New York Review of Books."* New York: Charterhouse, 1974.

Rahv, Philip. "The Editor Interviews Elizabeth Hardwick." *Modern Occasion* 2 (Sept. 1972), 159–67.

Rudikoff, Sonya. "Heroines of Literature and Life." *Hudson Review* 27 (Winter 1974–75), 615–19.

Mary Jane Holmes

Chafee, Zechariah, Jr. "Mary Jane Hawes Holmes." In *Dictionary of American Biography*, vol. 5: 168–69.

Ginsberg, Elaine K. "Mary Jane Hawes Holmes." In *American Women Writers.*

Papashvily, Helen Waite. *All the Happy Endings*, 145–51. New York: Harper, 1956.

Pattee, Fred Lewis. *The Feminine Fifties*. New York: Appleton-Century, 1940.

Felix Holt

Thompson, Lawrence. "Felix Holt, Kentucky Historical Novelist." *The Register of the Kentucky Historical Society* 53 (July 1955), 247–56.

Annie Fellows Johnston

Cook, Martha E. "Annie Fellows Johnston." In *American Women Writers.*

Kaye, Marilyn. "Annie Fellows Johnston." In *Dictionary of Literary Biography*, vol. 42: 251–57.

Kuntz, S.J., and H. Haycraft, eds. *The Junior Book of Authors*, 206–208. New York: H.W. Wilson Company, 1934.

Shumaker, Arthur W. "Annie Fellows Johnston." In *Notable American Women, 1607–1950*, edited by Edward T. James et al. Cambridge: Harvard University Press, Belknap Press, 1971.

Steele, Elizabeth. "Mrs. Johnston's Little Colonel." In *Challenges in American Culture*, edited by Ray B. Brown et al., 217–23. Bowling Green: Bowling Green Popular Press, 1970.

Vandercook, Margaret W. "Annie Fellows Johnston: The Beloved Writer of the Books for Young People." *St. Nicholas* 41 (Dec. 1913), 129–30.

Gayl Jones

Byerman, Keith E. "Black Vortex: The Gothic Structure of *Eva's Man*." *Melus* 7, no. 4 (1980), 93–101.

———. *Fingering the Jagged Grain: Tradition and Form in Recent Black Fiction.* Athens: University of Georgia Press, 1985.

———. "Gayl Jones." In *Dictionary of Literary Biography*, vol. 33: 128–134.

———. "Intense Behaviors: The Use of the Grotesque in *Eva's Man* and *The Bluest Eye*." *College Language Association Journal* 25 (June 1982), 447–57.

Fontenot, Chester J. "Black Fiction: Apollo or Dionysus." *Twentieth-Century Literature* 25 (1979), 73–84.

Harper, Michael. "Gayl Jones: An Interview." *Massachusetts Review* 18 (1977), 631–42.

Harris, Trudier. "A Spiritual Journey: Gayl Jones's Song for Annenko." *Callaloo* 5, no. 3 (1982), 105–11.

Jones, Judith F. "Gayl Jones." In *American Women Writers.*

Lee, Valerie Gray. "The Use of Folktale in Novels by Black Women Writers." *College Language Association Journal* 23 (March 1980), 266–72.

Tate, Claudia C. "*Corregidora*: Ursa's Blue Medley." *Black American Literature Forum* 13 (Fall 1979), 139–41.
Ward, Jerry W., Jr. "Escape from Trublem: The Fiction of Gayl Jones." *Callaloo* 5, no. 3 (1982), 95–104.
Wedeman, John. "Defining the Black Voice in Fiction." *Black American Literature Forum* 11 (1977), 79–82.

Edith Summers Kelley

Brett, Sally. "Edith Summers Kelley." In *American Women Writers.*
Bruccoli, Matthew J. "Afterword." *The Devil's Hand*, Carbondale: Southern Illinois University Press, 1974.
———. "Foreword." *Weeds.* Carbondale: Southern Illinois University Press, 1972.
Goodman, Charlotte. "Edith Summers Kelley." In *Dictionary of Literary Biography*, vol. 9: 154–56.
———. "Images of America. Rural Women in the Novel." *Michigan Papers in Women's Studies* 1 (June 1975), 57–70.
———. "Widening Perspectives, Narrowing Possibilities: The Trapped Woman in Edith Summers Kelley's *Weeds.*" *Regionalism and the Female Imagination* 3 (Spring 1977), 14–20.
Kelley, Patrick. "Edith Summers Kelley: A Postscript." In *The Devil's Hand*, 299–301. Carbondale: Southern Illinois University Press, 1974.
Shields, McIlwaine. "America Makes the Poor-White a Cause and a Literary Vogue . . . Edith S. Kelley, Elizabeth Madox Roberts, and Paul Green." In *The Southern Poor-White from Lubberland to Tobacco Land.* Norman: University of Oklahoma Press, 1939.

Eleanor Mercein Kelly

Hoeveller, Diane Long. "Eleanor Mercein Kelly." In *American Women Writers.*

David Madden

"A Conversation with David Madden." *Critique* 15 (1973), 5–14.
Dasher, Thomas E. "David Madden." *Dictionary of Literary Biography*, vol. 6: 192–200.
"An Interview with David Madden." *Southern Review* 11 (1975), 167–80.
Kibler, James E., ed. *American Novelists Since World War II. Second Series.* Detroit: Gale Research Company, 1980.

Mrs. George Madden Martin

Cook, Martha E. "George Madden Martin." In *American Women Writers.*
Clark, Thomas D. "George Madden Martin." In *Notable American Women*, edited by Edward T. James. Cambridge: Harvard University Press, Belknap Press, 1971.

Thomas Merton

Baker, James Thomas. *Thomas Merton, Social Critic.* Lexington: University Press of Kentucky, 1972.
Berrigan, Daniel. "The Seventy Times Seventy Seven Storey Mountain." *Cross Currents* 27 (Winter 1977–78), 385–93.
Boenig, Robert E. "Thomas Merton." In *Critical Survey of Poetry*, edited by Frank N. Magill, vol. 5: 1970–78. Englewood Cliffs, N.J.: Salem Press, 1982.
Boyd, John D., S.J. "Christian Imaginative Patterns and the Poetry of Thomas Merton." *Greyfriar-Siena Studies in Literature* 13 (1972), 3–14.

Glimm, James York. "Thomas Merton's Last Poem: *The Geography of Lograire*." *Renascence* 26 (Winter 1974), 95–104.
Kramer, Victor A. *Thomas Merton*. Boston: Twayne, 1984.
———. "Thomas Merton." In *Dictionary of Literary Biography*, vol. Y81: 217–27.
Labrie, Ross. *The Art of Thomas Merton*. Fort Worth: Texas Christian University Press, 1979.
———. "Thomas Merton." In *Dictionary of Literary Biography*, vol. 48: 290–98.
Lentfoehr, Thérèse, Sr. *Words and Silence: On the Poetry of Thomas Merton*. New York: New Directions, 1979.
Malits, Elena. "Thomas Merton: Symbol and Synthesis of Contemporary Catholicism." *Critic* 35 (Spring 1977), 26–33.
Sutton, Walter. *American Free Verse: The Modern Revolution in Poetry*, 198–203. New York: New Directions, 1973.
Thielen, James A. "Thomas Merton—Poet of the Contemplative Life." *Catholic World* 169 (1949), 86–89.
Woodcock, George. *Thomas Merton: Monk and Poet*. New York: New Directions, 1978.

Jim Wayne Miller

Magill, Frank N. "Jim Wayne Miller." In *Critical Survey of Fiction*, vol. 7: 2723. Englewood Cliffs, N.J.: Salem Press.

Marsha Norman

"Conversations with Marsha Norman." *Dramatists' Guild Quarterly* 21, no. 3 (1984), 9–21.
"Five Dramatists Discuss the Value of Criticism." *Dramatists' Guild Quarterly* 21, no. 1 (1984), 11–25.
Murry, Timothy. "Patriarchal Panopticism, or the Seduction of a Bad Joke: Getting Out in Theory." *Theatre Journal* 35 (1983), 376–88.
Salem, James M. *A Guide to Critical Reviews. Part I: American Drama, 1909–1982*, 380. Metuchen, N.J.: Scarecrow Press, 1984.
Simon, John. "Theatre Chronicle: Kopit, Norman, and Shepard." *Hudson Review* 32 (1979), 77–88.
Stahl, Linda. "The Storyteller." *The Courier-Journal Magazine*, May 20, 1984.
Stone, Elizabeth. "An Optimist Writes about Suicide, Confinement, and Despair." *Ms* 12 (July 1983).

John Patrick

Marion, John. "John Patrick." In *Dictionary of Literary Biography*, vol. 7: 166–71.
Salem, James M. *A Guide to Critical Reviews. Part I: American Drama, 1909–1982*, 419–22. Metuchen, N.J.: Scarecrow Press, 1984.

Burton Rascoe

Benét, William Rose. "A Bookman's Daybook." *The Bookman* 69 (June 1929), 440–41.
Boyd, Ernest. "Literary Journalism." *The Nation* 106 (Jan. 4, 1933), 22.
Chamberlain, John. "Eye Opener." *New Republic* 29 (May 31, 1937), 228–29.
Cleaton, Irene and Allen. *Books and Battles, American Literature, 1920–1930*. Boston: Houghton Mifflin, 1937.
Cowley, Malcolm. *Exile's Return: A Literary Odyssey of the 1920s*. New York: Viking, 1951.

Gray, James. "Fun, All the Way." *Saturday Review* 30 (Oct. 18, 1947), 13–18.
Wilson, Edmund. "The All-Star Literary Vaudeville." In *A Literary Chronicle: 1920–1950*. Garden City, N.Y.: Doubleday Anchor, 1956.

Alice Hegan Rice

Axton, William F., ed. "Foreword." *Mrs. Wiggs of the Cabbage Patch, by Alice Hegan Rice*, v–xxii. Lexington: University Press of Kentucky, 1979.
DeMarr, Mary Jean. "Alice Hegan Rice." In *American Women Writers*.
Norman, Charles M. "Alice Caldwell Hegan Rice." In *Notable American Women, 1607–1960*, edited by Edward T. James et al. Cambridge: Harvard University Press, Belknap Press, 1971.

Elizabeth Madox Roberts

Adams, J. Donald. "Elizabeth Madox Roberts." *Virginia Quarterly Review* 12 (June 1936), 80–90.
Auchincloss, Louis. *Pioneers and Caretakers: A Study of Nine Women Writers*. Minneapolis: University of Minnesota Press, 1965.
Campbell, Harry Modean, and Ruel E. Foster. *Elizabeth Madox Roberts, American Novelist*. Norman: University of Oklahoma Press, 1956.
Goeller, Alison D. "Elizabeth Madox Roberts." *Dictionary of Literary Biography*, vol. 9: 310–13.
Janney, Lamar F. "Elizabeth Madox Roberts." *Sewanee Review* 45 (Oct.–Dec. 1937), 388–410.
McDowell, Frederick P. W. "Elizabeth Madox Roberts." In *Dictionary of American Biography*, suppl. 3: 636–38.
———. *Elizabeth Madox Roberts*. New York: Twayne, 1963.
Rouse, H. Blair. "Time and Place in Southern Fiction." In *Southern Renascence: The Literature of the Modern South*, edited by Louis D. Rubin and Robert D. Jacobs, 126–50. Baltimore: The Johns Hopkins University Press, 1953.
Rovit, Earl H. *Herald to Chaos; the Novels of Elizabeth Madox Roberts*. Lexington: University Press of Kentucky, 1960.
Rowe, Ann E. "Elizabeth Madox Roberts." In *Dictionary of Literary Biography*, vol. 54: 361–65.
Simpson, Lewis P. "The Sexuality of History." *Southern Review* 30 (Fall 1984), 785–802.
Slavick, William H. "Elizabeth Madox Roberts." In *Fifty Southern Writers after 1900: a Bio-Bibliographical Sourcebook*, edited by Joseph N. Flora and Robert Ban, 411–22. New York: Greenwood Press, 1987.
Van Doren, Mark. "Elizabeth Madox Roberts: Her Mind and Style." In *The Private Reader*, 97–109. Henry Holt and Company, 1942.
Wagenknecht, Edward. "The Inner Vision: Elizabeth Madox Roberts." In *Cavalcade of the American Novel*, 389–96. New York: Henry Holt and Company, 1952.
Warren, Robert Penn. "Life Is from Within." *Saturday Review* 46 (March 2, 1963), 20–21, 38.

I.J. Schwartz

Jones, Joseph R. "I.J. Schwartz in Lexington." *Kentucky Review* 3, no. 1 (1981), 23–40.

Ellen Churchill Semple

Brooker-Gross, Susan R. "Ellen Churchill Semple." In *American Women Writers*.

James Still

Cadle, Dean. "Man on Troublesome." *Yale Review* 57, no. 2 (1968), 236–55.

Chappell, Fred. "The Seamless Vision of James Still." *Appalachian Journal* 8 (1981), 196–202.
Driskell, Leon V. "James Still." *Dictionary of Literary Biography*, vol. 9: 68–72.
Hall, Wade. "James Still: An Introduction." *Kentucky Poetry Review* 14 (Winter/Spring, 1978), 25–26.
Kobler, Dayton. "Jesse Stuart and James Still: Mountain Regionalists." *College English* 3 (March 1942), 523–33.
Miller, Jim Wayne. "James Still." In *Critical Survey of Poetry*, edited by Frank N. Magill, 2759–66. Englewood Cliffs, N.J.: Salem Press, 1982.
Williams, Shirley. "Still Writing after All This Time." *The Courier-Journal Magazine*, July 9, 1978, pp. 25–31.

Jesse Stuart

Blair, Everetta Love. *Jesse Stuart: His Life and Works.* Columbia: University of South Carolina Press, 1967.
Clarke, Mary Washington. *Jesse Stuart's Kentucky.* New York: McGraw-Hill, 1967.
Foster, Ruel E. *Jesse Stuart.* New York: Twayne, 1968.
———. "Jesse Stuart's Way with Short Fiction." *Kansas Quarterly* 9, no. 2 (1977), 21–29.
Leavell, Frank H. "Jesse Stuart." *Dictionary of Literary Biography*, vol. 9: 79–85.
Le Master, J. R. "Jesse Stuart." *Dictionary of Literary Biography*, vol. 48: 411–18.
———. *Jesse Stuart: Kentucky's Chronicler-Poet.* Memphis: Memphis State University Press, 1980.
———, ed. *Jesse Stuart: Selected Criticism.* St. Petersburg, Fla.: Valkyrie Press, 1978.
Le Master, J. R., and Mary W. Clarke, eds. *Jesse Stuart: Essays on His Work.* Lexington: University Press of Kentucky, 1977.
Richardson, Harold Edward. *Jesse: The Biography of an American Writer, Jesse Hilton Stuart.* New York: McGraw-Hill, 1984.

Hollis Summers

Hester, Carol C. "Hollis Summers." In *Dictionary of Literary Biography*, vol. 6: 330–36.

Allen Tate

Arnold, Willard S. *The Social Ideas of Allen Tate.* Boston: Bruce Humphries, 1955.
Beatty, Richmond C. "Allen Tate as a Man of Letters." *South Atlantic Quarterly* 47 (April 1943), 226–41.
Bishop, Ferman. *Allen Tate.* New York: Twayne, 1967.
Broughton, Irv. "An Interview with Allen Tate." *Western Humanities Review* 32 (1978), 317–36.
Dupree, Robert S. *Allen Tate and the Augustinian Imagination: A Study of the Poetry.* Baton Rouge: Louisiana State University Press, 1983.
Feder, Lillian. "Allen Tate's Uses of Classical Literature." *Centennial Review* 4, no. 1 (1960), 89–114.
Hart, James A. "Allen Tate." In *Dictionary of Literary Biography*, vol. 45: 381–95.
Hemphill, George. *Allen Tate.* Pamphlet Series on American writers, no. 39. Minneapolis: University of Minnesota Press, 1964.
Johnson, Carol H. *The Heroism of the Rational: The Poetry of Allen Tate. Renascence* 17 (Winter 1964), 89–96.
Krieger, Murray. *The New Apologists for Poetry.* Minneapolis: University of Minnesota Press, 1956.
Meiners, R.K. *The Last Alternatives: A Study of the Works of Allen Tate.* Denver: Swallow Press, 1962.

Rubin, Louis D. *The Wary Fugitives: Four Poets and the South*. Baton Rouge: Louisiana State University Press, 1978.

Squires, Radcliffe. *Allen Tate: A Literary Biography*. New York: Pegasus, 1971.

———, ed. *Allen Tate and His Work: Critical Evaluations*. Minneapolis: University of Minnesota Press, 1972.

Wilkie, Everett C., Jr. "Allen Tate." In *Dictionary of Literary Biography*, vol. 4: 278–82.

Robert Penn Warren

Bedient, Calvin. *In the Heart's Last Kingdom: Robert Penn Warren's Major Poetry*. Cambridge: Harvard University Press, 1984.

Beatty, Richmond C. "The Poetry and Novels of Robert Penn Warren," In *Vanderbilt Studies in the Humanities*, vol. 1, edited by Richmond C. Beatty, J. Philip Hyatt, and Monroe K. Spears, 142–60. Nashville: Vanderbilt University Press, 1957.

Bentley, Eric. "The Meaning of Robert Penn Warren's Novels." *Kenyon Review* 10 (Summer 1948), 407–24.

Bohner, Charles H. *Robert Penn Warren*. New York: Twayne, 1964; rev. 1981.

Bradbury, John M. *The Fugitives: A Critical Account*. Chapel Hill: University of North Carolina Press, 1985.

Casper, Leonard. *Robert Penn Warren: The Dark and Bloody Ground*. Seattle: University of Washington Press, 1960.

Chambers, Robert H. *Twentieth-Century Interpretations of "All the King's Men." A Collection of Critical Essays*. Englewood Cliffs, N.J.: Prentice-Hall, 1977.

Guttenberg, Barnett. *Web of Being: The Novels of Robert Penn Warren*. Nashville: Vanderbilt University Press, 1975.

Justus, James H. *The Achievement of Robert Penn Warren*. Baton Rouge: Louisiana State University Press, 1981.

Longley, John Lewis, Jr., ed. *Robert Penn Warren: A Collection of Critical Essays*. New York: New York University Press, 1965.

Shepherd, Allen. "Robert Penn Warren as a Philosophical Novelist." *Western Humanities Review* 24 (1970), 157–68.

Stitt, Peter. "Robert Penn Warren, the Poet." *Southern Review* 12 (1974), 261–76.

Strandberg, Victor. *The Poetic Vision of Robert Penn Warren*. Lexington: University Press of Kentucky, 1977.

———. "Robert Penn Warren." In *Dictionary of Literary Biography*, vol. 48: 425–44.

Watkins, Floyd C., and John T. Hiers, eds. *Robert Penn Warren Talking: Interviews, 1950–1978*. New York: Random House, 1980.

West, Paul. *Robert Penn Warren*. Pamphlet Series on American writers, no. 44. Minneapolis: University of Minnesota Press, 1964.

Wilkie, Everett C., Jr. "Robert Penn Warren." In *Dictionary of Literary Biography*, vol. Y80: 120–24.

Wilkie, Everett C., Jr., and Josephine Helterman. "Robert Penn Warren." In *Dictionary of Literary Biography*, vol. 2: 513–24.

Amelia Welby

Watts, Emily Stipes. *The Poetry of American Women from 1632 to 1943*. Austin: University of Texas Press, 1977.

Leane Zugsmith

Landman, Isaac. "Leane Zugsmith." In *The Universal Jewish Encyclopedia*. New York: The Universal Jewish Encyclopedia, 1943–48.

Index

A Literary History of Kentucky was designed by Dariel Mayer, composed by Tseng Information Systems, Inc., and printed by Thomson-Shore, Inc. The cloth and deluxe editions were bound by John H. Dekker and Sons, Inc.; the paperback edition was bound by Thomson-Shore, Inc. Text stock is 60-lb. Glatfelter Smooth Eggshell. The book is set in Aldus, with Palatino display type. Calligraphy by T. Oberright Kelly.